Lecture Notes in Computer Science 6026

Commenced Publication in 1973
Founding and Former Series Editors:
Gerhard Goos, Juris Hartmanis, and Jan van Leeuwen

Reneta P. Barneva   Valentin E. Brimkov
Herbert A. Hauptman   Renato M. Natal Jorge
João Manuel R.S. Tavares (Eds.)

Computational Modeling of Objects Represented in Images

Second International Symposium, CompIMAGE 2010
Buffalo, NY, USA, May 5-7, 2010
Proceedings

 Springer

Volume Editors

Reneta P. Barneva
State University of New York at Fredonia
Fredonia, NY, USA
E-mail: barneva@cs.fredonia.edu

Valentin E. Brimkov
SUNY Buffalo State College
Buffalo, NY, USA
E-mail: brimkove@buffalostate.edu

Herbert A. Hauptman
Hauptman-Woodward Institute
Buffalo, NY, USA
E-mail: hauptman@hwi.buffalo.edu

Renato M. Natal Jorge
University of Porto
Porto, Portugal
E-mail: rnatal@fe.up.pt

João Manuel R.S. Tavares
University of Porto
Porto, Portugal
E-mail: tavares@fe.up.pt

Library of Congress Control Number: 2010925271

CR Subject Classification (1998): I.4, I.5, I.2, C.2, F.1, J.3

LNCS Sublibrary: SL 6 – Image Processing, Computer Vision, Pattern Recognition, and Graphics

ISSN	0302-9743
ISBN-10	3-642-12711-8 Springer Berlin Heidelberg New York
ISBN-13	978-3-642-12711-3 Springer Berlin Heidelberg New York

springer.com

© Springer-Verlag Berlin Heidelberg 2010
Printed in Germany

Typesetting: Camera-ready by author, data conversion by Scientific Publishing Services, Chennai, India
Printed on acid-free paper   06/3180

Preface

It is indeed a great pleasure to welcome you to the proceedings of the International Symposium "Computational Modeling of Objects Represented in Images. Fundamentals, Methods and Applications" (CompIMAGE 2010) held in Buffalo, NY, May 5-7, 2010. This was the second issue of CompIMAGE symposia, the first one being held in Coimbra, Portugal.

The purpose of CompIMAGE 2010 was to provide a common forum for researchers, scientists, engineers, and practitioners around the world to present their latest research findings, ideas, developments, and applications in the area of computational modeling of objects represented in images. In particular, the symposium aimed to attract scientists who use various approaches – such as finite element method, optimization methods, modal analysis, stochastic methods, principal components analysis, independent components analysis, distribution models, geometrical modeling, digital geometry, grammars, fuzzy logic, and others – to solve problems that appear in a wide range of areas as diverse as medicine, robotics, defense, security, astronomy, material science, and manufacturing.

CompIMAGE 2010 was highly international. Its Program Committee members are renowned experts coming from 25 different countries. Submissions to the symposium came from 22 countries from Africa, Asia, Europe, North and South America. Overall, representatives of 32 countries contributed to the symposium in different capacities.

The present volume includes the papers presented at the symposium. Following the call for papers, CompIMAGE 2010 received 77 submissions; 28 of them are included in this volume. The review process was rigorous, involving three to four independent double-blind reviews. A Scientific Committee of several world-leading experts was formed to help resolve possible controversial cases. *OpenConf* provided a convenient platform for smoothly carrying out the review process. The most important selection criterion for acceptance or rejection of a paper was the overall score received. Other criteria were: relevance to the symposium topics, correctness, originality, mathematical depth, clarity, and presentation quality. We believe that as a result, only high-quality papers were accepted for presentation at CompIMAGE 2010 and for publication in this volume. We hope that many of these papers are of interest to a broader audience.

The program of the symposium included presentations of contributed papers, as well as invited talks by five distinguished scientists: Chandrajit L. Bajaj, Venu Govindaraju, Dinggang Shen, Sargur N. Srihari, and Yongjie (Jessica) Zhang. The participants enjoyed a recent film about the life and the achievements of Dr. Herbert Hauptman, Nobel Laureate.

In addition to the main track of CompIMAGE 2010, a Special Track on Object Modeling, Algorithms, and Applications was organized. In this track, researchers presented their recent work and made software demonstrations.

Many individuals and organizations contributed to the success of the symposium. First of all, the Chairs are indebted to CompIMAGE 2010's Steering Committee for endorsing the candidacy of Buffalo for the second edition of the symposium. Our most sincere thanks go to the Program Committee and the Scientific Committee whose cooperation in carrying out high quality reviews was essential in establishing a strong symposium program. We express our sincere gratitude to the invited speakers Chandrajit L. Bajaj, Venu Govindaraju, Dinggang Shen, Sargur N. Srihari, and Yongjie (Jessica) Zhang for their remarkable talks and overall contribution to the symposium. We wish to thank everybody who submitted their work to CompIMAGE 2010. Thanks to their contributions, we succeeded in having a technical program of high scientific quality. We are indebted to all participants and especially to the contributors to this volume.

The success of the symposium would not be possible without the hard work of the local Organizing Committee. We are grateful to Boris V. Brimkov, Daniel W. Cunningham, Bonita R. Durand, Khalid J. Siddiqui, and Michael Szocki for their valuable work. We are obliged to SUNY Buffalo State College and SUNY Fredonia for the continuous support through their designated offices. Special thanks go to Dennis K. Ponton, Interim President of SUNY Buffalo State College, and Dennis L. Hefner, President of SUNY Fredonia, for endorsing CompIMAGE 2010, to Kevin J. Railey, Interim Provost of SUNY Buffalo State College, Mark W. Severson, Dean of the School of Natural and Social Sciences at SUNY Buffalo State College, and Kevin P. Kearns, Associate Vice President of Graduate Studies & Research at SUNY Fredonia, for their strong support. In addition to our main sponsors, SUNY Buffalo State College, SUNY Fredonia, and the University of Porto, many thanks for endorsing the event go to a number of foundations and associations, such as APMTAC, FCT, INEGI, and IDMEC."

Finally, we wish to thank Springer for the pleasant cooperation in the timely production of this volume.

May 2010

Reneta P. Barneva
Valentin E. Brimkov
Herbert A. Hauptman
Renato M. Natal Jorge
João Manuel R.S. Tavares

Organization

The Second International Symposium on Computational Modeling of Objects Represented in Images: Fundamentals, Methods, and Applications, CompIMAGE 2010, was held in Buffalo, NY, USA, May 5-7, 2010.

General Chairs

Reneta P. Barneva	SUNY Fredonia, USA
Valentin E. Brimkov	SUNY Buffalo State College, USA
Renato M. Natal Jorge	University of Porto, Portugal
João Manuel R.S. Tavares	University of Porto, Portugal

Steering Committee

Valentin E. Brimkov	SUNY Buffalo State College, USA
Renato M. Natal Jorge	University of Porto, Portugal
João Manuel R.S. Tavares	University of Porto, Portugal

Invited Speakers

Chandrajit L. Bajaj	Univeristy of Texas at Austin, USA
Venu Govindaraju	University at Buffalo, USA
Dinggang Shen	University of North Carolina–Chapel Hill, USA
Sargur N. Srihari	University at Buffalo, USA
Yongjie (Jessica) Zhang	Carnegie Mellon University, USA

Scientific Committee

Jake Aggarwal	University of Texas at Austin, USA
Robert H. Blessing	Hauptman-Woodward Institute, USA
Venu Govindaraju	University at Buffalo, USA
Edwin Hancock	University of York, UK
Eaton E. Lattman	Hauptman-Woodward Institute, USA

Program Committee

Amr Abdel-Dayem	Laurentian University, Canada
Lyuba Alboul	Sheffield Hallam University, UK
Constantino Carlos Reyes-Aldasoro	University of Sheffield, Sheffield, UK
Fernando Alonso-Fernandez	Universidad Autonoma de Madrid, Spain
Luís Amaral	Polytechnic Institute of Coimbra, Portugal

Diamantino Freitas	University of Porto, Portugal
Irene M. Gamba	University of Texas at Austin, USA
Jose M. García Aznar	University of Zaragoza, Spain
Joaquim Silva Gomes	University of Porto, Portugal
Jordi González	Computer Vision Center, Spain
Bernard Gosselin	Faculte Polytechnique de Mons, Belgium
Christos Grecos	University of West of Scotland, UK
Mislav Grgic	University of Zagreb, Croatia
Enrique Alegre Gutiérrez	University of León, Spain
John C. Handley	Xerox Corporation, USA
Gerhard A. Holzapfel	Royal Institute of Technology, Sweden
Daniela Iacoviello	Università degli Studi di Roma "La Sapienza", Italy
Khan M. Iftekharuddin	The University of Memphis, USA
Joaquim A. Jorge	Instituto Superior Técnico, Portugal
Kamen Kanev	Shizuoka Univesity, Japan
Constantine Kotropoulos	Aristotle University of Thessaloniki, Greece
Maria Elizete Kunkel	Universität Ulm, Germany
Nguyen Dang Binh Kyushu	Institute of Technology, Japan
Slimane Larabi	U.S.T.H.B. University, Algeria
Chang-Tsun Li	University of Warwick, UK
Rainald Lohner	George Mason University, USA
Javier Melenchón Maldonado	Universitat Ramon Llull, Barcelona, Spain
Andre R.S. Marcal	Faculty of Sciences of University of Porto, Portugal
Jorge S. Marques	Instituto Superior Técnico, Portugal
Teresa Mascarenhas	University of Porto, Portugal
Ana Maria Mendonça	University of Porto, Portugal
Luis Metello	ESTSP, Portugal
Lionel Moisan	Université Paris V, France
Helcio R.B. Orlande	Federal University of Rio de Janeiro, Brazil
Todd Pataky	University of Liverpool, UK
Francisco Perales	Balearic Islands University, Spain
Nicolai Petkov	University of Groningen, The Netherlands
Raquel Ramos Pinho	University of Porto, Portugal
João Rogério Caldas Pinto	Instituto Superior Técnico, Portugal
Axel Pinz	TU Graz, Austria
Eduardo Borges Pires	Instituto Superior Técnico, Portugal
Hemerson Pistori	Dom Bosco Catholic University, Brazil
Ioannis Pitas	Aristotle University of Thessaloniki, Greece
Giuseppe Placidi	Università dell'Aquila, Italy
José Carlos Príncipe	University of Florida, USA
Xiaojun Qi	Utah State University, USA
Petia Radeva	Autonomous University of Barcelona, Spain

Organizing Committee

Reneta P. Barneva	SUNY Fredonia, USA
Boris V. Brimkov	University at Buffalo, USA
Daniel W. Cunningham	SUNY Buffalo State College, USA
Bonita R. Durand	SUNY Buffalo State College, USA
Khalid J. Siddiqui	SUNY Fredonia, USA
Michael Szocki	SUNY Fredonia, USA

Table of Contents

Theoretical Foundations of Image Analysis and Processing

Generalized Perpendicular Bisector and Circumcenter 1
Marc Rodríguez, Sere Abdoulaye, Gaëlle Largeteau-Skapin, and Eric Andres

Digital Stars and Visibility of Digital Objects 11
Valentin E. Brimkov and Reneta P. Barneva

Ω-Arithmetization of Ellipses 24
Agathe Chollet, Guy Wallet, Eric Andres, Laurent Fuchs, Gaëlle Largeteau-Skapin, and Aurélie Richard

Connectedness of Offset Digitizations in Higher Dimensions 36
Valentin E. Brimkov

Curvature Estimation for Discrete Curves Based on Auto-adaptive Masks of Convolution 47
Christophe Fiorio, Christian Mercat, and Frédéric Rieux

An Algorithm to Decompose n-Dimensional Rotations into Planar Rotations 60
Aurélie Richard, Laurent Fuchs, and Sylvain Charneau

Tile Pasting Systems for Tessellation and Tiling Patterns 72
T. Robinson, S. Jebasingh, Atulya K. Nagar, and K.G. Subramanian

Polyoisominoes 85
Mary Jemima Samuel, V.R. Dare, and T. Kalyani

Collage of Iso-Picture Languages and P Systems 95
S. Annadurai, V.R. Dare, T. Kalyani, and D.G. Thomas

Online Tessellation Automaton Recognizing Various Classes of Convex Polyominoes 107
H. Geetha, D.G. Thomas, and T. Kalyani

A New Method for Generation of Three-Dimensional Cubes 119
R. Arumugham, K. Thirusangu, and D.G. Thomas

Methods and Applications. Medical Imaging, Bioimaging, Biometrics, and Imaging in Material Sciences

Surface-Based Imaging Methods for High-Resolution Functional
Magnetic Resonance Imaging 130
David Ress, Sankari Dhandapani, Sucharit Katyal,
Clint Greene, and Chandra Bajaj

Characterization of a SimMechanics Model for a Virtual Glove
Rehabilitation System 141
Danilo Franchi, Alfredo Maurizi, and Giuseppe Placidi

Numerical Methods for the Semi-automatic Analysis of Multimodal
Wound Healing Images 151
Giuseppe Placidi, Maria Grazia Cifone, Benedetta Cinque,
Danilo Franchi, Maurizio Giuliani, Cristina La Torre,
Guido Macchiarelli, Marta Maione, Alfredo Maurizi,
Gianfranca Miconi, and Antonello Sotgiu

Customizable Visualization on Demand for Hierarchically Organized
Information in Biochemical Networks 163
Peter Droste, Eric von Lieres, Wolfgang Wiechert, and
Katharina Nöh

Improved Kernel Common Vector Method for Face Recognition Varying
in Background Conditions 175
C. Lakshmi, M. Ponnavaikko, and M. Sundararajan

Compact Binary Patterns (CBP) with Multiple Patch Classifiers for
Fast and Accurate Face Recognition 187
Hieu V. Nguyen and Li Bai

Graph-Theoretic Image Alignment Using Topological Features 199
Waleed Mohamed, A. Ben Hamza, and Khaled Gharaibeh

Fast Automatic Microstructural Segmentation of Ferrous Alloy Samples
Using Optimum-Path Forest 210
João Paulo Papa, Victor Hugo C. de Albuquerque,
Alexandre Xavier Falcão, and João Manuel R.S. Tavares

Numerical Simulations of Hypoeutectoid Steels under Loading
Conditions, Based on Image Processing and Digital Material
Representation 221
Łukasz Rauch, Łukasz Madej, and Bogdan Pawłowski

Surface Finish Control in Machining Processes Using Haralick
Descriptors and Neuronal Networks 231
Enrique Alegre, Rocío Alaiz-Rodríguez, Joaquín Barreiro,
Eduardo Fidalgo, and Laura Fernández

Methods and Applications. Image Reconstruction, Computed Tomography, and Other Applications

Direction-Dependency of a Binary Tomographic Reconstruction
Algorithm.. 242
  László Varga, Péter Balázs, and Antal Nagy

Circular Acquisition to Define the Minimal Set of Projections for
Optimal MRI Reconstruction 254
  Giuseppe Placidi

Surface Reconstruction with an Interactive Modification of Point
Normals 263
  Taku Itoh

On the Effects of Normalization in Adaptive MRF Hierarchies 275
  Albert Y.C. Chen and Jason J. Corso

Topology Preserving Parallel Smoothing for 3D Binary Images......... 287
  Gábor Németh, Péter Kardos, and Kálmán Palágyi

Coding a Simulation Model of the 3D Structure of Paper 299
  Eduardo L.T. Conceição, Joana M.R. Curto,
  Rogério M.S. Simões, and António A.T.G. Portugal

Crowd Behavior Surveillance Using Bhattacharyya Distance Metric 311
  Md. Haidar Sharif, Sahin Uyaver, and Chabane Djeraba

Author Index 325

Generalized Perpendicular Bisector
and Circumcenter

Marc Rodríguez[1], Sere Abdoulaye[2], Gaëlle Largeteau-Skapin[1],
and Eric Andres[1]

[1] Laboratory XLIM-SIC,
University of Poitiers BP 30179, UMR CNRS 6712
86962 Futuroscope Chasseneuil Cedex, France
[2] University of Ouagadoudou 03 BP 7021, Burkina Faso
{rodriguez,glargeteau,andres}@sic.univ-poitiers.fr

Abstract. This paper presents a theoretical generalization of the circumcenter as the intersection of generalized perpendicular bisectors. We define generalized bisectors between two regions as an area where each point is the center of at least one circle crossing each of the two regions. These new notions should allow the design of new circle recognition algorithms.

1 Introduction

Euclidean and discrete space have different behaviors. One of the principal issues in discrete geometry is to define discrete equivalents to Euclidean objects or transforms with as many useful (for a given application) properties as possible. In this paper, we are interested in the definition of a perpendicular bisector for discrete space. In Euclidean geometry, the intersection of the perpendicular bisectors of three points defines the circumcenter of the circumcircle. In this paper we are considering the problem of defining a perpendicular bisector adapted to discrete space for discrete circle recognition purposes. Classically, parameter space approaches are used for circle recognition [7]. The problem with these Hough transform type approaches is that there are three parameters (abscissa, ordinate of the center and radius) which makes it a three dimensional accumulator matrix. Various methods have been proposed to circumvent this problem [6]. These methods however are adapted for circle recognition in image analysis but not so much for problems such as invertible reconstruction. The discrete geometry community works for many years now on the problem of 2D and 3D invertible reconstruction of discrete objects. Discretization is the transform that associates a discrete object to a continuous one. Reconstruction is the transform that associates a continuous object to a discrete one. A reconstruction method is invertible if the discretization of the reconstructed object is equal to the original discrete object. Straight line segment recognition have been the main focus of research when it comes to invertible reconstruction [11,12,1,4]. There have been relatively few papers so far that could be used for invertible circle reconstruction [9].

R.P. Barneva et al. (Eds.): CompIMAGE 2010, LNCS 6026, pp. 1–10, 2010.

Bisectors appear several times in the literature with usually a definition based on the notion of equidistance. For instance, definitions of discrete bisector functions are used to analyze and filter medial axis [3,10] where the medial axis of a Jordan curve is defined as the all the points equidistant to its borders. Bisectors between points and curves or between two curves have also been discussed in detail in the literature [5,8] but to our knowledge, no definition for the bisector between two coplanar surfaces such as pixels has been proposed so far.

There are various ways of considering points in discrete geometry. In this paper, where we focus on dimension two, we consider that a discrete point is represented by a continuous surface element (pixel). We are extending the notion of perpendicular bisector as the bisector between two regions. The generalized bisector of two 2D regions A and B is defined as the union of the perpendicular bisectors of all the couple of points (p, q) where p and q are respectively points of the regions A and B. This new definition extends the main property of the Euclidean perpendicular bisector of two points that is to be equidistant to both points. However, contrary to a Voronoi diagram, the generalized bisector is a surface and not simply a line as we will see. The new definition also extends the circumcircle property. For n regions, the intersection of all the generalized bisectors corresponds to the center of all the circles that cross all n regions. The definition is general and fits all type of regions and can be easily extended to higher dimensions. It gets however complicated very fast as illustrated in the paper with the generalized bisector of two disks which is a hyperbola. Even for pixels, as we will see, the generalized bisector is a complicated region bordered by straight line segments and pieces of parabolas. We propose a simplification that can be used for circle recognition.

The starting point of this paper is the definition of the perpendicular bisector between two regions. We examine the properties that are extended from usual perpendicular bisectors. In Section 3, we extend the circumcenter notion to surfaces, at first between three and after between an arbitrary number of surfaces. At the end of this section, we discuss what still needs to be done in order to obtain an efficient discrete circle arc recognition and reconstruction algorithm.

2   The Perpendicular Bisector of Two Regions

In this section, we focus on the perpendicular bisector of two regions. We will present two ways of defining the generalized perpendicular bisector.

2.1   Definition and Properties

The idea is to extend the perpendicular bisector definition to regions. The perpendicular bisector of two points p and q in $\mathbb{R}^n$ corresponds to all the points that are equidistant from the two points. The perpendicular bisector is a hyperplane that is perpendicular to the straight line pq and that passes through its midpoint. All the points of this perpendicular bisector are equidistant to both points p and q and each of them is therefore the center of a hypersphere that passes through both points. The idea here is to replace p and q by regions. This defines the generalized bisector (see Figure 1):

Definition 1 (Generalized perpendicular bisector). *Let S_1 and S_2 be two regions. The generalized perpendicular bisector of S_1 and S_2 is the union of all the perpendicular bisectors of each couple of point (X,Y) where $X \in S_1$ and $Y \in S_2$.*

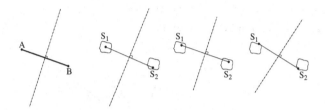

Fig. 1. A Euclidean couple of point has only one perpendicular bisector but a couple of regions has an infinity of bisectors

From this definition we can deduce two immediate properties:

Property 1: The generalized perpendicular bisector of two overlapping regions is the whole space even if they only share one point.

Proof. The bisector of two identical points is the whole space since all the points of space are equidistant to both (identical) points. Therefore, as soon as two regions overlap, the generalized perpendicular bisector is the whole space.   □

Property 2: Each point of the generalized perpendicular bisector of two regions is the center of a hypersphere crossing them.

This property is an immediate and direct consequence of the generalized bisector definition. This property leads to an alternative definition of the generalized bisector of two regions.

Definition 2 (Alternative definition of the generalized bisector). *Let S_1 and S_2 be two regions. Let $d_i(X) = \min(d(X, S_i))$, $D_i(X) = \max(d(X, S_i))$ where d is the classical Euclidean distance.*

Every Euclidean point $X \in \mathbb{R}^n$ such that the intervals $[d_1(X), D_1(X)] \cap [d_2(X), D_2(X)] \neq \emptyset$ belong to a region called the generalized perpendicular bisector of S_1 and S_2.

These two definitions are equivalent and define the same area. This second definition shows that, for each point of the generalized bisector, there is, in general, an interval of radii for which hyperspheres centered on the point will cut both regions.

2.2   Generalized Perpendicular Bisector between Two 2D Discs

The generalized perpendicular bisector (GPB) of two 2D regions is not a straight line but an infinite set of straight lines that form a region. The shape of the generalized bisector depends, of course, on the shape of both regions.

For example, let $C_1 = (O_1, r_1)$ and $C_2 = (O_2, r_2)$ be two disks. The generalized bisector of both discs is a region bordered by a hyperbola (see Figure 2) defined by the asymptotes d_1 and d_2 and passing through I and J. The straight lines d_1 and d_2 are the perpendicular bisectors of t_2 and t_1 which are the common tangents to both circles. $\overrightarrow{O_1I} = \frac{(1-r_1-r_2)}{2}\overrightarrow{O_1O_2} = -\overrightarrow{O_2J}$. As we can see, the GPB is, in general, a complicated region.

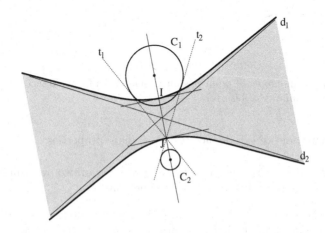

Fig. 2. Example of a generalized perpendicular bisector of two discs

2.3   Generalized Perpendicular Bisector between Two Pixels

We are now interested in 2D discrete spaces where each discrete point is represented a region classically called a pixel (a square region). While the generalized bisector is defined in arbitrary dimensions, we are focusing here on the dimension two. In the following, we explain how the generalized perpendicular bisector of two pixels can be piecewise computed.

Let $P_1(x_1, y_1)$ and $P_2(x_2, y_2)$ be two pixels of which we want to compute the generalized bisector area. The pixel is the unit square region centered on a $\mathbb{Z}^2$ point : $\{(x, y),\ x \in [x_i - 0, 5, x_i + 0, 5]\ and\ y \in [y_i - 0, 5, y_i + 0, 5]\}$. Let $X(x, y)$ be another point in $\mathbb{R}^2$. To know if the point X belongs to the generalized bisector area, we have to compute $d_1(X) = min(d(X, P_1))$, $D_1(X) = max(d(X, P_1))$, $d_2(X) = min(d(X, P_2))$ and $D_2(X) = max(d(X, P_2))$.

We can see on figure 3 that the point of the pixel P that is closest to X can be either: X itself if X belongs to the pixel P, a point on an edge of P if X can be orthogonally projected on an edge of P or a vertex of P in all the other cases. The point F of the pixel P that is furthest from X is always a vertex of P. Each

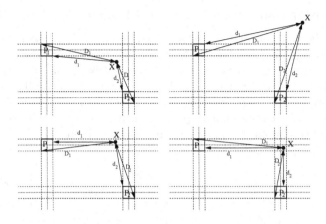

Fig. 3. X is a possible circle center if $[d_1(X), D_1(X)] \bigcap [d_2(X), D_2(X)] \neq \emptyset$

pixel splits the space into 16 areas and so two non aligned pixels divide space in 49 areas where each area has a different formula for $d_1(X), d_2(X), D_1(X)$, and $D_2(X)$ (with symmetries).

Let us now examine what the intersection of intervals means in terms of equations. $[d_1(X), D_1(X)] \bigcap [d_2(X), D_2(X)] \neq \emptyset$ is equivalent to $\neg ([d_1(X), D_1(X)] \bigcap [d_2(X), D_2(X)] = \emptyset)$ which occurs only if $D_1(X) < d_2(X)$ or $D_2(X) < d_1(X)$.

Let $C_i(C_{ix}, C_{iy})$ be the closest point of X in the pixel P_i and let $F_i(F_{ix}, F_{iy})$ be the furthest point of X in P_i. In each area, a constraint $d_i \leq D_j$ can be writen:

$$\sqrt{(x - C_{i_x})^2 + (y - C_{i_y})^2} \leq \sqrt{(x - F_{j_x})^2 + (y - F_{j_y})^2}$$

where $C_{i_x} \in \{x, x_i + 0.5, x_i - 0.5\}$, $C_{i_y} \in \{y, y_i + 0.5, y_i - 0.5\}$, $F_{j_x} \in \{x, x_j + 0.5, x_j - 0.5\}$ and $F_{j_y} \in \{y, x_j + 0.5, x_j - 0.5\}$.

For the areas where X is not orthogonally projected on an edge of a pixel, we know that $x \neq C_{i_x}$, $x \neq F_{j_x}$, $y \neq C_{i_y}$, $y \neq F_{j_y}$. The two constraints can then be reduced to half planes inequations of type $\alpha x + \beta y + \gamma \leq 0$ where $\alpha, \beta, \gamma \in \mathbb{R}^*$.

For example, for the first case of Figure 3, we have $C_1 = (x_1 + 0, 5, y_1 - 05)$, $F_1 = (x_1 - 0, 5, y_1 + 0, 5)$ and $C_2 = (x_2 - 0, 5, y_2 + 0, 5)$, $F_2 = (x_2 + 0, 5, y_2 - 0, 5)$. The distance constraint $d_1 \leq D_2$ is therefore :

$$\sqrt{(x - (x_1 + 0, 5))^2 + (y - (y_1 - 05))^2} \leq \sqrt{(x - (x_2 + 0, 5))^2 + (y - (y_2 - 0, 5))^2}$$

$$= 2(x_2 - x_1)x + 2(y_2 - y_1)y + \left(x_1^2 - x_2^2 + x_1 - x_2 + y_1^2 - y_2^2 - y_1 + y_2\right).$$

In the other areas, we are at least in one of the cases where $C_{i_x} = x$, $F_{j_x} = x$, $C_{i_y} = y$ or $F_{j_y} = y$. There are no simplifications during the calculation. The constraints correspond to pieces of parabolas of the form: $(x - \alpha)^2 + (y - \beta)^2 - \gamma \leq 0$.

2.4   Approximation of the Generalized Bisector for Two Pixels

To simplify the description of the generalized perpendicular bisector of two pixels, we are going simply to ignore the pieces of parabolas in the piecewise description of the generalized bisector. The pieces of parabolas are actually very small (not larger than a pixel side). We consider here that each pixel divides space into only four areas by doing as if the closest point of a pixel is always one of the vertices. The approximated generalized perpendicular bisector border is therefore only composed of straight line pieces (see Figure 4).

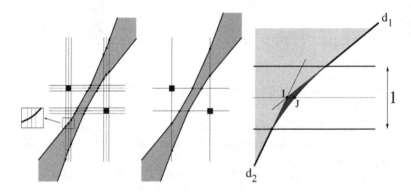

Fig. 4. On the left, the exact perpendicular bisector and the approximation where the parabolic pieces have been dropped by extending the straight lines. The generalized bisector is slightly reduced.

With this approximation, we reduce (very slightly) the solution space (the possible circle centers). If a circle is recognized with help of the simplified generalized bisectors it means that it is also a solution to the generalized bisector. We might reject some valid solution and not recognize a valid circle but since the approximation is so minimal, this would probably fall into the margin of error of the computations anyway.

3   The Generalized Circumcenter

The Euclidean circumcenter of a set of Euclidean points is defined by the intersection of all the bisectors from pairing the points two by two. Its main property is to be the center of the circle passing through all the points of the set. In this section, we naturally extend this notion to 2D regions.

Definition 3 (Generalized Circumcenter (GC) of a set of regions). *The generalized circumcenter (GC) of set of n regions $\mathcal{S} = (S_i)_{i \in [1,n]}$ is the intersection of the generalized perpendicular bisectors (GPB) of every two regions of the set:*

$$GC(\mathcal{S}) = \bigcap_{i,j \in [1,n], i<j} (GPB(S_i, S_j)).$$

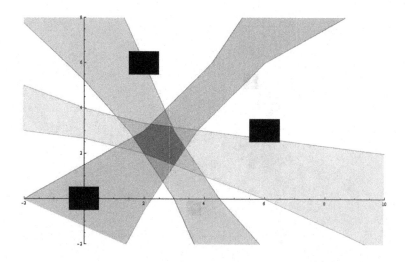

Fig. 5. Generalized circumcenter of $P_1 = (0,0)$, $P_2 = (2,6)$ and $P_3 = (6,3)$

We can see on Figure 5 the generalized circumcenter of three pixels and on Figure 6 the generalized circumcenter of four pixels.

For the Euclidean circumcenter, if the points are aligned they belong to a Euclidean straight line which forms a circular arc of an infinite radius. In discrete space things are a little bit different as we can see on Figure 7: discrete straight line segments belong to discrete circles. The generalized circumcenter is, in this case, a disconnected infinite region.

One of the last remaining question is the existence of a general solution. All the points in the generalized circumcenter of a pixel set are the center of at least one circle crossing every two pixels of the set. That does not mean that there exists a circle that crosses every pixels of the set. We need to ensure that a common radius exists. Actually, there always exists a solution:

Theorem 1 (Circle existence). *If the generalized circumcenter $GC(\mathcal{S})$ of a set of regions $\mathcal{S}$ is not empty, then for all $X \in GC(\mathcal{S})$ there exists at least one circle centered in X that crosses all the regions of the set $\mathcal{S}$.*

Proof. The radius intervals (as defined in definition 2) are of dimension 1. The generalized circumcenter of a set of regions is the intersection of the generalized circumcenters for every two regions of the set. This defines a non empty interval of radii for the intersection of all the radius intervals. □

Note that if the circumcenter area is empty then there is no circle that intersects all the regions. This is not completely true if we use the simplified generalized perpendicular bisector. The area of solutions that are neglected are however, as we have already stated, very small.

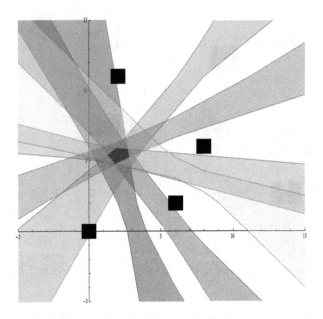

Fig. 6. The generalized circumcenter of $\{(0,0),(2,11),(6,2),(8,6)\}$

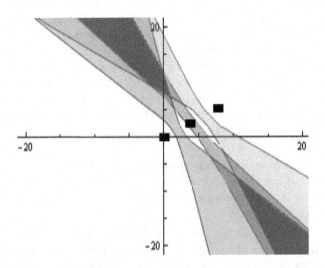

Fig. 7. When the pixels are aligned, the generalized circumcenter (dark region) is not connected. The pixels are marked in black.

4 Conclusion and Perspectives

In this paper, we have proposed a generalization of perpendicular bisectors and circumcenters to regions in an arbitrary dimensional space. This extension is very interesting because many properties from classical segment bisectors are preserved. We have shown that, in 2D, all the points of the generalized circumcenter of a set of regions are the center of at least one circle that crosses all the regions of the set. We have described the generalized bisector of two pixels. We have also proposed a slight simplification of the generalized bisector of two pixels in order to avoid the pieces of parabola on its border.

The generalized circumcenter is a new interesting approach to digital circles recognition and reconstruction because it contains all the centers of all the Euclidean circles that pass through all the pixels. It can be used for full discrete circle recognition or only for discrete circular arc recognition [2,9]. The generalized perpendicular bisector is easily defined in upper dimensions. The n dimensional circumcenter of a voxel set will be a volume containing the centers of all the Euclidean hyperspheres crossing all the voxels of the set. One of the last advantages of this approach is that the pixels/voxels in the recognition process do not need to all be of the same size. This could allow multiscale or noisy circle/hypersphere recognition.

Much work remains to be done however. There are some complicated algorithmic problems that need to be solved before an efficient circle recognition algorithm can be proposed. The intersection of the simplified generalized bisectors is algorithmically costly because (despite the fact that they are defined by straight lines) they are typically not convex. Secondly, for n regions we have $O(n^2)$ generalized bisectors to intersect in order to compute the generalized circumcenter. We are looking right now into some simplification in the recognition process that should allow us, at least, to be able to fast reject cases where there are no solutions. The long term goal of all this is to be able to have an invertible circle recognition algorithm that can be paired with straight line recognition algorithms.

References

1. Breton, R., Sivignon, I., Dexet, M., Andres, E.: Towards an invertible Euclidean reconstruction of a discrete object. In: Nyström, I., Sanniti di Baja, G., Svensson, S. (eds.) DGCI 2003. LNCS, vol. 2886, pp. 246–256. Springer, Heidelberg (2003)
2. Coeurjolly, D., Gerard, Y., Reveills, J.-P., Tougne, L.: An elementary algorithm for digital arc segmentation. Discrete Applied Mathematics 139(1-3), 31–50 (2004)
3. Couprie, M., Coeurjolly, D., Zrour, R.: Discrete bisector function and Euclidean skeleton in 2D and 3D. Image and Vision Computing 25(10), 1543–1556 (2007)
4. Dexet, M., Andres, E.: A generalized preimage for the digital analytical hyperplane recognition. Discrete Applied Mathematics 157(3), 476–489 (2009)
5. Farouki, R.T., Johnstone, J.K.: Computing point/curve and curve/curve bisectors. In: Fisher, R.B. (ed.) The Mathematics of Surfaces V, pp. 327–354. Oxford University, Oxford (1994)

6. Gonzalez, R.C., Woods, R.E., Eddins, S.L.: Digital Image Processing Using MAT-LAB(R). Prentice-Hall, Englewood Cliffs (2004)
7. Ioannou, D., Huda, W., Laine, A.F.: Circle recognition through a 2D Hough transform and radius histogramming. Image and Vision Computing 17(1), 15–26 (1999)
8. Peternell, M.: Geometric properties of bisector surfaces. Graphical Models 62(3), 202–236 (2000)
9. Roussillon, T., Tougne, L., Sivignon, I.: On three constrained versions of the digital circular arc recognition problem. In: Brlek, S., Reutenauer, C., Provençal, X. (eds.) DGCI 2009. LNCS, vol. 5810, pp. 34–45. Springer, Heidelberg (2009)
10. Talbot, H., Vincent, L.: Euclidean skeletons and conditional bisectors. In: Visual Comm. and Image Pricessing. SPIE, vol. 1818, pp. 862–876 (1992)
11. Vittone, J., Chassery, J.-M.: (n,m)-cubes and farey nets for naive planes understanding. In: Bertrand, G., Couprie, M., Perroton, L. (eds.) DGCI 1999. LNCS, vol. 1568, pp. 76–90. Springer, Heidelberg (1999)
12. Vittone, J., Chassery, J.-M.: Recognition of digital naive planes and polyhedrization. In: Nyström, I., Sanniti di Baja, G., Borgefors, G. (eds.) DGCI 2000. LNCS, vol. 1953, pp. 296–307. Springer, Heidelberg (2000)

Digital Stars and Visibility of Digital Objects

Valentin E. Brimkov[1] and Reneta P. Barneva[2]

[1] Mathematics Department, SUNY Buffalo State College, Buffalo, NY 14222, USA
brimkove@buffalostate.edu
[2] Department of Computer Science, SUNY Fredonia, NY 14063, USA
barneva@cs.fredonia.edu

Abstract. Starshaped sets (or stars) are objects defined and studied since early 20th century. Stars are closely related to convexity issues. Results about stars have found numerous applications in several mathematical disciplines, such as computational and convex geometry. With the present paper we are initiating a study on digital stars. This is particularly motivated by possible applications in computer vision. We derive several basic properties of digital stars and consider relations between digital starshapedness, continuous starshapedness, and digital convexity.

Keywords: Star, digital star, convex set, digitally convex set.

1 Introduction

Convexity and related issues are fundamental to different facets of pure and applied mathematics. A great number of classical concepts and theorems are germane to the subject. Within the framework of digital geometry, "discrete," or "digital" versions of those have been investigated within the last two or three decades. See Chapter 13 of [7] and the extensive bibliography therein.

Starshaped sets (or stars, for short) are objects defined and studied since early 20th century. Originally, problems related to stars have been formulated in a popular form in terms of visibility within an art gallery. With some updating, one can say that an art gallery is starshaped if and only if there is a location in it, from where a security camera can observe every point of the gallery. Stars are closely related to convexity issues and results, such as the classical Helly's theorem. Results about stars have found numerous applications in several mathematical disciplines, such as computational and convex geometry.

A bit surprisingly (to our knowledge of the available literature on digital geometry), digital versions of stars and their properties have not been introduced and studied so far. With the present paper we are initiating such a study. This is particularly motivated by possible applications in computer vision, to which considerations in a digital setting are even more relevant than in the continuous one.

The main purpose of the paper is to attract some attention to this interesting subject and to appear as a starting point for future research on that. To this end, we define digital stars and study their basic properties. In particular, we obtain a necessary and sufficient conditions for a digital object to be a star.

R.P. Barneva et al. (Eds.): CompIMAGE 2010, LNCS 6026, pp. 11–23, 2010.

However, we also show that star characterizations, which parallel by approach certain characterizations of a digitally convex set, are not always possible. We also show that some digital analogs of certain basic theorems about stars (such as the well-known Krasnoselśkii's theorem [9]) do not hold, in general.

In the next section we introduce some basic notions and results to be used in the sequel. In Section 3 we present the main results of the paper. We conclude with some remarks in Section 4.

2   Preliminaries

In this section we introduce some basic notions to be used in the sequel. We conform to terminology used in [7] and [11,15].

2.1   Basic Notions of Digital Geometry

All considerations take place in the *grid cell model* that consists of the grid squares, called *pixels*, together with the related topology. Pixels are centered at the grid points that are the elements of $\mathbb{Z}^2$. Thus a pixel is identified by its center; so, all notions in terms of pixels apply to sets of integer points.

Pixels, pixel edges, and pixel vertices are also referred to as 2-*cells*, 1-*cells* and 0-*cells*, respectively. For every $i = 0, 1, 2$, the set of all cells of dimension i (or i-cells) is denoted by $\mathbb{C}_2^{(i)}$. Further, we define the space $\mathbb{C}_2 = \bigcup_{k=0}^{2} \mathbb{C}_2^{(i)}$.

We say that two 2-cells e, e' are k-adjacent for $k = 0$ or $k = 1$ if they share a k-cell. Two 2-cells are *strictly* k-adjacent if they are k-adjacent but not $(k+1)$-adjacent. A k-adjacency relation is denoted by A_k. If pixels p and q are A_k-adjacent, this is denoted by pA_kq. For a given pixel p, the set $\{q : pA_kq\}$ is the *adjacency set* of p, denoted by $A_k(p)$.

A digital object $D \subseteq \mathbb{C}_2^{(2)}$ is a set of pixels[1] (or, equivalently, it can be thought as a set of integer points). A k-*path* (where $k = 0$ or $k = 1$) in D is a sequence of pixels from D such that every two consecutive pixels on the path are k-adjacent. Two pixels p and q of a digital object D are k-*connected* (in D) iff there is a k-path of points from D between p and q. A subset G of D is k-*connected* (in D) iff there is a k-path connecting any two pixels of G. The maximal (by inclusion) k-connected subsets of a digital object D are called k-*(connected) components* of D. Components are nonempty, and distinct k-components are disjoint. Clearly, a digital object may be 0-connected but not 1-connected.

A pixel $p \in D$ is called a k-*inner pixel* for D ($k = 0, 1$) iff $A_k(p) \subseteq D$. Otherwise, it is a k-*border pixel*.

Let D be a finite digital object in $\mathbb{C}_2^{(2)}$ and let $\bar{D}$ be its complement[2] to the whole space $\mathbb{C}_2^{(2)}$. It is clear (and well-known) that if D is finite, $\bar{D}$ has exactly one infinite connected component with respect to an adjacency relation A_k ($k = 0$ or 1) and, possibly, a number of finite components. The latter are

---

[1] Sometimes, digital objects are considered to be finite sets of points. Here we do not impose such a restriction.

[2] Sometimes $\bar{S}$ is called the *background* of D.

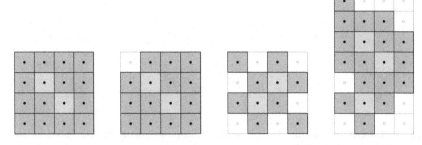

Fig. 1. *From left to right:* a 1-connected digital object with one 0-hole that constitutes two (proper) 1-holes; a 1-connected digital object with no 0-hole and with two (improper) 1-holes; a 0-connected digital object with no 0-hole and with two (improper) 1-holes; a 0-connected digital object with one 0-hole that constitutes two (proper) 1-holes, and with another (improper) 1-hole

called *k-holes* of D. That is, 0-holes are components of $\bar{D}$ with respect to 0-adjacency, while 1-holes are components of $\bar{D}$ with respect to 1-adjacency.[3] If D is infinite, its complement may consist of any number of finite and/or infinite connected components. A 0-hole may also be a 1-hole (if it is 1-connected) or, otherwise, it is a union of several 1-holes (see Figure 1). We also have

Fact 1. *A digital object D that has a 0-hole, has also 1-hole(s).*

Proof. Let H be a 0-hole of D, i.e., H is a 0-component of $\bar{D}$. Then, no point of H is 0-adjacent to an infinite component of $\bar{D}$, hence, no point of H is 1-adjacent to an infinite component of $\bar{D}$. Since H is either 1-connected or a union of 1-connected sets, it follows that H is either a 1-hole or a union of several 1-holes of D.   □

Further important comments follow.

A 0-connected set of points $G \subset \bar{D}$ may form a 1-hole or a number of 1-holes of D, but may not constitute a 0-hole of D. See Figure 1 (second subfigure). Such 1-holes are called in [7] *improper holes* of D.

As already mentioned, it is possible a 0-connected set $G \subset \bar{D}$ to form a 1-hole or a number of 1-holes of D, as well as a 0-hole of D (see Figure 1 (left)). Such a 1-hole is called in [7] a *proper hole*.[4]

---

[3] Note that different adjacencies may be used in defining the connectedness of a digital object and its background (e.g., A_0 for S and A_1 for $\bar{S}$ or vice-versa). In fact, this is often the preferred approach, since 0- and 1-adjacencies form a *good pair* of adjacency relations. Basically, good pairs characterize separation of the holes of the digital object from the infinite background. For details and discussion about the usefulness of this notion we refer to [8,3,7]. However, as the examples in Figure 1 demonstrate, sometimes it may make sense to speak about 0-holes in 0-connected digital objects and 1-holes in 1-connected digital objects.

[4] Proper/improper holes are defined in [7] in a different way that seems too complex to us, as it requires several other definitions as a background.

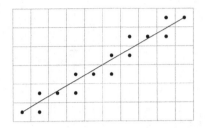 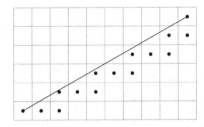

Fig. 2. *Left:* Centered standard digitization of a line segment. *Right:* One-side (lower) standard digitizations of a line segment.

The *boundary* of a closed set $M \subseteq \mathbb{R}^2$ will be denoted by $\partial(M)$. Given a set of pixels (unit squares) $D \subseteq \mathbb{C}_2^{(2)}$, their union forms a rectilinear set $P(D) = \cup_{q \in D} q$.

A (parametrized) *path* in $\mathbb{R}^2$ from $p \in \mathbb{R}^2$ to $q \in \mathbb{R}^2$ is a continuous function $\phi : [0,1] \to \mathbb{R}^2$ with $\phi(0) = p$ and $\phi(1) = q$. A *Jordan curve* in the plane is defined as a set $\gamma = \{(x,y) : \phi(t) = (x,y), a \le t \le b\}$, where $\phi : [a,b] \to \mathbb{R}^2$ is a path in $\mathbb{R}^2$ with $a \ne b$, $\phi(a) = \phi(b)$, $\phi(s) \ne \phi(t)$ for all s, t, $a \le s < t \le b$. The following is a classical result in the theory of curves.

Theorem 1. *(Jordan-Veblen curve theorem [16]) Let γ be a Jordan curve in $\mathbb{R}^2$. Then the open set $\mathbb{R}^2 \setminus \gamma$ consists of two disjoint connected open sets R_1 and R_2 with a common frontier γ. Moreover, any path that connects a point from R_1 with a point of R_2 intersects γ.*

2.2   Digital Lines

Recall that a *digital line*[5] is a set of integer points (pixels) $L(a_1, a_2, b, \mu, \omega) = \{(x_1, x_2) \in \mathbb{Z}^2 | 0 \le a_1 x_1 + a_2 x_2 + \mu < \omega\}$, where $a_1, a_2, b, \mu \in \mathbb{Z}, \omega \in \mathbb{Z}_+$. The parameter ω is the *arithmetic thickness* of the line and μ its digital *intercept*. If $\omega = \max(|a_1|, |a_2|)$, the line is called *naive*, and if $\omega = |a_1| + |a_2|$, it is called *standard*. These lines can be considered as discretizations of a straight line with equation $ax_1 + ax_2 + \mu = 0$. For more details about digital lines the reader is referred to [13], [12].

All following results hold for any of the above two types of digital lines. For definiteness, we will consider standard lines. A discrete line with $\mu = \lfloor \frac{\omega}{2} \rfloor$ is known as a *Bresenham line* [2]. Such a line is "centered" about the continuous one. If $\mu = 0$ or $\mu = \omega$, the digital line is on the one side of the continuous one. We will call it *one-side digitization* (which may be *upper* or *lower*; in the trivial case of a vertical straight line digitization, the latter consists of a vertical column of pixels). See Figure 2. Further we will use both types of digitizations.

Any connected set of pixels that is a subset of a certain digital line is called *digital straight line segment* (DSS). A DSS with end-points p and q will be denoted by $[pq]$, while the segment with endpoints p and q will be denoted by $\overline{pq}$.

---

[5] Also called "arithmetic line."

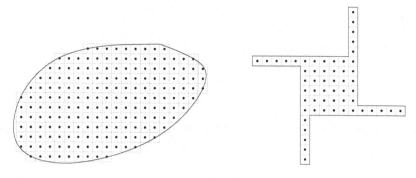

Fig. 3. *Left:* A digitally convex set. *Right:* A row- and column-convex set that is not digitally convex and is not a digital star.

2.3 Digital Convexity

Let $S \subseteq \mathbb{R}^2$. The *Gauss digitization* of S is the union of pixels with centers in S. Gauss digitization of S can be viewed as the set $S_{\mathbb{Z}} = S \cap \mathbb{Z}^2$. The following is a well-known fact [7].

Fact 2. *The Gauss digitization of any nonempty bounded set $S \subset \mathbb{R}^2$ is a union of a finite number of rectilinear polygons.*

It is well-known that $S_{\mathbb{Z}}$ may be a disconnected digital object even for a connected S.

A connected digital object $D \subseteq \mathbb{C}^2$ is called *digitally convex* if it is the Gauss digitization of some convex set $M \subseteq \mathbb{R}^2$. See Figure 3 (left). Note that a Gauss digitization of a convex subset of $\mathbb{R}^2$ is not necessarily connected.

Digital convexity can be characterized in several different ways (see Theorem 13.2 in [7]). We list one of them for future references.

Fact 3. *A digital object D is digitally convex if and only if for any two elements $p, q \in D$, at least one DSS that has p and q as end-pixels, is contained in D.*

A set $M \subseteq \mathbb{Z}^2$ is called *row-convex* (*column-convex*) iff each row (column) contains at most one run of pixels of M.

It is easy to see that every digitally convex set is both row- and column-convex, but the opposite does not hold, in general (see Figure 3 (right)).

A *staircase path* is a 1-connected path that has x- and y- coordinates that are monotonically nonincreasing or nondecreasing. One can easily see that the 0-border of a row and column-convex digital 1-connected set can be partitioned into at most four staircase paths.

2.4 Stars and Art Gallery Problems

A set $S \subset \mathbb{R}^n$ is called *starshaped* if it contains a point x_0, such that for every point $x \in S$ the segment $\overline{x_0 x}$ is contained in S. One also says that every point x

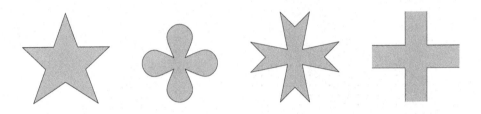

Fig. 4. Examples of stars in R^2. The rightmost example is an unbounded cross-shaped star.

of S is *visible* from x_0. We will call starshaped sets *stars*, for short. See Figure 4 for a number of examples.

The concept of starshapedness and visibility have been introduced by Brunn in 1913 [6]. It has found numerous applications in computational geometry [10,11] and convex geometry [1,14]. A basic result related to stars is a theorem of Krasnoselśkii from 1946 (Krasnoselśkii's art gallery theorem [9]), that characterizes compact stars in $\mathbb{R}^n$. It states that a compact set $S \subset \mathbb{R}^n$ is a star if and only if every $n + 1$ points of S are visible from a certain point of S. Over the years, several different versions of Krasnoselśkii's theorem have been proved, in particular for the case when S is a rectilinear polygon in $\mathbb{R}^2$, and visibility through a monotone staircase path has been investigated [4,5,10].

In the following section we define digital stars and study their basic properties.

3   Digital Stars and Their Properties

We start by introducing the definition of a digital star.

Definition 1. *A set $D \subseteq \mathbb{Z}^2$ is called a digital star if there is a point $p \in D$ (which we call a star center), such that for every other point $q \in D$, there is a (centered or one-sided) DSS $[pq]$ that is contained in D.*

Examples of digital stars are presented in Figure 5. Note that a digital star may have more than one center. Note also that digital stars may be both finite or infinite digital objects.

Remark 1. As already mentioned, we will assume 1-connectivity of the considered digital objects. In particular, in the above definition we mean a standard DSS. All results hold if 0-connectivity is assumed instead.

Our first observation is the following.

Proposition 1. *1. A digital star may have improper 1-holes.*
 2. A digital star cannot have proper 1-holes.

Fig. 5. *Left, Middle:* Two digital stars that are Gauss digitizations of the two leftmost stars in Figure 4. Note that the one to the right has 1-holes. *Right:* An unbounded digital star that is the Gauss digitization of the unbounded cross-shaped star of Figure 4 (right).

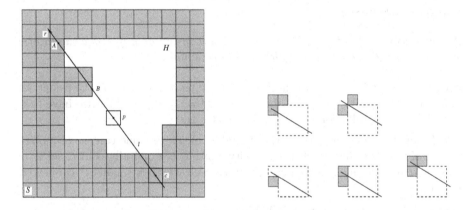

Fig. 6. Illustration to the proof of Proposition 1

Proof. 1. See the examples exposed in Figure 5 (middle), and Figure 7 (right).

2. Let S be a digital star. Reasoning by contradiction, assume that there is a finite set $G \subset \bar{S}$ that is a proper hole of S.

Consider the rectilinear set $P(G)$. Since G is finite, $P(G)$ is bounded and its boundary $\gamma = \partial(P(G))$ is a closed simple curve.

Now choose a pixel $p \in G$. Let $c \in S$ be a center of S. Let l be the straight line through the centers of pixels c and p, and r the ray (part of l) with origin p and direction opposite to c (see Figure 6 (left)). Since γ is a bounded simple and closed curve, there is a point $A \in r$ that belongs to the exterior of γ. Then, by Jordan-Velben theorem, $\gamma \cap r \neq \emptyset$. Let, for definiteness, B be the first intersection point of γ and r between p and A.

Now consider the central, upper, and lower standard digitizations L, L_1, and L_2, respectively, of the straight line l. Since l goes through the centers of pixels c and p, both c and p belong to each of L, L_1, and L_2.

Since point s belongs to $P(G)$'s boundary, it belongs to $P(S)$'s boundary as well. Hence it belongs to the boundary of one, two, or three pixels of S (see Figure 6 (right), for illustration of different cases). Then at least one of L, L_1, or L_2 above will contain at least one such pixel $p' \in S$. Denote by $[pp']$ the corresponding standard DSS with end-points p and p'. Then the star center c will see p' if and only if $[pp'] \subseteq S$. The latter, however, is not the case, since the pixel $p \in [pp']$ but $p \notin S$—a contradiction.   □

It is also easy to notice that every digitally convex set is a star. However, we have:

Fact 4. *A digital object that is both row- and column-convex, is not necessarily a digital star. A digital star is not necessarily row- and column-convex.*

Examples are given in Figure 3 (right), and Figure 5 (left, middle), respectively.

The following statements demonstrate the relation between digital convexity and starshapedness.

Proposition 2. *A set $D \subseteq \mathbb{Z}^2$ is a digital star if and only if it is a union of a family of digitally convex sets which have a common point.*

Proof. 1. Let D be a digital star and let p_0 be a center of D. Consider all standard DSSs $[p_0 p]$ over all $p \in D$. Clearly, $D = \cup_{p \in D} [p_0 p]$. We also have that every $[p_0 p]$ is digitally convex, which completes the proof.

2. From the common point of the digitally convex sets one can see all points of each of them because of their convexity. Since every digitally convex set is 1-connected and they share a common point, then clearly their union is 1-connected as well.   □

Note that an analogous statement holds for stars in $\mathbb{R}^2$ as well, as every segment is a convex set.

Remark 2. An infinite digital star may be a union of finitely many digitally convex sets with a common point. For example, the digital star in Figure 5 (right) can be represented as a union of two digital strips.

Fact 5. *The set of all centers of a digital star is digitally convex.*

Follows from the observation that every center of a digital star "must see" all others via standard DSSs.

We also have the following

Fact 6. *The union of digital stars that have a common center is a digital star. However, the intersection of digital stars with a common center may be disconnected and, therefore, not a digital star.*

A connected intersection of digital stars with a common center is a digital star.

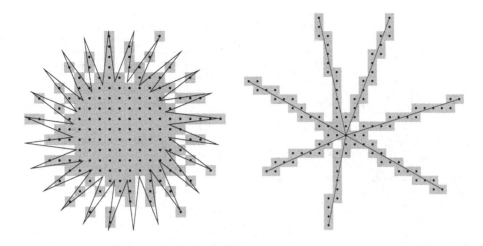

Fig. 7. *Left:* Digitization of a star in R^2 which is a disconnected digital object. *Right:* A digital star that consists of seven standard line segments with a common point. If the segments are extended to infinite standard digital rays, then the star complement would feature seven infinite connected components. *Note:* If 0-adjacency is assumed for the background, then the latter has exactly seven components; if 1-adjacency is adopted, the background has nine components: seven infinite and two finite (one pixel each).

The first part of Fact 6 follows directly from the definition of a digital star. Note that the statement holds even for a union/intersection of infinitely many distinct digital stars. For the second part, it suffices to consider the intersection of the two digital straight segments from Figure 2. Obviously, a connected intersection of digital stars with a common center is a digital star.

Next, we study the relation between stars in $\mathbb{R}^2$ and their digitizations. In view of the discussion in Section 2.3, the following fact is no surprise.

Fact 7. *The Gauss digitization of a star in $\mathbb{R}^2$ may be disconnected. See Figure 7 (left).*

Recall that a digitally convex set is a connected digital object that is a digitization of a convex set, and, equivalently (by Fact 3), it is a digital object that contains a DSS between any two points of the object. One may expect that a similar theorem holds for digital stars, i.e., that a connected set $D \subseteq \mathbb{Z}^2$ is a digital star if and only if it is a digitization of a star in $\mathbb{R}^2$. However, with stars the situation is different: the above statement holds only in one direction. More precisely, we have:

Proposition 3. *Every digital star $D \subseteq \mathbb{Z}^2$ is a digitization of a star in $\mathbb{R}^2$.*

Proof. Let D be a digital star and $c \in D$ a center of D. Hence, a standard DSS $[cp]$ exists between c and every $p \in D$.

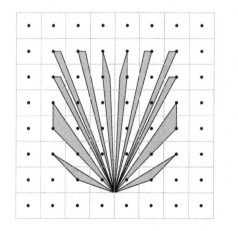 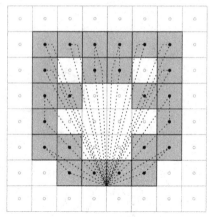

Fig. 8. Illustration to Fact 8. *Left:* A star in R^2. *Right:* The pixels that constitute the star digitization. Because of the large hole, the obtained 1-connected digital object is not a digital star.

Define

$$P = \cup_{p \in D} conv([cp]),$$

where $conv([cp])$ denotes the convex hull of $[cp]$.

All polygons $conv([cp])$ have a common point c. Then, P is a simple polygon which is a star in $\mathbb{R}^2$. By construction, its Gauss digitization is precisely D. $\quad\square$

As mentioned, the converse of Proposition 3 is not true, i.e., we have:

Fact 8. *A 1-connected digitization of a star in $\mathbb{R}^2$ may not be a digital star.*

A counterexample is provided in Fig 8.

Fact 8 is important: it demonstrates, in particular, that, unlike with digital convexity, intuitively "obvious" statements about starshapedness may actually be false. The reason seems to be rooted in the higher intrinsic complexity of digital stars, coupled with the specificity of the discrete spaces.

We conclude this section by one more negative result, revealing the essential differences in the nature of the discrete and continuous spaces. It may be tempting to try to prove a digital analog of the Krasnoselśkii's theorem recalled in Section 2.4. Unfortunately, we have the following

Proposition 4. *Krasnoselśkii's theorem does not hold for digital stars.*

Proof. With a reference to Figure 9, one can directly verify that for any triple of integer points of the given digital object D there is at least one point of S that sees all the three points through a certain standard segment. However, no point of D sees all the other seven points of D, as no point can see the point across the hole in the middle of D. Hence, D is not a digital star. $\quad\square$

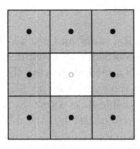

Fig. 9. Illustration to the proof of Proposition 4

Stars and Visibility of Digital Objects

Let D be an arbitrary digital object. We will call a subset $U \subseteq D$ a *surveillance set* for D if every point of D is visible from at least one point of U. In terms of art galleries, *surveillance set* can be interpreted as a set of locations of the cameras, so that every point of the gallery can be observed. The *surveillance number* $v(D)$ for a set D is the minimum cardinality of a surveillance set for D, i.e., $v(D) = \min\{k : \text{there is a surveillance set } U \text{ for } D \text{ with } |U| = k\}$.

Now let $S_1, S_2, \ldots, S_m$ be a family of stars such that $D = S_1 \cup S_2 \cup \cdots \cup S_m$. We say that $S_1, \ldots, S_m$ form a *star decomposition* for D. The *star decomposition number* $s(D)$ for a set D is the minimum possible number of stars in a star decomposition for D, i.e., $s(D) = \min\{m : D = S_1 \cup S_2 \cup \cdots \cup S_m, S_i \text{ are digital stars}, 1 \le i \le m\}$.

We have the following important result.

Proposition 5. *For any digital object D, $v(D) = s(D)$.*

Proof. 1. Let $M = \{p_1, p_2, \ldots, p_k\}$ be an arbitrary surveillance set for D. Let S_{p_i}, $1 \le i \le k$, be the maximal (by inclusion) subset of M whose points are visible from p_i. Clearly, S_{p_i} is a star. Moreover, since M is a surveillance set for D, it follows that $D = S_{p_1} \cup S_{p_2} \cup \cdots \cup S_{p_k}$. Hence, $s(D) \le k$. Since the surveillance set M was arbitrary, we obtain

$$s(D) \le v(D). \tag{1}$$

2. Now let $D = S_1 \cup S_2 \cup \cdots \cup S_m$ be an arbitrary star decomposition for D. Let $c_1, c_2, \ldots, c_m$ be arbitrary centers of $S_1, S_2, \ldots, S_m$, respectively. Then the set $C = \{c_1, c_2, \ldots, c_m\}$ is a surveillance set for D. Hence, $v(D) \le m$. Since the star decomposition $D = S_1 \cup S_2 \cup \cdots \cup S_m$ was arbitrary, it follows that

$$v(D) \le s(D). \tag{2}$$

Then (1) and (2) imply the stated equality. □

Note that Proposition 5 applies to both finite and infinite digital objects.

4   Concluding Remarks

In this paper we defined digital stars and studied their basic properties. We have also seen that the Krasnoselśkii's theorem does not hold for digital stars, in general. Work in progress is aimed at proving the following digital version of the Krasnoselśkii's art gallery theorem. A set $D \subset \mathbb{Z}^2$ is a digital star if and only if every four points of D are visible from a certain point of D.

Another interesting theoretical question is the following. According to Proposition 2, any digital star S is a union of digitally convex sets. Denote by $c(S)$ the minimal number of digitally convex sets whose union constitutes S. We call $c(S)$ the *complexity* of S. For example, one can easily realize that the complexities of the digital stars in Figs. 5 and 7 (right), and 6 are 3, 4, 2, and 7, respectively.

Problem: Construct an efficient algorithm for computing a star complexity or prove that this problem is NP-hard.

We also conjecture that computing the surveillance/star decomposition number is NP-hard.

Future work is aimed at constructing a time and space-efficient algorithm for finding a center of a digital star. Extending the considerations to higher dimensions is seen as another important task.

Acknowledgements

The authors thank the three anonymous referees for their useful remarks and suggestions. The work was partly supported by the Cooperative Research Project of RIE, Shizuoka University, Japan.

References

1. Boltianskii, V.G., Soltan, P.S.: Combinatorial Geometry of Various Classes of Convex Sets. Chişinău, Stiinţa (1978)
2. Bresenham, J.: Algorithm for computer control of a digital plotter. IBM Systems Journal 4, 25–30 (1965)
3. Brimkov, V.E., Klette, R.: Border and surface tracing – theoretical foundations. IEEE Transactions on Pattern Analysis and Machine Intelligence 30(4), 577–590 (2008)
4. Breen, M.: A Krasnosel'skii theorem for staircase paths in orthogonal polygons. J. Geometry 51, 22–30 (1994)
5. Breen, M.: An improved Krasnosel'skii-type theorem for orthogonal polygons which are stairshaped via staircase paths. J. Geometry 51, 31–35 (1994)
6. Brunn, H.: Über Kerneigebiete. Matt. Ann. 73, 436–440 (1913)
7. Klette, R., Rosenfeld, A.: Digital Geometry – Geometric Methods for Digital Picture Analysis. Morgan Kaufmann, San Francisco (2004)
8. Kong, T.Y., Roscoe, A.W., Rosenfeld, A.: Concepts of digital topology. Topology and its Applications 46, 219–262 (1992)
9. Krasnoselśkii, M.A.: Sur un critère pour qu'un domain soit étoilé. Mat. Sb. 19, 309–310 (1946)

10. Motwani, R., Raghunathan, A., Saran, H.: Covering orthogonal polygons with star polygons: the perfect graph approach. J. Comput. System Sci. 40, 19–48 (1990)
11. O'Rourke, J.: Art Gallery Theorems and Algorithms. Oxford University Press, New York (1987)
12. Reveillès, J.-P.: Géométrie Discrète, Calcul en Nombres Entiers et Algorithmique. Thèse d'État. Univ. Louis Pasteur, Strasbourg (1991)
13. Rosenfeld, A., Klette, R.: Digital straightness. Electronic Notes in Theoretical Computer Science, vol. 46. Elsevier, Amsterdam (2001)
14. Valentine, F.A.: Convex Sets. McGraw-Hill, New York (1964)
15. van der Vel, M.: Theory of Convex Structures. Elsevier, Amsterdam (1993)
16. Veblen, O.: Theory on plane curves in non-metrical analysis situs. Transactions of the American Mathematical Society 6(1), 83–98 (1905)

Ω-Arithmetization of Ellipses

Agathe Chollet[1], Guy Wallet[1], Eric Andres[2], Laurent Fuchs[2],
Gaëlle Largeteau-Skapin[2], and Aurélie Richard[2]

[1] Laboratoire MIA,
Université de La Rochelle,
Avenue Michel Crépeau 17042 La Rochelle cedex, France
{achollet01,Guy.Wallet}@univ-lr.fr
[2] Laboratoire XLIM SIC, UMR 6172,
Université de Poitiers,
BP 30179 86962 Futuroscope Chasseneuil cédex, France
{fuchs,glargeteau,andres,arichard}@sic.univ-poitiers.fr

Abstract. Multi-resolution analysis and numerical precision problems
are very important subjects in fields like image analysis or geometrical
modeling. In the continuation of our previous works, we propose to apply the method of Ω-arithmetization to ellipses. We obtain a discrete
multi-resolution representation of arcs of ellipses. The corresponding algorithms are completely constructive and thus, can be exactly translated
into functional computer programs. Moreover, we give a global condition
for the connectivity of the discrete curves generated by the method at
every scale.

Keywords: discrete geometry, multi-resolution analysis, nonstandard
analysis.

1 Introduction

Discrete analytical geometry has been somewhat accidently founded in 1988
by Jean-Pierre Reveillès [18] when he proposed the analytical description of a
discrete straight line. This was an unexpected result that came out of theoretical
research in nonstandard analysis (NSA). Nonstandard analysis [20,17] provides
an explicit framework for the manipulation of infinitely large and infinitely small
numbers. The authors, in this paper and several previous papers, have decided
to go back to the roots of Reveillès' discovery: the arithmetization method.
The arithmetization process is a way to discretize a continuous curve that is a
solution of a differential equation. The general idea is to transform a classical
approximation scheme (such as the Euler scheme for instance) of the continuous
solution of a differential equation defining a curve, into an equivalent discrete
scheme. This is possible because, given an infinitely large (nonstandard) number
ω (the global scale), it is possible to establish an equivalence between the set of
limited real numbers and a subset $\mathcal{HR}_\omega$ of $\mathbb{Z}$. The set $\mathcal{HR}_\omega$, with an additional
structure, is called the Harthong-Reeb line. The intuitive idea is that, in some
way, the real line $\mathbb{R}$ is similar to the discrete line $\mathbb{Z}$ seen from far away.

R.P. Barneva et al. (Eds.): CompIMAGE 2010, LNCS 6026, pp. 24–35, 2010.

In a previous work, the authors re-examined the circle of Holin [9,10]. The corresponding arithmetization process was based on infinitely large integers that had only an axiomatic status. Hence, the method was not constructive in nature and it was impossible to give an exact numerical representation of the result. In a past paper [5], we tried to tackle the issue of the constructivity of our model by using Ω-numbers of Laugwitz and Schmieden [12]. Roughly speaking, an Ω-number (natural, integer or rational) is a serie of numbers of same nature, with an adapted equality relation. The sets of Ω-numbers are extending the corresponding sets of usual numbers with the added advantage of providing naturally infinitely large integer numbers: for instance, an Ω-integer α represented by a sequence (α_n) of integers is such that $\alpha \approx +\infty$ if $lim_{n \to +\infty} \alpha_n = +\infty$ in the usual meaning. Clearly, these infinite numerical entities are constructive . It was a pleasant surprise to discover that the corresponding Ω-arithmetization method is also a discrete multi-scale representation of the real function on which the method is applied.

The goal of the present paper is to apply the Ω-arithmetization to the case of an ellipse and to study some connectivity properties of the corresponding discrete curve. The first result is a constructive algorithm which gives an exact discrete multi-resolution representation of an arc of ellipse. In Figure 1, we give a graphical illustration of this kind of representation. In fact, this multi-resolution aspect is a normal consequence of the Ω-arithmetization: this is in relation with the nature of the scaling parameter ω of the method. Since ω is now an infinitely large Ω-integer, it encodes an infinity of increasing scales. The arithmetization process gives simultaneously a discretization of the initial real function at each of these scales. Since nowadays many developments in image analysis, geometrical modelling, etc. comprise multi-resolution approaches and must deal with numerical precision problems, the Ω-arithmetization is a new tool which has the interesting property of taking into account these two aspects. The second main result of this paper is about the discrete connectivity: we show that the connectivity of the corresponding discrete ellipse arcs is a global property and that there is a rectangle within which these curves are connected at every scale. Such global properties for a step-by-step integration process is unexpected. It extends a similar result we already had for circles but here, the property extends through all the scales. The paper is organized as follows: in Section 2, we introduce the Ω-numbers and the associated Harthong-Reeb line. In Section 3, we propose an Ω-arithmetization of ellipse arcs. Properties and graphical representation are discussed in Section 4. We conclude and provide perspectives for this work in Section 5.

2   Theoretical Basis : The Ω-Numbers and the Associated Harthong-Reeb Line

The aim of this section is to present the basis of the nonstandard theory of Laugwitz and Schmieden [12,13]. Our goal is to implement such a theory using the Ocaml language [11] and use it to build conic arcs.

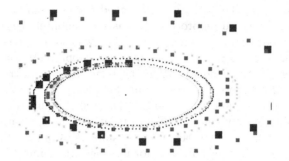

Fig. 1. Graphical representations of the multiresolution aspects of the Ω-arithmetization of an arc of ellipse. (Full explanation in Section 3).

Globally, this theory permits the definition of a nonstandard model of the integer number set that can be used to build a discrete model of real numbers. This discrete model of the continuum is called the Harthong-Reeb line [8]. The main interest of this nonstandard model (compared to other nonstandard theories such as, for instance, Internal Set Theory [17]) is that it is constructive [3]. Therefore, the implementation in a programming language is possible. In this section, we will not describe the whole theory but only introduce the basic notions that are essential to the understanding of the Harthong-Reeb line. For more details about our approach please refer to [5].

2.1 The Ω-Numbers of Laugwitz and Schmieden

To extend a theory of integer numbers, Laugwitz and Schmieden introduced a new symbol, Ω, to the classical ones $(0, 3, 9, +, /, ...)$. The only thing that we know about it is that Ω verifies the following propriety named the *Basic Definition (BD)*:

Definition 1. *Let $S(n)$ be a statement in $\mathbb{N}$ depending of $n \in \mathbb{N}$. If $S(n)$ is true for almost $n \in \mathbb{N}$, then $S(\Omega)$ is true.*

We specify that here and in all this article, the expression "*almost $n \in \mathbb{N}$*" means "for all $n \in \mathbb{N}$ from some level N", i.e. "($\exists N \in \mathbb{N}$) such that ($\forall n \in \mathbb{N}$) with $n > N$". Since Ω can be substituted to any natural number, it denotes an Ω-number which is the first example of Ω-integer. Immediately, we can verify that Ω is infinitely large, i.e. greater than every element of $\mathbb{N}$. Indeed, for $p \in \mathbb{N}$, we apply (BD) to the statement $p < n$ which is true for almost $n \in \mathbb{N}$; thus $p < \Omega$ for each $p \in \mathbb{N}$. One simple such example is Ω defined by the sequence $(n)_{n \in \mathbb{N}}$.

Hence, each element a of this theory will be declined as a sequence $(a_n)_{n \in \mathbb{N}}$. To compare such Ω-numbers, we put the following equivalence relation:

Definition 2. *Let $a = (a_n)_{n \in \mathbb{N}}$ and $b = (b_n)_{n \in \mathbb{N}}$ be two Ω-numbers, a and b are equal if it exists $N \in \mathbb{N}$ such that for all $n > N$, $a_n = b_n$.*

The definition of the operations and relations between $\mathbb{Z}_\Omega$, the set of Ω-numbers are the following:

Definition 3. *Let $a = (a_n)_{n \in \mathbb{N}}$ and $b = (b_n)_{n \in \mathbb{N}}$ two Ω-numbers,*

- $a + b =_{def} (a_n + b_n)_{n \in \mathbb{N}}$ *and* $-a =_{def} (-a_n)$ *and* $a \times b =_{def} (a_n \times b_n)_{n \in \mathbb{N}}$;
- $a > b =_{def} [(\exists N \forall n > N)\, a_n > b_n]$ *and* $a \geqslant b =_{def} [(\exists N \forall n > N)\, a_n \geqslant b_n]$;
- $|a| =_{def} (|a_n|)$.

As in all nonstandard theories, there exist two classes of elements, the standard ones and the nonstandard ones. We recall that in classical IST nonstandard theory, this second class exists only in an axiomatic way: there are the infinitely small and large numbers. Here, the two classes of elements can be distinguished:

- the class of *standard* elements are the elements $\alpha = (\alpha_n)_{n \in \mathbb{N}}$ which verify $\exists p \in \mathbb{Z}$ such that $\exists N \in \mathbb{N}$, $\forall n > N, \alpha_n = p$ (example: $(2)_{n \in \mathbb{N}}$).
- the class of *nonstandard* elements are all the other elements of $\mathbb{Z}_\Omega$ (examples: $(-1)_{n \in \mathbb{N}}^n$, $(n)_{n \in \mathbb{N}}$)

Among the nonstandard elements, we focus on the *infinitely large* numbers which are the sequences $\alpha = (\alpha_n)_{n \in \mathbb{N}}$ such that $\lim_{n \to +\infty} \alpha_n = +\infty$ (example: $(n)_{n \in \mathbb{N}}$).

2.2   The Harthong-Reeb Line Based on Ω-Numbers

The Harthong-Reeb line ($\mathcal{HR}_\omega$) is built upon the usual nonstandard axiomatic theory IST [8]. This kind of formalism was introduced by Diener in [6]. It is defined as a scaling on the integer numbers. We consider a new unit which is an infinitely large integer named $\omega = (\omega_n)_{n \in \mathbb{N}}$, which can be Ω himself. This scaling strongly contracts $\mathbb{Z}$ so that the result looks like $\mathbb{R}$ [7].

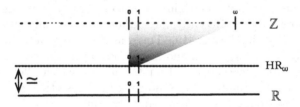

Fig. 2. Intuitive representation of the Harthong-Reeb line

More formally, we defined the Harthong-Reeb with Ω-numbers as follows.

Definition 4. *We consider the set*

$$\mathcal{HR}_\omega = \{x \in \mathbb{Z}_\Omega,\ \exists p \in \mathbb{N},\ |x| \leq p\omega\}$$

and the relations, operations and constants on $\mathcal{HR}_\omega$ described by the following definitional equalities: for all $(x, y) \in \mathcal{HR}_\omega^2$, we set

- $(x =_\omega y) =_{def} (\forall p \in \mathbb{N})\, (p|x - y| \leq \omega)$;
- $(x >_\omega y) =_{def} (\exists p \in \mathbb{N})\, (p(x - y) \geq \omega)$;

- $(x \neq_\omega y) =_{def} (x >_\omega y) \vee (x <_\omega y)$;
- $(x \leq_\omega y) =_{def} (\forall z \in \mathcal{HR}_\omega)(z <_\omega x \Rightarrow z <_\omega y)$;
- $(x +_\omega y) =_{def} (x + y)$ and $0_\omega =_{def} 0$ and $-_\omega x =_{def} -x$;
- $(x \times_\omega y) =_{def} ((x \times y) \div \omega)$ and $1_\omega =_{def} \omega$ and $x^{(-1)_\omega} =_{def} (\omega^2 \div x)$ for $x \neq_\omega 0$.

Then, the Harthong-Reeb line is the numerical system $(\mathcal{HR}_\omega, =_\omega, \leq_\omega, +_\omega, \times_\omega)$.

We can say that $\mathcal{HR}_\omega$ is the set of Ω-integers which are limited at the scale ω. We can describe all these relations and operations with integers, for instance, $x =_\omega y \Longleftrightarrow \forall p \in \mathbb{N} \, \exists M_p \in \mathbb{N} \, \forall n \geq M_p \quad p|x_n - y_n| \leq \omega_n$.

The goal of the construction of this line is to obtain a discrete model of the continuum. To understand that the Harthong-Reeb line is a kind of continuum, we can compare it to $(\mathcal{R}_\Omega^{lim}, \simeq, \lesssim, +, \times)$. This is the set of limited Ω-rational numbers of Laugwitz and Schmieden defined considering sequences of rational numbers. The two following maps:

$$\left\{ \begin{matrix} \varphi_\omega : \mathcal{HR}_\omega \to \mathcal{R}_\Omega^{lim} \\ x \mapsto x/\omega \end{matrix} \right\} \text{ and } \left\{ \begin{matrix} \psi_\omega : \mathcal{R}_\Omega^{lim} \to \mathcal{HR}_\omega \\ u \mapsto (\lfloor \omega u \rfloor) \end{matrix} \right\}$$

are the isomorphic maps necessary to pass from the classical real world to the discrete one. The following section uses the Harthong-Reeb line to define the *arithmetization* process based on the well known Euler scheme.

3   The Discrete Ellipse Arcs

In this section we revisit and extend recent work about the arithmetization method. The arithmetization is basically a way of transforming a continuous Euler scheme into a discrete one. This leads to a step-by-step generation algorithm of a discrete object. Recently the authors have arithmetized differential equations defining a circular arc [19]. This was done with an axiomatic definition of infinitely large integers. In another recent paper, the authors introduced the Ω-arithmetization method based on Ω-numbers which allows a constructive representation of infinitely large integers. In this section we apply the Ω-arithmetization to circles and more generally to ellipses.

We consider an axis-aligned ellipse of equation

$$\frac{x(t)^2}{a'^2} + \frac{y(t)^2}{b'^2} = 1 \tag{1}$$

with a' and $b' \in \mathbb{Q}$. The parametric form of this set is

$$\begin{cases} x = a' \cos(t) \\ y = b' \sin(t) \end{cases} \tag{2}$$

and is the solution of the differential system

$$\begin{cases} x' = -a'/b' \, y(t) \\ y' = b'/a' \, x(t). \end{cases} \tag{3}$$

As a' and b' are in $\mathbb{Q}$, so there exist $p, q, \in \mathbb{Z}$ and $r, s \in \mathbb{N}^*$ such that $a' = p/r$ and $b' = q/s$. We can define two integer numbers a an b thus that $a/b = a'/b'$ and $b/a = b'/a'$. So, now only integers are manipulated in the differential system.

To obtain a solution we use the well known Euler method. In this case, we have:

$$\begin{cases} (x_0, y_0) & = (0, b') \\ (x_{n+1}, y_{n+1}) = (x_n, y_n) + (-\dfrac{a}{b}h\ y_n, \dfrac{b}{a}h\ x_n). \end{cases} \tag{4}$$

We know that the smaller the integration step h, the better the approximation. In some meaning, the better choice is an infinitesimal h.

We want to embed this scheme in $\mathcal{HR}_\Omega$ line. Using the idea of the isomorphism ψ_ω

$$\psi_\omega : \mathcal{R}_{lim} \longrightarrow \mathcal{HR}_\omega$$
$$x \longmapsto \lfloor \omega x \rfloor$$

and replace the step h by $1/\beta$ we can write the following scheme

$$\begin{cases} (x_0, y_0) & = (0, \lfloor \omega b' \rfloor) \\ (x_{n+1}, y_{n+1}) = (x_n, y_n) + ((-ay_n) \div (b\beta), bx_n \div (a\beta)) \end{cases} \tag{5}$$

where

- $\exists \alpha$ such that $\alpha, \beta, \omega \in \mathcal{HR}_\omega$; $\alpha, \beta, \omega \simeq +\infty$ and $\omega = \alpha\beta$ (we say that ω is the global scale)
- $\lfloor \omega b' \rfloor = (\lfloor \omega_0 b' \rfloor, \lfloor \omega_1 b' \rfloor, \ldots)$
- $\forall u, v \in \mathcal{HR}_\omega, u \div v = (\lfloor u_0 \div v_0 \rfloor, \lfloor u_1 \div v_1 \rfloor, \ldots)$
- $(x_0, y_0) \in \mathcal{HR}_\omega^2$

As presented in [4,19], the problem of this scheme is that it generates values that are infinitely far from each other and thus the corresponding discrete curve is strongly (infinitely) non-connected. To avoid this problem, we divide everything by β in order to bring the discrete points close together. It is equivalent to work at a scale α which is named the intermediary scale.[1] Let us introduce the following notations to describe the decomposition $x = \tilde{x}\beta + \hat{x}$: for any integer $x \in \mathcal{HR}_\omega$ so $\tilde{x} = x \div \beta \in \mathcal{HR}_\alpha$ and $\hat{x} = x \bmod \beta \in \{0, \ldots, \beta - 1\}$. The integer $\tilde{x} \in \mathcal{HR}_\alpha$ is interpreted as the result of the rescaling on x. This decomposition produces the following scheme:

$$\begin{cases} (\tilde{x}_0, \tilde{y}_0) & = (0, \lfloor \omega b' \rfloor \div \beta) \\ (\hat{x}_0, \hat{y}_0) & = (0, \lfloor \omega b' \rfloor \bmod \beta) \\ (f_n^1, f_n^2) & = ((-a(\tilde{y}_n\beta + \hat{y}_n)) \div (b\beta), b(\tilde{x}_n\beta + \hat{x}_n) \div (a\beta)) \\ (\tilde{x}_{n+1}, \tilde{y}_{n+1}) = (\tilde{x}_n + (\hat{x}_n + f_n^1) \div \beta, \tilde{y}_n + (\hat{y}_n + f_n^2) \div \beta) \\ (\hat{x}_{n+1}, \hat{y}_{n+1}) = ((\hat{x}_n + f_n^1) \bmod \beta, (\hat{y}_n + f_n^2) \bmod \beta) \end{cases} \tag{6}$$

the relevant variables are $\tilde{x}$ and $\tilde{y} \in \mathcal{HR}_\alpha$ while $\hat{x}$ and $\hat{x}$ only conserve the accumulated error.

---

[1] We could of course as well work at the intermediary scale β. The equations would be slightly different because of the role of β as $1/h$ but the principle would remain the same.

Let us call $E_d^\alpha(0, a, b)$ the discrete curve defined by the solution $(\widetilde{x}_n, \widetilde{y}_n)$ of (6). $E_d^\alpha(0, a, b)$ is the arithmetization at the intermediate scale α of the initial ellipse (1).

Observe that the algorithm (6) is standard. This means that for α, β and ω standard we get a usual scheme in $\mathbb{Z}^2$. Nevertheless, in this paper, we have to consider that all objects are Ω-numbers, i.e. infinite sequences of integers operating with the relations and operations defined in Section 2, for instance, $a = (a)_{m \in \mathbb{N}}$, $b = (b)_{m \in \mathbb{N}}^2$ and $\beta = (\beta_m)_{m \in \mathbb{N}}$ and $(\widetilde{x}_n, \widetilde{y}_n)_{n \in \mathbb{N}} = ((\widetilde{x}_{m,n}), (\widetilde{y}_{m,n}))_{n \in \mathbb{N}}$.

Let us note that n represents the iteration in the algorithm and that m the level in the sequence.

4   Properties and Graphical Results

In this section we present some theoretical results on the connectivity of the elliptical arcs and some graphical illustrations of the algorithm which result of an implementation in Ocaml. Let us first start with an extension of the theorem on the connectivity of circular arcs proposed in [19] by A. Richard and al.

4.1   Connectivity Properties

Before proving connectivity properties, we need some definitions.

Definition 5. *An arc of $E_d^\alpha(0, a, b)$ is a sequence of the following form $(\widetilde{x}_n, \widetilde{y}_n)_{k < n < k+p}$ for k and p fixed in $\mathbb{N}$*

Then, we define the notion of connectedness with Ω-intergers and call it 8_Ω-connectedness:

Definition 6. *A curve defined by the Ω-points $((\widetilde{x}_{m,n}), (\widetilde{y}_{m,n}))_{(m \in \mathbb{N}, \ k \le n \le k+p)}$ is 8_Ω-connexe if*

$$\forall n, \ \forall m, \ |x_{m,n+1} - x_{m,n}| \le 1 \ and \ |y_{m,n+1} - y_{m,n}| \le 1.$$

This is equivalent to the classical 8-connectedness for each level m of the underlying sequences. This is the natural generalization to the Ω-numbers of the discrete connectivity. We also need the definition of a rectangle that is defined in $\mathbb{Z}_\Omega^2$. A *rectangle in $\mathbb{Z}_\Omega^2$*, centered in zero and with length $2l = (2l, 2l, ...)$ and width $2w = (2w, 2w, ...)$ is defined by :

$$R_{l,w} = \{(x, y) \in \mathbb{Z}_\Omega^2 \ ; \ -l \le x < l \ and \ -w \le y < w\}.$$

If we remember that Ω-numbers are sequences, this definition becomes:

$$R_{l,w} = \{((x_m)_{(m \in \mathbb{N})}, (y_m)_{(m \in \mathbb{N})}) \in \mathbb{Z}_\Omega^2 \ ; \forall n \in \mathbb{N} \ (-l \le x_m < l \ and \ -w \le y_m < w)\}.$$

---

[2] Here a and b are standard Ω-numbers because of φ_Ω, hence the sequences are constant ones.

The following theorem is an extension of the connectivity theorem given in [19]. This is a double extension: firstly to the axis aligned elliptical arcs and secondly to the Ω-numbers. The proof is very close to the one proposed in [19]. It is however remarkable that, since we are working with Ω-integers, the result is a multi-scale result that is valid at all scales at the same time.

Theorem 1. *Every arc of $E_d^\alpha(0, a, b)$ in the square $R_{l,w}$ is 8-Ω-connected for $l = a\beta \div b$ and $b\beta \div a$.*

Proof. Let $\Gamma = ((\widetilde{x}_n, \widetilde{y}_n))_{k \leq n \leq k+p}$ an arc of $E_d^\alpha(0, a, b)$ such that $(\widetilde{x}_n, \widetilde{y}_n) \in R_\beta$ for each $n = k, \ldots, k+p$.

The proof is in two parts: in part (a) we will give a necessary and sufficient condition for the connectedness of Γ and in part (b) we will show that the condition $\Gamma \subset R_{l,w}$ with $(l, w) = (a\beta \div b, b\beta \div a)$ is sufficient.

(a) *Equivalent conditions:* using the two schemes (5) and (6) and properties of the Euclidean division, we can see that the following conditions are equivalent:

$$-1 \leq \widetilde{x}_{m,n+1} - \widetilde{x}_{m,n} \leq 1$$

$$-1 \leq (\widehat{x}_{m,n} + f_n^1) \div \beta_m \leq 1$$

$$-\beta_m \leq \widehat{x}_n + f_n^1 < 2\beta_m$$

$$-\beta_m - \widehat{x}_{m,n} \leq (-a(\widetilde{y}_{m,n}\beta_m + \widehat{y}_{m,n})) \div (b\beta_m) < 2\beta_m - \widehat{x}_{m,n}$$

$$-b\beta_m^2 - b\widehat{x}_{m,n}\beta_m \leq -a(\widetilde{y}_n\beta_m + \widehat{y}_{m,n}) < 2b\beta_m^2 - b\widehat{x}_{m,n}\beta_m$$

$$-b\beta_m^2 - b\widehat{x}_{m,n}\beta_m \leq -ay_{m,n} < 2b\beta_m^2 - b\widehat{x}_{m,n}\beta_m$$

$$-\frac{b}{a}(\beta_m^2 + \widehat{x}_{m,n}\beta_m) \leq -y_{m,n} < \frac{b}{a}(2\beta_m^2 - \widehat{x}_{m,n}\beta_m)$$

Hence with a similar proof for $(\widetilde{y}_{m,n+1} - \widetilde{y}_{m,n})$, Γ is 8Ω-connected if and only if, for each $n = k, \ldots, k+p-1$ for all m, we have:

- $\dfrac{b}{a}(-2\beta_m^2 + \widehat{x}_{m,n}\beta_m) < y_{m,n} \leq \dfrac{b}{a}(\beta_m^2 + \widehat{x}_{m,n}\beta_m)$
- $\dfrac{a}{b}(\beta_m^2 + \widehat{y}_{m,n}\beta_m) \leq x_{m,n} < \dfrac{a}{b}(2\beta_m^2 - \widehat{y}_{m,n}\beta_m)$.

(b) *Sufficient condition:* We prove here that if $\Gamma \subset R_{a\beta \div b, b\beta \div a}$, then the previous condition is verified. Since $0 \leq \widehat{x}_n \leq \beta - 1$ and $0 \leq \widehat{y}_n \leq \beta - 1$, we get the two following sequences of inequalities:

$$\frac{b}{a}(-2\beta_m^2 + \widehat{x}_{m,n}\beta_m) \leq \frac{b}{a}(-\beta_m^2 - \beta_m) < -\frac{b}{a}\beta_m^2 < \frac{b}{a}\beta_m^2 \leq \frac{b}{a}(\beta_m^2 + \widehat{x}_{m,n}\beta_m)$$

$$-\frac{a}{b}(\beta_m^2 + \widehat{y}_{m,n}\beta_m) \leq -\frac{a}{b}\beta_m^2 < \frac{a}{b}\beta_m^2 < \frac{a}{b}(\beta_m^2 + \beta_m) \leq \frac{a}{b}(2\beta_m^2 - \widehat{y}_{m,n}\beta_m).$$

From $-\dfrac{b}{a}\beta_m^2 \leq y_n < \dfrac{b}{a}\beta_m^2$, we derive[3] $\left(-\dfrac{b}{a}\beta_m^2\right) \div \beta \leq y_n \div \beta < \dfrac{b}{a}\beta_m^2 \div \beta$ which imply $-\dfrac{b}{a}\beta_m \leq \widetilde{y}_n < \dfrac{b}{a}\beta_m$. This implies $-(b\beta_m \div a) \leq \widetilde{y}_n < b\beta_m \div a$.

---

[3] Usually, the division algorithm operates on integer numbers. Here we need to extend it to rational numbers. Hence we defined $u \div v$ where u and v are rational fractions by $u \div v =_{def} \lfloor u/v \rfloor$.

For $\widetilde{x}$, applying the same property, if $-\dfrac{a}{b}\beta_m^2 \leq x_n < \dfrac{a}{b}\beta_m^2$, then $-(a\beta_m \div b) \leq \widetilde{x}_n < a\beta_m \div b$. This is the condition of the inclusion in the rectangle $R_{a\beta \div b, b\beta \div a}$ and so for the 8_Ω-connectedness. $\qquad\qquad\qquad\qquad\qquad\qquad\qquad\qquad\square$

The section (4.2) shows some representations and interpretations of this theorem.

4.2   Graphical Illustrations

In this section, we present different representations of axis-aligned elliptical arcs which illustrate our connectivity theorem and our arithmetization method in general. The Ω-integers are implemented in Ocaml language. Firstly, some words about this language: Ocaml is a functional programming language i.e. a programming paradigm that treats computation as the evaluation of mathematical functions and avoids state and mutable data. It prefers the application of functions, contrarily to the imperative programming style, which emphasizes changes in state. Hence, objects are functions which permits the manipulation of infinite ones. For instance, Ω-integers are viewed as a function of integers: sequences which associate a value a_n to n for all n.

The multiresolution aspect is graphic ally represented by the different colors which encode the level m in the Ω-integers. We can observe that there is a correlation between the level of resolution and the size of the error. It is important to understand that the Ω-numbers contain all the scales at the same time and that the model as such is inherently multiscale. In fact, the algorithm handle entities which are infinite, but for the graphical illustration, we just extract some of them.

According to the theorem of Section 4.1, we have here two Ω-arithmetization of circle arcs. In Figure 3(a), the arc is connected and satisfies $\alpha R < \beta$, $(R, \alpha, \beta) = ((2)_n, (2n)_n, (9n)_n)$, hence we have indeed $\forall n \in \mathbb{N}$, $R\alpha_n = 2*2n = 4n < 9n$. The second example, in Figure 3(b) is not connected. Its parameters are $(R, \alpha, \beta) = ((2)_n, (4n)_n, (3n)_n)$.

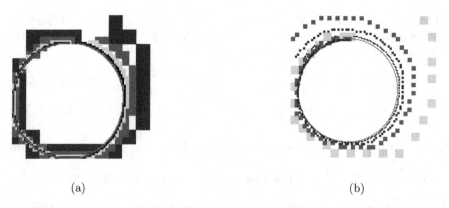

(a)   (b)

Fig. 3. Graphical representations of the Ω-arithmetization of connected and non-connected circle arcs

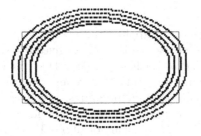

Fig. 4. Illustration of the theorem with an ellipse $E_d^{(2n)_{n \in \mathbb{N}}}(0,3,2)$ with $\beta = (80n)_{n \in \mathbb{N}}$

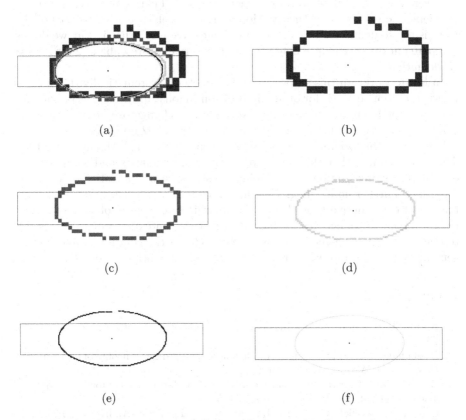

Fig. 5. Graphical representations of ellipse with the associated rectangle-connectedness

The Figure 4. shows that all the parts (arcs) of the ellipse that are located inside the rectangle $R_{(2\beta; \lfloor 0.5\beta \rfloor)}$ are connected.

In Figure 5. we can see in (a) a multiresolution representation of a discrete ellipse $E_d^{(2n)_{n \in \mathbb{N}}}(0,4,2)$ with $\beta = (7n)_{n \in \mathbb{N}}$. The pictures (b), (c), (d), (e), (f) are the different scales presented separately in Figure 5.(a). The rectangle $R_{(2\beta; \lfloor 0.5\beta \rfloor)}$ is also displayed for each picture.

5   Conclusion

In the present paper, we have applied the new concept of Ω-arithmetization to the case of an arc of ellipse. This method gives a discrete and multi-scale representation of this kind of Euclidean object. Due to the structure of the Ω-integers, we obtain a completely constructive algorithms which can be exactly translated into functional computer programs. It follows that these programs do not generate any numerical error and they provide an exact discrete multi-resolution representation of the given arc of ellipse. Furthermore, we have shown that a discrete ellipse arc is connected inside a global region of the discrete plane.

The connectivity properties of a one-revolution ellipse is here not studied however. The accumulated error of Euler scheme still exists and does, of course, not depend on the applied theory. Moreover, we emphasize that the goal of this work is not to define discrete objects in an intuitive way. That is why we do not compare our discrete ellipse definition with others like Bresenham [2] or Andres [1] definitions.

In future works on this subject, we plan to study systematically this form of multi-resolution analysis for other kinds of continuous curves such as polynomial ones and spline curves. In addition, we intend to change our general theoretical framework; we want to move from the theory of Ω-numbers of Laugwitz-Schmieden to the formalism of constructive type theory of P. Martin-Löf [14,15]. The first reason is that this stark approach of mathematics and computer science is well suited for both developing constructive mathematics and writing programs. Furthermore, Martin-Löf has already developed a nonstandard extension of constructive type theory [16] in which we dispose of infinitely large natural numbers. Hence, in this more satisfactory context, it would be possible to define an Harthong-Reeb line as a new model of the continuum and build a general tool for discrete multi-resolution analysis of continuous objects.

References

1. Andres, E.: Discrete circles, rings and spheres. Computer and Graphics 18(5), 695–706 (1994)
2. Bresenham, J.E.: A linear algorithm for incremental digital display of circular arcs. Comm. of ACM 20(2), 100–106 (1977)
3. Bridges, D.S.: Constructive mathematics: A foundation for computable analysis. Theor. Comput. Sci. 219(1-2), 95–109 (1999)
4. Chollet, A., Wallet, G., Fuchs, L., Largeteau-Skapin, G., Andres, E.: Insight in discrete geometry and computational content of a discrete model of the continuum. Pattern Recognition 42(10), 2220–2228 (2009)
5. Chollet, A., Wallet, G., Fuchs, L., Largeteau-Skapin, G., Andres, E.: ω-arithmetization: a discrete multi-resolution representation of real functions. In: Wiederhold, P., Barneva, R.P. (eds.) IWCIA 2009. LNCS, vol. 5852, pp. 316–329. Springer, Heidelberg (2009)
6. Diener, M.: Application du calcul de Harthong-Reeb aux routines graphiques. In: Salanskis, J.-M., Sinaceurs, H. (eds.) Le Labyrinthe du Continu, pp. 424–435. Springer, Heidelberg (1992)

7. Fuchs, L., Largeteau-Skapin, G., Wallet, G., Andres, E., Chollet, A.: A first look into a formal and constructive approach for discrete geometry using nonstandard analysis. In: Coeurjolly, D., Sivignon, I., Tougne, L., Dupont, F. (eds.) DGCI 2008. LNCS, vol. 4992, pp. 21–32. Springer, Heidelberg (2008)

8. Harthong, J.: Éléments pour une théorie du continu. Astérisque (109/110), 235–244 (1983)

9. Holin, H.: Harthong-Reeb circles. Séminaire Non Standard, Univ. de Paris 7 (89/2), 1–30 (1989)

10. Holin, H.: Harthong-Reeb analysis and digital circles. The Visual Computer 8(1), 8–17 (1991)

11. INRIA-consortium. Le langage Caml, http://www.ocaml.org/

12. Laugwitz, D.: Ω-calculus as a generalization of field extension. In: Hurd, A. (ed.) Nonstandard Analysis – Recent Developments. Lecture Notes in Mathematics, vol. 983, pp. 144–155. Springer, Heidelberg (1983)

13. Schmieden, C., Laugwitz, D.: Eine erweiterung der Infinitesimalrechnung. Mathematische Zeitschrift 69(1), 1–39 (1958)

14. Martin-Löf, P.: Constructive mathematics and computer programming. In: Logic, Methodology and Philosophy of Science VI, pp. 153–175 (1980)

15. Martin-Löf, P.: Intuitionnistic Type Theory. Bibliopolis, Napoli (1984)

16. Martin-Löf, P.: Mathematics of infinity. In: Gilbert, J.R., Karlsson, R. (eds.) COLOG 1988. LNCS, vol. 417, pp. 146–197. Springer, Heidelberg (1990)

17. Nelson, E.: Internal set theory: A new approach to nonstandard analysis. Bulletin of the American Mathematical Society 83(6), 1165–1198 (1977)

18. Reveillès, J.-P.: Géométrie Discrète, Calcul en Nombres Entiers et Algorithmique. PhD thesis, Université Louis Pasteur, Strasbourg, France (1991)

19. Richard, A., Wallet, G., Fuchs, L., Andres, E., Largeteau-Skapin, G.: Arithmetization of a circular arc. In: Brlek, S., Reutenauer, C., Provençal, X. (eds.) DGCI 2009. LNCS, vol. 5810, pp. 350–361. Springer, Heidelberg (2009)

20. Robinson, A.: Non-standard Analysis, 2nd edn. American Elsevier, New York (1974)

Connectedness of Offset Digitizations
in Higher Dimensions

Valentin E. Brimkov

Mathematics Department, SUNY Buffalo State College, Buffalo, NY 14222, USA
brimkove@buffalostate.edu

Abstract. In this paper we investigate properties of a digital object obtained by taking the integer points within an offset of a certain radius of the object. Our considerations apply to digitizations of arbitrary path-connected sets in an arbitrary dimension n. Corollaries are derived for the important special case of surfaces, as well as for offsets of disconnected sets.

Keywords: digital geometry, digital curve, digital surface, digital object connectedness, set offset, path-connected set, edge-connected/ disconnected graph, spanning tree.

1 Introduction

A basic approach to modeling curves and surfaces in computer aided geometric design is the one based on computing the *offset* of a curve/surface Γ – the locus of points at a given distance d from Γ (see, e.g., [5,6,15] and the bibliography therein). As a rule, such sort of considerations resort to results from algebraic geometry (see, e.g., [4,10]). Usually, when looking for an offset defined by a distance d, one does not keep track of the properties of the set of integer points enclosed by the offset. Offset approach has also been used to define digital circles and spheres, whose connectedness properties have been studied, as well [2,3].

In a recent paper [8] we provided a complete answer (from a digital geometry point of view) to some basic theoretical questions concerning digital curves defined by offsets. We showed that, in dimension n, if the offset radius is greater than or equal to $\sqrt{n}/2$, the obtained digital curve features maximal connectedness. We also demonstrated that the radius value $\sqrt{n}/2$ is the minimal possible that always guarantees such a connectedness. Moreover, we proved that a radius length greater than or equal to $\sqrt{n-1}/2$ guarantees 0-connectedness, and that this is the minimal possible value with this property. Note that assuring connectedness of a digital curve, surface, or other digital primitives is an important issue in digital geometry (see [1,7,9,11,12,13,14,16,17,22,23,24]).

In the present work we extend the considerations to an offset digitization of an arbitrary set $S \subset \mathbb{R}^n$. First we show that the results from [8] apply to the case when S is a general curve. Then we use this last fact to obtain a similar result

R.P. Barneva et al. (Eds.): CompIMAGE 2010, LNCS 6026, pp. 36–46, 2010.

for the case of an arbitrary path-connected set. We also consider the special case of surfaces in view of the questions about their connectedness and presence of gaps and tunnels. We also consider the case of an arbitrary (not necessarily path-connected) set.

The paper is organized as follows. In the next section we recall some basic notions of digital geometry to be used in the sequel, as well as the geometric interpretation of offset construction and the basic results of [8]. In Sections 3 and 4 we present the main theoretical results. We conclude with some final remarks in Section 5.

2   Preliminaries

2.1   Some Definitions and Notations

Throughout we conform to terminology used in [18] (see also [19,22]).

Our considerations take place in the *grid cell model* which consists of the grid cells of $\mathbb{Z}^n$, together with the related topology. In this model, a regular orthogonal grid subdivides $\mathbb{R}^n$ into n-dimensional hypercubes (e.g., unit squares for $n = 2$ or unit cubes for $n = 3$, also considered as n-*cells*) defining a class $\mathbb{C}_n^{(n)}$. These are usually called *hypervoxels*, or *voxels*, for short. Let $\mathbb{C}_n^{(k)}$ be the class of all k-dimensional cells of n-dimensional hypercubes, for $0 \leq k \leq n$. The grid-cell space $\mathbb{C}_n$ is the union of all classes $\mathbb{C}_n^{(k)}$, for $0 \leq k \leq n$. The $(n-1)$-cells, 1-cells, and 0-cells of a voxel are referred to as *facets*, *edges*, and *vertices*, respectively.

We say that two voxels v, v' are k-adjacent for $k = 0, 1, \ldots, n-1$, if they share a k-cell.

An n-dimensional (nD) digital object S is a finite set of voxels. A k-*path* (where $0 \leq k \leq n - 1$) in S is a sequence of voxels from S such that every two consecutive voxels of the path are k-adjacent. Two voxels of S are k-*connected* (in S) iff there is a k-path in S between them. A subset G of S is k-*connected* iff there is a k-path connecting any two voxels of G.

A maximal (by inclusion) k-connected subset of a digital object S is called a k-*(connected) component* of S. Components are non-empty and distinct k-components are disjoint.

Given a set $M \subseteq \mathbb{R}^n$, by $|M|$ we denote its cardinality and by $M_{\mathbb{Z}}$ its *Gauss digitization* $M \cap \mathbb{Z}^n$.

Throughout the paper, the Euclidean norm is assumed. For a hyperball in $\mathbb{R}^n$ we will also use the term an n-*ball*. An n-ball of radius r and center c will be denoted by $B(c, r)$, and the corresponding sphere by $S(c, r)$.

A *curve* $\gamma \in \mathbb{R}^n$ is a continuous mapping $\gamma : I \to \mathbb{R}^n$, where I is a closed interval of real numbers.

A set $A \subseteq \mathbb{R}^n$ is *path-connected* if for any two points $p, q \in \mathbb{R}^n$ there is a path (continuous curve) $\gamma \subseteq A$ with endpoints p and q.

By $d(x, y)$ we denote the *Euclidean distance* between two points $x, y \in \mathbb{R}^n$. Given two sets $A, B \subset \mathbb{R}^n$, the Euclidean distance between them is defined by $d(A, B) = \inf_{x,y} \{d(x, y) : x \in A, y \in B\}$.

2.2 Geometric Interpretation of the Offset Concept

We first briefly recall the dynamic geometric interpretation of the concept of a curve offset used in [8].

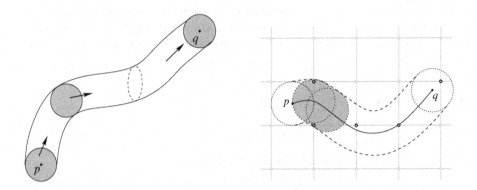

Fig. 1. *Left:* Geometric interpretation. The curve offset as a trace of a moving ball along a curve with endpoints p and q. *Right:* A 2D example of a 0-connected digital curve obtained by an offset of radius $\sqrt{n-1}/2 = 1/2$. The points of the digital curve are marked by small circles.

Let γ be a curve in $\mathbb{R}^n$ with endpoints p and q. Place an n-ball B of a radius r at p. The space included in the n-ball is part of the offset.

Now move B so that its center continuously runs over γ until it reaches the other endpoint q. See Figure 1, left. The space traced by B while its center is moving from p to q constitutes the r-offset of γ. It will be denoted by $\mathit{Off}(\gamma, r)$. We will identify ball's position by the position of its center.

The above geometric interpretation extends to arbitrary sets. Given a set $S \subseteq \mathbb{R}^n$, imagine that one moves a ball of radius r over all points of S. Then $\mathit{Off}(S, r)$ is the entire space traced by the ball during its motion.

The set $D(S, r)$ of integer points within an r-offset $\mathit{Off}(S, r)$ will be called r-offset digitization of S.

In what follows, we will make use of the following results from [8].

Theorem 1. *Let γ be a curve in $\mathbb{R}^n$, $n \geq 2$. If $r \geq \sqrt{n}/2$, then $D(\gamma, r)$ is $(n-1)$-connected.*

Moreover, the value $r = \sqrt{n}/2$ is the minimal possible that guarantees $(n-1)$-connectedness of $D(\gamma, r)$.

Theorem 2. *Let γ be a curve in $\mathbb{R}^n$, $n \geq 2$. If $r \geq \sqrt{n-1}/2$, then $D(\gamma, r)$ is at least 0-connected.*

Moreover, the value $r = \sqrt{n-1}/2$ is the minimal possible that guarantees 0-connectedness of $D(\gamma, r)$.

3   Generalization for Arbitrary Path-Connected Sets

We first consider the case of an offset digitization of more general curves than those considered in [8]. More specifically, a *general curve* γ is a one-dimensional continuum[1] [25,20]. See Figure 2 (left).

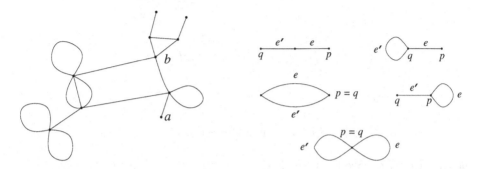

Fig. 2. *Left:* A general curve in the plane with cycles, parallel edges, pending edges/vertices, and loops. Point a is a pending vertex with branching index 1, while point b is a vertex with branching index 4. *Right:* Illustration to the proof of Proposition 1.

Let a general curve γ and a point $p \in \gamma$ be given. Informally speaking, a *branching index* of γ at p is the number of different directions within γ to which one can move from p. See Figure 2 (left) and the comments in the caption. The formal definition (which is available, e.g., in [18], Ch. 8) requires certain preparation (as well as space). It is omitted here since the notion is classical, intuitively clear, and defining it formally goes beyond the purposes of this paper.

Proposition 1. *Let γ be a general curve in $\mathbb{R}^n$, $n \geq 2$. If $r \geq \sqrt{n}/2$, then $D(\gamma, r)$ is $(n-1)$-connected. If $r \geq \sqrt{n-1}/2$, then $D(\gamma, r)$ is (at least) 0-connected.*

Moreover, the values $r = \sqrt{n}/2$, resp. $r = \sqrt{n-1}/2$, are the minimal possible that always guarantee $(n-1)$-connectedness/resp. 0-connectedness of $D(\gamma, r)$.

Proof. We consider the part of the statement for $r \geq \sqrt{n}/2$, the proof of the other parts being analogous.

Let V be the set of points of γ (if any) with branching index different than two. We call these *vertices* of γ. The portion of γ between two of its vertices, which does not contain another vertex of γ, is an *edge* of γ. Denote by E the set of all edges of γ. Two edges that join the same pair of vertices are *parallel*. An edge that starts and ends at the same vertex will be called a *loop* of γ. An edge that has a vertex with a branching index 1 (as well as the vertex itself) will

---

[1] I.e., a nonempty subset of a topological space that is compact and topologically connected.

Fig. 3. A connected set in R^2

be called *pending*. See Figure 2 (left). Clearly, the sets V and E define a graph $G_\gamma(V, E)$ embedded in $\mathbb{R}^n$.

The proof proceeds by induction on the number m of edges of γ. If $m = 1$, then γ is a simple closed curve or a simple arc, and the statement follows from Theorem 1. Assume that it is true for any integer $m \geq 1$ and consider a curve with $m + 1$ edges.

By *removing an edge e* from γ (denoted $\gamma - e$) we will mean that all points of e but its endpoints are removed from γ. It is easy to see that a connected curve γ always contains an edge e, such that $\gamma - e$ is still connected. (For example, if $G_\gamma(V, E)$ is a tree, e may be any pending edge of γ; Otherwise, e may either be an edge that is parallel to another edge (if any), or an edge that belongs to a cycle (if any) including more than two edges, or a loop (if any). Obviously, at least one of these is always the case.)

Remove such an edge e from γ and denote $\gamma' = \gamma - e$.

By the induction hypothesis and Theorem 1, $D(\gamma', r)$ and $D(e, r)$ are both $(n-1)$-connected for $r \geq \sqrt{n}/2$.

Let e' be an edge of γ' incident to e. It is easy to see that then $e \cup e'$ is a curve that can continuously be traversed starting from a point $p \in e \cup e'$ and ending at a point $q \in e \cup e'$ (possibly, $p = q$; see Figure 2 (right) for illustration of different cases). By Theorem 1, $D(e \cup e', r)$ is $(n-1)$-connected for $r \geq \sqrt{n}/2$. This, coupled with the $(n-1)$-connectedness of $D(\gamma', r)$, implies the $(n-1)$-connectedness of $D(e \cup \gamma', r) = D(\gamma, r)$.   □

Using the above proposition, we can prove the following theorem that applies to an arbitrary connected set, e.g., such as the one in Figure 3.

Theorem 3. *Let A be a path-connected set in $\mathbb{R}^n$, $n \geq 2$. If $r \geq \sqrt{n}/2$, then $D(A, r)$ is $(n-1)$-connected. If $r \geq \sqrt{n-1}/2$, then $D(A, r)$ is at least 0-connected.*

Moreover, the values $r = \sqrt{n}/2$, resp. $r = \sqrt{n-1}/2$, are the minimal possible that always guarantee $(n-1)$-connectedness/resp. 0-connectedness of $D(A, r)$.

Proof. Let $M = A_{\mathbb{Z}}$. Denote $N = D(A, r)$. For any $p \in N$ there is at least one point $q \in A$, such that $p \in B(q, r)$. (If there are more than one point with this property, we choose an arbitrary one.) Let Q be the set of all q's chosen as above for all elements of N.

Now consider the set $M \cup Q$. It is a finite proper subset of A. Since A is path-connected, there is a general curve C, such that $M \cup Q \subset C \subseteq A$.

By construction, we have $D(C, r) = D(A, r)$ and the theorem follows from Proposition 1. $\qquad \square$

4 Other Results and Corollaries

4.1 Hypersurface Offset Digitization and Their Gaps and Tunnels

A *Jordan surface* is defined by a parametrization $\Gamma(u, v) = (x(u, v), y(u, v), z(u, v))$ that establishes a homeomorphism with the surface of a unit sphere. So, a Jordan surface is a closed, hole-free surface. See [18] (Sec. 7.4) for a more detailed discussion.

Let $S \subset \mathbb{R}^n$ be a Jordan surface and $D(S, r)$ its r-offset digitization. By the Jordan theorem for surfaces [18], S partitions $\mathbb{R}^n$ into two sets: interior $int(S)$ and exterior $ext(S)$ with respect to S. Denote by $int(D(S, r))$ the set of voxels with centers in $\mathbb{Z}^n \setminus D(S, r)$ that belong to $int(S)$ and by $ext(S)$ those voxels with centers in $\mathbb{Z}^n \setminus D(S, r)$ that belong to $ext(S)$.

We will say that $D(S, r)$ has a k-*gap*, $0 \le k \le n - 2$, if there are voxels $u \in int(D(S, r))$ and $v \in ext(D(S, r))$ that are k-connected. If u and v are $(n-1)$-connected, we say that $D(S, r)$ has a *tunnel*. $D(S, r)$ is k-*gap-free/tunnel-free* if it has no k-gaps/tunnels. If $int(D(S, r)) = \emptyset$, then $D(S, r)$ is k-gap/tunnels-free by definition.

Clearly, if $D(S, r)$ has tunnels or k-gaps for some k, $1 \le k \le n - 2$, then it also has $(k - 1)$-gaps, and if $D(S, r)$ is k-gap-free for some k, $0 \le k \le n - 3$, then it is also $(k + 1)$-gap-free and tunnel-free.

Theorem 4. *Let M be a hole-free closed hypersurface in $\mathbb{R}^n$, $n \ge 2$. Then $D(S, r)$ is $(n - 1)$-connected/0-connected, provided that $r \ge \sqrt{n}/2$/resp. $r \ge \sqrt{n-1}/2$, as the values $r = \sqrt{n}/2$, resp. $r = \sqrt{n-1}/2$, are the minimal possible that always guarantee $(n - 1)$-connectedness/resp. 0-connectedness.*

Moreover, if $r \ge \sqrt{n}/2$, then $D(S, r)$ is 0-gap-free. If $r \ge \sqrt{n-1}/2$, then $D(S, r)$ is 1-gap-free.

Proof. The first part of the theorem follows directly from Theorems 1 and 2, so only the second part needs proof.

Let $r \ge \sqrt{n}/2$. Assume that $D(S, r)$ has a 0-gap. From the definition of a 0-gap it follows that there must be voxels $u' \in int(D(S, r))$ and $v' \in ext(D(S, r))$ that are 0-adjacent. Then the distance between u' and v' is at most $\sqrt{n}$. Since $u' \in int(S)$ and $v' \in ext(S)$, we have that at least one of u' or v' is at distance at most $\sqrt{n}/2$ from S. Then one of these voxels belongs to $D(S, r)$ - a contradiction.

The statement about the case $r \ge \sqrt{n-1}/2$ can be handled analogously. $\quad \square$

Remark 1. It is easy to see that a more general statement holds:

If $r \geq \sqrt{n-k}/2$, where $0 \leq k \leq n-2$, then $D(S,r)$ is $(n-k)$-gap-free. If $r \geq 1/2$, then $D(S,r)$ is tunnel-free.

Note that if $k \geq 2$, then $D(S,r)$ may be a disconnected set. Note also that the statement holds if S is a hyperplane. However, in that case $D(S,r)$ cannot be disconnected. Details on the above will be provided in the full-length journal version of the paper.

4.2   Connected Offset Digitizations of Disconnected Sets

In this section we consider the general case of arbitrary (not necessarily connected) sets.

Let M be a closed disconnected subset of $\mathbb{R}^n$, $n \geq 2$. Let M_i, $i \in \Lambda$, be the connected components of M, where $\Lambda = \{1, 2, \ldots, m\}$ for some positive integer m. Denote by $\Delta_j(M)$, $j = 0$ or $n-1$, the minimal value of an offset radius for which $D(M, \Delta_j(M))$ is j-connected. We call $\Delta(M)$ the *radius of digital offset connectedness* of M. The rest of this section will be devoted to $\Delta_j(M)$ estimation.

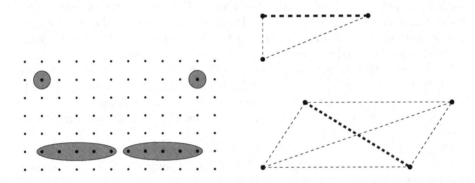

Fig. 4. *Top-left:* A set consisting of two discs at distance 8 from each other. Its offset becomes connected for a radius greater than or equal to 4. *Bottom-left:* A disconnected set whose Gauss digitization is 1-connected. *Top-right:* A set consisting of three points. For it, $\delta(M)/2$ is the least offset radius for which the offset of M is path-connected. This is the half length of the dashed segment in bold. *Bottom-right:* A set consisting of four points. For it, $\delta(M)/2$ is *not* the least offset radius for which the offset of M is path-connected. The minimal value is the half length of the dashed segment in bold, while $\delta(M)$ is the length of the longer side of the parallelogram.

As Figure 4 (left) demonstrates, given a disconnected set $M \subset \mathbb{R}^n$, its Gauss digitization $M_\mathbb{Z}$ may either be disconnected or connected digital set. In the former case it is possible $\Delta_j(M)$ be arbitrarily large (Figure 4, top-left), while in the latter case $\Delta_j(M) = 0$ (Figure 4, bottom-left). Therefore, it makes sense to look for lower bounds for the offset radius r that guarantee $(n-1)$- (resp. 0-) connectedness of $D(M, r)$ *for any set M.*

We assume that the input to the problem consists of the space dimension n and an $(m \times m)$-array $A_M = [d_{ij} : 1 \leq i, j \leq m]$, where $d_{ij} = d(M_i, M_j)$ is the Euclidean distance between components M_i and M_j. So, we will look for an estimation for $\Delta_j(M)$ in terms of these parameters.

It is clear that if $Off(M, r_1)$ becomes connected for a certain radius r_1, then $D(M, r_1 + \sqrt{n}/2)$ (resp. $D(M, r_1 + \sqrt{n-1}/2)$) will be $(n-1)$-connected (resp. 0-connected). For example, we have the following straightforward proposition.

Proposition 2. Let M be a closed subset of $\mathbb{R}^n$, $n \geq 2$. Denote $\delta(M) = \min_i \max_j d_{ij}$ for d_{ij} as defined above. Then we have:
$\Delta_{n-1}(M) \leq (\delta(M) + \sqrt{n})/2$. That is, if $r \geq (\delta(M) + \sqrt{n})/2$, then $D(M, r)$ is $(n-1)$-connected.
$\Delta_0(M) \leq (\delta(M) + \sqrt{n-1})/2$. That is, if $r \geq (\delta(M) + \sqrt{n-1})/2$, then $D(M, r)$ is 0-connected.

Proof. Clearly, for any $M \subseteq \mathbb{R}^n$, $Off(Off(M, r_1), r_2) = Off(M, r_1 + r_2)$. By the definition of $\delta(M)$, $Off(M, \delta(M))$ is path-connected. Then the statement follows from Theorem 3.   □

Figure 4 (top-right) illustrates that there are sets for which the value $r = \delta(M)$ is the best possible in a sense of assuring connectedness of $Off(M, r)$. However, Figure 4 (bottom-right) illustrates that for other sets this is not the case. In what follows, we investigate the problem of finding that least offset radius value for which $Off(M, r)$ is path-connected for an arbitrary $M \subset \mathbb{R}^n$. We call it the *radius of offset connectedness* of M and denote it by $\rho(M)$. Having $\rho(M)$ found, one can easily estimate $\Delta_i(M)$ with the help of Theorem 3.

Given the array A_M defined above, one can find $\rho(M)$, as follows.

Consider a complete weighted graph $K_m(V, E)$ on m vertices, so $|V| = m$ and $|E| = \frac{m(m-1)}{2}$. The vertices of K_m label the sets $M_1, M_2, \ldots, M_m$ and the edges e_{ij}, $1 \leq i, j \leq m, i \neq j$, label pairs of sets (M_i, M_j). Weights are assigned by $w(e_{ij}) = d_{ij}$ (recall that $d_{ij} = d(M_i, M_j)$).

Consider the set T of all spanning trees of K_m. For every $t \in T$ denote by e^t an edge of t with a maximal weight. It is easy to realize that $w(e^t) \geq \rho(M)$ and that

$$\rho(M) = \min_{t \in T} w(e^t).$$

A spanning tree t can be found in $O(m^2)$ time, e.g., by Prim's algorithm [21], and meanwhile the longest edge can be identified. Note however that a complete graph on m vertices has m^{m-2} distinct spanning trees, so $\rho(M)$ cannot be efficiently computed by generating all of them and taking the minimum of the maxima. Nevertheless, below we show that this can be done in polynomial time. We have the following theorem.

Theorem 5. Let M be a closed subset of $\mathbb{R}^n$, $n \geq 2$, with m connected components. Given the array of distances A_M, one can compute $\rho(M)$ in $O(m^4)$ time.

Proof. First we describe the procedure of computing $\rho(M)$, then analyze its complexity and correctness.

Algorithm. Order A_M. Then, starting from the heaviest edge and proceeding in decreasing order, consecutively remove edges from A_M. After an edge removal, test the remaining graph for edge-connectivity. Stop as soon as removal of an edge causes edge-disconnectedness and report its weight as $\rho(M)$.

Running time. Ordering of A_M takes $O(m^2 \log m)$ operations. Each connectivity test takes $O(m^2)$ operations. Since $O(m^2)$ tests are performed, the overall time-complexity of the algorithm is $O(m^4)$.

Correctness. Let e be the heaviest edge whose removal (after the removal of all heavier edges and possibly some edges with the same weight as of e) makes the graph edge-disconnected. Denote by K^e the graph obtained after the removal of e. Then the graph $K' = K^e \cup \{e\}$ is edge-connected and e is its heaviest edge. Then every spanning tree of K' contains e, and e is the heaviest edge in all these spanning trees (which are spanning trees for K_m, as well). This demonstrates that $\rho(M) = w(e)$. □

Remark 2. Note that in the procedure described in the proof of Theorem 5, after the removal of the first $m - 2$ edges from K_m the remaining graph will still be edge-connected, since a complete graph on m vertices is $(m-1)$-edge-connected. Moreover, the graph K' contains at least $m - 1$ edges (K' may have exactly $m - 1$ edges only if K' itself is a spanning tree of K_m).

Theorem 5 implies the following

Corollary 1. *Let M be a closed subset of $\mathbb{R}^n$, $n \geq 2$, with m connected components and $\rho(M)$ its radius of offset connectedness. Then:*
$\Delta_{n-1}(M) \leq (\rho(M) + \sqrt{n})/2$. *That is, if $r \geq (\rho(M) + \sqrt{n})/2$, then $D(M, r)$ is $(n - 1)$-connected.*
$\Delta_0(M) \leq (\rho(M) + \sqrt{n-1})/2$. *That is, if $r \geq (\rho(M) + \sqrt{n-1})/2$, then $D(M, r)$ is 0-connected.*
Moreover, given the array of distances between the components of M, $\rho(M)$ can be computed in $O(m^4)$ time.

5   Concluding Remarks

In the present work we investigated the offset approach for digitizing arbitrary subsets of $\mathbb{R}^n$. We showed that certain results known about curves are also valid in this more general settings.

Further work is expected to elaborate the case of digital surfaces (in particular digital planes) obtained through offsets, in view of Remark 1. In particular, one can look for conditions that would guarantee connectedness of $D(S, r)$.

Another interesting question is: Is there a more efficient way to compute the radius of offset connectedness?

Computer implementation and testing the practical worth and visual appearance of offset digitizations is considered as another important task.

Acknowledgements

The author thanks the three anonymous referees for their useful remarks and suggestions.

References

1. Andres, E.: Discrete linear objects in dimension n: the standard model. Graphical Models 65(1-3), 92–111 (2003)
2. Andres, E.: Discrete circles, rings and spheres. Computers & Graphics 18(5), 695–706 (1994)
3. Andres, E., Jacob, M.-A.: The discrete analytical hyperspheres. IEEE Trans. Vis. Comput. Graph. 3(1), 75–86 (1997)
4. Anton, F.: Voronoi Diagrams of Semi-algebraic Sets. Ph.D. thesis, The University of British Columbia, Vancouver, British Columbia, Canada (2004)
5. Anton, F., Emiris, I., Mourrain, B., Teillaud, M.: The offset to an algebraic curve and an application to conics. In: Gervasi, O., Gavrilova, M.L., Kumar, V., Laganá, A., Lee, H.P., Mun, Y., Taniar, D., Tan, C.J.K. (eds.) ICCSA 2005. LNCS, vol. 3480, pp. 683–696. Springer, Heidelberg (2005)
6. Arrondo, E., Sendra, J., Sendra, J.R.: Genus formula for generalized offset curves. J. Pure and Applied Algebra 136(3), 199–209 (1999)
7. Brimkov, V.E., Barneva, R.P., Brimkov, B., de Vieilleville, F.: Offset approach to defining 3D digital lines. In: Bebis, G., Boyle, R., Parvin, B., Koracin, D., Remagnino, P., Porikli, F., Peters, J., Klosowski, J., Arns, L., Chun, Y.K., Rhyne, T.-M., Monroe, L. (eds.) ISVC 2008, Part I. LNCS, vol. 5358, pp. 678–687. Springer, Heidelberg (2008)
8. Brimkov, V.E., Barneva, R.P., Brimkov, B.: Minimal offsets that guarantee maximal or minimal connectivity of digital curves in nD. In: Brlek, S., Reutenauer, C., Provençal, X. (eds.) DGCI 2009. LNCS, vol. 5810, pp. 337–349. Springer, Heidelberg (2009)
9. Cohen-Or, D., Kaufman, A.: 3D line voxelization and connectivity control. IEEE Computer Graphics & Applications 17(6), 80–87 (1997)
10. Cox, D., Little, J., O'Shea, D.: Using Algebraic Geometry. Springer, New York (1998)
11. Debled-Rennesson, I.: Etude et Reconnaissance des Droites et Plans Discrets. Ph.D. Thesis, Université Louis Pasteur, Strasbourg, France (1995)
12. Debled-Rennesson, I., Domenjoud, E., Jamet, D.: Arithmetic discrete parabolas. In: Bebis, G., Boyle, R., Parvin, B., Koracin, D., Remagnino, P., Nefian, A., Meenakshisundaram, G., Pascucci, V., Zara, J., Molineros, J., Theisel, H., Malzbender, T. (eds.) ISVC 2006. LNCS, vol. 4292, pp. 480–489. Springer, Heidelberg (2006)
13. Figueiredo, O., Reveillès, J.-P.: New results about 3D digital lines. In: Melter, R.A., Wu, A.Y., Latecki, L. (eds.) Internat. Conference Vision Geometry V. SPIE, vol. 2826, pp. 98–108 (1996)
14. Fiorio, C., Jamet, D., Toutant, J.-L.: Discrete circles: An arithmetical approach based on norms. In: Internat. Conference Vision-Geometry XIV. San Jose, CA. SPIE, vol. 6066, 60660C (2006)
15. Hoffmann, C.M., Vermeer, P.J.: Eliminating extraneous solutions for the sparse resultant and the mixed volume. J. Symbolic Geom. Appl. 1(1), 47–66 (1991)

16. Jonas, A., Kiryati, N.: Digital representation schemes for 3D curves. Pattern Recognition 30(11), 1803–1816 (1997)
17. Kim, C.E.: Three dimensional digital line segments. IEEE Transactions on Pattern Analysis and Machine Intelligence 5(2), 231–234 (1983)
18. Klette, R., Rosenfeld, A.: Digital Geometry – Geometric Methods for Digital Picture Analysis. Morgan Kaufmann, San Francisco (2004)
19. Kong, T.Y.: Digital topology. In: Davis, L.S. (ed.) Foundations of Image Understanding, pp. 33–71. Kluwer, Boston (2001)
20. Menger, K.: Kurventheorie. Teubner (1932)
21. Prim, R.C.: Shortest connection networks and some generalizations. Bell System Technical Journal 36, 1389–1401 (1957)
22. Rosenfeld, A.: Connectivity in digital pictures. Journal of the ACM 17(3), 146–160 (1970)
23. Rosenfeld, A.: Arcs and curves in digital pictures. Journal of the ACM 20(1), 81–87 (1973)
24. Toutant, J.-L.: Characterization of the closest discrete approximation of a line in the 3-dimensional space. In: Bebis, G., Boyle, R., Parvin, B., Koracin, D., Remagnino, P., Nefian, A., Meenakshisundaram, G., Pascucci, V., Zara, J., Molineros, J., Theisel, H., Malzbender, T. (eds.) ISVC 2006. LNCS, vol. 4291, pp. 618–627. Springer, Heidelberg (2006)
25. Urysohn, O.: Über die allegemeinen Cantorischen Kurven. In: Proc. Ann. Meeting, Deutsche Mathematiker Vereinigung (1923)

Curvature Estimation for Discrete Curves Based on Auto-adaptive Masks of Convolution

Christophe Fiorio[1], Christian Mercat[1,2], and Frédéric Rieux[1,2]

[1] LIRMM, Université Montpellier 2, 161 rue Ada,
F-34392 MONTPELLIER, France
[2] I3M, Université de Montpellier 2 c.c. 51
F-34095 Montpellier Cedex 5, France

Abstract. We propose a method that we call auto-adaptive convolution which extends the classical notion of convolution in pictures analysis to function analysis on a discrete set. We define an averaging kernel which takes into account the local geometry of a discrete shape and adapts itself to the curvature. Its defining property is to be local and to follow a normal law on discrete lines of any slope. We used it together with classical differentiation masks to estimate first and second derivatives and give a curvature estimator of discrete functions.

1 Introduction

The discretization of a smooth object loses some features of the original geometrical characteristics. An important problem is in estimating derivatives of digital functions, for example the tangent space at a point or the curvature of the shape. Many approaches exist based on line segmentation [7,11,14] or on filtering [8,13,19]. New approaches to derivative estimation [8,12] are based on convolution product with a diffusion kernel and give striking estimations of derivatives of noisy curves. Those convolutions use binomial kernels which are not adaptive to the local geometry of the discrete object. In [8], a surface kernel has been proposed where the weights computed take into account the local disposition of the adjacent voxels. Ours work builds on this approach.

The main issue is to compute convolution masks best suited for a particular discrete object. We propose kernels that adapt themselves to the geometry. Those masks enable us to give a good estimation of derivative and curvature of discretized functions.

This article is laid out as follows: We introduce convolution product in Section 3 and define our auto-adaptive process in Section 4 as a random process defining our convolution kernel. We investigate discrete lines in Section 5 and prove that their masks are equivalent to normal laws. We normalize their deviations by allowing some optimized tunnel effect in Section 5.3, recovering Euclidean properties for lines of any slopes. Finally we show the usefulness of our approach by giving estimations of derivative and curvature of discretized functions in Section 6.

R.P. Barneva et al. (Eds.): CompIMAGE 2010, LNCS 6026, pp. 47–59, 2010.
© Springer-Verlag Berlin Heidelberg 2010

2   Diffusion Processes

Heat kernel or random walks have been widely used in image processing, for example lately by Sun, Ovsjanikov and Guibas [18] and Gebal, Bærentzen, Aanæs and Larsen [9] in shape analysis. It is indeed a very precious tool because two manifolds are isometric if and only if their heat kernels are the same (in the non degenerate case).

The heat kernel k_t of a manifold M maps a couple of points $(x, y) \in M \times M$ to a positive real number $k_t(x, y)$ which describes the transfer of heat from y to x in time t. Starting from a (real) temperature T on M, the temperature after a time t at a point x is given by a convolution of the initial temperature distribution with the diffusion kernel:

$$H^t f(x) = \int_M f(y) \, k_t(x, y) \, dy.$$

The heat equation is driven by the diffusion process, the evolution of the temperature in time is governed by the (spatial) Laplace-Beltrami operator Δ_M: $\frac{\partial f(t,x)}{\partial t} = -\Delta_M f(t, x)$ which presides to the diffusion on the manifold, for example random walks.

The first issue when using these ideas in the discrete setup is to define a good discrete Laplacian, or equivalently, a good diffusion process. It should be reasonably robust to noise, to outliers (points which are added by mistake) and to missing data.

This situation is understood in the realm of polyhedral surfaces and triangulations, and a time appraised discrete Laplacian, based on sound theoretical grounds has been understood for a long time, the so-called *cotangent weights* Laplacian [15].

In this article, we are going to define a diffusion process in 2D-Digital Geometry, where the space is composed of pixels, and show how it can be used to compute estimates of tangencies and curvatures of discrete curves in the plane $\mathbb{Z}^2$. In subsequent articles, we will describe a generalization to higher dimensions, in particular discrete surfaces in $\mathbb{Z}^3$.

3   Convolution Products

Estimation of geometrical properties is an important goal of discrete geometry. Many methods exist to estimate the length [4], or the curvature of discrete curves [3,7,11,14]. In this work, we are interested in the estimation of geometrical properties of a noisy set of pixels, for example the discretized graph of a function, or a discrete curve. A whole set of methods use digital straight segments recognition algorithm [6] to compute maximal line segments and estimate the length of a curve or tangent vectors. Those methods are sensitive to noise. Our aim is to extend the pioneer work of [8] on product convolution technique to produce *adaptive masks*. Convolution with averaging masks is used in image analysis to smooth contours or functions and estimate tangent vectors or curvature of a discrete object.

We introduce here the convolution product in the discrete case. This work describes a method to compute a convolution kernel, adapted to an arbitrary connected set of pixels representing the quantization of a curve in the plane. Commonly, the convolution product *smooths* a function g by an averaging function f, usually concentrated around the origin which slides along the line, $\mathbb{Z}$ in the discrete setup: $f * g(x) = \sum_{t \in \mathbb{Z}} f(x - t).g(t)$.

In the case of functions defined on a less homogeneous set of pixels E, no simple addition is defined, so there is no easy way to slide a function, which has to be defined as a 2-point kernel:

Definition 1 (Mask product)
The product $f * g$ of a kernel $f : E \times E \to \mathbb{R}$ and a discrete function $g : E \to \mathbf{F}$ to a vector space $\mathbf{F}$, is given by:

$$f * g : E \to \mathbf{F} \tag{1}$$

$$x \mapsto \sum_{y \in \mathbf{E}} f(x, y).g(y). \tag{2}$$

The kernel function is usually of limited support, hence the name *mask*. A small support mask can be convolved with itself to widen its range: $f^{(n)} * g = f * (f^{(n-1)} * g)$. The averaging kernel $\boxed{}\boxed{\frac{1}{2}}\boxed{\frac{1}{2}}\boxed{}$ is for example widened into the binomial $\frac{1}{2^n} \boxed{}\boxed{1}\boxed{n} \cdots \boxed{\binom{n}{p}} \cdots \boxed{n}\boxed{1}\boxed{}$.

These definitions can be extended to the 2D case where such convolution masks are used to limit the noise in a picture, by smoothing the intensity vector of colors, blurring sharp details but otherwise limiting the effect of noise.

On an object like a 1D-curve, we do not have a regular structure therefore the main problem which arises, is in choosing the suitable weights that preserve the intrinsic geometry of the curve.

In this work we introduce masks whose weights are suitable for any curve and any shape. Rémy Malgouyres and Sébastien Fourey [8] define mask weights for discrete surfaces in 3D-space that are computed taking into account the neighbors of the voxels. Likewise, our masks are computed according to the local geometry of a set of pixels. Those masks are adaptive and allow us to smooth a function with suitable weights for the studied curve. They are based on auto-adaptive diffusion processes.

4   Auto-adaptive Process

We setup the diffusion of a walker wandering on the object, in order to recover its local geometry. This auto-adaptive process is a local Markov process, a stochastic process where the probability of transition between states depends only on the immediate past. We restrain ourselves to the discrete case where the Markov chain is executed in discrete time and where the set $\mathcal{E}$ of possible states are the pixels of the discrete object we consider.

Our Markov process governs a random walker moving along the object. This character will undergo transition according to the possibilities provided by the geometry of the object, our walker goes from a pixel to another through its four corners.

Definition 2 (Standard adaptive process)

We call standard adaptive process, *the Markov chain with the probabilities of transition from pixel to pixel defined by the composition of transitions from a pixel of the set to its corners and back from a corner to adjacent pixels of the set constrained by:*

1. Equiprobability $\frac{1}{4}$ *to go from a pixel to one of its corners;*
2. Equiprobability *to move from a corner to an adjacent pixel of the set.*

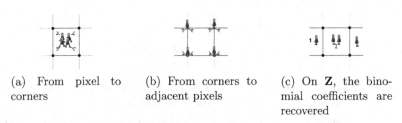

(a) From pixel to corners

(b) From corners to adjacent pixels

(c) On **Z**, the binomial coefficients are recovered

Fig. 1. A walker has a probability of $\frac{1}{4}$ to pick up a corner of a pixel, then $\frac{1}{k}$ to select a pixel among k possible, ending up in the binomial coefficients $\{1, 2, 1\}$ for the random walk on **Z**

This standard choice amounts to walkers with no memory and only local knowledge, the celebrated short-sighted drunken man. *We note this process A_s^m for a walker starting at any given point, with m the number of iterations of the process.*

Remark 1. A_s^m is the stochastic matrix of the studied discrete object. We obtain a mask of length $2m + 1$ centered on the pixel i if we multiply the matrix A_s^m by a position vector $v_i = (0, \ldots, 0, \underbrace{1}_{i-th\ position}, 0, \ldots, 0)^T$. In the sequel, we call v_x the position vector of the pixel x.

We illustrate the definition with examples (see Figure 2b) of masks computed on discrete lines. After m steps the process builds a mask of length $2m + 1$.

We call our process *standard* because of the equiprobability condition. In the next section, we will modify these probabilities to uniformize the diffusion on discrete lines. Note that the standard adaptive process on a finite connected discrete object is *ergodic*.

On the integer line $\mathbb{Z}$, the diffusion leads to the Gaussian binomial masks $A_s^n(x, y) = \binom{n}{|x-y|}$. We prove next that on discrete lines, it is a more involved Gaussian mask.

5   Convolution Masks on Discrete Lines

Let us investigate here the auto-adaptive standard masks on discrete lines of different slopes.

We recall the definition of arithmetic discrete lines and we prove that the weights of the associated auto-adaptive masks have a Gaussian distribution. But their deviations differ for different slopes.

5.1   Auto-adaptive Masks on Discrete Lines

Definition 3 (Discrete line [16])

A discrete line of slope $\dfrac{a}{b}$ *with* $a \wedge b = 1$, *inferior limit* μ *and arithmetic thickness* ω *is the set of pairs* $(x,\ y) \in \mathbb{Z}^2$ *such that*

$$\mu \leq ax\ -\ by < \mu\ +\ \omega$$

where a, b, ω *and* μ *are integers.*

In discrete geometry there are two adjacencies commonly used, the connectivity by edge, called 4-adjacency and the connectivity by vertex, called 8-adjacency. We are interested in naive lines ($\omega\ =\ \max(|a|, |b|)$), i.e. the thinner 8-adjacent connected lines for a given slope.

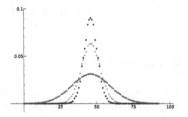

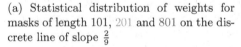

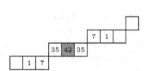

(a) Statistical distribution of weights for masks of length 101, 201 and 801 on the discrete line of slope $\frac{2}{9}$

(b) Example of standard adaptive process on the discrete line of slope $\frac{3}{9}$ with 128 walkers.

Fig. 2. Examples of walkers diffusion on discrete lines

Example results in Figure 2a show that for a mask large enough, the statistical distribution can be estimated by a continuous normal law with the same mean and deviation. The proof of this observation resides on ergodicity and the application of the Central Limit Theorem. We first need a technical definition:

Definition 4 (Equivalence class)

We assign to a pixel i *the pair of adjacencies of its left and right neighbors and denote* $[i]$ *its induced equivalence class.*

Theorem 1. *The standard auto-adaptive process* A_s^m *computed on a discrete line* $\mathcal{D}(a, b, \mu, \omega)$ *is equivalent to a normal law when* $m \to \infty$.

See its proof in the appendix on p.59.

(a) 4-4

(b) 8-8

(c) 8-4

(d) 4-8

Fig. 3. There are only four equivalence classes appearing on an 8-connected line in the first octant

5.2   Curvilinear Abscissa versus Integer Index

The standard adaptive process gives us good normal laws but they are not completely satisfactory because their deviation depends on the line slope: pixels which are only 8-connected act as filters (see Figure 4b). We measure the dispersion of walkers on a discrete line to compare the dispersion between two discrete lines of different slopes. In Figure 4b, we have used a discrete index i with respect to which we computed the spatial deviation. It is a relevant index for *graphs* of discrete functions $f : \mathbb{Z} \rightarrow \mathbb{Z}$, but it is not for arbitrary curves. We need to take into consideration the curvilinear abscissa of the underlying curve. This abscissa is easy to compute for lines with the help of the projection (see Figure 9a) on p. 54.

The difference between the index and the curvilinear abscissa can be as big as a speeding factor $\sqrt{2}$ for diagonal lines, which are no longer the minimum of this curvilinear deviation (see Figure 4a).

5.3   Standardization of Standard Deviation for Any Slope

To balance the effect of digitization which creates narrow links for diagonal lines and links for horizontal and vertical lines, we will allow the walker to step *outside* the discrete line. We thicken discrete lines and we modify the probability transition in this thick virtual, fuzzy part. We consider three natural sets associated with a thin discrete line, the line itself (see Figure 5), a thicker one obtained by adding all the 4-adjacent pixels (see Figure 6), and a larger one by adding all the 8-adjacent pixels (see Figure 7).

By definition of discrete lines, we could increase the arithmetic thickness ω. But ω depends on the discrete line under study, and the number of pixels added depends on the slope as well. We want, on the contrary, to define a local thickening procedure without taking into account global features like the arithmetic thickness, to apply it on arbitrary set.

We build in this way three Markov processes, associated with matrices, M_0, M_1 and M_2 of increasing dimensions by adding all the pixels neighbors.

Definition 5 (Fuzzy Matrix)

Let M_0, M_1 and M_2 represent the matrices of the discrete lines respectively the naive thin line, its thickened version with the addition of 4-connected neighbors and the fatter line with 8-connected neighbors. Let M_0' and M_1' the matrices induced by M_0 and M_1, padded by columns and rows of zeros and a diagonal of

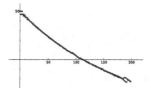
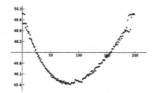
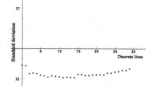

(a) Curves of deviation obtained from two hundred lines of increasing slope. The minimum is reached for the line of slope 1 with only 8-connected pixels acting as filters that slowdown the walkers.

(b) The minimum dispersion is reached for lines mixing 4 and 8-connectivities, where the low slope doesn't increase yet the curvilinear abscissa but where enough upwards steps disrupt the diffusion

(c) Comparison of the standard deviation computed on thirty discrete lines, between the standard (thin) mask and the fuzzy matrix corresponding to $\lambda = 0.3$ and $\mu = 0.4$, at the same vertical scale

Fig. 4. Standard deviation of mask for curvilinear abscissa and integer index

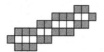
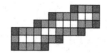

Fig. 5. Discrete standard line of slope $\frac{2}{5}$

Fig. 6. Add the 4-connected pixels

Fig. 7. Add the 8-connected pixels

1 for pixels not belonging to these sets, so that the three matrices have the same dimension as M_2. We define F a function with two parameters λ and μ defined by:

$$F : (\lambda, \mu) \mapsto (1 - (\lambda + \mu))M_0' + \lambda M_1' + \mu M_2'$$

We call F the fuzzy matrix of parameters λ and μ.

The fuzzy matrix is still associated with a stochastic process but on a larger set of pixels: we allow the walker to go outside the main discrete line so that the process, when restricted to the discrete line, is no longer stochastic, because at the end of the process, many walkers appear in *ghost* pixels. We bring them back on line by a simple projection onto the associated real line of the same slope, as illustrated in Figure 9a. We obtain two sets of points; the first corresponds to points belonging to the original naive discrete line called *primary points*, and the others correspond to the ghost points (see Figure 8). We assign ghost walkers to primary points according to the distance between their projection point and the two nearest primary points (see Figure 9b). We do not lose any walker and we take into account the position of their ghost pixels.

For fixed λ and μ, we computed the deviations of our fuzzy diffusion process on lines of increasing slopes and computed the standard deviation of these deviations. We plotted this dispersion as a function of λ and μ (see Figure 10a). We found experimentally the best values for λ and μ to have minimal dispersion.

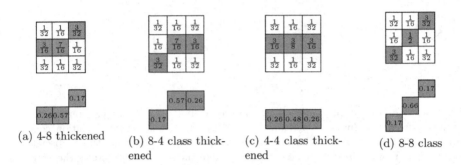

(a) 4-8 thickened   (b) 8-4 class thickened   (c) 4-4 class thickened   (d) 8-8 class

Fig. 8. Computed projection masks of the four equivalent classes on naive discrete lines (Figure 3). First, we compute the thickened mask of the fuzzy matrix for $\lambda = 0$, $\mu = 0.5$, close to the minimum dispersion. In white we have the ghost pixels, in blue the primary points. Then, to give an example we project on the line $2x - 5y = 0$ to obtain the final mask on the line.

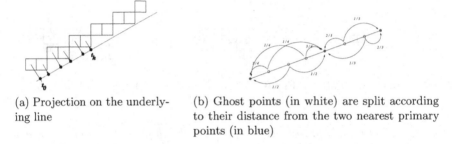

(a) Projection on the underlying line

(b) Ghost points (in white) are split according to their distance from the two nearest primary points (in blue)

Fig. 9. Projection of walkers on the underlying line and repartition onto primary points

The general shape of this dispersion and the location of its minima do not depend heavily on the size of the mask once it is large enough (a few pixels wide) and on the number of lines (we used up to 50 lines): We found (see Figure 10a) $\lambda = 0.3$ and $\mu = 0.4$, with a long valley of acceptable values up to $\lambda = 0$, $\mu = 0.5$. In particular, good values are given when there are not much differences in probability between the 4 and 8-connected added neighbors.

As we can see in Figure 4c, the fuzzy process with suitable λ and μ gives masks with approximately the same standard deviation for any line.

With these values, we have now a local fuzzy process, which is adaptive to the shape of the underlying set and which has been tailored to recover the Euclidean geometry of discrete lines.

Therefore, given a curve, which is by definition locally modeled on a line, its discretization with a step finer than its feature size, can be analyzed by our mask, of a proper standard deviation between the discretization step and the feature size, and thus giving back the Euclidean geometry of the curve. We are going to show in the next section that it indeed allows us to compute derivatives and second derivatives of discrete functions with great accuracy.

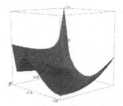

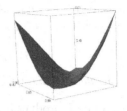

(a) Computation of the values of the dispersion of standard deviations as a function of λ and μ

(b) Zoom on the minimum part of the graph

Fig. 10. We get a minimal dispersion for the values $\lambda = 0.3$ and $\mu = 0.4$

6 Derivative and Curvature Estimation

Fuzzy processes are expensive in terms of computation because we need to increase significantly the number of points of the studied object. We will show that, in order to compute derivatives of discretized functions, the standard auto-adaptive kernel, which is cheaper, is already very efficient. However fuzzy processes are clearly the most suitable and we can improve the results. We will study tangent estimation and we will show our results on the function $x \mapsto \sin(x)$.

First we will introduce how we obtained the set of studied pixels for the discretized graph of a real function, then we will show how we compute the derivation kernel according to the standard auto-adaptive process on a digital curve. Finally we will give a curvature estimator and we will display the results computed on the discrete sinus function.

6.1 Derivative Function Estimation

We use a classical method of discretization called grid intersect quantization (GIQ) [17].

In order for this procedure to give us a connected set of pixels, we rely here on a pre-processing that *flattens* the function in order to have a derivative of magnitude less than 1. We will describe in a future article how to deal with supercover graphs [1].

Let φ be a digital function defined on $I \subset \mathbb{Z}$, and $A_s^m(\varphi)$ the fuzzy process on its digital graph. We want to approximate the derivative function φ' according to the discrete values of φ.

There are three popular discrete derivation masks: the centered δ_0 :

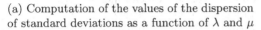

, the right-sided δ_+ :

and the left-sided δ_- :

. We will specify for each estimation the mask used. Our convolution kernel $A_s^m(\varphi)$ smooths the function φ, before and after the application of the derivation operator D_1.

Definition 6 (Derivative estimator). *Let φ be a discrete function and $A_s^m(\varphi)$ be the kernel of the auto-adaptive process. Then the estimated derivative of the function φ at the point x is given by:*

$$D_1(x) \ = [A_s^m(\varphi) * \delta_* * A_s^m(\varphi)] \, (x)$$

with δ_* one of the three derivation kernels.

The convolution product is not commutative, and we can increase several times the support of the mask to the right or the left of D_1 in order to raise the smoothing effect of the kernel and improve the estimation on noisy functions to the price of an erosion of the small scale data. As an example in Figure 11, we give an estimation of the derivative function $x \mapsto \sin(x)$ with the centered kernel δ_0.

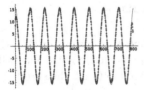

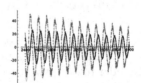

(a) Comparison between the derivative estimation of $x \mapsto sin(x)$ and the values of the real function $x \mapsto cos(x)$ computed according a mask of length 61

(b) Estimation of the discrete derivative function of $x \mapsto \frac{20}{x} sin(2x)$ of order one and two, computed according a mask of length 30

Fig. 11. Estimation of derivative for different functions

6.2   Curvature Estimation

We define a derivation kernel to compute derivatives of higher order used in the curvature.

Definition 7 (Derivative of higher order). *Let φ be a discrete function and $A_s^m(\varphi)$ be the auto-adaptive process computed on φ. Let δ_* be a derivation kernel, then the derivation kernel of order n is defined as*

$$D_n(x) \ = \left[A_s^m(\varphi) \underbrace{*\delta_* * A_s^m(\varphi) * \ldots * A_s^m(\varphi)}_{n \ times} \right] (x)$$

As an example we give the estimated second derivative of $x \mapsto \sin(x)$ (see Figure 12a) for the centered derivation kernel.

We recall the classical definition of the curvature for a real function in the plane. Let $(x, y(x))$ be a function graph with $x \in I \subset \mathbb{R}$. Then the curvature is given by $\Gamma(x) \ = \dfrac{y''(x)}{(1 + y'^2(x))^{\frac{3}{2}}}$. The curvature estimation for a discrete function is based on this formula and the estimation of φ' and φ'':

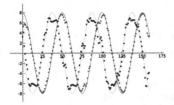 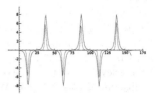

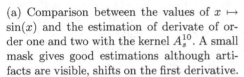

(a) Comparison between the values of $x \mapsto \sin(x)$ and the estimation of derivate of order one and two with the kernel A_s^{10}. A small mask gives good estimations although artifacts are visible, shifts on the first derivative.

(b) Comparison between the real (blue) and discretised (red) curvatures of the function shown in Figure 12a. The smoothing reduces the curvature value.

Fig. 12. Second order derivative and curvature are amazingly accurate (mask of size 10)

$$\Gamma(x) = \frac{D_2(x)}{(1 + D_1(x)^2)^{\frac{3}{2}}}.$$

We computed the estimated curvature of the discretised function $x \mapsto \sin(x)$ and we compared it with the real curvature. As we can see in Figure 12b, for a typical mask of convolution, we obtain a curvature close to the exact curvature.

The result is encouraging because we recover, in spite of the noise induced by the discretization, a good estimate of the curvature. Moreover, experiments reveal that our estimator gives results comparable to many other estimators: Tangent estimators based on recognition discrete lines [7,11,14] are sensitive to noise and our Gaussian approach should not. On the other hand, methods based on filtering [13,19] use convolution masks which are not adaptive to the local geometry. Our approach is more faithful to the discrete object and is versatile: we can intensify the smoothing or reduce it according to prior knowledge on the data or revise the data once the local feature size has been roughly estimated. The performance of the fitting in comparison to the size of the masks, the local feature size and the intensity of the final convolution will be studied in a forthcoming paper.

7   Conclusion

We defined an averaging operator based on diffusion on a discrete set. The distribution of weights on discrete lines is equivalent to a normal law and we standardize its diffusion to have approximately the same standard deviation for any slopes, recovering their Euclidian geometry. The computed masks smooth out correctly discretisation noise, and provide a first step in recovering the intrinsic 1D-geometry of the underlying object: convolved with differentiation kernel, we build a derivative estimator that we use to estimate tangent vector and curvature.

This estimator will be investigated in the future to account for discretised functions with non-connected discretised function graphs. More generally, we will describe in a forthcoming paper how to define a parameterisation of discrete curves by curvilinear abscissa for an arbitrary discrete set modeled on an unknown 1D curve.

References

1. Andres, E.: Modélisation Analytique Discrète d'Objets Géométriques. Habilitation à diriger des recherches, UFR Sciences Fondamentale et Appliquées, Université de Poitiers, France (2000)
2. Billingsley, P.: Convergence of probability measures, 2nd edn. Wiley Series in Probability and Statistics. John Wiley & Sons Inc., New York (1999)
3. Coeurjolly, D., Debled-Rennesson, I., Teytaud, O.: Segmentation and length estimation of 3D discrete curves. In: Bertrand, G., Imiya, A., Klette, R. (eds.) Digital and Image Geometry. LNCS, vol. 2243, pp. 299–317. Springer, Heidelberg (2002)
4. Coeurjolly, D., Klette, R.: A comparative evaluation of length estimators of digital curves. IEEE Trans. Pattern Anal. Mach. Intell. 26(2), 252–257 (2004)
5. Coeurjolly, D., Sivignon, I., Tougne, L., Dupont, F. (eds.): DGCI 2008. LNCS, vol. 4992. Springer, Heidelberg (2008)
6. Debled-Rennesson, I., Reveillès, J.P.: A linear algorithm for segmentation of digital curves. IJPRAI 9(4), 635–662 (1995)
7. Feschet, F., Tougne, L.: Optimal time computation of the tangent of a discrete curve: Application to the curvature. In: Bertrand, G., Couprie, M., Perroton, L. (eds.) DGCI 1999. LNCS, vol. 1568, pp. 31–40. Springer, Heidelberg (1999)
8. Fourey, S., Malgouyres, R.: Normals and curvature estimation for digital surfaces based on convolutions. In: Coeurjolly, D., et al. (eds.) [5], pp. 287–298
9. Gebal, K., Bærentzen, J.A., Aanæs, H., Larsen, R.: Shape Analysis Using the Auto Diffusion Function. Computer Graphics Forum 28(5), 1405–1413 (2009)
10. Konrad, P., Marc, A., Michael, K. (eds.): Symposium on Graphics Processing. Eurographics Association (2009)
11. Lachaud, J.O., Vialard, A., de Vieilleville, F.: Fast, accurate and convergent tangent estimation on digital contours. Image Vision Comput. 25(10), 1572–1587 (2007)
12. Malgouyres, R., Brunet, F., Fourey, S.: Binomial convolutions and derivatives estimation from noisy discretizations. In: Coeurjolly, et al. (eds.) [5], pp. 370–379
13. Matas, J., Shao, Z., Kittler, J.: Estimation of curvature and tangent direction by median filtered differencing. In: Braccini, C., Vernazza, G., DeFloriani, L. (eds.) ICIAP 1995. LNCS, vol. 974, pp. 83–88. Springer, Heidelberg (1995)
14. Nguyen, T.P., Debled-Rennesson, I.: Curvature estimation in noisy curves. In: Kropatsch, W.G., Kampel, M., Hanbury, A. (eds.) CAIP 2007. LNCS, vol. 4673, pp. 474–481. Springer, Heidelberg (2007)
15. Pinkall, U., Polthier, K.: Computing discrete minimal surfaces and their conjugates. Experiment. Math. 2(1), 15–36 (1993)
16. Reveillès, J.P.: Géométrie Discrète, Calcul en Nombres Entiers et Algorithmique. Ph.D. Thesis, Université Louis Pasteur, Strasbourg, France (1991)
17. Rosenfeld, A.: Digital straight line segments. IEEE Transactions on Computers 23(12), 1264–1269 (1974)
18. Sun, J., Ovsjanikov, M., Guibas, L.: A concise and provably informative multi-scale signature based on heat diffusion. In: Konrad, et al. (eds.) [10], pp. 1383–1392, http://www.eg.org/EG/DL/CGF/volume28/issue5/v28i5pp1383-1392.pdf
19. Worring, M., Smeulders, A.W.: Digital curvature estimation. CVGIP: Image Understanding 58(3), 366–382 (1993)

Appendix. Proof of Theorem 1

Proof. Contrary to the case on $\mathbb{Z}$ the random variable $X_t \in \{-1, 0, +1\}$ that drives the wandering at time t, (left, stay put or right), is not equal for each pixel, hence for each time. These pixels are distributed in few classes determined by the ring of pixels nearby (see Definition. 4 on p. 51). The position evolution at time t, $P_t = P_{t-1} + X_{P_{t-1}}$ brings into play the random variable X_t that depends on t through the position P_{t-1}. We can write it in the form of:

$$\frac{1}{T}P_T = \frac{1}{T}\sum_{t=1}^{T}X_t$$

Since the system is *ergodic* [2], this time average of X along a trajectory up to T is equal to its space average at the given time T. Therefore we can find an equivalent of this form according to the position i:

$$\frac{1}{T}P_T = \frac{1}{T}\sum_{t=1}^{T}X_t \simeq_{T\to\infty} \sum_{i=-\infty}^{+\infty}\mathbb{P}(P_T = i)X_i$$

$\mathbb{P}(P_T = i)$ represents the probability for the walker to be at time T on pixel i. The transition random variable X_i depends on the position i only through its equivalence class $[i]$. Let $\lambda_{[i]}$ be the proportion of pixels in the equivalence class $[i]$ on the discrete line. Then we can write this sum in the form of:

$$\sum_{i=-\infty}^{+\infty}\mathbb{P}(P_T = i)X_i = \sum_{[i]}\left(\sum_{i\in[i]}\mathbb{P}(P_T = i)\right)X_{[i]} \simeq_{T\to\infty}\sum_{[i]}\lambda_{[i]}X_{[i]}$$

We build a sequence of random variables P_t with $\lambda_{[i]}$ proportion of pixels in the class $[i]$ on the discrete line, independent of the time. We have:

$$P_T \simeq T\sum_{[i]}\lambda_{[i]}X_{[i]}$$

We conclude by using the Central Limit Theorem, that $\frac{1}{\sqrt{T}}P_T$ follows a normal law.   □

An Algorithm to Decompose n-Dimensional Rotations into Planar Rotations

Aurélie Richard, Laurent Fuchs, and Sylvain Charneau

Laboratoire XLIM-SIC, Université de Poitiers, 86360 Chasseneuil, France
{arichard,Laurent.Fuchs}@sic.univ-poitiers.fr

Abstract. In this paper, we present an algorithm that decomposes an n-dimensional rotation into planar rotations. The input data are n points and their images by the rotation to be decomposed. An evaluation of the existing methods and numerical examples are also provided.

Keywords: n-dimensional rotations, planar rotations, Cartan-Dieudonné theorem.

1 Introduction

In this paper we propose an algorithm to determine nD rotations from n points and their images. From the Cartan-Dieudonné theorem [2], we know that an nD rotation can be decomposed into planar rotations. Our algorithm finds the planar rotations and the angle of each of these planar rotations. This fully characterizes the rotation.

Rotation characterization is very useful in many application domains such as Computer Vision [16] to determine object positions and camera position, in medicine [6,5] to determine limb movements, in procrustes analysis [10] where geometric shapes are analyzed up to rotations (and others transformations). Other applications should also be cited such as global visibility computation [4].

In many cases, estimating 3D rotations is sufficient, but there are some cases where higher dimensions are needed such as in color image analysis, where 4D rotations are used or in global visibility computation where 5D or 6D spaces (Plücker space) are needed. Moreover, due to the dimension increase of new acquisition techniques, new trends about higher dimensions appear in such application domains.

Unfortunately, in the available literature we did not find many methods that determine the characteristics of a rotation. To our knowledge some methods only characterize 3D rotations [5,6,19] and they cannot be extended to higher dimensions. Other methods [15] estimate an algebraic quantity (a rotor). But a rotor describes the rotation in a form such that rotation planes cannot be computed easily. This is not well adapted to our targeted application, viz., describing nD discrete rotations by extension of hinge angles for 3D discrete rotations [18].

The only existing approach, to our best knowledge, that could provide an algorithm to characterize nD rotations by their decomposition into planar rotations,

R.P. Barneva et al. (Eds.): CompIMAGE 2010, LNCS 6026, pp. 60–71, 2010.
© Springer-Verlag Berlin Heidelberg 2010

comes from a constructive proof of the Cartan-Dieudonné theorem [1]. However, we show in this paper that this solution is not practical.

The paper is organized as follow. In Section 2, we recall previous methods for determining rotation parameters. In Section 3, we present our method and show how geometric algebra can simplify the determination of rotation angles and planes in arbitrary dimensions. Numerical experiments in 3, 4, 5 and 6D are proposed to show the validity of our method.

2   Related Work

In this section, we present a quick overview of methods that determine rotation characteristics from points and their images.

The first group we consider, consists of methods that determine 3D rotation characteristics and cannot be generalized to higher dimensions. To illustrate these methods, we outline three papers found in the literature.

The first one, by Cheng & al. [6], decomposes a 3D rotation into two rotations such that the composition order does not matter. A drawback of this method is that the rotation must start from a position where the orientation of the local coordinate system coincides with a reference coordinate system. Another method, also by Cheng [5], is based on the expression of a vector by a longitude and a latitude according to the reference coordinate system. Hence, movement from a point to another one can be described by changes of longitude and latitude in the spherical rotation coordinate system. The last method uses the Helmert transformation [19] that transforms a set of points into another one by rotation, scaling, and translation. In [19], Watson explains how to estimate this transformation when both sets of points are given using least squares approximation.

The second group of methods works in the geometric algebra framework [3, 7, 12, 15, 17]. It is based on the geometric product that, for vectors, is a combination of the usual scalar product and the outer product[1]. The outer product can be seen as an algebraic operation that geometrically connects elements. Hence, if $\mathbf{u}$ and $\mathbf{v}$ are vectors then $\mathbf{u} \wedge \mathbf{v}$ (a 2-blade) could be used to define the vector plane generated by $\mathbf{u}$ and $\mathbf{v}$. More generally the outer product of n independent vectors defines the subspace spanned by these vectors. It is called an n-blade [7]. This gives an algebra over subspaces of a vector space. The geometric interpretation of these subspaces defines geometric elements such as lines or planes [7, 12, 15, 17]. Vectors could also be used to represent reflection operators. Then, if $\mathbf{a}$ is a unit vector, the reflection of the vector $\mathbf{x}$ in the line of $\mathbf{a}$ is given by $\mathbf{a}\mathbf{x}\mathbf{a}^{-1}$. In 3D space, it is well known that two reflections make a 3D rotation (see Figure 1(b)). If $\mathbf{b}$ defines a second reflection the rotation of vector $\mathbf{x}$ is written as $\mathbf{b}(\mathbf{a}\mathbf{x}\mathbf{a}^{-1})\mathbf{b}^{-1}$, hence $R = \mathbf{b}\mathbf{a}^{-1}$ is an algebraic element that represents the rotation. This element is called a rotor. Rotors define rotations in any dimension[2] as a geometric product of an even number of reflections.

---

[1] If $\mathbf{u}$ and $\mathbf{v}$ are vectors then $\mathbf{u}\mathbf{v} = \mathbf{u}.\mathbf{v} + \mathbf{u} \wedge \mathbf{v}$.

[2] In 4D, they are equivalent to quaternions [7].

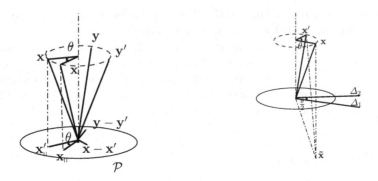

Fig. 1. (a) Graphical illustration of rotation plane and angle. $\mathbf{x}, \mathbf{x}'$ (resp. $\mathbf{y}, \mathbf{y}'$) represent a vector and its image by a rotation. The rotation plane $\mathcal{P}$ is generated by $\mathbf{x} - \mathbf{x}'$ and $\mathbf{y} - \mathbf{y}'$. The angle between $\mathbf{x}$ and $\mathbf{x}'$ is the same as the one between $\mathbf{x}_{\parallel}$ and $\mathbf{x}'_{\parallel}$ in $\mathcal{P}$, (b) Rotation decomposition into two reflections. The rotation from $\mathbf{x}$ to $\mathbf{x}'$ can be seen as the composition of the reflections through Δ_1 and Δ_2.

The second group of methods estimates rotors from geometric data [15]. But this does not solve our decomposition problem because from the estimated rotor we must still deduce the planar rotation decomposition, which leads to tricky computations. However, here is a short description of how these computations can be made. One way is to express the rotor in a matrix form, as the images of the basis are the columns of the rotation matrix, and then use our algorithm.

From our input data there is no gain to estimate the rotor first. Another way is to use the exponential form of a rotor R. We have $R = e^{-B/2}$ where B is a bivector[3] that can be decomposed into a sum of 2-blades $B = B_1 + \cdots + B_k$ with $k \leq n/2$. These 2-blades define the planar rotations. However, the drawback of this approach is that we need to obtain the bivector B by a logarithm computation and then decompose it. These two computations are not so straightforward [7, 11].

The last group of methods tries to compute directly the planar rotation decomposition of a rotation from points and their images. One approach is to reconstruct reflections that compose the planar rotations. It is based on the constructive proof of the Cartan-Dieudonné theorem given in [1]. In an Euclidean space E, a reflection ϕ is uniquely determined by a vector $\mathbf{a}$ and the image $\phi(\mathbf{a}) = \mathbf{b}$ such that $\mathbf{a}$ and $\mathbf{b}$ are non-null vectors with $\mathbf{b} \neq \mathbf{a}$ and $||\mathbf{a}|| = ||\mathbf{b}||$. This reflection can be expressed as:

$$\phi(x) = \begin{cases} \phi_{\mathbf{a}}(x) \text{ if } \mathbf{b} = -\mathbf{a} \\ \phi_{\mathbf{a}-\mathbf{b}}(x), \text{ otherwise} \end{cases} \tag{1}$$

where $\phi_{\mathbf{v}}(x)$ denotes the reflection of x through the hyperplane $\mathbf{v}^{\perp}$ of orthogonal vectors to $\mathbf{v}$ as shown in the Figure 2(a). The reflection $\phi_{\mathbf{v}}(x)$ is defined as

---

[3] An algebraic element that is a combination of $e_i \wedge e_j$, $i \neq j$ where e_i $i = 1, \ldots, n$ are basis vectors and n the space dimension.

Fig. 2. (a) Reflection of vector **y** through the hyperplane $\mathbf{x}^\perp$, (b) Rotation that brings the vector a onto vector b can be seen as the composition of the rotation through the hyperplanes $(a+b)^\perp$ and $b^\perp$

$$\phi_{\mathbf{v}}(x) = x - 2\frac{\mathbf{v}.x}{||\mathbf{v}||^2}\mathbf{v} = x - 2r\mathbf{v}.$$

The reflection decomposition of the rotation[4] R can be determined by an incremental process that constructs a reflection at each step as shown in Figure 2(b). Suppose that we have chosen a basis $(e_1, \ldots, e_n)$ in E. For the first step, we choose $\mathbf{a} = e_1$ and $\mathbf{b} = R(e_1)$ which define the first reflection ϕ_1. At the k-th step, $\mathbf{a} = e_k$ and $\mathbf{b} = \phi_{k-1} \circ \ldots \circ \phi_1 \circ R(e_k)$ are chosen in order to obtain the k-th reflection ϕ_k. Finally, we obtain $R = \phi_1^{-1} \circ \phi_2^{-1} \circ \ldots \phi_n^{-1} = \phi_1 \circ \phi_2 \circ \ldots \phi_n$. If the space dimension n is odd, at least one reflection is the identity because we decompose a rotation.

Based on this approach we have performed experiments with MatLab using the Geometric Algebra package Gable [8]. This works well when using data without any noise. However, when perturbations are introduced we are faced with the problem of recognizing the reflection that should be the identity, actually the hyperplane that must be ignored. Even if this problem could be more or less solved in 3D, this comes to be very difficult in higher dimensions. For example, consider a 5D-rotation that could be composed of two or four reflections. One cannot determine how many hyperplanes must by ignored. Moreover, this incremental approach is a cumulative one. So a small error into the determination of ϕ_k introduces errors to the determination of the following ϕ_{k+i}. Hence, a direct algorithmic translation of the proof of the Cartan-Dieudonné theorem, as it is provided in [1], is not practical.

This is why, in this paper, we propose a new approach that computes directly the planar rotation decomposition of an nD rotation.

3   Decomposition of nD Rotations

In this section, we give some results about the nD rotations, and we describe our method to obtain a planar rotation decomposition of an nD rotation in Euclidean space E.

In the following, the n dimensional space E (usually $\mathbb{R}^n$) is considered with a basis (not necessarily an orthogonal one) denoted by $(x_i)_{i=1...n}$. The space E

---

[4] Or more generally of an orthogonal transformation.

must be equipped with a non-degenerated quadratic form and the associated bilinear form is denoted by $\mathcal{B}$. In standard cases, $\mathcal{B}$ corresponds to the usual scalar product. Thus, the space E is a metric space upon which isometries can be defined.

3.1   Some Results about nD-Rotations

In this section, we recall useful properties of the nD rotations. Let R be a rotation in $SO(E)$, the rotation group of E. The fixed-point subspace of R is denoted by F. Its orthogonal subspace[5] in E is denoted by $\mathcal{P}$ or $F^{\perp}$. The respective images of $(x_i)_{i=1...n}$ by R are denoted by $(y_i)_{i=1...n}$. Since $\mathcal{B}$ is non-degenerate, the space E can be decomposed into $E = \mathcal{P} \oplus F$. Moreover, E can also be decomposed into another direct sum given by the following well-known proposition [2]:

Proposition 1. *Let f be a linear isometry of E. The vector space E is an orthogonal direct sum:*

$$E = V \oplus W \oplus P_1 \oplus \cdots \oplus P_r$$

where the subspaces V, W and P_i are stable under f, and $f \mid_V = Id_V$, $f \mid_W = -Id_W$, and every P_i is a plane such that $f \mid_{P_i}$ is a rotation.

In term of matrices, proposition 1 shows us that there exists an orthonormal basis of E such that the matrix of f can be written as

$$\mathcal{F} = \begin{pmatrix} I_p & & & & \\ & -I_q & & & \\ & & R_{\theta_1} & & \\ & & & \ddots & \\ & & & & R_{\theta_r} \end{pmatrix}$$ where I_p denotes the identity matrix of order p and

R_{θ_i} the 2×2 planar rotation matrix. As we deal with rotations, W has an even dimension q. Thus, we can consider the submatrix $-I_q$ as the concatenation of $q/2$ rotations of angle π. So, we can set $V = F$, $W = 0$ and $\mathcal{P} = P_1 \oplus \cdots \oplus P_r$.

As an example, in $4D$, a rotation can be decomposed into one or two planar rotations. In the case that we have two rotations (i.e. $r = 2$ in the matrix $\mathcal{F}$), if the angles θ_1 and θ_2 have the same magnitude[6] then the 4D rotation is said to be isoclinic[7] [14]. These particular rotations are only defined in an even dimensional space[8]. For the purpose of this paper, we introduce the term pseudo-isoclinic rotation in order to define n-dimensional rotations that have at least two planar rotation angles of the same magnitude. In our algorithm, it is presupposed that the input data $((x_i)_{i=1...n}$ and $(y_i)_{i=1...n})$ do not represent an isoclinic or pseudo isoclinic rotation.

---

[5] $F = \{x \in E | R(x) = x\}$ and $F^{\perp} = \{x \in E \mid \forall y \in F, \mathcal{B}(x, y) = 0\}$.

[6] $|\theta_1| = |\theta_2| \in [0, \pi]$, if θ_1 and θ_2 have same (resp. opposite) signs then the rotation is called left (resp. right) isoclinic rotation.

[7] This is also called a Clifford displacement.

[8] In an odd dimension space, the unique isoclinic rotation is the identity transformation.

3.2 Determination of the Rotation Parameters

Our method is in three steps. We begin by the determination of $\mathcal{P}$, which is the orthogonal subspace to the rotation fixed-points set. From it, we can construct the rotation planes and finally we can retrieve the rotation angles.

Determination of $\mathcal{P}$. To characterize $\mathcal{P}$, we need to prove first that the vectors $y_i - x_i$ are in this space and then that the family $(y_i - x_i)_{i=1...n}$ generates it.

We proceed in two steps. Firstly, we prove that the vectors $y_i - x_i$ are in $\mathcal{P}$. Since $\mathcal{P}$ and F are in direct sum, every vector $x \in E$ can be uniquely decomposed into two vectors, $x_{\shortparallel} \in \mathcal{P}$ and $x_{\perp} \in F$ such that $x = x_{\shortparallel} + x_{\perp}$. Let $x_i = x_{i_{\shortparallel}} + x_{i_{\perp}}$ and $y_i = y_{i_{\shortparallel}} + y_{i_{\perp}}$ be the unique decomposition of x_i and $y_i = R(x_i)$ (Figure 1(b)). Rotations are linear transformations, so we have: $R(x_i) = R(x_{i_{\shortparallel}}) + R(x_{i_{\perp}}) = y_{i_{\shortparallel}} + x_{i_{\perp}}$ because $y_{i_{\shortparallel}} = R(x_{i_{\shortparallel}})$ and $y_{i_{\perp}} = x_{i_{\perp}}$. From this, we have:

$$y_i - x_i = y_{i_{\shortparallel}} + x_{i_{\perp}} - x_{i_{\shortparallel}} - x_{i_{\perp}} = x_{i_{\perp}} - x_{i_{\perp}} - x_{i_{\shortparallel}} + y_{i_{\shortparallel}} = y_{i_{\shortparallel}} - x_{i_{\shortparallel}}.$$

Since $\mathcal{P}$ is a plane, the difference between $y_i \in \mathcal{P}$ and $x_i \in \mathcal{P}$ is in $\mathcal{P}$ too.

As a second step we prove that $y_i - x_i$ generate $\mathcal{P}$. We set Id as the identity function. The subspace F is the kernel of the application $(R - Id)$, so $F = Ker(R - Id) = \{x \in E | (R - Id)(x) = 0\}$. As the kernel and the image sets of an application are in direct sum, we have: $E = Ker(R - Id) \oplus Im(R - Id) = F \oplus Im(R - Id)$ and also

$$E = F \oplus \mathcal{P} = Ker(R - Id) \oplus \mathcal{P} = Ker(R - Id) \oplus Ker(R - Id)^{\perp}.$$

Hence, $\mathcal{P} = Im(R - Id)$ and, as (x_i) form a basis of E, the family of vectors $((R - Id)(x_i))_{i=1...n} = (y_i - x_i)_{i=1...n}$ generates $Im(R - Id)$. So we proved that the $y_i - x_i$ generate $\mathcal{P}$.

Determination of the Rotation Planes. The goal here is to build a basis of $\mathcal{P}$ in order to be able to determine the rotation planes. Using Proposition 1, $\mathcal{P}$ can be decomposed as $\mathcal{P} = P_1 \oplus \cdots \oplus P_r$. Then, if we compute an orthogonal basis of $\mathcal{P}$, couples of basis elements will determine P_i.

To explain this, let us recall that a rotation R can be written in an exponential form [7,11] $R = e^{-B/2}$ where B is a bivector such that $B = B_1 + \cdots + B_r$ with $r \leq n/2$. The planes defined by the B_i's are mutually orthogonal and define the rotation planes. With respect to an orthonormal basis $(b_{2r}, b_{2r-1}, \cdots, b_2, b_1)$, we have $B_i = \|B_i\| b_{2i-1} \wedge b_{2i}$ and:

$$e^{-B/2} = e^{-B_r/2} \cdots e^{-B_1/2}$$

where $e^{-B_i/2} = \cos(\|B_i\|) - (b_{2i-1} \wedge b_{2i}) \sin(\|B_i\|)$ are the planar rotations. This means that $\mathcal{P}$ is spanned by the b_i, i.e. $\mathcal{P} = b_{2r} \wedge b_{2r-1} \wedge \cdots \wedge b_2 \wedge b_1$. We can choose $P_i = b_{2i-1} \wedge b_{2i}$. The most obvious choice to compute the orthogonal basis would be to use the Gram-Schmidt process over the $y_i - x_i$. However, in case of noisy data, it is difficult to obtain a matrix of correct rank[9]. An alternative

---

[9] The $(y_i - x_i)_{(i=1...n)}$ family generates $\mathcal{P}$. So, the obtained matrix must be of rank $2r \leq n$ that is at most $2r = n - 1$ if n is odd.

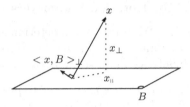

Fig. 3. Contraction of a vector x by a 2-blade B

is to use a SVD decomposition over the matrix involved by the $y_i - x_i$. The approximation property of the SVD [9] ensures to obtain a matrix with rank $2r$ that is the dimension of $\mathcal{P}$. Hence, following the usual presentation of the SVD decomposition, the first $2r$ columns form the desired basis.

Determination of the Rotation Angles. The last step of the algorithm finds the rotation angle of each planar rotation. For each rotation plane P_i, rotation angle between x_j and y_j is the same as the angle between their projections $x_{j_{\shortparallel}}$ and $y_{j_{\shortparallel}}$ in P_i (see Figure 1(a)). Then, for each P_i we have to determine these two vectors $x_{j_{\shortparallel}}$ and $y_{j_{\shortparallel}}$. To do so, we suppose that we have chosen x_j and y_j such that their projections are not null. To avoid cumbersome indexes, throughout of this section we simply set $P_i = P$, $x_j = x$ and $y_j = y$. For all $a \in P$, we have:

$$a.x = a.(x_{\shortparallel} + x_{\perp}) = a.x_{\shortparallel} + a.x_{\perp} = a.x_{\shortparallel} + 0 = a.x_{\shortparallel}.$$

The relation $a.x = 0$ defines the set $x^{\perp} \cap P = \{a : a \in P \text{ and } a \in x^{\perp}\}$ and the relation $a.x_{\shortparallel} = 0$ defines $x_{\shortparallel}^{\perp} \cap P$, so we have:

$$x^{\perp} \cap P = x_{\shortparallel}^{\perp} \cap P. \tag{2}$$

Now, we use the orthogonal contraction operation [7]. The orthogonal contraction of an a-blade A by a b-blade B defines the subspace of dimension $(b - a)$ in B which is orthogonal to A. It is denoted by $< A, B >_{\perp}$. In the particular case where B defines a plane and A a vector, this operator defines the subspace of the plane perpendicular to $A_{\shortparallel}$ (cf Figure 3). Thus, here $x^{\perp} \cap P$ is denoted by $< x, P >_{\perp}$ and $x_{\shortparallel}^{\perp} \cap P$ by $< x_{\shortparallel}, P >_{\perp}$. So, from the equality (2) we obtain:

$$< x, P >_{\perp} = < x_{\shortparallel}, P >_{\perp}$$

This intersection is a hyperplane contained in P and orthogonal to $x_{\shortparallel}$ (cf Figure 3). Using again the orthogonal contraction between $< x, P >_{\perp}$ and P, we obtain the intersection between the subspace $(x^{\perp} \cap P)^{\perp}$ and the plane P that is the subspace generated by $x_{\shortparallel}$. The same process with the vector y provides the projection $y_{\shortparallel}$ on P up to a scalar factor. Then, the rotation angle θ in P is the angle between x and y and is given by:

$$\cos(\theta) = \frac{x_{\shortparallel}.y_{\shortparallel}}{||x_{\shortparallel}||||y_{\shortparallel}||} \text{ and } \sin(\theta) = \frac{x_{\shortparallel} \wedge y_{\shortparallel}}{||x_{\shortparallel}||||y_{\shortparallel}||P}.$$

The computation is applied to all rotation planes in order to find all the rotation angles. Our method is summarized in Algorithm 1, below.

Algorithm 1. Find P_i (rotation plane) and θ_i (rotation angle)

Require: $(x_i)_{i=1...n}$, $(y_i)_{i=1...n}$
Ensure: P_i, θ_i
  // *Orthogonal basis construction*
  $z_i = y_i - x_i$
  $B = Orthogonalize[z_1 \ldots z_n]$
  $k = rank(B)$
  // *Build the rotation planes*
  for all i such that $1 \leq i \leq \frac{k}{2}$ **do**
    $P_i = B(2i-1) \wedge B(2i)$
  end for
  // *Compute rotation angles*
  for all P_i **do**
    Find $x_{j_\parallel} = \ll x_j, P_i >_\perp, P_i >_\perp$ and $y_{j_\parallel} = \ll y_j, P_i >_\perp, P_i >_\perp$ non null
    $\cos(\theta_j) = \frac{x_{j_\parallel} \cdot y_{j_\parallel}}{||x_{j_\parallel}||||y_{j_\parallel}||}$ and $\sin(\theta_j) = \frac{x_{j_\parallel} \wedge y_{j_\parallel}}{||x_{j_\parallel}||||y_{j_\parallel}|| P_i}$.
  end for

---

4 Examples and Numerical Results

4.1 Examples

Figure 4 provides examples in 3D and 4D spaces. They have been computed with the Matlab package Gable [8]. The frame axis are denoted by capital letters, the canonical basis vectors by x_i and their rotated images by y_i.

Example in a 3D space. Let us consider the space $E = \mathbb{R}^3$ equipped with the canonical basis (x_1, x_2, x_3).

We consider the composition of a rotation of angle $\pi/4$ around the X-axis and a rotation of angle $\pi/6$ around the Y-axis. The vectors y_i are thus given by: $y_1 = (\sqrt{3}/2, 0, -1/2), y_2 = (\sqrt{2}/4, \sqrt{2}/2, \sqrt{6}/4)$ and $y_3 = (\sqrt{2}/4, -\sqrt{2}/2, \sqrt{6}/4)$.

From our algorithm, it is easy to show that the rotation plane (which is unique in 3D) is represented by the 2-blade $P = x'_{j1} \wedge x'_{j2}$ where $x'_{j1} = (\sqrt{3}/2-1, 0, -1/2)$ and $x'_{j2} = (\sqrt{2}/8, \sqrt{2}/2 - 1, -(4\sqrt{6} - 7\sqrt{2})/(8\sqrt{3} - 16))$. The angle rotation is given by the angle between $x_{1_\parallel}$ and $y_{1_\parallel}$, the projection of x_1 and y_1 in P (Figure 1(b)). These results are illustrated in Figure 4(a).

Example in a 4D space. In 4D, we consider the space $E = \mathbb{R}^4$ and its canonical basis (x_1, x_2, x_3, x_4). These vectors rotate in the plane XY of angle $\pi/4$ and in the plane ZT of angle $\pi/6$. The vectors $(y_i)_{i=1...4}$ are thus given by $y_1 = (\sqrt{2}/2, \sqrt{2}/2, 0, 0), y_2 = (-\sqrt{2}/2, \sqrt{2}/2, 0, 0), y_3 = (0, 0, \sqrt{3}/2, 1/2)$, and $y_4 = (0, 0, -1/2, \sqrt{3}/2)$. It is easy to show that this 4D-rotation can be decomposed into two planar rotations. Actually, our algorithm provides four vectors which constitute the basis of $\mathcal{P}$. From these four vectors, three couples of two vectors

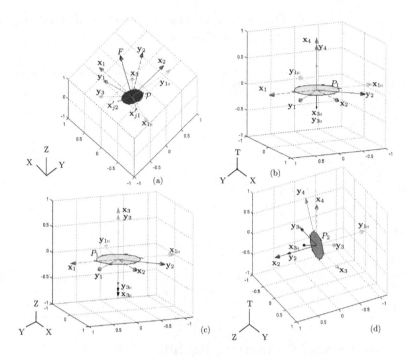

Fig. 4. (a) Graphical representation in a 3D-space of canonical basis vectors (x_1, x_2, x_3), their images by a 3D-rotation (y_1, y_2, y_3), the invariant vector space (F), the rotation plane $\mathcal{P}$. $x_{1\parallel}$ (resp. $y_{1\parallel}$) is the projection in $\mathcal{P}$ of x_1 (resp. y_1). The vectors x'_{j1} and x'_{j2} constitute a basis of $\mathcal{P}$. (b)(c)(d) Projections in a 3D-space of canonical basis vectors their images by a 4D-rotation and the rotation plane.

(which corresponds to the rotation planes) can be formed (the solution is not unique). Arbitrarily, in this example, the first (resp. the second) rotation plane is represented by the outer product between the two first output vectors (resp. the two last) resulting from the SVD. Finally, rotation angles are computed by projection onto the rotation planes as defined in the algorithm.

Since the graphical representation in a 4D space is somewhat complicated, in Figure 4, the vectors generated by our algorithm are projected according to the first three coordinates (fig. 4(c)), first, second and fourth coordinates (fig. 4(b)) and the last three (fig. 4(d)). The basis vectors (x_1, x_2, x_3 and x_4) are drawn with dotted lines and their images (y_1, y_2, y_3 and y_4) with continuous line. In the projections (b) and (c) we have represented the plane P_1 and in projection (d) the plane P_2 is represented. Since P_1 and P_2 are orthogonal, the vectors $x_{3\parallel}$ and $y_{3\parallel}$ ($\in P_2$) are normal to the plane P_1 in (b) and (c) and the vector $y_{1\parallel}$ ($\in P_1$) is normal to the plane P_2 (d). Projections of $x_{1\parallel}$ in the space which correspond to the configuration (d) are null. Rotation angles are angles between the vectors $x_{1\parallel}$ and $y_{1\parallel}$ in P_1 and between the vectors $x_{3\parallel}$ and $y_{3\parallel}$ in P_2 as explained before. Some vectors are rescaled ($y_{1\parallel}$ is increased and $x_{3\parallel}$ and $y_{3\parallel}$ are decreased) in order to obtain readable graphics.

4.2   Numerical Experiments

We have also experimented our algorithm in higher dimensions with the library developed in [3] using the OCaml language [13]. In order to be analyzed, the data are retrieved and handled with Matlab.

The following numerical experiments have been carried out. The rotation planes and angles are randomly chosen and the rotation matrices A_i are thus generated. Then, these matrices are biased with a random perturbation of a decimal. The biased matrices are denoted by B_i. The perturbation of the matrix A_i can be estimated by computing the usual Frobenius norm[10] of the matrix $(B_i - A_i)$. Afterward, our method is applied to these matrices. The estimated

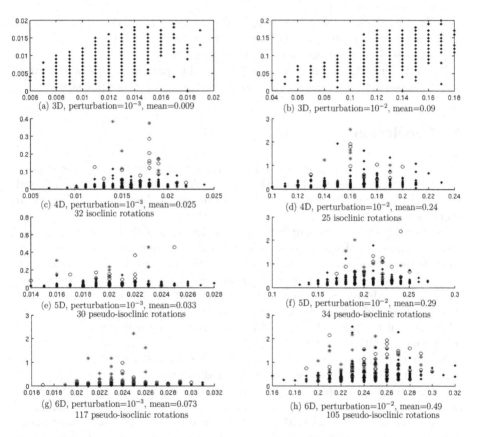

(a) 3D, perturbation=10^{-3}, mean=0.009

(b) 3D, perturbation=10^{-2}, mean=0.09

(c) 4D, perturbation=10^{-3}, mean=0.025
32 isoclinic rotations

(d) 4D, perturbation=10^{-2}, mean=0.24
25 isoclinic rotations

(e) 5D, perturbation=10^{-3}, mean=0.033
30 pseudo-isoclinic rotations

(f) 5D, perturbation=10^{-2}, mean=0.29
34 pseudo-isoclinic rotations

(g) 6D, perturbation=10^{-3}, mean=0.073
117 pseudo-isoclinic rotations

(h) 6D, perturbation=10^{-2}, mean=0.49
105 pseudo-isoclinic rotations

Fig. 5. Plot of the Frobenius norm of the matrix $(E_i - A_i)$ with respect to the perturbation (Frobenius norm of the matrix $(B_i - A_i)$). Points with a marker "*" (resp. "o") correspond to pseudo-isoclinic rotations such that the absolute value of the difference of the two angles is less than 5 (resp. 15) degrees.

---

[10] Let A a $m \times n$ matrix, its Frobenius norm is defined by $||A||_F = \sqrt{\sum_{i=1}^{m} \sum_{j=1}^{n} a_{ij}^2}$.

rotation planes and angles are thus obtained (resp. P_i and θ_i). In order to estimate the error of our method, we successively compute the rotor corresponding
to these parameters[11] and the image of each basis vector x_k using Rx_kR^{-1}.
The matrix whose k-th column is the vector Rx_kR^{-1} is denoted by E_i and is
compared with the initial matrix A_i.

The tests have been conducted with 500 matrices in 3D, 4D, 5D and 6D. In
each case, the second and the third decimals of initial matrices A_i were per-
turbed. In Figure 5, the Frobenius norm of the matrices $(E_i - A_i)$ are plotted
with respect to the norm of $(B_i - A_i)$.

In 3D, the error is almost null as shown in Figures 5(a,b). The mean of the
error is of the same order as of the perturbation. Even if the data are biased,
rotation parameters (plane and angle) which are given by our algorithm are very
close to the exact solution.

In four and higher dimensions results are also good but there exists "isolated
plots" as shown in Figures 5(c-g). These points correspond to the particular case
of pseudo-isoclinic rotations (see the paragraph 3.1).

Actually, our algorithm is not adapted to this particular case and further
investigations are under consideration in order to bypass this drawback.

5   Conclusion

In this paper, we have proposed an algorithm that computes the decomposition into planar rotations of an nD rotation. The input data are n points and
their images. Using the geometric algebra framework this algorithm is easy to
implement.

We found in the literature only two propositions that could be used to compute
the decomposition of nD rotation. The method that could be deduced from the
constructive proof of the Cartan Dieudonné theorem given in [1] leads to an
algorithm that only determines the hyperplanes of the reflections that compose
the rotation. Moreover, when the data are biased the decomposition can not
be computed and due to its incremental nature the error is accumulated. The
adaptation of the method proposed in [15] leads to complex computations and
finally our algorithm must be used.

So, to the authors' best knowledge, the proposed algorithm is the unique
method that gives this decomposition in an efficient way.

If the data do not represent a pseudo-isoclinic rotation, the calculated planes
and angles are very close to the exact ones even if the input data are biased.

An adaptation of our algorithm to the pseudo-isoclinic case is being studied.
Actually, in the case of isoclinic rotation, the planes spanned by half-lines and
their corresponding displaced half-lines are invariant under that rotation [14].
Extension to the pseudo-isoclinic case must be studied. And then, this can be
used as preprocessing of the input data. We have to detect if there exists indices
i and j such that the planes $y_i \wedge x_i$ and $y_j \wedge x_j$ are orthogonal. Hence, rotation

---

[11] The rotor R is given by $R = \cos(\theta_i) - P_i \sin(\theta_i)$.

planes are directly found and the angle (such that $\theta_i = \theta_j$) can be computed using orthogonal contractions.

As an application of this work, we plan to use it in order to describe nD discrete rotations by extending the hinge angle notion developed for 3D rotations in [18].

References

1. Aragon-Gonzalez, G., Aragon, J., Rodriguez-Andrade, M., Verde-Star, L.: Reflections, rotations, and pythagorean numbers. Advances in Applied Clifford Algebra 19(1), 1–14 (2009)
2. Audin, M.: Geometry. Springer, Heidelberg (2003)
3. Charneau, S.: Étude et Application des Algèbres Géométriques pour le Calcul de la Visibilité Globale dans un Espace Projectif de Dimension n $\geq$ 2. Ph.D. Thesis, Université de Poitiers, France (2007)
4. Charneau, S., Aveneau, L., Fuchs, L.: Exact, robust and efficient full visibility computation in the Plücker space. The Visual Computer Journal 23, 773–782 (2007)
5. Cheng, P.: Joint rotation between two attitudes in the spherical rotation coordinate system. Journal of Biomechanics 37(10), 1475–1482 (2004)
6. Cheng, P., Nicol, A., Paul, J.: Determination of axial rotation angles of limb segments – a new method. Journal of Biomechanics 33(7), 837–843 (2000)
7. Dorst, L., Fontijne, D., Mann, S.: Geometric Algebra for Computer Science: An Object-Oriented Approach to Geometry. Morgan Kauffmann Publishers, San Francisco (2007)
8. Dorst, L., Mann, S., Bouma, T.: Gable: A Matlab Tutorial for Geometric Algebra (2003)
9. Golub, G., Van Loan, C.: Matrix Computations, 3rd edn. Johns Hopkins Studies in Mathematical Sciences (1996)
10. Gower, J.C., Dijksterhuis, G.B.: Procrustes Problems. Oxford University Press, Oxford (2004)
11. Hestenes, D., Sobczyk, G.: Clifford Algebra to Geometric Calculus: A Unified Language for Mathematics and Physics. D.Reidel Pub. Co., Dordrecht (1984)
12. Hildebrand, D., Fontijne, D., Perwass, C., Dorst, L.: Geometric algebra and its application to computer graphics. In: 25th Annual Conference of the European Association for Computer Graphics – Interacting with Virtual Worlds (2004)
13. The Calm Language, http://www.ocaml.org
14. Mebius, J.: The Four-dimensional Rotation Group SO(4) (2008), http://www.xs4all.nl/~jemebius/so4-wiki.pdf
15. Perwass, C., Sommer, G.: Numerical evaluation of versors with Clifford Algebra. In: Dorst, L., Doran, C., Lasenby, J. (eds.) Applications of Geometric Algebra in Computer Science and Engineering, pp. 341–350. Birkhauser, Boston (2002)
16. Shapiro, L.G., Stockman, G.C.: Computer Vision. Prentice-Hall, Englewood Cliffs (2001)
17. Sommer, G.: Geometric Computing with Clifford Algebra. Springer, Heidelberg (2001)
18. Thibault, Y., Kenmochi, Y., Sugimoto, A.: Computing upper and lower bounds of rotation angles from digital images. Pattern Recognition 42(8), 1708–1717 (2009)
19. Watson, G.: Computing Helmert transformations. Journal of Computational and Applied Mathematics 197 (2006)

Tile Pasting Systems for Tessellation and Tiling Patterns

T. Robinson[1,3], S. Jebasingh[2], Atulya K. Nagar[3], and K.G. Subramanian[4]

[1] Department of Mathematics, Madras Christian College
Tambaram, Chennai - 600 059, India
[2] Department of Mathematics, Saveetha Engineering College
Thandalam, Chennai - 602 105, India
[3] Department of Computer Science, Liverpool Hope University
Hope Park, Liverpool, L16 9JD, United Kingdom
[4] School of Mathematical Sciences, Universiti Sains Malaysia
11800 Penang, Malaysia

Abstract. Pasting System (PS) and Extended Pasting Scheme (EPS) are new techniques to generate tiling patterns by using pasting rules for gluing tiles at their edges. In this paper we introduce a Tabled Pasting System (TPS) based on the technique of suitably grouping the rules of a pasting system into different sets of rules. We compare the generative power of TPS with PS and EPS. We propose theoretical models of P-system, called tile pasting P-system, with active membranes ($TPPS - AM$) and tissue-like evolution communication tile pasting P system ($t - ECTPPS$) to generate tiling patterns made of polygon tiles and compare the generative power of TPS with $TPPS - AM$ and $t - ECTPPS$.

Keywords: syntactic methods, two-dimensional pattern, pasting system, picture languages, P system.

1 Introduction

Syntactic methods have been found useful in the generation of two dimensional arrays and polygons [5]. Puzzle grammars and array grammars are linguistic tools, studied extensively in the literature, for the description and analysis of two dimensional structures. Rewriting rules and pasting catenation [6] are certain important techniques for picture generation and analysis. Recently, extending a new generating technique known as pasting system, a variant called extended pasting scheme has been introduced by Robinson [12], by the use of the notion of a pasting rule that allows the edges of the corresponding tiles to get glued or attached at those edges. In this paper we introduce a tabled pasting system (TPS) employing the technique of suitably grouping the rules of a pasting system into different sets of rules. This technique is known to be powerful in string and array generation. We find that TPS generates interesting tiling patterns. We compare the generative power of TPS with (PS) and (EPS).

R.P. Barneva et al. (Eds.): CompIMAGE 2010, LNCS 6026, pp. 72–84, 2010.

Membrane computing (or P-system) [7,9] is an area of computer science aiming to abstract computing models from the structure and functioning of living cells. A P-system consists of a membrane structure, multisets of objects placed inside the membranes, evolution rules governing the modification of these objects in time, and transfer of objects from one membrane to another membrane (inter-cellular communication). In recent years, generation of two dimensional picture languages using P-systems is extensively studied. P-systems generating arrays and Indian folk designs (kolam patterns) are considered in [11]. Tissue-like P-systems with active membranes that generate local picture languages are considered in [1,3].

Recently, Subramanian et al. [10] proposed a theoretical model of a P-system called Tile pasting P-system, for generating two dimensional patterns that are formed by gluing square tiles, wherein the application of pasting rule to a picture pattern is sequential. i.e., one rule is applied at a time. In this paper we propose variants of tile pasting P-system wherein the application of pasting rule to a picture pattern is in a maximally parallel manner i.e., all the rules are applied to the edges of the pattern simultaneously. We find that the picture languages generated by TPS are contained in the family of the new tile pasting P systems presented in this paper.

2 Preliminaries

We recall certain notions relating to pasting systems [6,12,10]. By a tile we mean a two dimensional topological disk (region) whose boundary is a simple closed curve, whose ends join up to form a loop without crossing or branches. We are concerned here with labeled regular polygons of unit length. Each edge of the tile is also labeled. For example, for a square tile labeled a with the right, up, left, down edges respectively labeled b, c, d, e, we write such a tile as a pair $(a, bcde)$ with the first component indicating the label of the tile and the symbols in the word in the second component indicating edge labels of the right, up, left, down edges in this order. If the edge labels are not needed we simply refer to a tile with label a as a itself. We also consider tiling patterns p or simply patterns made up of tiles, 'glued' (or pasted edge to edge) together. The intersection of any finite set of tiles in a tiling has necessarily zero area. Such an intersection will consist of a set of points called vertices and lines called edges. Two tiles are adjacent in a pattern if they have a common edge. A decorated tile is one whose region is engraved or drawn with any picture/coloured pattern/design.

A pasting rule (pr) [10,12] is a pair (x, y) of edge labels of two (not necessarily different) tiles a and b. Again x and y need not be different. If x is the label of the right (respectively left) edge of a and y is the label of the left (respectively right) edge of b, then an application of the rule (x, y) pastes side by side (or joins edge to edge) the two tiles a and b. We can likewise define pasting of two tiles one above the other. Rotation of tiles is not allowed while pasting two tiles.

A pasting system (PS) [10,12] is $S = (\Sigma, P, t_0)$, where Σ is a finite non-empty set of (labeled regular polygons) tiles, P is a finite set of pasting rules and t_0 is the axiom pattern of tiles. A pattern p_2 is generated from a pattern p_1 by applying the pasting rules in parallel to all the boundary edges of p_1 where pasting is possible. Note that the labels of pasted edges in a pattern are ignored once the tiles are pasted. The set of all patterns generated from the axiom t_0 constitutes the pattern language $T(S)$ of S.

A variation of pasting system has been introduced in [12] by defining extended pasting scheme (EPS) wherein the application of pasting rules is done either sequentially or in parallel and the sequence of edge labels of the boundary of a picture pattern generated is required to satisfy a constraint. This feature increases the generative power of the system.

An extended pasting scheme (EPS) is $G = (\Sigma, P, t_0, \Delta)$, where Σ is a finite non empty set of (labeled regular polygons) tiles, P is a finite set of pasting rules and t_0 is the axiom pattern of tiles and Δ is a finite set of constraints on the edge labels of Σ.

Example 1. Consider the extended pasting scheme $G = (\Sigma, P, t_0, \Delta)$ where $P = \{(a, c), (b, d)\}$, axiom t_0 is the same tile in Σ where the tile is a decorated type with a kolam pattern drawn in it. $\Delta = \{(ab)^n(cb)^{n-1}(cd)^n(ad)^{n-1}/n = 1, 2, \dots\}$. Note that the boundary $abcd$ of the axiom tile belongs to Δ. Since the edges with labels a and c can be pasted edge-to-edge and the edges with labels b and d can be pasted edge-to-edge, the tile in Σ, in one step from the axiom, will get pasted up, left, down right to itself yielding a pattern whose boundary will be $ababcbcdcdad$ which is a word in Δ for $n = 2$ so that the generated pattern satisfies the constraint. The process can be repeated.

A member of the "kambi kolam" patterns generated in parallel in one step starting with the axiom is shown in Figure 1.

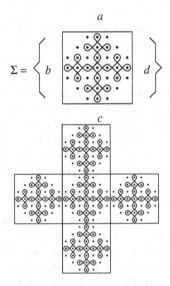

Fig. 1. A kolam pattern generated by G in Example 1

3 Tabled Pasting System

Considering many sets of pasting rules at every step of derivation, a generalization is obtained viz. table pasting System - such that at each step of a computation one table is used, nondeterministically chosen (the rules of the selected table are applied in the maximally parallel manner as mentioned in the previous section). The application of sets of pasting rules can be governed by a control set.

A tabled pasting system (TPS) is $TS = (\Sigma, P, t_0, C)$, where Σ is a finite non-empty set of (labeled regular polygons) tiles, P is a finite set of tables $\{t_1, t_2, \ldots, t_k\}$ and each table t_i contains pasting rules to glue the tiles and t_0 is the axiom pattern and C is a control over P.

Example 2. Consider the tabled pasting system $TS = (\Sigma, P, t_0, C)$ where

$$\Sigma = \left\{ \begin{array}{c} R_1 \quad R_6 \\ R_2 \quad R_5 \\ R_3 \quad R_4 \end{array}, \begin{array}{c} G_1 \quad G_6 \\ G_2 \quad G_5 \\ G_3 \quad G_4 \end{array}, \begin{array}{c} B_1 \quad B_6 \\ B_2 \quad B_5 \\ B_3 \quad B_4 \end{array} \right\}$$

$P = \{t_1, t_2, t_3\}$ and
$t_1 = \{(R_2, G_5), (R_4, G_1), (R_6, G_3), (G_6, B_3), (G_4, B_1), (G_2, B_5)\}$
$t_2 = \{(B_1, G_4), (B_2, R_5), (B_3, G_6), (B_4, R_1), (B_5, G_2), (B_6, R_3)\}$
$t_3 = \{(R_1, B_4), (R_2, G_5), (R_3, B_6), (R_4, G_1), (R_5, B_2), (R_6, G_3)\}$

$$t_0 = \left\{ \begin{array}{c} R_1 \quad R_6 \\ R_2 \quad R_5 \\ R_3 \quad R_4 \end{array} \right\}$$

$C = \{(t_1 t_2 t_3)^n / n \geq 1\}$

For $n = 1$, the tiling pattern is derived in three steps. In step 1, starting from the axiom tile, applying the pasting rules given in the set t_1 to the edges of the red hexagon tile in a maximally parallel manner, the green hexagon tiles are glued at the edges R_2, R_4, R_6 of the red hexagon. In step 2, applying the pasting rules in the set t_2 to the edges of the pattern obtained in step 1,the blue hexagon tiles are pasted at the edges of the $G_2, G_4, G_6, R_1, R_3, R_5$. While pasting a blue hexagon tile between a red hexagon tile and green hexagon tile, we require that pasting rules are defined for the edges of blue hexagon with the edges of the green and red hexagon involved in the pasting of tiles. In a similar manner, a tiling pattern is obtained for the application of pasting rules from the table t_3. The process can be repeated. The tessellation pattern generated is shown in Figure 2.

In the following, we compare the generative power of PS, EPS and TPS. Let $\mathcal{F}_{PS}, \mathcal{F}_{EPS}, \mathcal{F}_{TPS}$ denote the families of languages/tiling patterns generated by pasting system (PS), extended pasting scheme (EPS) and tabled pasting system (TPS) respectively.

Lemma 1. $\mathcal{F}_{EPS} \cap \mathcal{F}_{TPS} \neq \phi$

Fig. 2. Tessellation pattern for TPS

Proof. Consider the extended pasting scheme $G = (\Sigma, P, t_0, \Delta)$ where

$$\Sigma = \left\{ A \begin{array}{c} D \\ \boxed{} \\ B \end{array} C \right\} \text{ ; the axiom tile.}$$

$P = \{(A, C)\}$ and $\Delta = \{AD^n CB^n / n = 3, 5, \dots\}$
The language thus generated has the set of all rectangles as shown below.

$$L(G) = \left\{ \boxed{} \ , \dots \right\}$$

The language $L(G)$ can be generated by tabled pasting system $G' = (\Sigma', P', t_0, C)$

$$\Sigma' = \left\{ A_1 \begin{array}{c} A_4 \\ \boxed{} \\ A_2 \end{array} A_3 \ , \ B_1 \begin{array}{c} B_4 \\ \boxed{} \\ B_2 \end{array} B_3 \ , \ C_1 \begin{array}{c} C_4 \\ \boxed{} \\ C_2 \end{array} C_3 \right\}$$

where
$P = \{t_1, t_2\}, \quad t_1 = \{(A_1, B_3), (B_1, B_3)\}, \quad t_2 = \{(A_3, C_1), (C_3, C_1)\}$
$C = \{(t_1 t_2)^n / n = 1, 2, \dots\}$
It can be easily seen that $L(G) = L(G')$. Hence the proof.

Lemma 2. $\mathcal{F}_{EPS} \cap \mathcal{F}_{PS} \neq \phi$

Proof. Consider the language $L(G)$ generated in lemma 1 by the extended pasting scheme. $L(G)$ can be generated by pasting system $G' = (\Sigma', P', t_0)$ where Σ' and t_0 is same as given in lemma 1.

$P' = \{(A, C)\}$. It can be easily seen that $L(G) = L(G')$. Hence the proof.

Lemma 3. $\mathcal{F}_{PS} - \mathcal{F}_{EPS} \neq \phi$

Proof. The tiling pattern generated using Wang tiles [4] can be generated using pasting system. In the generation of tessellation patterns using Wang tiles [4], the edge label set of the tiling could not be generalized as the pattern is non repeating one. The tessellation pattern generated using Wang tiles cannot be generated using extended pasting scheme, as it is not possible to define the constraint for the edge label set of the tiling. If $\Delta = \phi$, then the extended pasting scheme reduces to pasting system.

Lemma 4. $\mathcal{F}_{EPS} - \mathcal{F}_{PS} \neq \phi$

Proof. Consider the extended pasting system EPS $G = (\Sigma, P, t_0, \Delta)$ where

$$\Sigma = \left\{ \; , \; , \; \right\}$$

$t_0 = $ $, \Delta = \{B^*\},$
$P = \{(R, R), (R, B)\}.$

For the given set of production rules, starting from the axiom tile, different types of patterns are generated. By the defintion of extended pasting scheme, patterns which satisfy the constraints given by Δ are included in the language $L(G)$.

Therefore $L(G) = \left\{ \; , \; , \; ... \right\}$

However $L(G)$ cannot be generated by a pasting system as the language generated by a pasting system will contain all patterns generated from the axiom tile. Here the language generated by a pasting system will contain different kind of patterns including the patterns generated by the EPS.

From the above lemma 2, 3 and 4 we have the following result.

Theorem 1. *Pasting system and extended pasting scheme are incomparable.*

Theorem 2. $\mathcal{F}_{TPS} - \mathcal{F}_{EPS} \neq \phi$

Proof. Consider the tabled pasting system $TS = (\Sigma, P, t_0, C)$ where Σ contains red, green and blue hexgons and each side of the red hexagon (respectively green and blue) is labelled by the letter R respectively G and B). The red hexagon is the axiom tile.

$C = \{(t_1^2 t_2^2)^n / n \geq 1\}.$
$P = \{t_1, t_2\}$ and $t_1 = \{(R, B)\}, t_2 = \{(R, G)\}.$

A tessellation pattern generated is shown in Figure 3.

Let $G' = (\Sigma', P', t_0, \Delta)$ be the EPS generating the language $L(G)$. We show that $L(G')$ has tiling patterns t' such that $t' \notin L(G)$.

Consider a pattern $t_i \in L(G)$ obtained for some $n > 0$, of the control P. Since G' generates $L(G)$, the pattern t_i is obtained for some constraint Δ'. The

Fig. 3. A tessellation pattern

pasting rule P' will contain rules to paste red hexagon with blue hexagon and green hexagons. For the given constraint Δ' and pasting rules, we can derive various tiling patterns satisfying the constraint Δ'.

$$w_0 \to T_1 \to T_2 \to \cdots \to T_n \to t_i'$$

since the constraint is applied to the outer edges of the tiling, there is no control in the scheme to generate the desired tiling in the intermediate derivations T_i $i \in \{1,\ldots,n\}$. Hence for a given constraint Δ' we can derive different tilings $\{t_i'\}$, $i = 1,\ldots,n$. Now the required tiling t_i will be one of the tilings $\{t_i'\}$, $i \in \{1,\ldots,n\}$ and the remaining tiling $t_i' \notin L(G)$ (with $t_i \neq t_i'$, $i \in \{1,\ldots,n\}$). Due to the pattern (repeated appearance of the red hexagons with other colour hexagons in an orderly manner) and the lack of control of the EPS in the intermediate derivations T_i, G' will always generate a set of tilings $\{t_i'\}$, $i = 1,\ldots,n$ for the given constraint. This shows that $L(G')$ contains tiling patterns, which are not members of $L(G)$. Therefore $L(G') \neq L(G)$. Hence there is no EPS to generate the language $L(G)$.

Theorem 3. $\mathcal{F}_{PS} \subset \mathcal{F}_{TPS}$

Proof. The inclusion is straight forward.

Consider the tabled pasting system $TS = (\Sigma, P, t_0, C)$ discussed in theorem 2. Let $G' = (\Sigma, P', t_0)$ be the PS generating the language $L(G)$. We show that $L(G')$ has tiling patterns t' such that $t' \notin L(G)$.

Consider a pattern $t_i \in L(G)$ obtained for some $n > 0$, of the control P. Since G' generates $L(G)$, the pattern t_i is obtained after repeated application of the rules from P'. The production set P' will contain rules to paste blue hexagon with red hexagon and green hexagons. Starting from the axiom tile, all the patterns generated in the intermediate derivations are also included in the languge $L(G')$

$$w_0 \to T_1 \to T_2 \to \cdots \to T_n \to T_i'$$

This shows that $L(G')$ contains tiling patterns, $T_1, T_2, \ldots, T_n$ which are not members of $L(G)$. Therefore $L(G') \neq L(G)$. Hence there is no PS to generate the language $L(G)$. Hence the family of languages generated by PS is properly contained in the family of TPS.

4   Tile Pasting P System for Generating Tiling Patterns

Tile pasting P-system ($TPPS$) which uses pasting rules in a sequential manner in its regions and has labeled square tiles as objects to generate picture patterns are considered by Subramanian et al. in [10]. We introduce here tile pasting P-system with active membranes where development sets are assigned for each membrane [3] and the application of pasting rules is in a maximally parallel manner at each step of the computation of the pattern.

A tile pasting P system with active membranes ($TPPS - AM$) is a construct of the form

$$\Pi = (O, H, \mu, (t_0)_i, \Sigma, T_k, (k \in \{1, \ldots, n\}), R_i, m_j)$$

where

- O is an alphabet of labels of the edges of the tiles
- $m \geq 1$, is the initial degree of the system
- H is a finite set of labels for the membranes
- $(t_0)_i$, $i \in \{1, \ldots, m\}$ is the axiom tile present in the membrane m_i.
- μ is the membrane structure, consisting of m membranes labeled from the set H (not necessarily in a one-one manner)
- Σ is a finite set of tiles associated with the regions of the membranes m_i, $i \in \{1, \ldots, m\}$.
- T_k, $k \in \{1, \ldots, n\}$, are the finite sets of tables containing evolution rules. An evolution rule is a pair (α, β), $\alpha, \beta \in O$, concerned with a pair of edges of tiles, which allows the edges of the corresponding tiles to get glued (pasting rule).
- R_i is a finite set of developmental rules associated with the membrane m_i. The developmental rules can be in the following form:

  (a) Object evolution rule: $[_i p_i]_i \rightarrow_{T_k} [_i p_{i+1}]_i$
  The evolution rules in T_k are applied to the edges of the pattern p_i, present in the membrane m_i, and the resultant pattern p_{i+1} is retained in the same membrane. Here the membranes are neither taking part in the application of these rules nor are they modified by them.

  (b) Object evolution and communication/creation rule: $[_i p_i]_i \rightarrow_{T_k} [_j p_{i+1}]_j$
  The effect of the rule is, the evolution rules contained in table T_k are applied to the pattern p_i present in the membrane m_i and the resultant pattern p_{i+1} is transferred to the membrane m_j (symport communication). The rule is applied only if both m_i and m_j are elementary membranes. If membrane m_j does not exist, then it is created adjacent to m_i (membrane creation) and the pattern is transferred to it.

(c) Evolution rule with dissolution: $[_i p_i]_i \rightarrow_{T_{k\delta}} p_{i+1}$

If a rule of the form $T_{k\delta}$ is used in a region m_i, then the evolution rules in table T_k are applied to the edges of the pattern p_i, present in the membrane m_i, and the resultant pattern p_{i+1} is placed in the region, directly outside the membrane, and the membrane m_i is dissolved as a consequence of δ, where $\delta \notin O$ is a special symbol (dissolving capability). The skin membrane cannot be dissolved.

(d) Out communication rule: $[_i p_i]_i \rightarrow_{T_k} [_i]_i p_{i+1}$

The evolution rules in T_k are applied to the edges of the pattern p_i, present in the membrane m_i, and the resultant pattern p_{i+1} is sent out to the region, directly outside the membrane m_i. If this rule is applied to the skin membrane then the pattern sent out of the skin membrane is lost from the system.

- m_j, is the output membrane.

The computation starts with the membrane m_i, containing the axiom pattern t_0. The evolution rules present in the tables T_k are applied to the edges of the tiles in a maximally parallel manner. For instance during a computation if pasting is possible at all the edges of the given pattern p_i then the evolution rules present in the table T_k are applied to all possible edges simultaneously. If R_j contains two or more developmental rules, then any one of them, chosen non deterministically is applied in the membrane. A sequence of transitions forms a computation and the result of a halting computation is the set of patterns sent to the output membrane. The set of all such picture patterns computed by a $TPPS - AM$ Π is denoted by $PL - AM(\Pi)$. The family of all such languages $PL - AM(\Pi)$ generated by systems Π as above, with at most m membranes is denoted by $PL_m(TPPS - AM)$.

Example 3. Consider a tile pasting P system with active membranes with the following specification:

$$\Pi = (O, H, \mu, (t_0)_1, \Sigma, T_k, (k \in \{1,2\}), R_i, (i \in \{1,2,3\}), m_3)$$

- $O = \{R, B\}$, $m = 2$, $H = \{m_1, m_2, m_3\}$
- $(t_0)_1$ and Σ are same as given in Lemma 4
- μ is the membrane structure, consisting of elementary membrane m_1 inside a skin membrane
- $T_1 = \{(R, R)\}$, $T_2 = \{(R, B)\}$
- $R_1 = \{[_1 p_i]_1 \rightarrow_{T_1} [_1 p_{i+1}]_1, [_1 p_i]_1 \rightarrow_{T_1} [_2 p_{i+1}]_2\}$
- $R_2 = \{[_2 p_i]_2 \rightarrow_{T_2} [_3 p_{i+1}]_3\}$
- $R_3 = \{\phi\}$, m_3 is the output membrane

Therefore the language of patterns generated is

$$L(G) = \left\{ \quad \begin{array}{c}\bigstar\end{array} \quad , \ ... \right\}$$

We introduce a variant of $TPPS$ such as tissue-like P-system involving evolution and communication. The method proposed here for the generation of families of tiling patterns using pasting rules is a combination of tissue-like P System [3,8] and Evolution-communication P System [7]. Although some features of these two models are not used in our proposed system, a new feature namely tables containing evolution and communication rules for each membrane is introduced in this model.For the generation of tiling patterns/tessellations, the (pasting) rules are evolution and communication rules, which allow the edges of a tile to be attached with the edges of another (possibly the same) tile/tiling and the resultant tiling pattern is transferred to a designated membrane (uniport communication). Like in the case of tissue P system [8] all membranes are elementary membranes but the system has no skin membrane nor environment and the result of the computation is collected in the output membrane.

Formally a tissue-like, evolution-communication tile pasting P system ($t - ECTPPS$)is a construct

$$\Pi = (O, T, M, (t_0)_i, \Sigma, syn, T_i(i = 1, \ldots, m), m_j)$$

where

- O is an alphabet of labels of the edges of the tiles.
- $T \subseteq O$ is the terminal alpahabet.
- M is a finite set of membranes with labels from the set $\{1, \ldots, m\}$.
- $(t_0)_i$, $i \in \{1, \ldots, m\}$ is the axiom tile present in the membrane m_i.
- $Syn = \{(i,j)/i, j \in \{1, \ldots, m\}\}$ is the set of links among the membranes (synapses)
- Σ is the finite set of tiles associated with the region of the membranes m_i, $i \in \{1, \ldots, m\}$.
- T_i, $i \in \{1, \ldots, m\}$, are the finite sets of tables, containing rules of the form $\{R_{(i,j)}/(i,j) \in syn, i, j \in (1, \ldots, m)\}$. $R_{(i,j)}$ is a finite set containing evolution rules. An evolution rule is a pair (α, β), $\alpha, \beta \in O$ concerned with a pair of edges of tiles, which allows the edges of the corresponding tiles to get glued (pasting rule).
- m_j, is the output membrane.

The computation starts with the membrane m_i, containing the axiom tile $(t_0)_i$. In each time unit, a rule $R_{(i,j)}$ is used in the region of membrane i, containing the pattern p_i, and the resultant pattern p_{i+1} is transferred to the membrane m_j. Therefore the use of rules $R_{(i,j)}$ is sequential at the level of membranes. The evolution rules, present in the set $R_{(i,j)}$, are applied simultaneously to all the edges of the tiling present in the membrane region. It is clear that the application of evolution rules has priority over communication. We first apply the evolution rules to the pattern p_i and only after that we communicate the pattern p_{i+1} to another membrane.

If T_i contains two or more sets, then any one of the sets $R_{(i,j)}$, chosen non deterministically will be applied to the pattern p_i. A sequence of transitions forms a computation and the result of a halting computation is the set of patterns over

T sent to the output membrane during the computation. A system is said to be non-extended if $O = T$. In the case of all non-extended systems, all tilings sent to the output membrane are accepted. A tiling which remains inside the system or in the case of extended system, which reaches the output membrane but contains labels not in T does not contribute to the generated language. The set of all such picture patterns computed or generated in this way by a $t-ECTPPS$ Π is denoted by $PL-EC(\Pi)$. The family of all such languages $PL-EC(\Pi)$ generated by systems Π as above, with at most m membranes, is denoted by $PL_m(TECTPPS)$.

Example 4. Consider a tissue-like, evolution-communication tile pasting P system with the following specification:

$$\Pi = (O, T, M, (t_0)_1, \Sigma, syn, T_i(i = 1, \ldots, 4), m_4)$$

where

- $O = \{R_1, R_2, R_3, R_4, R_5, R_6, G_1, G_2, G_3, G_4, G_5, G_6, B_1, B_2, B_3, B_4, B_5, B_6\}$ is the alphabet of labels of the edges of the tiles
- $T = O$ is the terminal alphabet.
- $M = \{m_1, m_2, m_3, m_4\}$ is the finite set of membranes, $(t_0)_1$, is the axiom tile present in the membrane m_1.
- $Syn = \{(1,2), (2,3), (3,1), (3,4)\}$ is the set of links among the membranes (synapses).
- Σ is the finite set of tiles associated with the regions of the membranes m_i, $i \in \{1, \ldots, 4\}$.
- m_4, is the output membrane.

The axiom tile $(t_0)_1$ and the set of tiles in the set Σ are same as given in the Example 2, given in Section 3.

$T_1 = \{R_{(1,2)}\}$ $T_2 = \{R_{(2,3)}\}$ $T_3 = \{R_{(3,4)}, R_{(3,1)}\}$ $T_4 = \{R_{(4,4)}\}$
$R_{(1,2)} = \{(R_2, G_5), (R_4, G_1), (R_6, G_3), (G_6, B_3), (G_4, B_1), (G_2, B_5)\}$
$R_{(2,3)} = \{(B_1, G_4), (B_2, R_5), (B_3, G_6), (B_4, R_1), (B_5, G_2), (B_6, R_3)\}$
$R_{(3,4)} = \{(R_1, B_4), (R_2, G_5), (R_3, B_6), (R_4, G_1), (R_5, B_2), (R_6, G_3)\}$
$R_{(3,1)} = \{(R_1, B_4), (R_2, G_5), (R_3, B_6), (R_4, G_1), (R_5, B_2), (R_6, G_3)\}$
$R_{(4,4)} = \{\phi\}$
The tiling patterns generated is same as shown in Figure 2.

In the following, we compare the generative power of TPS with $t-ECTPPS$ and $TPPS-AM$. Let $PL_m(TPPS-AM)$, $PL_m(ECTPPS)$ denote the families of languages/tiling patterns generated in tile pasting P system with active membranes and tissue-like evolution communication tile pasting P system respectively.

Theorem 4. $\mathcal{F}_{TPS} \subseteq PL_m(ECTPPS)$ *and* $\mathcal{F}_{TPS} \subseteq PL_m(TPPS-AM)$

Proof. Let $C = (t_1 t_2^l \ldots t_n)^k$,$l \geq 1, k \geq 1$ be the control over the production rules of a tabled pasting system G. Let us define a tissue like, evolution communication P system,

$$\Pi = (O, T, M, (t_0)_1, \Sigma, syn, T_i(i = 1, \ldots, n+1), m_{n+1})$$

where

- O and T are as given in the definition.
- M is a finite set of membranes with labels from the set $\{1, \ldots, n+1\}$.
- $(t_0)_1$, is the axiom tile present in the membrane m_1.
- Σ is the finite set of tiles associated with the regions of the membranes m_i, $i \in \{1, \ldots, n+1\}$.
- $Syn = \{(1,2), (2,2), (2,3), \ldots, (n,1), (n,n+1)\}$ is the set of links among the membranes (synapses).
- $T_1 = \{R_{(1,2)}\}, T_2 = \{R_{(2,2)}, R_{(2,3)}\}, \ldots, T_n = \{R_{(n,n+1)}, R_{(n,1)}\}, T_{n+1} = \{\phi\}$
- $R_{(1,2)} = t_1, R_{(2,2)} = t_2, R_{(2,3)} = t_2, \ldots, R_{(n,1)} = t_n, R_{(n,n+1)} = t_n$
- m_{n+1}, is the output membrane.

For a given tabled pasting system, the tissue like evolution communication P system defined above will generate the same tessellation pattern and language. In a similar manner we can prove that the family of languages generated by tabled pasting system is contained in the family of tile pasting P system with active membranes.

5 Conclusion

A new type of generating mechanism called tabled pasting system and certain variants of tile pasting P system with tile objects to generate tiling patterns have been introduced and their generative power compared.

Acknowledgements

The authors thank the referees for useful comments. The first and third authors would like to acknowledge the support rendered by the Leverhulme Trust,UK and the fourth author, an FRGS grant of Universiti Sains Malaysia.

References

1. Annadurai, S., Kalyani, T., Dare, V.R., Thomas, D.G.: P Systems generating iso-picture languages. Progress in Natural Science 18, 617–622 (2008)
2. Bottoni, P., Labela, A., Martin-Vide, C., Paun, G.: Rewriting P Systems with Conditional Communication. In: Brauer, W., Ehrig, H., Karhumäki, J., Salomaa, A. (eds.) Formal and Natural Computing. LNCS, vol. 2300, pp. 325–353. Springer, Heidelberg (2002)
3. Ceterchi, R., Gramatovici, R., Jonaska, N., Subramanian, K.G.: Tissue-like P systems with active membranes for picture generation. Fundamenta Informaticae 56(4), 311–328 (2003)
4. Culik, K.: An aperiodic set of 13 Wang tiles. Discrete Math. 160, 245–251 (1996)
5. Fu, K.S.: Syntactic Pattern Recognition and Applications. Prentice-Hall Inc., Englewood Cliffs (1982)

6. Kalyani, T., Sasikala, K., Dare, V.R., Abisha, P.J., Robinson, T.: Triangular pasting system. In: Formal Models, Languages and Application. Series in Machine Perception and Artificial Intelligence, vol. 66, pp. 195–211 (2006)
7. Krithivasan, K., Rama, R.: Introduction to Formal Languages, Automata and Computation. Pearson Education, New Delhi (2009)
8. Martin-Vide, C., Paun, G., Pazos, J., Rodriguez-Paton, A.: Tissue P systems. Theoretical Computer Science 296(2), 295–326 (2003)
9. Paun, G.: Computing with Membranes: An Introduction. Springer, Berlin (2002)
10. Subramanian, K.G., Robinson, T., Nagar, A.K.: Tile pasting P system model for pattern generation. In: Proc. Third Asia International Conference on Modelling and Simulation, Indonesia (2009)
11. Subramanian, K.G., Saravanan, R., Robinson, T.: P system for array generation and application to kolam patterns. Forma 22, 47–54 (2007)
12. Robinson, T.: Extended pasting scheme for kolam pattern generation. Forma 22, 55–64 (2007)

Polyoisominoes

Mary Jemima Samuel[1], V.R. Dare[2], and T. Kalyani[3]

[1] Department of Mathematics
Anna Adarsh College for Women
Anna Nagar, Chennai - 600 040, India
dr_pjaya@yahoo.com
[2] Department of Mathematics
Madras Christian College
Tambaram East, Chennai - 600 059, India
rajkumardare@yahoo.com
[3] Department of Mathematics
St. Joseph's College of Engineering
Jeppiaar Nagar, Chennai - 600 119, India
kalphd02@yahoo.com

Abstract. We observe that two-dimensional array languages are useful in Image Processing and Analysis. We represent two-dimensional iso-picture languages in terms of various classes of polyoisominoes. Polyoisominoes are related to tiling. The art of tiling has played an important role in the field of architecture since early civilization. A parallel generating model called pasting system was proposed in order to form coloured patterns over square grid (1999). This model allows two cells (tiles) to get glued on their sides depending upon some rules. Two tiles are called adjacent if they have an edge in common. We prove that various classes of polyoisominoes defined are tiling recognizable languages and local language. Local languages are introduced by Giammarresi and Restivo (1997).

Keywords: convex polyoisominoe, ferrers diagram, stack polyoisominoe, parallelogram polyoisominoe.

1 Introduction

In this paper we consider the problem of representing, in terms of two-dimensional iso-picture languages, various classes of polyoisominoes. We give some fundamental ideas of gluing the tiles and catenating them in different ways.

We have four distinct labelled or coloured isoceles right angled triangular tiles denoted by A, B, C and D of dimensions $1/\sqrt{2}, 1/\sqrt{2}$ and 1 unit obtained by intersecting a unit square by its diagonals.

Definition 1. *[2] Let Σ be the finite alphabet of tiles A, B, C and D. An iso-picture of size (n, m), $(n, m \geq 1)$ over Σ is a picture formed by catenating n-iso arrays of size m. The number of tiles in any iso-picture of size (n, m) is nm^2.*

R.P. Barneva et al. (Eds.): CompIMAGE 2010, LNCS 6026, pp. 85–94, 2010.
© Springer-Verlag Berlin Heidelberg 2010

We recall some definitions of local and recognizable iso-picture language and iso-triangular tiling system.

Definition 2. *[2]*

1. *Let p be an iso-picture of size (n, m). We denote by $B_{n',m'}(p)$, the set of all sub iso-pictures of p of size (n', m') where $n' \leq n$, $m' \leq m$.*
2. *Let p be an iso-picture over Σ. Then $\hat{p}$ is an iso-picture obtained by surrounding p with a special boundary symbols $\triangle_{\#A}$, $\nabla^{\#B}$, $\triangleleft_{\#C}$, $\triangleright^{\#D}$ $\notin \Sigma$.*
3. *An iso-picture language $L \subseteq \Sigma_I^{**}$ is called local if there exists a finite set θ of iso-arrays of size 2 over $\Sigma \cup \{ \triangle_{\#A}, \nabla^{\#B}, \triangleleft_{\#C}, \triangleright^{\#D} \}$ such that $L = \{p \in \Sigma_I^{**}/B_{1,2}(\hat{p}) \subseteq \theta\}$ and is denoted by $L(\theta)$.*
4. *Let $p \in \Sigma_I^{**}$ be an iso-picture. $p(i, j, k)$ is the kth element of jth row of the ith iso-array.*
5. *Let Σ and Γ be two finite alphabets and $\pi : \Gamma \to \Sigma$ be a projection. Let $L \subset \Gamma_I^{**}$ be an iso-picture language. The projection by mapping π of L is the language. $L' = \{p'/p' = \pi(p), \text{ for all } p \in L\} \subseteq \Sigma_I^{**}$. We denote by $\pi(L)$ the projection by mapping π of an iso-picture language L.*
6. *Let Σ be a finite alphabet. An iso-picture language $L \subseteq \Sigma_I^{**}$ is called recognizable if there exists a local iso-picture language L' over an alphabet Γ and a mapping $\pi : \Gamma \to \Sigma$ such that $L = \pi(L')$ where $L' = L(\theta)$.*
7. *An iso-triangular tiling system is a 4-tuple $(\Sigma, \Gamma, \pi, \theta)$ where Σ and Γ are two finite sets of symbols, $\pi : \Gamma \to \Sigma$ is a projection and θ is a set of iso-arrays of size 2 over the alphabet $\Gamma \cup \{ \triangle_{\#A}, \nabla^{\#B} \}$.*
8. *An iso-picture language $L \subseteq \Sigma_I^{**}$ is tiling recognizable if there exists an iso-triangular tiling system $(\Sigma, \Gamma, \pi, \theta)$ such that $L = \pi(L(\theta))$. If $L = L(\Sigma, \Gamma, \pi, \theta)$ then L is the language recognized by iso-triangular tiling system.*
9. *The language L of rhombuses is recognizable by iso-triangular tiling system.*

2   Polyosiominoes

In this section we introduce polyoisominoes and prove that some classes of polyoisominoes are represented by tiling recognizable languages.

We define polyosiomino, column of a polyoisomino, row of a polyoisomino.

Definition 3. *In the plane $\mathcal{Z} \times \mathcal{Z}$ a cell is an isosceles right angled triangular tile of the form $\triangle_A$, ∇^B, $\triangleleft_C$, $\triangleright^D$. of dimensions $1/\sqrt{2}, 1/\sqrt{2}$ and 1 unit. A polyoisomino is a connected subset of the plane which is an isopicture made up of finite union of gluable cells of $\triangle_A$ and ∇^B or $\triangleleft_C$ and $\triangleright^D$ having no cut set, that is the interior is also connected.*

Definition 4. *A column of a polyoisomino is the intersection between the polyoisomino and an infinite strip of $\triangleleft_C$ and $\triangleright^D$ tiles whose centroids lie on a vertical line see Figure 1.*

Fig. 1. Column of a polyoisomino

Similarly row of a polyoisomino can be defined.

A right slanting i.e., S_1 of polyosiomino is the intersection between the polyoisomino and a right infinite strip of ◁A and B▷ tiles or ◁C and D▷ tiles whose centroids lie on a right slanting line shown in Figure 2.

Fig. 2.

A polyoisomino is said to be column convex (row convex) when its intersection with any vertical line (horizontal line) is convex. See Figures 3 and 4.

A polyoisomino is said to be right / (left) slanting convex when its intersection with any right / (left) slanting line is convex.

Definition 5. *A polyoisomino is said to be column right / (left) slanting convex or cr / (cl) convex if it is both column convex and right / (left) slanting convex. See Figure 5.*

Similarly row right slanting convex or rr convex and row left slanting convex or rl convex polyoisominoes can be defined.

Definition 6. *A polyoisomino P is said to be directed when every cell of P can be reached from a distinguished cell (usually the leftmost at the lowest ordinate) by a path in P which uses north, north-east and north-west steps.*

Figure 6 depicts a polyoisomino that is both directed and right slanting convex.

We define three types of directed and convex polyoisominoes.

1. *Stack polyoisominoes is a self avoiding convex polyoisominoe containing two opposite corners of its minimal bounding rhombus. This is directed and right slanting convex.*

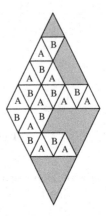

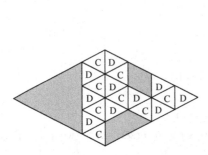

Fig. 3. Column convex polyoisominoe   **Fig. 4.** Row convex polyoisominoe

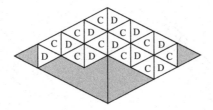

Fig. 5. cr-convex polyoisominoe

2. *Ferrers diagram is a directed row-convex polyoisomino such that it is made of ℓ columns or rows such that the ith column or row is made up of p_i tiles where $p_1 \geq p_2 \geq \cdots \geq p_\ell$.*

3. *Parallelogram or staircase polyoisominoes is a polyoisominoe such that the intersection of every line drawn from the vertices of each tile is perpendicular to the main diagonal and this line passes through the centroid of each tile is a connected segment. It can also be characterized with the border formed with two paths, having only east and north elementary steps, having the same initial and final points and being disjoint except at the extreme points.*

All these three types are depicted in Figure 7.

3 Polyoisominoes and Tiling Systems

In this section we prove that some classes of polyoisominoes are represented by iso-tiling recognizable languages. Let us consider the following two-dimensional iso-picture languages on the alphabet $\{0, 1\}$. $\mathcal{F}$, S, P is the class of pictures that represent Ferrers diagrams, Stack polyoisomionoes, Parallelogram polyoisominoes. We prove that $\mathcal{F}$ is a local language and S, P are tiling recognizable languages.

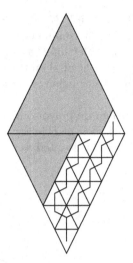

Fig. 6.

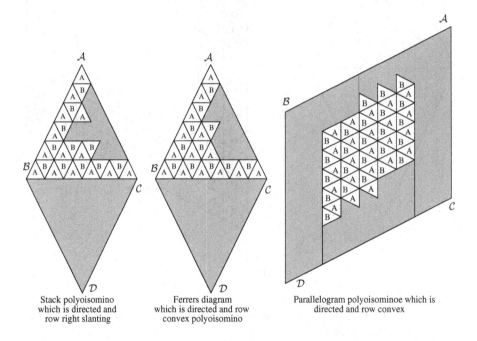

Stack polyoisomino
which is directed and
row right slanting

Ferrers diagram
which is directed and row
convex polyoisomino

Parallelogram polyoisominoe which is
directed and row convex

Fig. 7.

Let P be a convex polyoisomino, and $R(P)$ be its minimal bounding rhombus. We observe that there are four disjoint (possibly empty) sets of tiles in $R(P)\backslash P$. These tiles can be easily designated each of them to be located at one of the four sides of $R(P)$. $R(P)$ is named as the rhombus $\mathcal{ABCD}$ as given in Figure 8.

The four sides of $R(P)$ namely $\mathcal{AB}, \mathcal{AC}, \mathcal{BD}$ and $\mathcal{DC}$ are located as follows. We first designate the tiles for stack polyisominoes and Ferrers diagram. Join the vertices $\mathcal{B}$ and $\mathcal{C}$. The region to the left of P and above the line $\mathcal{BC}$ is located as side $\mathcal{AB}$ and the region to the right of P and above the line $\mathcal{BC}$ is located as side $\mathcal{AC}$. The region below $\mathcal{BC}$ either belongs to side $\mathcal{BD}$ or side $\mathcal{DC}$. Here we have taken it as side $\mathcal{BD}$.

We now designate for parallelogram polyoisomino. Side $\mathcal{AB}$ and side $\mathcal{AC}$ are described above. The region to the left of P below the line $\mathcal{BC}$ is located as side $\mathcal{BD}$ and the region to the right of P is located as side $\mathcal{CD}$ as shown in Figure 8.

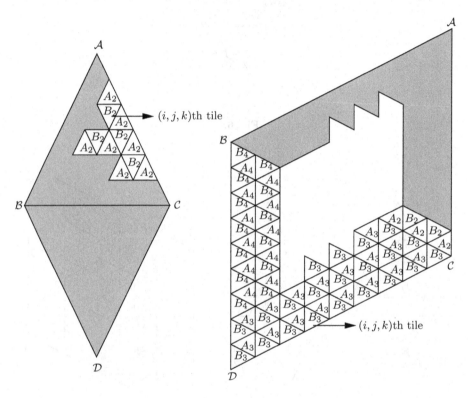

Fig. 8.

Proposition 1. *Polyoisomino is convex if and only if for each tile (i, j, k) of $R(P)$ the following holds:*

1. *Consider the side $\mathcal{AC}$, if $p(i, j, k)$ tile is $\underset{B}{\triangledown} \in \mathcal{AC}$ then $p(i, j+1, k)$th tile is $\underset{A}{\triangle} \in \mathcal{AC}$.*

2. *Consider the side $\mathcal{CD}$, if $p(i, j, k)$ tile is $\underset{B}{\triangledown} \in \mathcal{CD}$ then $p(i, j+1, k)$th tile is $\underset{A}{\triangle} \in \mathcal{CD}$.*

3. *Similarly it can be defined for the side $\mathcal{AB}$ and $\mathcal{BD}$.*

Similarly the above statement can also be stated for a column convex polyoisomino.

Proof follows from the definition.

Let $\mathcal{L}_{\mathcal{C}_1}$ be the language of these minimal rhombuses over the alphabet $\Sigma_{\mathcal{C}_1} = \{A, B, A_1, B_1, A_2, B_2, A_3, B_3, A_4, B_4\}$ containing $\mathcal{C}_1$ where $\mathcal{C}_1 = S, \mathcal{F}, P$.

Theorem 1. *Let $\mathcal{L}_S$ be the language over the alphabet $\Sigma_S = \{A, B, A_1, B_1, A_2, B_2, A_4, B_4\}$ for stack polyoisominoes. Then $\mathcal{L}_S$ is a local language and $L_S = L(\theta_R \cup \theta_{AB} \cup \theta_{AC} \cup \theta_{BD})$ where R is the region of the stack polyoisomino. Also the stack polyoisomino S is tiling recognizable.*

Proof. To the stack polyoisomino we associate the picture obtained by representing with a A for $\triangle$ tile and B for $\triangledown$ tile, every tile belonging to the polyoisomino and with the symbol $\{A_1, B_1\}$ (respectively $\{A_2, B_2\}$; $\{A_4, B_4\}$ to each tile in $\mathcal{AB}$ (respectively $\mathcal{AC}$, $\mathcal{BD}$) as shown in Figure 9. Let $\mathcal{L}_S$ be the language obtained from these tiles over the alphabet $\{A, B, A_1, B_1, A_2, B_2, A_4, B_4\}$. We now consider the following set of tiles.

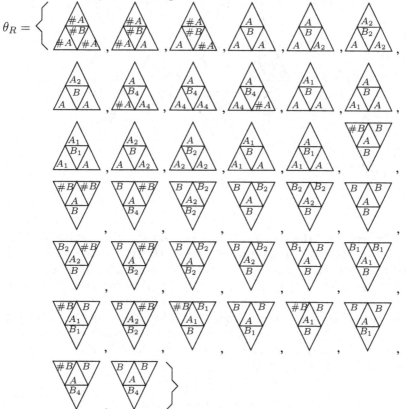

$$\theta_{AB} = \left\{ \ldots \right\}$$

$$\theta_{AC} = \left\{ \ldots \right\}$$

$$\theta_{BD} = \left\{ \ldots \right\}$$

It is easily seen that the sets θ_{AB}, θ_{AC}, θ_{BD} satisfy the conditions of the proposition given above with respect to the tiles of AB, AC and BD respectively and so together with θ_R the internal part of stack polyosiomino is obtained. $\mathcal{L}_S$ is a local language and $\mathcal{L}_S = L(\theta_R \cup \theta_{AB} \cup \theta_{AC} \cup \theta_{BD})$. Using these θ's sets we cannot obtain any other picture other than stack polyisomino.

To prove that S is tiling recognizable, we consider the projection mapping given as $\pi_S : \Sigma_S \to \{0,1\}$ such that $\pi(A_1) = \pi(A_2) = \pi(A_4) = 0$, $\pi(B_1) = \pi(B_2) = \pi(B_4) = 1$, $\pi(A) = A$, $\pi(B) = B$ so that we have $\pi_S(\mathcal{L}_S) = S$ thus S is tiling recognizable. See Figure 10.

In a similar way the following results have been proved.

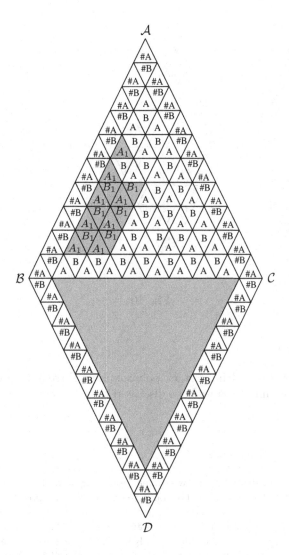

Fig. 9. Stack polyoisominoe which is directed and row right slanting

Theorem 2. *Let $\mathcal{L}_{\mathcal{F}}$ be the language over the alphabet $\Sigma_{\mathcal{F}} = \{A, B, A_1, B_1,$ $A_2, B_2, A_4, B_4\}$ for Ferrers diagram. Then $\mathcal{L}_{\mathcal{F}}$ is a local language and $L_F =$ $L(\theta_R \cup \theta_{\mathcal{A}B} \cup \theta_{\mathcal{A}C} \cup \theta_{\mathcal{B}D})$ where R is the region of the Ferrers diagram.*

Theorem 3. *Let $\mathcal{L}_P$ be the language over the alphabet $\Sigma_P = \{A, B, A_1, B_1,$ $A_2, B_2, A_3, B_3, A_4, B_4\}$ for parallelogram polyoisominoe. Then $\mathcal{L}_P$ is a local language and $L_P = L(\theta_R \cup \theta_{\mathcal{A}B} \cup \theta_{\mathcal{B}D} \cup \theta_{\mathcal{C}D})$ where R is the region of the parallelogram polyoisominoe. Also the parallelogram polyoisominoe P is tiling recognizable.*

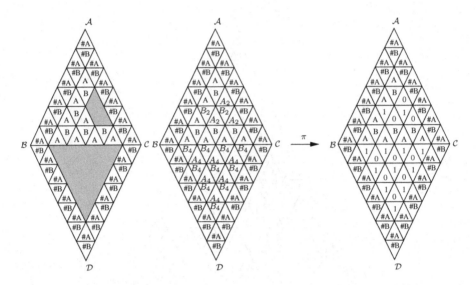

Fig. 10.

4   Conclusion

In this paper we have defined stack polyisominoe, Ferrers diagram, and parallelogram polyisominoe and we have discussed their local and tiling recognizable properties.

References

1. Giammarresi, D., Restivo, A.: Two-dimensional languages. In: Salomaa, A., Rozenberg, G. (eds.) Handbook of Formal Languages, vol. 3, pp. 215–267. Springer, Heidelberg (1997)
2. Kalyani, T.: A Study on Iso-picture Languages. Ph. D. Thesis (2006)
3. Robinson, T., Dare, V.R., Subramanian, K.G.: A parallel pattern generating system. In: Proceedings of 6th International Workshop on Parallel Image Processing and Analysis, pp. 23–32 (1999)

Collage of Iso-Picture Languages and P Systems

S. Annadurai[1], V.R. Dare[2], T. Kalyani[1], and D.G. Thomas[2]

[1] Department of Mathematics
St. Joseph's College of Engineering, Chennai - 119
annadurai_70@yahoo.co.in
[2] Department of Mathematics
Madras Christian College, Chennai - 59

Abstract. A new operation called collage on one-dimensional (respectively two-dimensional) word languages, obtained by piling up, one on top of the other, words of a given recognizable language on a previously empty one-dimensional (respectively two-dimensional) array, was introduced (2005). In this paper we extend the operation to iso-picture languages. We show that if L is an iso-picture language over a two letter alphabet then collage of L is recognizable. We introduce a new P system which consists of membrane structure in which the object in each membrane is a collection of iso-picture languages and the evolutionary rules are given in terms of collage operations. We obtain some properties of this P system using recognizability of collage of L.

Keywords: Membrane computing, iso-picture languages, collage, recognizable languages.

1 Introduction

Syntactic methods play an important role in picture generation and description on account of their structure handling ability [4]. There has been considerable interest in studying array grammars that generate two-dimensional pictures. Many models of array grammars were introduced to generate two-dimensional pictures [10]. Giammarresi and Restivo [4] have provided a definition of recognizability in terms of local array languages. In [5,6], the authors have introduced the notion of iso-arrays, iso-pictures and local and recognizable iso-picture languages. Iso-arrays are made up of isosceles right angled triangles and iso-picture is a picture formed by catenating iso-arrays of same size. A motivation for this study is that one can generate some interesting picture languages which cannot be generated by earlier models available in the literature. In particular iso-picture languages include more picture languages like hexagonal picture languages, rectangular picture languages, languages of rhombuses and triangles.

One application of the study of iso-picture languages is its use in the generation of interesting kolam patterns. Another application of this study lies in the area of tiling rectangular plane. In [7], we introduced triangular-tetromino, which is a figure formed by four isosceles triangular tiles arranged in the form of isosceles right angled triangle and proved that rectangles of size $2m \times 2n$ are tileable by triangular-tetrominoes.

R.P. Barneva et al. (Eds.): CompIMAGE 2010, LNCS 6026, pp. 95–106, 2010.

A new operation called collage was introduced on one-dimensional and two-dimensional recognizable languages [3]. The resulting language is the set of words seen from above, a position of the array is labeled by the topmost letter. Assume that we are given a collection of strips of wall papers of different textures in such a way that it forms a recognizable collection. Assume further that starting from an empty frame we can paste these strips one at a time, in any arbitrary way, with possible overlapping but without rotation. At each position, the visible pixel is that belonging to the last pasted strip. This is reminiscent of the so called painter's algorithm achieving fare elimination in computer graphics where the objects nearest to the observer are painted last.

On the other hand, membrane computing (P system) deals with distributed computing models inspired from the structure and the functioning of the living cell [8,9]. Very briefly, compartments (regions) defined by a hierarchical arrangement of membranes have multisets of objects together with evolution rules associated with the membranes. Rewriting P system is concerned with objects described by strings and sets of strings (languages) instead of multiset of objects. The evolution of an object will then correspond to a transformation of the string. The transformations are considered in the form of rewriting steps. Consequently, the evolution rules are given as rewriting rules. In [2] rewriting P systems to generate iso-picture languages have been introduced. Another kind of P system called tissue-like P system [1] has also been developed to generate iso-picture languages.

In this paper, we consider the collage operation on iso-picture languages. We show that if L is an iso-picture language over a two letter alphabet then collage of L is recognizable. Then we develop a P system called collage P system based on collage of iso-picture languages. The collage operation is used to create evolutionary rules in this P system. We obtain some interesting properties of the collage P systems using the recognizability of collage of iso-picture languages.

2   Preliminaries

In this section we recall the notions of iso-picture languages and iso-triangular tiling systems [5].

Let $\Sigma = \{$ $\overset{a_1\triangle a_3}{a_2}$, $\overset{b_2}{b_3 \nabla b_1}$, $c_3 \triangleleft c_2 \atop c_1$, $d_2 \overset{d_1}{\triangleright} \atop d_3 \}$ $\}$ be a finite set of labeled isosceles right angled triangular tiles of dimensions $\frac{1}{\sqrt{2}}, \frac{1}{\sqrt{2}}$ and 1 unit, obtained by intersecting a unit square by its diagonals.

Definition 1. *An iso-array of size $m(m \geq 1)$ is an isosceles right-angled triangular arrangement of elements of Σ, whose equal sides are denoted as S_1 and S_3 and the unequal side as S_2. It consists of m tiles along the side S_2 and it contains m^2 gluable elements of Σ. Iso-arrays can be classified as U-iso-array, D-iso-array, R-iso-array and L-iso-array, if tiles A, B, D and C are used in side S_2 respectively.*

Iso-arrays of same size can be catenated using the following catenation operations. *Horizontal catenation* $\ominus$ is defined between U and D iso-arrays of same size. *Right catenation* $\oslash$ is defined between any two gluable iso-arrays of same size. This catenation includes the following:
(a) $D \oslash U$ (b) $U \oslash R$ (c) $D \oslash L$ (d) $R \oslash L$.
In a similar way vertical $\odot$ and left $\oslash$ catenations can be defined.

Definition 2. *Let Σ be a finite alphabet of iso-triangular tiles. An iso-picture of size $(n,m), n, m \geq 1$ over Σ is a picture formed by catenating n-iso-arrays of size m. The number of tiles in any iso-picture of size (n,m) is nm^2.*

Definition 3. *Let p be an iso-picture of size (n,m). We denote by $B_{n',m'}(p)$, the set of all sub iso-pictures of p of size (n',m'), where $n' \leq n, m' \leq m$. $\hat{p}$ is an iso-picture obtained by surrounding p with a special boundary symbols*

$$\triangle_{\#A}, \nabla_{\#B}, \triangleleft_{\#C}, \triangleright_{\#D} \notin \Sigma.$$

Definition 4. *An iso-picture language $L \subseteq \Sigma_I^{**}$ is called local if there exists a finite set θ of iso-arrays of size 2 over $\Sigma \cup \{ \triangle_{\#A}, \nabla_{\#B}, \triangleleft_{\#C}, \triangleright_{\#D} \}$ such that $L = \{p \in \Sigma_I^{**} / B_{1,2}(\hat{p}) \subseteq \theta\}$ and is denoted by $L(\theta)$.*
The family of local iso-picture languages will be denoted by $ILOC$.

Definition 5. *Let Σ be a finite alphabet. An iso-picture language $L \subseteq \Sigma_I^{**}$ is called recognizable if there exists a local iso-picture language L' over an alphabet Γ and a mapping $\pi : \Gamma \to \Sigma$ such that $L = \pi(L')$. The family of all recognizable iso-picture languages will be denoted by $IREC$.*

Definition 6. *An iso-triangular tiling system IT is a 4-tuple $(\Sigma, \Gamma, \pi, \theta)$ where Σ and Γ are two finite sets of symbols, $\pi : \Gamma \to \Sigma$ is a projection and θ is a set of iso-arrays of size 2 over the alphabet $\Gamma \cup \{\triangle_{\#A}, \nabla_{\#B} \}$.*

Definition 7. *An iso-picture language $L \subseteq \Sigma_I^{**}$ is tiling recognizable if there exists an iso-triangular tiling system $IT = (\Sigma, \Gamma, \pi, \theta)$ such that $L = \pi(L'(\theta))$, where $L'(\theta)$ is a local iso-picture language. We write $L = L(IT)$, and we say that L is the language recognized by IT. We denote by $\mathcal{L}(ITS)$ the family of all iso-picture languages recognizable by iso-triangular tiling systems.*

It is easy to see that $IREC$ is exactly the family of iso-picture languages tiling recognizable by iso-triangular tiling systems ($\mathcal{L}(ITS)$). i.e., $IREC = \mathcal{L}(ITS)$.

The language of rhombuses over the iso-triangular tiles A and B is a recognizable iso-picture language [5].

3   Collage of Iso-Pictures

Here we extend the notion of collage of two-dimensional words introduced in [3] to iso-picture languages. It consists of "piling up" iso-pictures belonging to a given collection one on top of the other, above a horizontal surface filled with a blank symbol. The result is the picture seen from above, the top symbol at each position obscuring all symbols under it. Here for simplicity we consider iso-picture language of rhombuses of size $(2, m)$ over the alphabet $\Sigma = \{\triangle, \nabla\}$.

If P is an iso-picture of size $(2, 4)$ then the positions of the elements in P are represented as follows.

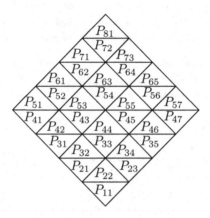

Fig. 1. Rhombus of size $(2, 4)$

Definition 8. *Let* $L \subseteq \Sigma_I^{**}$ *be a collection of iso-pictures, called patches, let* $(2, m)$ *be a pair of integers and let S be a finite sequence of triples* $(x, y, p) \in \mathbb{N}^2 \times P$, *called a stack. The collage* $Collage_S^{(2, M)}$ *is the iso-picture language of rhombuses of size* $(2, m)$ *with symbols in* $\Sigma \cup \{\triangle, \nabla\}$ *defined by induction on the number of elements in S as follows.*

If $S = \phi$ then $Collage_S^{(2, M)}$ *is the iso-picture language of rhombuses of size* $(2, m)$, *whose entries are all equal to the letters* $\triangle, \nabla$. *Otherwise let S' be the sequence S deprived of its last triple* (x, y, p).

$Collage_S^{(2, M)}[i, j]$

$$
= \begin{cases}
P(i - 2y + m, j - (2x + k_1)) & i > 0, \\
P(i + 1 - 2y + m, j - (2x + k_1)) & i < 0, \\
& i \in (2y - (m - 1), 2y + m) = (L, N) \\
& \text{if } i \leq 0, \text{ then } i = i - 1, \\
& j \in (2x + 1 + k_1, 2x + 2m - 1 - k_1) \\
& k_1 = 0, 1, 2, \ldots, m - 1 \text{ for} \\
& i = 2y, 2y + 1, \ldots, L - 1, N - 1, L, N. \\
Collage_{S'}^{(2, M)}[i, j] & \text{otherwise}
\end{cases}
$$

where i represents i^{th} row and j represents j^{th} element of the ith row.

Example 1. Consider the sequence of triples $S = \{(1, 1, P_1), (2, 4, P_2), (3, 3, P_3), (4, 2, P_4), (4, 3, P_5)\}$ with the following patches P_1, P_2, P_3, P_4, P_5 given below. Each P_i is an iso-picture of size $(2, m)$ where m is the number of rows in each iso-array.

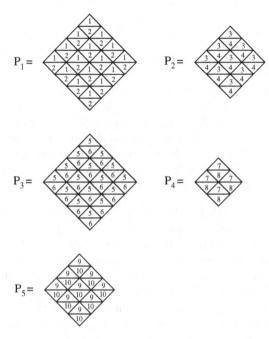

S defines the collage P where

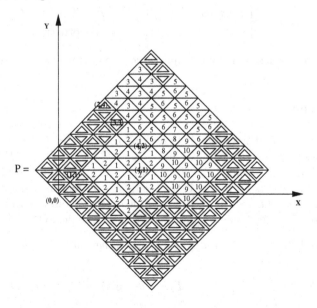

We are interested in studying the language of iso-pictures obtained by applying the collage operation from a recognizable iso-picture language. This requires extending the operation to subsets of pictures.

Definition 9. *Given a set of patches $L \subseteq \Sigma_I^{**}$, its collage closure is the set*

$$Collage(L) = \{p \in (\Sigma \cup \{\triangle, \triangledown\})_I^{**} | p = Collage_S^{(2,m)} \text{ for some } m \text{ and } S\}$$

When the resulting iso-picture p does not contain the symbols $\triangle$ and $\triangledown$, it is said to be completely covered by p.

The height of the stack is defined as follows. Let $S = \{(x_1, y_1, p_1), \ldots, (x_k, y_k, p_k)\}$ be a stack of k elements. Intuitively, we may consider the elements as falling on the ground and being prevented from hitting it only by previously fallen other elements occupying a position overlapping their own positions. The ℓth element of the stack is placed at a particular integer altitude $z_\ell \geq 0$ such that two elements at the same altitude do not overlap while minimizing maximum altitude, which by definition is the height of the stack.

Given a $Collage_S^{(2,M)}$, we define the height $h(i, j)$ of each pixel $2y_1 - (m - 1) \leq i \leq 2y_2 + m$ where $y_1 = min(y)$, $y_2 = max(y)$, and m is the size of the iso-array in the corresponding patch. If $i \leq 0$ then $i = i - 1$, $1 \leq j \leq 2x_1 + 2m - 1 - k_1$, where $x_1 = max(x)$, m is the size of the iso-array in the corresponding patch, and k_1 is the value corresponding to i, by induction on the cardinality k of the stack S. If $k = 0$, then $h(i, j) = 0$. Otherwise let S' be the stack deprived of its last triple (x, y, p) and let $h'(i, j)$ be the height of the pixel (i, j) in this collage. Let $I = [2y - (m - 1), 2y + m] \times [2x + 1 + k_1, 2x + 2m - 1 - k_1]$ provided $i = 2y - (m - 1) > 0$. If $i \leq 0$, then $i = i - 1$.

$$h(i, j) = \begin{cases} 1 + max\{h'(k, \ell) | (k, \ell) \in I\} & \text{if } (i, j) \in I \\ h'(i, j) & \text{otherwise.} \end{cases}$$

The height of the stack is the maximum value of $h(i, j)$ when (i, j) runs over the picture.

Closure Property

Let Σ_1, Σ_2 and Σ_3 be three alphabets and let $f : \Sigma_1 \times \Sigma_2 \to \Sigma_3$ be a function. Given two iso-pictures $P_1 \in \Sigma_{1I}^{m \times n}$ and $P_2 \in \Sigma_{2I}^{m \times n}$, define $F(P_1, P_2)$ as an iso-picture $P_3 \in \Sigma_{3I}^{m \times n}$ where $P_3[i, j] = f(P_1[i, j], P_2[i, j])$. On iso-pictures over the binary alphabet $\Sigma = \{0, 1\}$, if we take f to be logical disjunction and if $X, Y \subseteq \Sigma_I^{**}$, then $F(x, y)$ will be the set of iso-pictures obtained by combining one iso-picture of X and one iso-picture of Y with a logical OR operation.

Proposition 1. *If $X \subseteq \Sigma_{1I}^{**}$ and $Y \subseteq \Sigma_{2I}^{**}$ are recognizable iso-picture languages then $F(X, Y)$ is recognizable.*

Proof. Let $(\Sigma_1, \Gamma_1, \pi_1, \theta_1)$ and $(\Sigma_2, \Gamma_2, \pi_2, \theta_2)$ be iso-tiling systems recognizing X and Y. Define $\Gamma_3 = \Gamma_1 \times \Gamma_2$, $\theta_3 = \{t/h_1(t) \in \theta_1 \text{ and } h_2(t) \in \theta_2\}$ and

$\pi_3(x,y) = f(\pi_1(x), \pi_2(y))$ where $h_1 : \Gamma_1 \times \Gamma_2 \to \Gamma_1$ and $h_2 : \Gamma_1 \times \Gamma_2 \to \Gamma_2$ are projections. Then the system $(\Sigma_3, \Gamma_3, \pi_3, \theta_3)$ recognizes $F(X,Y)$.

Theorem 1. *Let $L \subseteq \Sigma_I^{**}$ be a recognizable iso-picture language of patches and let k be an integer. The set $collage_{h \leq k}(L)$ of collages of L which can be obtained by stacks of height k or less is recognizable.*

Proof. In the case where $k = 1$, the result is a consequence of asserting that tiles of recognizable iso-picture languages are recognizable. A tiling is a collage of patches such that no two patches overlap and the whole picture is covered by some patch. Then the tiling by the recognizable iso-picture language $(p \cup \{\triangle, \triangledown\})^{**}$ is precisely a collage of height 1. Let p' be the language. Let $f : (\Sigma \cup \{\triangle, \triangledown\})^2 \to \Sigma \cup \{\triangle, \triangledown\}$ be defined by $f(x,y) = x$ for $x \notin \{\triangle, \triangledown\}$ and $f(\triangle, y) = f(\triangledown, y) = y$ otherwise. This function allows us to combine layers of tiling of P by treating $\triangle, \triangledown$ as a transparent colour. We then have, with notations of proposition 1,

$$Collage_h(L) = \underbrace{F(p', F(p', \dots, F(p', p') \dots))}_{h-1\ times}$$

Using the closure under union, the proof is complete.

Theorem 2. *If $L \subseteq \Sigma_I^{**}$ is an arbitrary iso-picture language over two letter alphabet $\Sigma = \{\boxed{A}, \boxed{B}\}$ then the iso-picture language $Collage(L)$ is recognizable.*

Proof. If p belongs to L, then each occurrence of a rhombus q of size $(2, n)$ is contained in some occurrence of a rhombus p os size $(2, m)$ satisfying $m \leq n$. Thus $Collage(L)$ equals $Collage(L_1)$ where L_1 is the set of minimal patches in L where minimal is componentwise. The collage corresponds to taking the logical OR on pixels; thus by proposition 1 where the function f achieves the logical disjunction of the pixels, we see that it suffices to consider the case where L_1 is reduced to a unique element.

Let L be an iso-picture language of rhombuses over an alphabet $\{\boxed{A}, \boxed{B}\}$ of size $(2, m)$. Consider an element $p \in Collage(L)$. Every pixel (i,j) of L can belong to number of occurrences. The order in which these patches are laid is irrelevant. The number of times a given patch is laid on a given position is also irrelevant. However the position of the patches is relevant. Consider the set $B_{i,j}$ of pairs (k, ℓ) such that the rhombus $\{\boxed{A}, \boxed{B}\}^{2 \times m}$ can be placed in p with its left most corner at position $(i - k + 1, j - \ell + 1)$, that is the subpictures $[i - k + 1, i - k + 2, \dots, i - k + m] \times [2m - 1, 2m - 3, \dots, 1]$ and $[i - k - 1, i - k - 2, \dots, i - k - m] \times [2m - 1, 2m - 3, \dots, 1]$ of L is made of $\boxed{A}$'s and $\boxed{B}$'s. Let Γ be the power set of $\{1, 2\} \times \{1, \dots, m\}$.

An iso-triangular tiling $(\Sigma, \Gamma, \theta, \pi)$ recognizing $Collage(L)$ is specified as follows. The primary alphabet is $\Sigma = \{\boxed{A}, \boxed{B}, \triangle, \triangledown\}$ and the auxiliary alphabet is Γ. The projection π is defined as follows: (i) $\pi(\triangle_{\#A}) = \triangle$ (ii) $\pi(\nabla^{\#B}) = \nabla$ (iii) $\pi(\triangle_x) = \triangle_A$, $x \in \Gamma$ (iv) $\pi(\nabla^y) = \nabla^B$, $y \in \Gamma$.

Consider the following eight subsets of $\left(\Gamma \cup \left\{ \triangle_{\#A} \nabla^{\#B} \right\}\right)^{1\times 2}$

$$\theta_1 = \left\{ \triangle_{x\,y\,t}^{\;z} \middle/ \begin{array}{l} \forall\, k, \forall\, \ell, (k,\ell) \in x \wedge \ell < 2m - 2 \Rightarrow (k, \ell+1) \in y, \\ (k, \ell+2) \in t, (k+1, \ell+1) \in z \end{array} \right\}$$

$$\theta_2 = \left\{ \triangle_{x\,y\,t}^{\;z} \middle/ \begin{array}{l} \forall\, k, \forall\, \ell, (k,\ell) \in y \wedge \ell > 1 \Rightarrow (k, \ell-1) \in x, \\ (k, \ell+1) \in t, (k+1, \ell) \in z \end{array} \right\}$$

$$\theta_3 = \left\{ \triangle_{x\,y\,t}^{\;z} \middle/ \begin{array}{l} \forall\, k, \forall\, \ell, (k,\ell) \in z \wedge k < 2m \Rightarrow (k-1, \ell-1) \in x, \\ (k-1, \ell) \in y, (k-1, \ell+1) \in t \end{array} \right\}$$

$$\theta_4 = \left\{ \triangle_{x\,y\,t}^{\;z} \middle/ \begin{array}{l} \forall\, k, \forall\, \ell, (k,\ell) \in t \wedge k > 1, \ell \leq 2m - 1 \Rightarrow (k, \ell-2) \in x, \\ (k, \ell-1) \in y, (k+1, \ell-1) \in z \end{array} \right\}$$

$$\theta_5 = \left\{ \nabla_{\;\;z}^{x\,y\,t} \middle/ \begin{array}{l} \forall\, k, \forall\, \ell, (k,\ell) \in x \wedge \ell < 2m - 2 \Rightarrow (k, \ell+1) \in y, \\ (k, \ell+2) \in t, (k-1, \ell+1) \in z \end{array} \right\}$$

$$\theta_6 = \left\{ \nabla_{\;\;z}^{x\,y\,t} \middle/ \begin{array}{l} \forall\, k, \forall\, \ell, (k,\ell) \in y \wedge \ell > 1 \Rightarrow (k, \ell-1) \in x, \\ (k, \ell+1) \in t, (k-1, \ell) \in z \end{array} \right\}$$

$$\theta_7 = \left\{ \nabla_{\;\;z}^{x\,y\,t} \middle/ \begin{array}{l} \forall\, k, \forall\, \ell, (k,\ell) \in z \wedge k > 1 \Rightarrow (k+1, \ell-1) \in x, \\ (k+1, \ell) \in y, (k+1, \ell+1) \in t \end{array} \right\}$$

$$\theta_8 = \left\{ \nabla_{\;\;z}^{x\,y\,t} \middle/ \begin{array}{l} \forall\, k, \forall\, \ell, (k,\ell) \in t \wedge k \leq m, \ell \leq 2m - 1 \Rightarrow (k, \ell-2) \in x, \\ (k, \ell-1) \in y, (k-1, \ell-1) \in z \end{array} \right\}$$

We set $\theta = \left(\bigcap_{1 \leq i \leq 4} \theta_i\right) \cup \left(\bigcap_{4 \leq i \leq 8} \theta_i\right)$. We also make the assumption that a condition of the form $(k, \ell) \in x$ is false whenever $x = \triangle_{\#A}$ or $\nabla^{\#B}$. It is clear that all iso-pictures in $Collage(L)$ are recognized by an iso-triangular tiling system. Conversely assume that an iso-picture is recognized by the system. Then it suffices to observe that if (k, ℓ) is an element of a subset of Γ which labels the pixel at position (i, j), then all pixels at positions $(i + \alpha, j + \beta)$ satisfying $i - k + 1 \leq i + \alpha \leq i - k + m$ and $j - \ell + 1 \leq j + \beta \leq j - \ell + 2m - 1$ are labeled by a subset containing the element $(k + \alpha, \ell + \beta)$ proving thus that the iso-picture is a union of occurrences of the rhombus.

4   Collage P System

P system [8] is a new compatibility model of a distributed parallel type based
on the notion of a membrane structure. Such a structure consists of computing
cells which are organized hierarchically by the inclusion relation. Each cell is
enclosed by its membrane. Each cell is an independent computing agent with its
own computing program, which produces objects. The interaction between cells
consists of the exchange of objects through membranes.

A membrane structure can be represented in a natural way as a Venn diagram.
(Fig. 2).

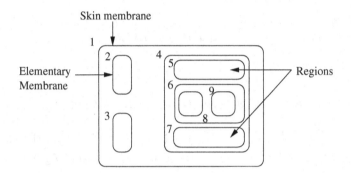

Fig. 2. A membrane structure

The membranes are labeled in one-to-one manner. Each membrane identifies
a region delimited by it and the membranes placed directly inside it (if any). A
membrane without any other membrane inside it is said to be elementary.

The membrane surrounding the cell which is the highest in the hierarchy is
called the skin membrane.

In the regions delimited by the membranes we place multisets of objects from
a specified finite set V together with evolution rules for these objects.

Now we define a P system based on collage operation.

Definition 10. *A collage P system is defined as*

$$\pi = (V, C, \mu, \mu_1, \mu_2, \ldots, \mu_n, (L_1, C, tar), (L_2, C, tar), \ldots, (L_n, C, tar))$$

where

- V *is an alphabet; its elements are called objects*
- C *is the collage* $_S^{(2,M)}$.
- μ *is a membrane structure consisting of n membranes $\mu_1, \mu_2, \ldots, \mu_n$*
- $tar \in \{here, in_j, out\}$, $j = 1, 2, \ldots, n$.

For each i, $1 \leq i \leq n$, let $L_i \subseteq \Sigma_I^{**}$ be the content of the ith membrane. The
$tar = out$ is attached with all the elementary membranes. The language L_i is sent

to the immediate successor. If j is the immediate successor of the ith membrane and j does not contain any membrane other than i, then collage operation C is applied to the languages L_i and L_j and the resultant language $C(L_i, L_j)$ is computed in the jth membrane. Depending on the target attached, $c(L_i, L_j)$ is sent to the inner membrane if $tar = in_i$ or sent to the outer membrane if $tar = out$ or stays in the same membrane if $tar = here$.

If j is the immediate successor of m elementary membranes $i_1, i_2, \ldots, i_m$, then the languages $L_{i_1}, L_{i_2}, \ldots, L_{i_m}$ are sent to the jth membrane and the language obtained is $C(L_{i_1}, L_{i_2}, \ldots, L_{i_m}, L_j)$. Depending on the target attached it is either sent to any one of the elementary membranes if the $tar = in_{i_k}$, $1 \le k \le m$ or sent to the outer membrane if the target is out or stays in the same membrane if $tar = here$.

This process is repeated till the language is sent to the skin membrane. The language obtained by skin membrane is denoted by $L(\pi)$.

Example 2. Consider the system

$$\pi = (V, C, \mu, \mu_1, \mu_2, (L_1, C, out), (L_2, C, in_1))$$

where $V = \{\triangle, \triangledown, \triangle, \triangledown\}$ Let $L_1 = \{P \in \Sigma_I^{**}/P$ is a rhombus of size $(2, m)$ over $\{\triangle, \triangledown\}$ fixed at the coordinate $(x, y)\}$ and $L_2 = \{P \in \Sigma_I^{**}/P$ is a rhombus of size $(2, m)$ over $\{\triangle, \triangledown\}$ fixed at the coordinate $(x, y)\}$.

Let $P_1 = $ 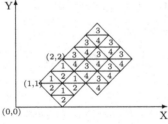 be fixed at $(1, 1)$ where $P_1 \in L_1$.

Now, the iso-picture P_1 is sent to membrane 2 since the target in the membrane

is out. Let $P_2 = $ be fixed at $(2, 2)$, where $P_2 \in L_2$.

Now $C(P_1, P_2)$ is computed in the membrane 2, where $C(P_1, P_2)$ is

Now $C(P_1, P_2)$ is sent to membrane 1 since the target is in_1.

Let $P_3 = $ 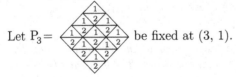 be fixed at $(3, 1)$.

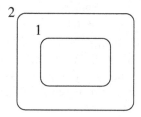

Fig. 3. Membrane structure of the system π

Now $C((P_1, P_2), P_3)$ is computed in membrane 1 and is shown below.

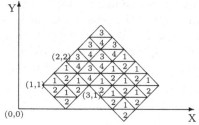

Now, $C((P_1, P_2), P_3)$ is sent to skin membrane (i.e., membrane 2).

Let $P_4 =$ be fixed at $(2, 0)$.

Now $C((P_1, P_2, P_3), P_4)$ is computed in membrane 2. The computation is stopped and the resultant collage obtained is shown in fig. 4.

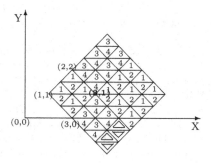

Fig. 4.

Theorem 3. *In a collage P system $\pi = (V, C, \mu, \mu_1, \mu_2, \ldots, \mu_n, (L_1, C, tar),$ $(L_2, C, tar), \ldots, (L_n, C, tar))$, suppose $L_1, L_2, \ldots, L_n$ are arbitrary iso-picture languages of rhombuses over $\{\triangle, \triangledown\}$. Then $L(\pi)$ is recognizable.*

Proof. Let $p_i \in L_i$ be the content of the ith elementary membrane where p_i is an arbitrary iso-picture language of rhombuses over $\{\triangle, \triangledown\}$. The contents of the elementary membranes are sent out to the immediate successor membrane μ_j. Let $p_j \in L_j$ be an arbitrary iso-picture language of rhombuses over $\{\triangle, \triangle\}$. $Collage(p_i, p_j)$ is computed in the jth membrane which is a recognizable iso-picture language by Theorem 2. $Collage(p_i, p_j)$ is either sent to the inner membrane or outer membrane based on the target. The process is continued till the objects reaches the skin membrane. The language collected in the skin membrane is $L(\pi)$ which is recognizable.

5   Conclusion

In this paper, we have extended the new operation called collage on pictures to iso-picture languages and proved that the collage of iso-picture languages on a two letter alphabet is recognizable. We have defined a P system based on collage operation which generates iso-picture languages. We have obtained some results using recognizability of collage of iso-picture languages.

References

1. Annadurai, S., Kalyani, T., Dare, V.R., Thomas, D.G.: P system generating iso-picture languages. Progress in Natural Science 18, 617–622 (2008)
2. Annadurai, S., Thomas, D.G., Dare, V.R., Kalyani, T.: Rewriting P systems generating iso-picture languages. In: Brimkov, V.E., Barneva, R.P., Hauptman, H.A. (eds.) IWCIA 2008. LNCS, vol. 4958, pp. 352–362. Springer, Heidelberg (2008)
3. Choffrut, C., Durak, B.: Collage of two-dimensional words. Theoretical Computer Science 340, 364–380 (2005)
4. Giammarresi, D., Restivo, A.: Two-dimensional languages. In: Salomaa, A., Rozenberg, G. (eds.) Handbook of Formal Languages, vol. 3, pp. 215–267. Springer, Heidelberg (1997)
5. Kalyani, T., Dare, V.R., Thomas, D.G.: Local and recognizable iso picture languages. In: Pal, N.R., Kasabov, N., Mudi, R.K., Pal, S., Parui, S.K. (eds.) ICONIP 2004. LNCS, vol. 3316, pp. 738–743. Springer, Heidelberg (2004)
6. Kalyani, T., Dare, V.R., Thomas, D.G., Robinson, T.: Iso-array acceptors and learning. In: Sakakibara, Y., Kobayashi, S., Sato, K., Nishino, T., Tomita, E. (eds.) ICGI 2006. LNCS (LNAI), vol. 4201, pp. 327–339. Springer, Heidelberg (2006)
7. Kalyani, T., Dare, V.R., Thomas, D.G.: Tilings of rectangles with triangular-tetrominoes. J. of Combinatorics, Information & System Sciences 33(3-4), 243–250 (2008)
8. Păun, G.: Computing with membranes. Journal of Computer and System Sciences 61(1), 108–143 (2000)
9. Păun, G., Rozenberg, G., Salomaa, A.: Membrane computing with external output. Fundamenta Informaticae 34, 313–340 (2000)
10. Rosenfeld, A., Siromoney, R.: Picture Languages - a survey. Languages of Design 1(3), 229–245 (1993)

Online Tessellation Automaton Recognizing Various Classes of Convex Polyominoes

H. Geetha[1], D.G. Thomas[2], and T. Kalyani[1]

[1] Department of Mathematics, St. Joseph's College of Engineering
Chennai - 600119
[2] Department of Mathematics, Madras Christian College
Chennai - 600059
dgthomasmcc@yahoo.com

Abstract. A polyomino is a finite connected union of cells having no cut points. Tiling and Wang recognizability of convex polyominoes have been studied in detail by De Carli et al. In this paper we define 2D polyomino online tessellation automaton to recognize a class of polyominoes and prove that the family of various classes of polyominoes recognized by tiling systems and 2D-polyomino online tessellation automata coincide. We also study the recognizability of convex polyominoes by domino systems.

Keywords: Polyominoes, 2D online tessellation automaton, domino system, tiling system.

1 Introduction

Two-dimensional recognizable picture languages was proposed by Blum and Hewitt, who in 1967 introduced a model of finite automaton that reads a two-dimensional tape [1]. Two important classes of two-dimensional languages, namely, local and recognizable picture languages were introduced by Giammarresi and Restivo [4]. They considered a particular model of 2D cellular automaton called the 2D online tessellation automaton (2OTA) introduced by Inoue and Nakamura [6]. Recognizability of two-dimensional picture languages using hv-domino systems were studied in depth in [7].

A polyomino is a finite connected union of cells having no cut points, where each cell is a unit square in the $Z \times Z$ plane. Polyominoes are well known combinatorial objects and are related to many different problems, such as tiling, games and enumeration. Polyominoes play an important role in the study of lattice models in physics and bio-chemistry as in models of polymers, cell-growth or cell structure etc. [5]. The way of tiling planar surfaces by polyominoes has shown interesting mathematical aspects connected with computational theory, mathematical logic and discrete geometry. Polyominoes are useful for the Ising model (modeling neural networks), beating heart cells, protein folds, biological membrane etc.

R.P. Barneva et al. (Eds.): CompIMAGE 2010, LNCS 6026, pp. 107–118, 2010.

Recently, representations of various classes of polyominoes in terms of two-dimensional languages using window movement of 2×2 array tiles (tiling system) and DNA Wang tiles have been studied [2,3]. Interesting information about various classes of polyominoes have been obtained.

This paper explores a relationship between various classes of convex polyominoes and a special kind of 2D online tessellation automata. We define a 2D polyomino online tessellation automaton (2DPOTA) to recognize a class of polyominoes and prove that the two families of polyomino languages recognized by polyomino tiling systems and 2DPOTA coincide. We study the recognizability of polyominoes by means of domino systems.

2 Preliminaries

In this section we deal with the basic concepts on arrays, tiling system, domino system and 2D online tessellation automaton [4] and convex polyominoes [3].

If p is a picture of size (m, n), then for any $h \le m, k \le n$, we denote by $B_{h,k}(p)$ the set of all blocks (or sub-pictures) of p of size (h, k). A tile is a sub-picture of size $(2, 2)$.

Definition 1. *Let Σ be a finite alphabet and Σ^{**} the set of all possible pictures over Σ. A two-dimensional language $L \subseteq \Sigma^{**}$ is local if there exists a finite set θ of tiles over the alphabet $\Sigma \cup \{\#\}$ such that $L = \{p \in \Sigma^{**} / B_{2,2}(\hat{p}) \subseteq \theta\}$. The set θ is usually called a representation by tiles for the local language L, and we write $L = L(\theta)$.*

Definition 2. *A tiling system (TS) is a 4-tuple $\mathcal{T} = (\Sigma, \Gamma, \theta, \pi)$, where Σ and Γ are two finite alphabets, θ is a finite set of tiles over the alphabet $\Gamma \cup \{\#\}$, and $\pi : \Gamma \to \Sigma$ is a projection (mapping).*

The tiling system $\mathcal{T}$ recognizes a language L over the alphabet Σ if $L = \pi(L')$ where $L' = L(\theta)$ is a local language over Γ. We write $L = L(\mathcal{T})$.

We say that the language $L \subseteq \Sigma^{**}$ is recognized by a tiling system if there exists a tiling system $\mathcal{T} = (\Sigma, \Gamma, \theta, \pi)$ such that $L = L(\mathcal{T})$. We denote the family of all two-dimensional languages recognizable by tiling systems as $\mathcal{L}(TS)$.

A domino is either a 2×1 picture (vertical domino) or a 1×2 picture (horizontal domino).

Definition 3. *A two-dimensional language $L \subseteq \Sigma^{**}$ is hv-local if there exists a finite set Δ of dominoes over the alphabet $\Sigma \cup \{\#\}$ such that the language $L = \{p \in \Sigma^{**} | B_{1,2}(\hat{p}) \cup B_{2,1}(\hat{p}) \subseteq \Delta\}$.*

The set Δ will be called a representation by dominoes for the hv-local language L and we will write $L = L(\Delta)$. It is true that if $L \subseteq \Sigma^{**}$ is a hv-local language then L is a local language.

Definition 4. *A domino system (DS) is a 4-tuple $D = (\Sigma, \Gamma, \Delta, \pi)$ where Σ and Γ are two finite alphabets, Δ is finite set of dominoes over the alphabet $\Gamma \cup \{\#\}$ and $\pi : \Gamma \to \Sigma$ is a projection from Γ to Σ.*

The domino system DS recognizes a language L over the alphabet Σ defined as $L = \pi(L')$ where $L' = L(\Delta)$ is a hv-local language over Γ corresponding to the set of dominoes Δ. We denote by $\mathcal{L}(DS)$ the family of two-dimensional languages recognized by domino systems.

Definition 5. *A non-deterministic (deterministic) two-dimensional online tessellation automaton, referred as 2OTA (2-DOTA), is defined as $\mathcal{A} = (\Sigma, Q, I, F, \delta)$ where Σ is the input alphabet, Q is the set of states, $I \subseteq Q$ is the set of initial states, $F \subseteq Q$ is the set of final (or accepting) states, $\delta : Q \times Q \times \Sigma \to 2^Q$, $(\delta : Q \times Q \times \Sigma \to Q)$ is the transition function.*

A run of $\mathcal{A}$ on a picture $p \in \Sigma^{**}$ consists of associating a state (from the set Q) to each of position (i, j) of p. Such state is given by the transition function δ and depends on the states already associated to positions $(i - 1, j)$ and $(i, j - 1)$ and on the symbol $p(i, j)$ (i.e., $(i, j)^{th}$ element in p).

A 2OTA $\mathcal{A}$ recognizes a picture p if there exists a run of $\mathcal{A}$ on p such that the state associated to the position $(\ell_1(p), \ell_2(p))$ is a final state, where $\ell_1(p)$ is the number of rows and $\ell_2(p)$ is the number of columns of p. The pair $(\ell_1(p), \ell_2(p))$ is the size of the picture p.

Convex Polyominoes

In the plane $Z \times Z$, a cell is a unit square and a polyomino is a finite connected union of cells having no cut point. A column (row) of a polyomino is the intersection between the polyomino and an infinite strip of cells whose centers lie on a vertical (horizontal) line.

A polyomino is said to be column-convex (row-convex) when its intersection with any vertical (horizontal) line is convex. A polyomino is convex if it is both column and row convex. Examples of classes of convex polyominoes are the classes of Ferrers diagrams ($\mathcal{F}$), parallelogram polyominoes ($\mathcal{P}$), stack polyominoes ($\mathcal{S}$) and directed polyominoes ($\mathcal{D}$) [3] (See Figure 1).

Let p be a convex polyomino and $R(p)$ be its minimal bounding rectangle. $\widehat{R(p)}$ is obtained by surrounding $R(p)$ by the boundary symbol #. We observe that four disjoint (possibly empty) sets of unit cells in $R(p) \backslash p$ are easily separated, each of them located at one of the four vertices of $R(p)$. Let us call these sets as A, B, C and D respectively. To each convex polyomino we associate a picture

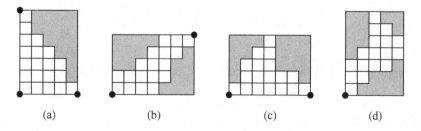

    (a)   (b)   (c)   (d)

Fig. 1. (a) A Ferrers diagram; (b) A parallelogram polyomino; (c) A stack polyomino; (d) A directed-convex polyomino

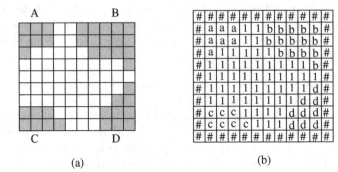

(a)   (b)

Fig. 2. (a) A convex polyomino p separates four disjoint sets of cells in $R(p)\backslash p$. (b) The representation of $\widehat{R(p)}$.

obtained by representing with '1' for every cell belonging to the polyomino and with the symbol a (respectively b, c, d) to every cell in A (respectively B, C, D) as depicted in Figure 2. Let $\mathcal{L}_c$ be the class of languages of these rectangles over the alphabet $\{1, a, b, c, d\}$.

3 Two-Dimensional Polyomino Online Tessellation Automaton

In this section we define 2D polyomino online tessellation automaton (2DPOTA) and proved that the class of all polyomino languages recognized by 2DPOTA coincides with the family of all polyomino languages recognized by tiling systems.

Definition 6. *A deterministic (non-deterministic) polyomino online tessellation automaton (2DPOTA) is $\mathcal{A} = (\Sigma, Q_1, Q_2, I, F, \delta)$ where $\Sigma = \Sigma_1 \cup \Sigma_2$ is the input alphabet, where $\Sigma_1 = \{1\}$ is the singleton set associated with the polyomino p, Σ_2 is the set of symbols associated with the region $R(p)\backslash p$, Q_1 and Q_2 are the finite sets of states associated with the region p and $R(p)\backslash p$ respectively. $I \subseteq Q_1 \cup Q_2$ is the set of initial states, $F \subseteq Q_1 \cup Q_2$ is the set of final states and the transition function $\delta : (Q_1 \cup Q_2) \times (Q_1 \cup Q_2) \times \Sigma \to Q_1 \cup Q_2(2^{Q_1 \cup Q_2})$ is defined as follows:*

(i) $\delta(q_1, q_2, 1) = q_3; q_1, q_2, q_3 \in Q_1$
(ii) $\delta(r, q_1, 1) = q_2; q_1, q_2 \in Q_1, r \in Q_2$
(iii) $\delta(q_1, r, 1) = q_2; q_1, q_2 \in Q_1, r \in Q_2$
(iv) $\delta(r_1, r_2, 1) = q; r_1, r_2 \in Q_2, q \in Q_1$
(v) $\delta(r_1, r_2, a) = r_3; a \in \Sigma_2, r_1, r_2, r_3 \in Q_2$
(vi) $\delta(q, r_1, a) = r_2; a \in \Sigma_2, r_1, r_2 \in Q_2, q \in Q_1$
(vii) $\delta(r_1, q, a) = r_2; a \in \Sigma_2, r_1, r_2 \in Q_2, q \in Q_1$
(viii) $\delta(q_1, q_2, a) = r; a \in \Sigma_2, q_1, q_2 \in Q_1, r \in Q_2$

The computation by a two-dimensional polyomino online tessellation automaton (2DPOTA) on $R(p)$ of size $m \times n$, where

$$\widehat{R(p)} = \begin{array}{cccccc} \# & \# & \# & \cdots & \# & \# \\ \# & a_{11} & a_{12} & \cdots & a_{1n} & \# \\ \# & a_{21} & a_{22} & \cdots & a_{2n} & \# \\ \cdots & & & \cdots & & \cdots \\ \# & a_{m1} & a_{m2} & \cdots & a_{mn} & \# \\ \# & \# & \# & \cdots & \# & \# \end{array}$$

with $a_{ij} \in \Sigma$ and $\#$ is a special symbol not in Σ is given as follows.

At time $t = 0$, an initial state $q_0 \in I$ is associated with all the positions of $\widehat{R(p)}$ holding $\#$. The state associated with each position (i, j) by the transition function δ, depends on the states already associated with the position $(i, j-1)$, $(i-1, j)$ and the symbol a_{ij}. Let s_{ij} be the state associated with the position (i, j) if $a_{ij} \in \Sigma_1$ and r_{ij} be the state associated with the position (i, j) if $a_{ij} \in \Sigma_2$. At time $t = 1$, a state from $\delta(q_0, q_0, a_{11})$ is associated to the position $(1, 1)$ holding a_{11}. If $a_{11} \in \Sigma_1$, then s_{11} is the state associated with the position $(1, 1)$ and if $a_{11} \in \Sigma_2$, then r_{11} is the state associated to the position $(1, 1)$. At time $t = 2$, states are associated simultaneously to the positions $(2, 1)$ and $(1, 2)$ respectively holding a_{21} and a_{12} of the next diagonal.

Case (i): If s_{11} is the state associated with the position $(1, 1)$ then the state associated to the position $(2, 1)$ is an element of $\delta(s_{11}, q_0, a_{21})$ and to the position $(1, 2)$, an element of $\delta(q_0, s_{11}, a_{12})$. If $a_{21} \in \Sigma_1$, then $\delta(s_{11}, q_0, a_{21}) = s_{21}$ and if $a_{21} \in \Sigma_2$ then $\delta(s_{11}, q_0, a_{21}) = r_{21}$.

 Similarly $\delta(q_0, s_{11}, a_{12}) = s_{12}$ *if* $a_{12} \in \Sigma_1$ *and* $\delta(s_{11}, q_0, a_{12}) = r_{12}$ *when* $a_{12} \in \Sigma_2$.

Case (ii): If r_{11} is the state associated with the position $(1, 1)$, then the state associated with the position $(2, 1)$ is an element of $\delta(r_{11}, q_0, a_{21})$ and to the position $(1, 2)$, an element of $\delta(q_0, r_{11}, a_{12})$ and they are given as follows:

(i) $\delta(r_{11}, q_0, a_{21}) = s_{21}$ *if* $a_{21} \in \Sigma_1$ *(ii)* $\delta(r_{11}, q_0, a_{21}) = r_{21}$ *if* $a_{21} \in \Sigma_2$
(iii) $\delta(q_0, r_{11}, a_{12}) = s_{12}$ *if* $a_{12} \in \Sigma_1$ *(iv)* $\delta(q_0, r_{11}, a_{12}) = r_{12}$ *if* $a_{12} \in \Sigma_2$

We then proceed to the next diagonal. The 2DPOTA stops its computation by reading the symbol a_{mn} and associating the state s_{mn} if $a_{mn} \in \Sigma_1$ and the state r_{mn} if $a_{mn} \in \Sigma_2$. A run for $R(p)$ is a sequence of states $q_{11}q_{12}q_{21}q_{13}q_{22}q_{31} \cdots q_{mn}$ where $q_{ij} \in Q_1 \cup Q_2$ and it is denoted by $\rho(\mathcal{A})$. The language of polyominoes recognized by 2DPOTA $\mathcal{A}$ is denoted by $L(\mathcal{A})$ and $\mathcal{L}(2DPOTA)$ is the family of languages of polyominoes recognized by 2DPOTA.

Example 1. A 2DPOTA recognizing the class of Ferrers diagrams is given below. A member of the class is, for instance, p whose

$$
\widehat{R(p)} = \begin{array}{c}
\# \; \# \; \# \; \# \; \# \; \# \; \# \\
\# \; 1 \; b \; b \; b \; b \; \# \\
\# \; 1 \; b \; b \; b \; b \; \# \\
\# \; 1 \; 1 \; b \; b \; b \; \# \\
\# \; 1 \; 1 \; 1 \; b \; b \; \# \\
\# \; 1 \; 1 \; 1 \; 1 \; b \; \# \\
\# \; 1 \; 1 \; 1 \; 1 \; b \; \# \\
\# \; 1 \; 1 \; 1 \; 1 \; 1 \; \# \\
\# \; \# \; \# \; \# \; \# \; \# \; \#
\end{array}
$$

$\mathcal{A} = (\Sigma, Q_1, Q_2, I, F, \delta)$, $\Sigma_1 = \{1\}$, $\Sigma_2 = \{b\}$, $Q_1 = \{q_1\}$, $Q_2 = \{q_0, r_1, q_p\}$, $F = \{q_p\}$, $I = \{q_0\}$.

The transition function δ is given as follows:

(i) $\delta(q_0, q_0, 1) = q_p$ (ii) $\delta(q_0, q_p, b) = r_1$ (iii) $\delta(q_p, q_0, 1) = q_p$

(iv) $\delta(q_0, r_1, b) = r_1$ (v) $\delta(r_1, q_p, b) = r_1$ (vi) $\delta(r_1, r_1, b) = r_1$

(vii) $\delta(q_0, q_p, 1) = q_p$ (viii) $\delta(q_p, q_p, 1) = q_p$ (ix) $\delta(q_p, q_p, b) = r_1$

(x) $\delta(q_p, r_1, b) = r_1$

Theorem 1. *The class of all polyomino languages recognized by 2DPOTA coincides with the class of all polyominoes recognized by tiling systems.*

The theorem follows by the following three lemmas.

Lemma 1. *If a polyomino language is recognized by a polyomino online tessellation automaton (2DPOTA) then it is recognized by a polyomino tiling system.*

Proof. Let $L \subseteq \Sigma^{**}$ be a language recognized by a 2DPOTA $\mathcal{A} = (\Sigma, Q_1, Q_2, I, F, \delta)$.

Let $\mathcal{T} = (\Sigma, \Gamma, Q, \pi)$ be a tiling system such that $\Gamma = (\Sigma \cup \{\#\}) \times (Q_1 \cup Q_2)$ where $\Sigma = \Sigma_1 \cup \Sigma_2$ and $\pi : \Gamma \to \Sigma$ is such that $\pi(1, q) = 1$, if $1 \in \Sigma_1$ and $q \in Q_1 \cup Q_2$ and $\pi(a, q) = a$ if $a \in \Sigma_2$.

For the transitions of the 2DPOTA corresponding to the region A, we define

$$
\theta_{A_1} = \left\{ \begin{array}{|c|c|}
\hline
(\#, q_0) & (\#, q_0) \\
\hline
(\#, q_0) & (a, r_1) \\
\hline
\end{array} \middle/ \begin{array}{l} a \in \Sigma_2 \\ r_1 \in \delta(q_0, q_0, a) \end{array} \right\}
$$

$$
\theta_{A_2} = \left\{ \begin{array}{|c|c|}
\hline
(\#, q_0) & (\#, q_0) \\
\hline
(a, r_1) & (a, r_1) \\
\hline
\end{array} \middle/ \begin{array}{l} a \in \Sigma_2 \\ r_1 \in \delta(q_0, r_1, a) \end{array} \right\}
$$

$$
\theta_{A_3} = \left\{ \begin{array}{|c|c|}
\hline
(\#, q_0) & (a, r_1) \\
\hline
(\#, q_0) & (a, r_1) \\
\hline
\end{array} \middle/ \begin{array}{l} a \in \Sigma_2 \\ r_1 \in \delta(r_1, q_0, a) \end{array} \right\}
$$

$$
\theta_{A_4} = \left\{ \begin{array}{|c|c|}
\hline
(a, r_1) & (a, r_1) \\
\hline
(a, r_1) & (a, r_1) \\
\hline
\end{array} \middle/ \begin{array}{l} a \in \Sigma_2 \\ r_1 \in \delta(r_1, r_1, a) \end{array} \right\}
$$

$$
\theta_{A_5} = \left\{ \begin{array}{|c|c|}
\hline
(\#, q_0) & (\#, q_0) \\
\hline
(a, r_1) & (1, q_p) \\
\hline
\end{array} \middle/ \begin{array}{l} a \in \Sigma_2 \\ q_p \in \delta(q_0, r_1, 1) \end{array} \right\}
$$

$$
\theta_{A_6} = \left\{ \begin{array}{|c|c|}
\hline
(\#, q_0) & (a, r_1) \\
\hline
(\#, q_0) & (1, q_p) \\
\hline
\end{array} \middle/ \begin{array}{l} a \in \Sigma_2 \\ q_p \in \delta(r_1, q_0, 1) \end{array} \right\}
$$

$$\theta_{A_7} = \left\{ \begin{array}{|c|c|} \hline (a,r_1) & (a,r_1) \\ \hline (a,r_1) & (1,q_p) \\ \hline \end{array} \middle/ \begin{array}{l} a \in \Sigma_2 \\ q_p \in \delta(r_1,r_1,1) \end{array} \right\}$$

$$\theta_{A_8} = \left\{ \begin{array}{|c|c|} \hline (a,r_1) & (1,q_p) \\ \hline (a,r_1) & (1,q_p) \\ \hline \end{array} \middle/ \begin{array}{l} a \in \Sigma_2 \\ q_p \in \delta(q_p,r_1,1) \end{array} \right\}$$

$$\theta_{A_9} = \left\{ \begin{array}{|c|c|} \hline (a,r_1) & (a,r_1) \\ \hline (1,q_p) & (1,q_p) \\ \hline \end{array} \middle/ \begin{array}{l} a \in \Sigma_2 \\ q_p \in \delta(r_1,q_p,1) \end{array} \right\}$$

$$\theta_{A_{10}} = \left\{ \begin{array}{|c|c|} \hline (a,r_1) & (1,q_p) \\ \hline (1,q_p) & (1,q_p) \\ \hline \end{array} \middle/ \begin{array}{l} a \in \Sigma_2 \\ q_p \in \delta(q_p,q_p,1) \end{array} \right\}$$

Let $\theta_A = \bigcup_{i=1}^{10} \theta_{A_i}$

For the transitions of the 2DPOTA corresponding to the region B, we define

$$\theta_{B_1} = \left\{ \begin{array}{|c|c|} \hline (b,r_2) & (b,r_2) \\ \hline (b,r_2) & (b,r_2) \\ \hline \end{array} \middle/ \begin{array}{l} b \in \Sigma_2 \\ r_2 \in \delta(r_2,r_2,b) \end{array} \right\}$$

$$\theta_{B_2} = \left\{ \begin{array}{|c|c|} \hline (\#,q_0) & (\#,q_0) \\ \hline (b,r_2) & (\#,q_0) \\ \hline \end{array} \middle/ \begin{array}{l} b \in \Sigma_2 \\ r_2 \in \delta(q_0,q,b) \text{ where } q \in Q_1 \cup Q_2 \end{array} \right\}$$

$$\theta_{B_3} = \left\{ \begin{array}{|c|c|} \hline (\#,q_0) & (\#,q_0) \\ \hline (b,r_2) & (b,r_2) \\ \hline \end{array} \middle/ \begin{array}{l} b \in \Sigma_2 \\ r_2 \in \delta(q_0,r_2,b) \end{array} \right\}$$

$$\theta_{B_4} = \left\{ \begin{array}{|c|c|} \hline (b,r_2) & (\#,q_0) \\ \hline (b,r_2) & (\#,q_0) \\ \hline \end{array} \middle/ \begin{array}{l} b \in \Sigma_2 \\ r_2 \in \delta(r_2,q,b) \text{ where } q \in Q_1 \cup Q_2 \end{array} \right\}$$

$$\theta_{B_5} = \left\{ \begin{array}{|c|c|} \hline (\#,q_0) & (\#,q_0) \\ \hline (1,q_p) & (b,r_2) \\ \hline \end{array} \middle/ \begin{array}{l} b \in \Sigma_2 \\ r_2 \in \delta(q_0,q_p,b) \end{array} \right\}$$

$$\theta_{B_6} = \left\{ \begin{array}{|c|c|} \hline (b,r_2) & (\#,q_0) \\ \hline (1,q_p) & (\#,q_0) \\ \hline \end{array} \middle/ \begin{array}{l} b \in \Sigma_2 \\ q_p \in \delta(r_2,q,1) \text{ where } q \in Q_1 \cup Q_2 \end{array} \right\}$$

$$\theta_{B_7} = \left\{ \begin{array}{|c|c|} \hline (b,r_2) & (b,r_2) \\ \hline (1,q_p) & (b,r_2) \\ \hline \end{array} \middle/ \begin{array}{l} b \in \Sigma_2 \\ r_2 \in \delta(r_2,q_p,b) \end{array} \right\}$$

$$\theta_{B_8} = \left\{ \begin{array}{|c|c|} \hline (1,q_p) & (b,r_2) \\ \hline (1,q_p) & (b,r_2) \\ \hline \end{array} \middle/ \begin{array}{l} b \in \Sigma_2 \\ r_2 \in \delta(r_2,q_p,b) \end{array} \right\}$$

$$\theta_{B_9} = \left\{ \begin{array}{|c|c|} \hline (b,r_2) & (b,r_2) \\ \hline (1,q_p) & (1,q_p) \\ \hline \end{array} \middle/ \begin{array}{l} b \in \Sigma_2 \\ q_p \in \delta(r_2,q_p,1) \end{array} \right\}$$

$$\theta_{B_{10}} = \left\{ \begin{array}{|c|c|} \hline (1,q_p) & (b,r_2) \\ \hline (1,q_p) & (1,q_p) \\ \hline \end{array} \middle/ \begin{array}{l} b \in \Sigma_2 \\ q_p \in \delta(r_2,q_p,1) \end{array} \right\}$$

Let $\theta_B = \bigcup_{i=1}^{10} \theta_{B_i}$

For the transitions of the 2DPOTA corresponding to the region C, we define

$$\theta_{C_1} = \left\{ \begin{array}{|c|c|} \hline (c,r_3) & (c,r_3) \\ \hline (c,r_3) & (c,r_3) \\ \hline \end{array} \middle/ \begin{array}{l} c \in \Sigma_2 \\ r_3 \in \delta(r_3,r_3,c) \end{array} \right\}$$

$$\theta_{C_2} = \left\{ \begin{array}{|c|c|} \hline (\#,q_0) & (c,r_3) \\ \hline (\#,q_0) & (\#,q_0) \\ \hline \end{array} \middle/ \begin{array}{l} c \in \Sigma_2 \\ r_3 \in \delta(q,q_0,c) \text{ where } q \in Q_1 \cup Q_2 \end{array} \right\}$$

$$\theta_{C_3} = \left\{ \begin{array}{|c|c|} \hline (c,r_3) & (c,r_3) \\ \hline (\#,q_0) & (\#,q_0) \\ \hline \end{array} \middle/ \begin{array}{l} c \in \Sigma_2 \\ r_3 \in \delta(q,r_3,c) \text{ where } q \in Q_1 \cup Q_2 \end{array} \right\}$$

$$\theta_{C_4} = \left\{ \begin{array}{|c|c|} \hline (\#,q_0) & (c,r_3) \\ \hline (\#,q_0) & (c,r_3) \\ \hline \end{array} \middle/ \begin{array}{l} c \in \Sigma_2 \\ r_3 \in \delta(r_3,q_0,c) \end{array} \right\}$$

$$\theta_{C_5} = \left\{ \begin{array}{|c|c|} \hline (c,r_3) & (1,q_p) \\ \hline (\#,q_0) & (\#,q_0) \\ \hline \end{array} \middle/ \begin{array}{l} c \in \Sigma_2 \\ q_p \in \delta(q,r_3,1) \text{ where } q \in Q_1 \cup Q_2 \end{array} \right\}$$

$$\theta_{C_6} = \left\{ \begin{array}{|c|c|} \hline (\#,q_0) & (1,q_p) \\ \hline (\#,q_0) & (c,r_3) \\ \hline \end{array} \middle/ \begin{array}{l} c \in \Sigma_2 \\ r_3 \in \delta(q_p,q_0,c) \end{array} \right\}$$

$$\theta_{C_7} = \left\{ \begin{array}{|c|c|} \hline (c,r_3) & (1,q_p) \\ \hline (c,r_3) & (c,r_3) \\ \hline \end{array} \middle/ \begin{array}{l} c \in \Sigma_2 \\ r_3 \in \delta(q_p,r_3,c) \end{array} \right\}$$

$$\theta_{C_8} = \left\{ \begin{array}{|c|c|} \hline (c,r_3) & (1,q_p) \\ \hline (c,r_3) & (1,q_p) \\ \hline \end{array} \middle/ \begin{array}{l} c \in \Sigma_2 \\ q_p \in \delta(q_p,r_3,1) \end{array} \right\}$$

$$\theta_{C_9} = \left\{ \begin{array}{|c|c|} \hline (1,q_p) & (1,q_p) \\ \hline (c,r_3) & (c,r_3) \\ \hline \end{array} \middle/ \begin{array}{l} c \in \Sigma_2 \\ r_3 \in \delta(q_p,r_3,c) \end{array} \right\}$$

$$\theta_{C_{10}} = \left\{ \begin{array}{|c|c|} \hline (1,q_p) & (1,q_p) \\ \hline (c,r_3) & (1,q_p) \\ \hline \end{array} \middle/ \begin{array}{l} c \in \Sigma_2 \\ q_p \in \delta(q_p,r_3,1) \end{array} \right\}$$

Let $\theta_C = \bigcup_{i=1}^{10} \theta_{C_i}$

For the transitions of the 2DPOTA corresponding to the region D, we define

$$\theta_{D_1} = \left\{ \begin{array}{|c|c|} \hline (d,r_4) & (d,r_4) \\ \hline (d,r_4) & (d,r_4) \\ \hline \end{array} \middle/ \begin{array}{l} d \in \Sigma_2 \\ r_4 \in \delta(r_4,r_4,d) \end{array} \right\}$$

$$\theta_{D_2} = \left\{ \begin{array}{|c|c|} \hline (d,r_4) & (\#,q_0) \\ \hline (\#,q_0) & (\#,q_0) \\ \hline \end{array} \middle/ \begin{array}{l} d \in \Sigma_2 \\ r_4 \in \delta(q_1,q_2,d) \text{ where } q_1,q_2 \in Q_1 \cup Q_2 \end{array} \right\}$$

$$\theta_{D_3} = \left\{ \begin{array}{|c|c|} \hline (d,r_4) & (\#,q_0) \\ \hline (d,r_4) & (\#,q_0) \\ \hline \end{array} \middle/ \begin{array}{l} d \in \Sigma_2 \\ r_4 \in \delta(r_4,q,d) \text{ where } q \in Q_1 \cup Q_2 \end{array} \right\}$$

$$\theta_{D_4} = \left\{ \begin{array}{|c|c|} \hline (d,r_4) & (d,r_4) \\ \hline (\#,q_0) & (\#,q_0) \\ \hline \end{array} \middle/ \begin{array}{l} d \in \Sigma_2 \\ r_4 \in \delta(q,r_4,d) \text{ where } q \in Q_1 \cup Q_2 \end{array} \right\}$$

$$\theta_{D_5} = \left\{ \begin{array}{|c|c|} \hline (1,q_p) & (d,r_4) \\ \hline (\#,q_0) & (\#,q_0) \\ \hline \end{array} \middle/ \begin{array}{l} d \in \Sigma_2 \\ r_4 \in \delta(q,q_p,d) \text{ where } q \in Q_1 \cup Q_2 \end{array} \right\}$$

$$\theta_{D_6} = \left\{ \begin{array}{|c|c|} \hline (1,q_p) & (\#,q_0) \\ \hline (d,r_4) & (\#,q_0) \\ \hline \end{array} \middle/ \begin{array}{l} d \in \Sigma_2 \\ r_4 \in \delta(q_p,q,d) \text{ where } q \in Q_1 \cup Q_2 \end{array} \right\}$$

$$\theta_{D_7} = \left\{ \begin{array}{|c|c|} \hline (1,q_p) & (d,r_4) \\ \hline (d,r_4) & (d,r_4) \\ \hline \end{array} \middle/ \begin{array}{l} d \in \Sigma_2 \\ r_4 \in \delta(r_4,r_4,d) \end{array} \right\}$$

$$\theta_{D_8} = \left\{ \begin{array}{|c|c|} \hline (1,q_p) & (d,r_4) \\ \hline (1,q_p) & (d,r_4) \\ \hline \end{array} \middle/ \begin{array}{l} d \in \Sigma_2 \\ r_4 \in \delta(r_4,q_p,d) \end{array} \right\}$$

$$\theta_{D_9} = \left\{ \begin{array}{|c|c|} \hline (1,q_p) & (1,q_p) \\ \hline (d,r_4) & (d,r_4) \\ \hline \end{array} \middle/ \begin{array}{l} d \in \Sigma_2 \\ r_4 \in \delta(q_p,r_4,d) \end{array} \right\}$$

$$\theta_{D_{10}} = \left\{ \begin{array}{|c|c|} \hline (1,q_p) & (1,q_p) \\ \hline (1,q_p) & (d,r_4) \\ \hline \end{array} \middle/ \begin{array}{l} d \in \Sigma_2 \\ r_4 \in \delta(q_p,q_p,d) \end{array} \right\}$$

Let $\theta_D = \bigcup_{i=1}^{10} \theta_{D_i}$

For the transitions of the 2DPOTA corresponding to the polyomino region R, we define

$$\theta_{R_1} = \left\{ \begin{array}{|c|c|} \hline (\#,q_0) & (\#,q_0) \\ \hline (\#,q_0) & (1,q_p) \\ \hline \end{array} \middle/ \begin{array}{l} 1 \in \Sigma_1 \\ q_p \in \delta(q_0,q_0,1) \end{array} \right\}$$

$$\theta_{R_2} = \left\{ \begin{array}{|c|c|} \hline (\#,q_0) & (\#,q_0) \\ \hline (1,q_p) & (\#,q_0) \\ \hline \end{array} \middle/ \begin{array}{l} 1 \in \Sigma_1 \\ q_p \in \delta(q_0,q,1) \text{ where } q \in Q_1 \cup Q_2 \end{array} \right\}$$

$$\theta_{R_3} = \left\{ \begin{array}{|c|c|} \hline (\#,q_0) & (1,q_p) \\ \hline (\#,q_0) & (\#,q_0) \\ \hline \end{array} \middle/ \begin{array}{l} 1 \in \Sigma_1 \\ q_p \in \delta(q,q_0,1) \text{ where } q \in Q_1 \cup Q_2 \end{array} \right\}$$

$$\theta_{R_4} = \left\{ \begin{array}{|c|c|} \hline (1,q_p) & (\#,q_0) \\ \hline (\#,q_0) & (\#,q_0) \\ \hline \end{array} \middle/ \begin{array}{l} 1 \in \Sigma_1 \\ q_p \in \delta(q_1,q_2,1) \text{ where } q_1,q_2 \in Q_1 \cup Q_2 \end{array} \right\}$$

$$\theta_{R_5} = \left\{ \begin{array}{|c|c|} \hline (\#,q_0) & (\#,q_0) \\ \hline (1,q_p) & (1,q_p) \\ \hline \end{array} \middle/ \begin{array}{l} 1 \in \Sigma_1 \\ q_p \in \delta(q_0,q_p,1) \end{array} \right\}$$

$$\theta_{R_6} = \left\{ \begin{array}{|c|c|} \hline (\#,q_0) & (1,q_p) \\ \hline (\#,q_0) & (1,q_p) \\ \hline \end{array} \middle/ \begin{array}{l} 1 \in \Sigma_1 \\ q_p \in \delta(q_p,q_0,1) \end{array} \right\}$$

$$\theta_{R_7} = \left\{ \begin{array}{|c|c|} \hline (1,q_p) & (\#,q_0) \\ \hline (1,q_p) & (\#,q_0) \\ \hline \end{array} \middle/ \begin{array}{l} 1 \in \Sigma_1 \\ q_p \in \delta(q_p,q,1) \text{ where } q \in Q_1 \cup Q_2 \end{array} \right\}$$

$$\theta_{R_8} = \left\{ \begin{array}{|c|c|} \hline (1,q_p) & (1,q_p) \\ \hline (\#,q_0) & (\#,q_0) \\ \hline \end{array} \middle/ \begin{array}{l} 1 \in \Sigma_1 \\ q_p \in \delta(q,q_p,1) \text{ where } q \in Q_1 \cup Q_2 \end{array} \right\}$$

$$\theta_{R_9} = \left\{ \begin{array}{|c|c|} \hline (1,q_p) & (1,q_p) \\ \hline (1,q_p) & (1,q_p) \\ \hline \end{array} \middle/ \begin{array}{l} 1 \in \Sigma_1 \\ q_p \in \delta(q_p,q_p,1) \text{ where } q \in Q_1 \cup Q_2 \end{array} \right\}$$

Let $\theta_R = \bigcup_{i=1}^{9} \theta_{R_i}$

Define $\theta = \theta_A \cup \theta_B \cup \theta_C \cup \theta_D \cup \theta_R$.

If L' is the local polyomino language represented by the set θ of tiles, then it is easy to verify that $\pi(L') = L$. Hence L is the polyomino language recognizable by a tiling system.

Lemma 2. *If a polyomino language is recognizable by a polyomino tiling system then it is recognizable by two-dimensional polyomino online tessellation automaton (2DPOTA).*

Proof. Let $L \subseteq \Sigma^{**}$ be a polyomino language recognized by a polyomino tiling system $(\Sigma, \Gamma, \theta, \pi)$ and L' be a local polyomino language represented by the set θ of tiles, then $\pi(L') = L$. It suffices to show that there exists a 2DPOTA recognizing $L' \subseteq \Gamma^{**}$.

Lemma 3. *If L is a local polyomino language then it is recognizable by a 2DPOTA.*

Proof. Let $L \subseteq \Sigma^{**}$ be a local polyomino language. Then $L = L(\theta)$, where θ is the set of tiles over $\Sigma \cup \{\#\}$. We construct a 2DPOTA as follows:
$\mathcal{A} = (\Sigma, Q_1, Q_2, I, F, \delta)$ where $\theta = Q_1 \cup Q_2$.

$$I = \left\{ \begin{smallmatrix} \# & \# \\ \# & a \end{smallmatrix}, \begin{smallmatrix} \# & \# \\ \# & 1 \end{smallmatrix} \middle/ \begin{matrix} 1 \in \Sigma_1 \\ a \in \Sigma_2 \end{matrix} \right\}, \quad F = \left\{ \begin{smallmatrix} a & \# \\ \# & \# \end{smallmatrix}, \begin{smallmatrix} 1 & \# \\ \# & \# \end{smallmatrix} \middle/ \begin{matrix} 1 \in \Sigma_1 \\ a \in \Sigma_2 \end{matrix} \right\}$$

The transition $\delta : (Q_1 \cup Q_2) \times (Q_1 \cup Q_2) \times \Sigma \to Q_1 \cup Q_2(2^{Q_1 \cup Q_2})$ is defined in a way that the run of $\mathcal{A}$ over $\widehat{R(p)}$ (where p is a polyomino) simulates a tiling of $R(p)$ by elements of $Q_1 \cup Q_2 = \theta$ given as follows: Given a polyomino p with $R(p) \in L(\theta)$, for each symbol 'a' in the $(i,j)^{th}$ position of $R(p)$, where $a \in \Sigma$, we first find two symbols α, β of $\Sigma \cup \{\#\}$ in $\widehat{R(p)}$ associated with 'a' using the following diagram.

Let us consider the following cases:

Case (i)a: If $a \in \Sigma$ and $\alpha = \beta = \#$ then

$(1)\ \delta\left(\begin{smallmatrix} \# & \# \\ \# & a \end{smallmatrix}, \begin{smallmatrix} \# & a \\ \# & a \end{smallmatrix}, a \right) = \begin{smallmatrix} a & a \\ a & a \end{smallmatrix}$
$\qquad (2)\ \delta\left(\begin{smallmatrix} \# & \# \\ \# & a \end{smallmatrix}, \begin{smallmatrix} \# & a \\ \# & 1 \end{smallmatrix}, a \right) = \begin{smallmatrix} a & a \\ 1 & 1 \end{smallmatrix}$

$(3)\ \delta\left(\begin{smallmatrix} \# & \# \\ \# & a \end{smallmatrix}, \begin{smallmatrix} \# & a \\ \# & a \end{smallmatrix}, a \right) = \begin{smallmatrix} a & a \\ a & 1 \end{smallmatrix}$
$\qquad (4)\ \delta\left(\begin{smallmatrix} \# & \# \\ \# & a \end{smallmatrix}, \begin{smallmatrix} \# & a \\ \# & a \end{smallmatrix}, a \right) = \begin{smallmatrix} a & 1 \\ a & 1 \end{smallmatrix}$

$(5)\ \delta\left(\begin{smallmatrix} \# & \# \\ \# & a \end{smallmatrix}, \begin{smallmatrix} \# & a \\ \# & 1 \end{smallmatrix}, a \right) = \begin{smallmatrix} a & 1 \\ 1 & 1 \end{smallmatrix}$

Case (i)b: If $a = 1$ and $\alpha = \beta = \#$

$(1)\ \delta\left(\begin{smallmatrix} \# & \# \\ \# & 1 \end{smallmatrix}, \begin{smallmatrix} \# & 1 \\ \# & 1 \end{smallmatrix}, 1 \right) = \begin{smallmatrix} 1 & 1 \\ 1 & 1 \end{smallmatrix}$
$\qquad (2)\ \delta\left(\begin{smallmatrix} \# & \# \\ \# & 1 \end{smallmatrix}, \begin{smallmatrix} \# & 1 \\ \# & 1 \end{smallmatrix}, 1 \right) = \begin{smallmatrix} 1 & b \\ 1 & b \end{smallmatrix}$

$(3)\ \delta\left(\begin{smallmatrix} \# & \# \\ \# & 1 \end{smallmatrix}, \begin{smallmatrix} \# & 1 \\ \# & 1 \end{smallmatrix}, 1 \right) = \begin{smallmatrix} 1 & b \\ 1 & 1 \end{smallmatrix}$

Case (ii)a: If $a \in \Sigma$ and $\alpha = \#, \beta \neq \#$

$(1)\ \delta\left(\begin{smallmatrix} \# & \# \\ a & a \end{smallmatrix}, \begin{smallmatrix} a & a \\ a & a \end{smallmatrix}, a \right) = \begin{smallmatrix} a & a \\ a & a \end{smallmatrix}$
$\qquad (2)\ \delta\left(\begin{smallmatrix} \# & \# \\ a & a \end{smallmatrix}, \begin{smallmatrix} a & a \\ a & a \end{smallmatrix}, a \right) = \begin{smallmatrix} a & 1 \\ a & 1 \end{smallmatrix}$

$(3)\ \delta\left(\begin{smallmatrix} \# & \# \\ a & a \end{smallmatrix}, \begin{smallmatrix} a & a \\ 1 & 1 \end{smallmatrix}, a \right) = \begin{smallmatrix} a & a \\ 1 & 1 \end{smallmatrix}$
$\qquad (4)\ \delta\left(\begin{smallmatrix} \# & \# \\ a & a \end{smallmatrix}, \begin{smallmatrix} a & a \\ 1 & 1 \end{smallmatrix}, a \right) = \begin{smallmatrix} a & 1 \\ 1 & 1 \end{smallmatrix}$

$(5)\ \delta\left(\begin{smallmatrix} \# & \# \\ a & a \end{smallmatrix}, \begin{smallmatrix} a & a \\ a & a \end{smallmatrix}, a \right) = \begin{smallmatrix} a & a \\ a & 1 \end{smallmatrix}$
$\qquad (6)\ \delta\left(\begin{smallmatrix} \# & \# \\ a & 1 \end{smallmatrix}, \begin{smallmatrix} a & 1 \\ a & 1 \end{smallmatrix}, 1 \right) = \begin{smallmatrix} 1 & 1 \\ 1 & 1 \end{smallmatrix}$

$(7)\ \delta\left(\begin{smallmatrix} \# & \# \\ a & 1 \end{smallmatrix}, \begin{smallmatrix} a & 1 \\ 1 & 1 \end{smallmatrix}, 1 \right) = \begin{smallmatrix} 1 & 1 \\ 1 & 1 \end{smallmatrix}$
$\qquad (8)\ \delta\left(\begin{smallmatrix} \# & \# \\ 1 & 1 \end{smallmatrix}, \begin{smallmatrix} 1 & 1 \\ 1 & 1 \end{smallmatrix}, 1 \right) = \begin{smallmatrix} 1 & 1 \\ 1 & 1 \end{smallmatrix}$

(9) $\delta\left(\begin{bmatrix}\# & \#\\ 1 & 1\end{bmatrix}, \begin{bmatrix}1 & 1\\ 1 & 1\end{bmatrix}, 1\right) = \begin{bmatrix}1 & b\\ 1 & 1\end{bmatrix}$

(10) $\delta\left(\begin{bmatrix}\# & \#\\ 1 & 1\end{bmatrix}, \begin{bmatrix}1 & 1\\ 1 & 1\end{bmatrix}, 1\right) = \begin{bmatrix}1 & b\\ 1 & b\end{bmatrix}$

(11) $\delta\left(\begin{bmatrix}\# & \#\\ 1 & b\end{bmatrix}, \begin{bmatrix}1 & b\\ 1 & 1\end{bmatrix}, b\right) = \begin{bmatrix}b & b\\ 1 & 1\end{bmatrix}$

(12) $\delta\left(\begin{bmatrix}\# & \#\\ 1 & b\end{bmatrix}, \begin{bmatrix}1 & b\\ 1 & 1\end{bmatrix}, b\right) = \begin{bmatrix}b & b\\ 1 & b\end{bmatrix}$

(13) $\delta\left(\begin{bmatrix}\# & \#\\ 1 & b\end{bmatrix}, \begin{bmatrix}1 & b\\ 1 & b\end{bmatrix}, b\right) = \begin{bmatrix}b & b\\ b & b\end{bmatrix}$

(14) $\delta\left(\begin{bmatrix}\# & \#\\ b & b\end{bmatrix}, \begin{bmatrix}b & b\\ b & b\end{bmatrix}, b\right) = \begin{bmatrix}b & b\\ b & b\end{bmatrix}$

(15) $\delta\left(\begin{bmatrix}\# & \#\\ b & b\end{bmatrix}, \begin{bmatrix}b & b\\ 1 & 1\end{bmatrix}, b\right) = \begin{bmatrix}b & b\\ 1 & 1\end{bmatrix}$

(16) $\delta\left(\begin{bmatrix}\# & \#\\ b & b\end{bmatrix}, \begin{bmatrix}b & b\\ 1 & 1\end{bmatrix}, b\right) = \begin{bmatrix}b & b\\ 1 & b\end{bmatrix}$

(17) $\delta\left(\begin{bmatrix}\# & \#\\ 1 & 1\end{bmatrix}, \begin{bmatrix}1 & 1\\ 1 & 1\end{bmatrix}, 1\right) = \begin{bmatrix}1 & \#\\ 1 & \#\end{bmatrix}$

(18) $\delta\left(\begin{bmatrix}\# & \#\\ 1 & 1\end{bmatrix}, \begin{bmatrix}1 & 1\\ d & d\end{bmatrix}, 1\right) = \begin{bmatrix}1 & \#\\ d & \#\end{bmatrix}$

(19) $\delta\left(\begin{bmatrix}\# & \#\\ 1 & 1\end{bmatrix}, \begin{bmatrix}1 & 1\\ 1 & d\end{bmatrix}, 1\right) = \begin{bmatrix}1 & \#\\ d & \#\end{bmatrix}$

(20) $\delta\left(\begin{bmatrix}\# & \#\\ b & b\end{bmatrix}, \begin{bmatrix}b & b\\ b & b\end{bmatrix}, b\right) = \begin{bmatrix}b & \#\\ b & \#\end{bmatrix}$

(21) $\delta\left(\begin{bmatrix}\# & \#\\ b & b\end{bmatrix}, \begin{bmatrix}b & b\\ 1 & b\end{bmatrix}, b\right) = \begin{bmatrix}b & \#\\ b & \#\end{bmatrix}$

(22) $\delta\left(\begin{bmatrix}\# & \#\\ b & b\end{bmatrix}, \begin{bmatrix}b & b\\ 1 & b\end{bmatrix}, b\right) = \begin{bmatrix}b & b\\ b & b\end{bmatrix}$

(23) $\delta\left(\begin{bmatrix}\# & \#\\ 1 & b\end{bmatrix}, \begin{bmatrix}1 & b\\ 1 & 1\end{bmatrix}, b\right) = \begin{bmatrix}b & \#\\ 1 & \#\end{bmatrix}$

(24) $\delta\left(\begin{bmatrix}\# & \#\\ 1 & b\end{bmatrix}, \begin{bmatrix}1 & b\\ 1 & b\end{bmatrix}, b\right) = \begin{bmatrix}b & \#\\ b & \#\end{bmatrix}$

Case (ii)b: If $a \in \Sigma$ and $\alpha \neq \#$, $\beta = \#$

(1) $\delta\left(\begin{bmatrix}\# & a\\ \# & a\end{bmatrix}, \begin{bmatrix}\# & a\\ \# & a\end{bmatrix}, a\right) = \begin{bmatrix}a & a\\ a & a\end{bmatrix}$

(2) $\delta\left(\begin{bmatrix}\# & a\\ \# & a\end{bmatrix}, \begin{bmatrix}\# & a\\ \# & a\end{bmatrix}, a\right) = \begin{bmatrix}a & a\\ a & 1\end{bmatrix}$

(3) $\delta\left(\begin{bmatrix}\# & a\\ \# & a\end{bmatrix}, \begin{bmatrix}\# & a\\ \# & a\end{bmatrix}, a\right) = \begin{bmatrix}a & 1\\ a & 1\end{bmatrix}$

(4) $\delta\left(\begin{bmatrix}\# & a\\ \# & 1\end{bmatrix}, \begin{bmatrix}\# & 1\\ \# & 1\end{bmatrix}, 1\right) = \begin{bmatrix}1 & 1\\ 1 & 1\end{bmatrix}$

(5) $\delta\left(\begin{bmatrix}\# & a\\ \# & a\end{bmatrix}, \begin{bmatrix}\# & a\\ \# & 1\end{bmatrix}, a\right) = \begin{bmatrix}a & a\\ 1 & 1\end{bmatrix}$

(6) $\delta\left(\begin{bmatrix}\# & a\\ \# & a\end{bmatrix}, \begin{bmatrix}\# & a\\ \# & 1\end{bmatrix}, a\right) = \begin{bmatrix}a & 1\\ 1 & 1\end{bmatrix}$

(7) $\delta\left(\begin{bmatrix}\# & 1\\ \# & 1\end{bmatrix}, \begin{bmatrix}\# & 1\\ \# & 1\end{bmatrix}, 1\right) = \begin{bmatrix}1 & 1\\ 1 & 1\end{bmatrix}$

(8) $\delta\left(\begin{bmatrix}\# & 1\\ \# & 1\end{bmatrix}, \begin{bmatrix}\# & 1\\ \# & c\end{bmatrix}, 1\right) = \begin{bmatrix}1 & 1\\ c & 1\end{bmatrix}$

(9) $\delta\left(\begin{bmatrix}\# & c\\ \# & c\end{bmatrix}, \begin{bmatrix}\# & c\\ \# & c\end{bmatrix}, c\right) = \begin{bmatrix}c & 1\\ c & c\end{bmatrix}$

(10) $\delta\left(\begin{bmatrix}\# & c\\ \# & c\end{bmatrix}, \begin{bmatrix}\# & c\\ \# & c\end{bmatrix}, c\right) = \begin{bmatrix}c & c\\ c & c\end{bmatrix}$

(11) $\delta\left(\begin{bmatrix}\# & c\\ \# & c\end{bmatrix}, \begin{bmatrix}\# & c\\ \# & \#\end{bmatrix}, c\right) = \begin{bmatrix}c & c\\ \# & \#\end{bmatrix}$

(12) $\delta\left(\begin{bmatrix}\# & c\\ \# & c\end{bmatrix}, \begin{bmatrix}\# & c\\ \# & \#\end{bmatrix}, c\right) = \begin{bmatrix}c & 1\\ \# & \#\end{bmatrix}$

(13) $\delta\left(\begin{bmatrix}\# & c\\ \# & c\end{bmatrix}, \begin{bmatrix}\# & c\\ \# & c\end{bmatrix}, c\right) = \begin{bmatrix}c & 1\\ c & 1\end{bmatrix}$

(14) $\delta\left(\begin{bmatrix}\# & 1\\ \# & c\end{bmatrix}, \begin{bmatrix}\# & c\\ \# & \#\end{bmatrix}, c\right) = \begin{bmatrix}c & c\\ \# & \#\end{bmatrix}$

(15) $\delta\left(\begin{bmatrix}\# & 1\\ \# & c\end{bmatrix}, \begin{bmatrix}\# & c\\ \# & \#\end{bmatrix}, c\right) = \begin{bmatrix}c & 1\\ \# & \#\end{bmatrix}$

(16) $\delta\left(\begin{bmatrix}\# & 1\\ \# & c\end{bmatrix}, \begin{bmatrix}\# & c\\ \# & c\end{bmatrix}, c\right) = \begin{bmatrix}c & 1\\ c & 1\end{bmatrix}$

$$(17)\ \delta\left(\begin{array}{|c|c|}\hline \# & 1\\\hline \# & c\\\hline\end{array},\begin{array}{|c|c|}\hline \# & c\\\hline \# & c\\\hline\end{array},c\right)=\begin{array}{|c|c|}\hline c & c\\\hline c & c\\\hline\end{array}$$

$$(18)\ \delta\left(\begin{array}{|c|c|}\hline \# & 1\\\hline \# & c\\\hline\end{array},\begin{array}{|c|c|}\hline \# & c\\\hline \# & c\\\hline\end{array},c\right)=\begin{array}{|c|c|}\hline c & 1\\\hline c & c\\\hline\end{array}$$

$$(19)\ \delta\left(\begin{array}{|c|c|}\hline \# & 1\\\hline \# & 1\\\hline\end{array},\begin{array}{|c|c|}\hline \# & 1\\\hline \# & c\\\hline\end{array},1\right)=\begin{array}{|c|c|}\hline 1 & 1\\\hline c & c\\\hline\end{array}$$

$$(20)\ \delta\left(\begin{array}{|c|c|}\hline \# & 1\\\hline \# & 1\\\hline\end{array},\begin{array}{|c|c|}\hline \# & 1\\\hline \# & \#\\\hline\end{array},1\right)=\begin{array}{|c|c|}\hline 1 & 1\\\hline \# & \#\\\hline\end{array}$$

Similarly we can do for the other combinations such as (i) $a = 1, \alpha = \#, \beta \neq \#$, (ii) If $a = 1, \alpha \neq \#, \beta = \#$, (iii) $\alpha \neq \#, \beta \neq \#, a = 1$, (iv) $\alpha \neq \#, \beta \neq \#, a \in \Sigma$. It can be easily verified that $L = L(\mathcal{A})$.

4   Domino Recognizability of Polyominoes

It is proved that various classes of convex polyominoes are both tiling and Wang recognizable [2,3]. In this section we prove the recognizability of classes of convex polyominoes by means of domino systems.

We are able to encode DS, the set of domino systems that represent $\mathcal{L}_c$ the class of languages as follows:

For each of the tiles of the region A, we have the corresponding set of hv-dominoes $\Delta_A = \left\{\begin{array}{|c|}\hline \#\\\hline a\\\hline\end{array},\begin{array}{|c|}\hline a\\\hline a\\\hline\end{array},\begin{array}{|c|}\hline a\\\hline 1\\\hline\end{array},\begin{array}{|c|c|}\hline a & a\\\hline\end{array},\begin{array}{|c|c|}\hline \# & a\\\hline\end{array},\begin{array}{|c|c|}\hline a & 1\\\hline\end{array},\dots\right\}$.

Similarly we construct the dominoes for the regions B, C, D and R respectively as $\Delta_B, \Delta_C, \Delta_D$ and Δ_R with $\Delta = \Delta_A \cup \Delta_B \cup \Delta_C \cup \Delta_D \cup \Delta_R$.

Theorem 2. *Let $\mathcal{L}_c = L(\Delta_A \cup \Delta_B \cup \Delta_C \cup \Delta_D \cup \Delta_R)$ be the local language over the alphabet $\Sigma_c = \{1, a, b, c, d\}$. Then the classes $\mathcal{F}, P, S, D$ are domino recognizable.*

Theorem 3. *The classes of polyomino languages recognizable by the tiling, Wang, domino systems and 2DPOTA all coincide.*

References

1. Blum, M., Hewitt, C.: Automata on a 2-dimensional tape. In: IEEE Symposium on Switching and Automata Theory, pp. 155–160 (1967)
2. De Carli, F., Frosini, A., Rinaldi, S., Vuillon, L.: How to construct convex polyominoes on DNA Wang tiles? LAMA report, Lama-Univ. Savoie, France (2009)
3. De Carli, F., Frosini, A., Rinaldi, S., Vuillon, L.: On the tiling system recognizability of various classes of convex polyominoes. Annals of Combinatorics 13, 169–191 (2009)
4. Giammarresi, D., Restivo, A.: Two-dimensional languages. In: Salomaa, A., Rozenberg, G. (eds.) Handbook of Formal Languages, vol. 3, pp. 215–267. Springer, Heidelberg (1997)
5. Castiglione, G., Vaglica, R.: Recognizable picture languages and polyominoes. In: Bozapalidis, S., Rahonis, G. (eds.) CAI 2007. LNCS, vol. 4728, pp. 160–171. Springer, Heidelberg (2007)
6. Inoue, K., Nakamura, A.: Some properties of two-dimensional on-line tessellation acceptors. Information Sciences 13, 95–121 (1977)
7. Latteux, M., Simplot, D.: Recognizable picture languages and domino tiling. Theoretical Computer Science 178, 275–283 (1997)

A New Method for Generation of Three-Dimensional Cubes

R. Arumugham[1], K. Thirusangu[2], and D.G. Thomas[3]

[1] Department of Mathematics, Tagore Engineering College
Chennai - 600048
`arumugham50@gmail.com`
[2] Department of Mathematics, SIVET College
Gowrivakkam, Chennai - 600073
`ktsangu@yahoo.com`
[3] Department of Mathematics, Madras Christian College
Tambaram, Chennai - 600059
`dgthomasmcc@yahoo.com`

Abstract. A chain code for representing three-dimensional (3D) curves was defined in [3]. In this paper we make use of Petri nets to generate a collection of three-dimensional graphs which yield three-dimensional cubes.

Keywords: chain code, Petri net, reachability tree, 3D pictures.

1 Introduction

Shape-of-object representation has always been an important topic in computer vision. The work deals with representation of shape based on a new boundary chain code introduced in [3]. Chain-code techniques are widely used because they preserve information and allow considerable data reduction. The first approach for representing digital curves using chain code was introduced by Freeman in [4].

Freeman [5] states that "in general, a coding scheme for line structures must satisfy three objectives: (1) it must faithfully preserve the information of interest; (2) it must permit compact storage and be convenient for display; and (3) it must facilitate any required processing. The three objectives are somewhat in conflict with each other, and any code necessarily involves a compromise among them". Bribiesca presented a chain code for representing 3D discrete curves. Discrete curves are composed of constant straight line segments, two contiguous straight line segments define a direction change and two direction changes define a chain element. There are only five possible orthogonal direction changes for representing any 3D discrete curve. This chain code only considers relative direction changes which allows us to have a curve description invariant under translation and rotation. Also, it may be a starting point normalized and invariant under mirroring transformation.

R.P. Barneva et al. (Eds.): CompIMAGE 2010, LNCS 6026, pp. 119–129, 2010.
© Springer-Verlag Berlin Heidelberg 2010

On the other hand we make use of Petri nets which generate a collection of graphs. Petri nets are graphical and mathematical models applicable to many systems. Various areas of applications of Petri nets include modeling and analysis of the distributed systems, parallel systems, formal languages and automata, learning theory and graph theory [6,7]. Interesting connections between Petri nets and graphs have been studied in the literature [1]. In a graphical representation of a Petri net the places are represented by circles and transitions are represented by boxes or bars. A marking of a Petri net is the distribution of tokens in the places of the Petri nets. The firing of an enabled transition will change the markings in a Petri net. A sequence of firing of transitions will result in a sequence of markings. This sequence of markings and the corresponding sequence of transitions fired can be represented by a graph. Thus a Petri net with initial markings yields a collection of graphs, which we call as a graph language associated with a Petri net (GLPN).

In this paper we construct a Petri net which generates a collection of graphs whose GLPN is a 3D picture language of cubes.

2   Basic Concepts and Definitions

In this section we give basic concepts and notions relevant to 3D discrete curves [3] and Petri nets [7].

Bribiesca introduced a new chain code model consisting of five possible direction changes for representing any 3D discrete curves which indicate relative direction changes in three dimensions [2,3]. The use of relative direction change allow to consider curve descriptions invariant under translation and rotation, and optimally under mirroring transformation [3]. These discrete curves are described by only five relative (orthogonal) direction changes which are shown in Figure 1.

The element labeled 0 represents the direction change which goes straight through the contiguous straight line segments following the direction of the last segment; the element labeled 1 represents a direction change to the right; the element labeled 2 represents a direction change upward (staircase fashion); the element labeled 3 represents a direction change to the left; and finally the element labeled 4 indicates a direction change of going back. The chain of a curve is a sequence of relative direction change calculated around the curve. Figure 2(A)

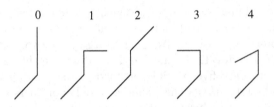

Fig. 1. Relative direction changes

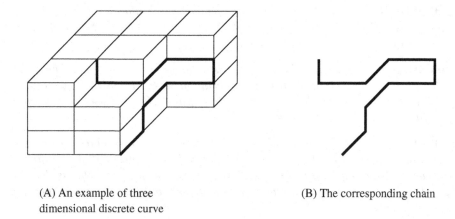

(A) An example of three
dimensional discrete curve

(B) The corresponding chain

Fig. 2. Discrete curve and corresponding chain

shows an example of three-dimensional discrete curve and Figure 2(B) shows the corresponding chain.

Definition 1. *An element a_i of a chain indicates the orthogonal direction changes of the contiguous straight line segments of the discrete curve in that element position.*

There are only five possible direction changes for representing any 3D discrete curve, which indicate relative direction changes, such as shape numbers, but specified in three dimensions. Freeman chains [5] use absolute directions for representing discrete curves.

Definition 2. *A chain A is an ordered sequence of elements, and is represented by*

$$A = a_1 a_2 \ldots a_n = \{a_i : 1 \leq i \leq n\}, \tag{1}$$

where n indicates the number of chain elements.

Definition 3. *The length L of a chain is the sum of the length of its elements, i.e., L may be expressed as*

$$L = (n+2)l, \tag{2}$$

where l is the length of each straight line segment, which is considered equal to one.

We now turn our attention to Petri nets.

Definition 4. *A Petri net $N = (P, T, F, W)$ is given by a finite set of places $P = \{p_1, \ldots, p_n\}$, a finite set of transitions $T = \{t_1, t_2, \ldots, t_k\}$ disjoint from P, a flow relation $F \subseteq (P \times T) \cup (T \times P)$ and weight function $W : F \to N_0$, where N_0 denotes the set of nonnegative integers.*

Definition 5. *Let $X = P \cup T$. For an element $x \in X$ the set ${}^\bullet x = \{v|(v, x) \in F\}$ is the set of input elements of x and $x^\bullet = \{u|(x, u) \in F\}$ is the set of output elements of x.*

Definition 6. *A marking of a Petri net is a function $m : P \rightarrow N_0$. The global state of a Petri net is represented by a marking $m \in N_0^n$. By $m(p)$ we denote the number of tokens of the place p in the marking $m \in N_0^n$. We use m_0 to denote the initial marking of a Petri net.*

Definition 7. *The dynamic behavior of a Petri net is represented by firing of transitions. A transition $t \in T$ of a Petri net N has a concession or can fire or is enabled at the marking m if $m(p) \geq W(p, t)$ for all $p \in {}^\bullet t$. This is denoted by $m[t >$. If t is enabled at the marking m, it fires and leads to a new marking $m' \in N^n$, where*

$$m'(p) = \begin{cases} m(p) - W(p, t) & \text{if } p \in {}^\bullet t \backslash t^\bullet \\ m(p) + W(t, p) & \text{if } p \in t^\bullet \backslash {}^\bullet t \\ m(p) - W(p, t) + W(t, p) & \text{if } p \in {}^\bullet t \cap t^\bullet \\ m(p) & \text{otherwise.} \end{cases}$$

This firing relation is denoted by $m[t > m'$.

Definition 8. *Let β denote a finite sequence of transitions. The firing relation is recursively extended to finite sequence of transitions by $m[\beta t > m' \Rightarrow m[\beta > m''$ and $m''[t > m'$ for all $m \in N^n$ and $t \in T$. The marking m' is said to be reachable from the marking m_0 if $\exists \beta$ such that $m_0[\beta > m'$. The set of all reachable markings from the initial marking m_0 of a Petri net N is denoted by $R(N, m_0)$ or $R(N)$.*

Example 1.   The reachable markings of Figure 3 are

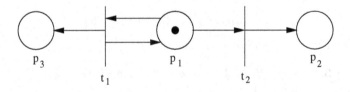

Fig. 3. A Petri net with an infinite reachability set

$M_0 = (1, 0, 0)$
$M_1 = (1, 0, 1)$ since $M_0[t_1 > M_1$
$M_2 = (0, 1, 0)$ as $M_0[t_2 > M_2$ from
M_2 no firing is possible
$M_3 = (1, 0, 2)$ as $M_1[t_1 > M_3$
$M_4 = (0, 1, 1)$ as $M_1[t_2 > M_4$ At M_4 no further firing is possible.
   The reachability set $R(N) = \{(1, 0, n)(0, 1, n)|n \geq 0\}$ is thus an infinite set.

The reachability problem of a Petri net is as follows:

Given a Petri net N with initial marking m_0, whether or not a marking $m' \in R(N)$? These problems have been studied using reachability graphs and there exists algorithms for the construction of reachability tree in the literature.

3 Petri Nets and Three-Dimensional Picture Languages

In this section we define the graph language associated with the Petri net (GLPN) and examine the existence of a Petri net whose GLPN is a three-dimensional picture language.

Definition 9. *Let $N = (P, T, F)$ be a Petri net with initial marking m_0. If $m_1, m_2, \ldots, m_k \in R(N, m_0)$ and $T = \{t_1, t_2, \ldots, t_n\}$ then the reachability graph is defined as $V = \{m_0, m_1, \ldots, m_k, \ldots\}$, $E = \{t_1, t_2, \ldots, t_k\}$, such that the edge $(m_{k-1}, m_k) = t_i$ if $m_{k-1}[t_i > m_k$. The graph language is recursively defined as follows:*

1. $G_1 = (V_1, E_1)$ where $V_1 = \{m_0, m_1\}$ and $E_1 = \{t\}$ if $m_0[t > m_1$.
2. $G_i = G_{i-1} \cup \{V_i, E_i\}$ where $V_i = \{m_{i-1}, m_i\}$ and $E_i = \{t'\}$ if $m_{i-1}[t' > m_i$, where $t, t', t_i \in T$.

This graph language associated with a Petri net N is denoted by GLPN.

Example 2. For the constructed Petri net given in Figure 4, the reachability set is denoted by $R(N, m_0)$ which is a subset of Z^4.
The initial marking is $m_0 : (1, 1, 1, 0)$ and the reachability tree is

$$(1,1,1,0) = m_0$$
$$| \, t_1$$
$$(2,1,0,1) = m_1$$
$$| \, t_2$$
$$(2,2,1,0) = m_2$$
$$| \, t_3$$
$$(3,2,0,1) = m_3$$
$$| \, t_2$$
$$\vdots$$

The reachability graph is given in Figure 5.

Define a projection mapping $\psi(a_1, a_2, a_3, a_4) = (a_1, a_2)$ where $(a_1, a_2, a_3, a_4) = m$ and $(a_1, a_2) = m^{(2)}$. i.e., $\psi(m) = m^{(2)}$. Thus every marking in $R(N, m_0)$ is a 4-tuple and the map ψ transforms every marking in $R(N, m_0)$ into a pair in Z^2 which will be plotted in two-dimensional plane.

We take the first and second coordinates of $m^{(2)}$ as x and y coordinates respectively in the two-dimensional plane. The firing $m_0[t_1 > m_1$ will result one move from $m_0^{(2)}$ to $m_1^{(2)}$ along x-axis only. Similarly $m_1[t_2 > m_2$ will result one move from $m_1^{(2)}$ to $m_2^{(2)}$ along y-axis only. Thus for each firing in the constructed petri net we have one move in Z^2.

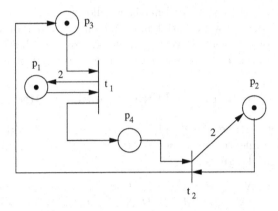

Fig. 4. Constructed Petri net

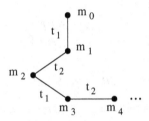

Fig. 5. The reachability graph

The mapping ψ yields a picture as shown in Figure 6.
We have the sequence of firing transitions as $t_1, t_1 t_2, t_1 t_2 t_1, t_1 t_2 t_1 t_2, \ldots$. This corresponds to moves in xoy plane as $r, ru, rur, ruru, \ldots$ respectively, where r stands for right move along x-axis and u stands for upward move along y-axis. Thus we have a picture language whose GLPN is given in Figure 7.

Theorem 1. *There exists a Petri net whose GLPN is a three-dimensional picture language of cubes.*

Proof. We first construct a Petri net. By definition every graph in *GLPN* is obtained by taking the markings of Petri net as vertices and the transitions fired as edges. Since the three-dimensional picture languages are drawn in the space, the required Petri net must have three transitions. We denote them as t_1, t_2 and t_3. In order to enable the transitions the required Petri net has atleast three places p_1, p_2, p_3 and to control the behaviour of the transitions there must be another three places. We call them as p_4, p_5 and p_6.

As p_4 controls t_1, draw an arc from p_4 to t_1 such that p_4 is included in the input of t_1 and to make the Petri net live, two more places p_7 and p_8 and a transition t_4 are introduced. The inputs of t_1 are the places p_1, p_4 and p_7 and the outputs are p_1, p_7 and p_8.

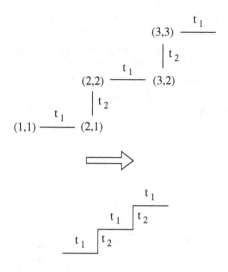

Fig. 6. Regular picture language

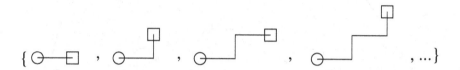

Fig. 7. GLPN of the constructed Petri net

Thus, we have the inputs and outputs for t_1, t_2, t_3 and t_4 as follows:

$$\begin{aligned}
{}^\bullet t_1 &= \{p_1, p_4, p_7\}, & t_1^\bullet &= \{p_1, p_7, p_8\} \\
{}^\bullet t_2 &= \{p_2, p_5, p_7\}, & t_2^\bullet &= \{p_2, p_7, p_8\} \\
{}^\bullet t_3 &= \{p_3, p_6, p_7\}, & t_3^\bullet &= \{p_3, p_7, p_8\} \\
{}^\bullet t_4 &= \{p_8, p_8, p_8\}, & t_4^\bullet &= \{p_4, p_5, p_6\}
\end{aligned}$$

Choose the initial marking m_0 so that t_4 can fire. Now as t_4 fires each of the places p_4, p_5, p_6 gets one token, making p_8 empty. Now, t_1, t_2 and t_3 are enabled for firing, we get the possible combination of sequence of firing as

$$\{t_1 t_2 t_3, t_1 t_3 t_2, t_2 t_1 t_3, t_2 t_3 t_1, t_3 t_1 t_2, t_3 t_2 t_1\}$$

The reachability set $R(N, m_0)$ is a subset of Z^8. We can define the projection map $\psi(m) = m^{(3)} = (a_1, a_2, a_3)$ where $m = (a_1, a_2, a_3, a_4, a_5, a_6, a_7, a_8)$. Thus every marking in $R(N, m_0)$ is a 8-tuple and ψ transforms every marking $R(N, m_0)$ into a triplet in Z^3 which will be plotted in three-dimensional space. We take the first, the second and the third components of $m^{(3)}$ as x, y, z coordinates respectively in three-dimensional space. Thus in the construction of the Petri net, $m_0[t_1 > m_1$ will increase one token in p_1, $m_0[t_2 > m_2$ will increase one token in p_2 and $m_0[t_3 > m_3$ will increase one token in p_3. As p_1, p_2 and p_3 represent x, y and z axes respectively for each firing in the constructed Petri net we have one move in Z^3. Thus by successive possible firings, we get, the sequences and each sequence will coincide with any one of the following sequences: $\{t_1t_2t_3, t_2t_1t_3, t_3t_2t_1\}$ and so on. Thus by connecting these points in space we get a set of graphs which is exactly the $GLPN$ of the constructed Petri net. This $GLPN$ generates the required three-dimensional cubes.

Illustration: We construct a Petri net as shown in Figure 8.

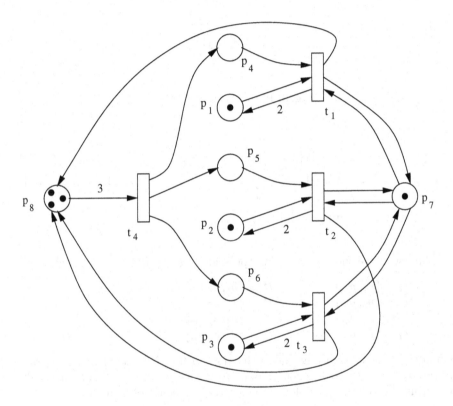

Fig. 8. A constructed Petri net

The reachability tree generated by the above Petri net is exhibited in Figure 9. We can write the sequences of firing obtained by the above reachability tree as:

$$S_1 : t_1t_2t_3, S_2 : t_2t_1t_3 \text{ and } S_3 : t_3t_2t_1$$

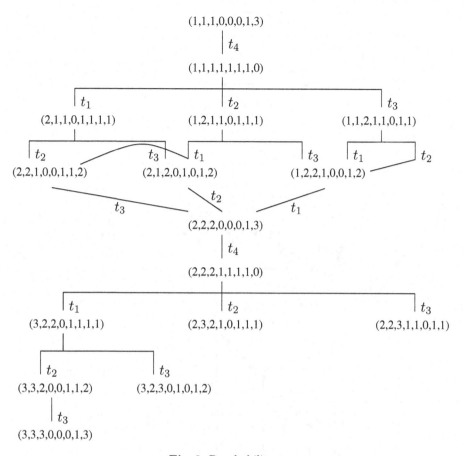

Fig. 9. Reachability tree

These sequences can be treated after ψ projections as follows:

$$
\begin{array}{ccc}
S_1 & S_2 & S_3 \\
(1,1,1) & (1,1,1) & (1,1,1) \\
\Big|\, t_1 & \Big|\, t_2 & \Big|\, t_3 \\
(2,1,1) & (1,2,1) & (1,1,2) \\
\Big|\, t_2 & \Big|\, t_1 & \Big|\, t_2 \\
(2,2,1) & (2,2,1) & (1,2,2) \\
\Big|\, t_3 & \Big|\, t_3 & \Big|\, t_1 \\
(2,2,2) & (2,2,2) & (2,2,2) \\
\cdots & \cdots & \cdots
\end{array}
$$

The corresponding graphs G_1, G_2, G_3 for these sequences S_1, S_2 and S_3 are drawn in Figure 10.

These sequences correspond to the moves in the XYZ space moving to the vertices of a cube.

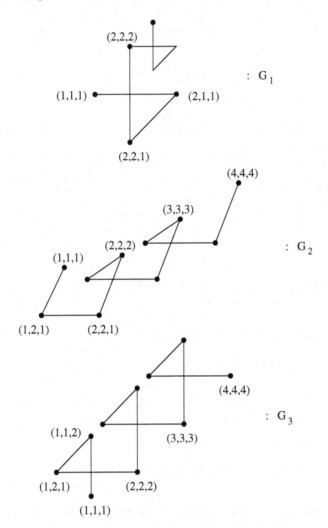

Fig. 10. Sequences of portions of cubes

Thus by connecting these coordinates, we get graphs which is exactly the *GLPN* of the constructed Petri net and this corresponds to the generation of three-dimensional cubes.

4   Conclusion

This paper shows the connection between Petri nets and three-dimensional pictures. We have constructed a Petri net whose *GLPN* is a three-dimensional language of graphs yielding cubes. A Petri net with initial marking generates a reachability tree. The analysis of Petri nets like liveness, deadlock freeness can be studied through the reachability tree. Petri nets has been used in various areas including the modeling of metabolic networks. In particular a test for liveness and deadlock freeness of a Petri net helps us to design whether the metabolic system can attain a situation where it is blocked. Thus the reachability tree is useful to decide a block in metabolic system. We have constructed a Petri net whose reachability tree is projected as a three-dimensional cube. It is worth examining to devise methods to construct shapes of other three-dimensional objects using Petri nets.

References

1. Arumugham, R., Thirusangu, K., David, N.G., Thomas, D.G.: Reachability graphs of Petri nets and graph grammars. Far East Journal of Mathematical Sciences 23(2), 193–200 (2006)
2. Bribiesca, E.: A new chain code. Pattern Recognition 32, 235–251 (1999)
3. Bribiesca, E.: A chain code for representing 3D curves. Pattern Recognition 33, 755–765 (2000)
4. Freeman, H.: On the encoding of arbitrary geometric configurations. IRE Trans. Electron Comput. EC 10, 260–268 (1961)
5. Freeman, H.: Computer processing of line drawing images. ACM Comput. Surveys 6, 57–97 (1974)
6. Murata, T.: Petri nets: properties, analysis and applications. Proceedings of the IEEE 77(4), 541–580 (1989)
7. Peterson, J.L.: Petri Net Theory and the Modeling of Systems. Prentice-Hall, Englewood Cliffs (1981)

Surface-Based Imaging Methods for High-Resolution Functional Magnetic Resonance Imaging

David Ress[1], Sankari Dhandapani[1], Sucharit Katyal[1], Clint Greene[1],
and Chandra Bajaj[2]

[1] Imaging Research Center, 3925B West Braker Lane, Austin TX, 78757 USA
ress@mail.utexas.edu
[2] Center for Computational Visualization, 201 E 24th Street, Austin TX, 78712 USA
University of Texas at Austin

Abstract. Functional magnetic resonance imaging (fMRI) has become an exceedingly popular technique for studies of human brain activity. Typically, fMRI is performed with >3-mm sampling, so that the imaging data can be regarded as two-dimensional samples that roughly average through the typically 1.5—4-mm thickness of cerebral cortex. The use of higher spatial resolutions, <1.5-mm sampling, complicates the use of fMRI, as one must now consider activity variations within the depth of the brain. We present a set of surface-based methods to exploit the use of high-resolution fMRI for depth analysis. These methods utilize white-matter segmentations coupled with deformable-surface algorithms to create a smooth surface representation at the gray-white interface. These surfaces provide vertex positions and surface normals, vector references for depth calculations. That information enables averaging schemes that can increase contrast-to-noise ratio, as well as permitting the direct analysis of depth profiles of functional activity in the human brain.

Keywords: MRI, fMRI, neuroimaging, brain, laminae.

1 Introduction

The human brain is a complex structure that exhibits neural activity on multiple spatial scales. The majority of human brain imaging research focuses on the laminated structure of the cerebral cortex gray matter. Cortical gray matter has a stereotypical 6-layer laminar structure that forms a sheet of tissue 1.5—4-mm thick upon the white matter [2, 4, 11]. The spatial structure of neural activity within cortex can be inferred from its hemodynamic correlates using functional magnetic resonance imaging (fMRI) with blood oxygen-level dependent contrast [10]. High-resolution fMRI can also be used to probe other laminated brain structures such as the superior colliculus and lateral geniculate nucleus [13, 14].

At standard spatial sampling, e.g., 3-mm, activity within cortical gray matter is not resolved. Moreover, these resolutions engender blurring of activity across sulcal boundaries. Because the convoluted shape of the brain brings regions with highly disparate functions into close proximity within the sulci, this kind of blurring can greatly diminish spatial localization. High resolution is also advantageous because it

R.P. Barneva et al. (Eds.): CompIMAGE 2010, LNCS 6026, pp. 130–140, 2010.

reduces contamination of cortical activity with noisy and mislocalized activity produced in superficial vascular regions adjacent to cortex. Thus high-resolution fMRI can enhance localization and signal quality for reasons that go beyond the measure of smaller sampling intervals.

In MRI, thermal signal-to-noise ratio varies linearly with voxel volume, so that high-resolution imaging must typically operate in a higher-noise regime for individual images. For example, a typical single T_2^*-weighted functional image with 3-mm sampling will typically have a signal-to-noise ratio (SNR) ~ 250 on a 3T MRI scanner, while at 1-mm-sampling the same image would yield an SNR < 10. Although there are a variety of methods available to improve the SNR, some measure of appropriate spatial averaging is generally essential.

To deal with these issues, our high-resolution methods generally seek to reconstruct the sampled signals into a very high-resolution (0.6- or 0.7-mm sampling) co-aligned reference anatomy that is segmented to precisely delineate the location of the active brain tissue (e.g., cortical gray matter). Analysis can then be restricted only to those spatial regions within cortex where we expect the best localization and signal quality. A smooth surface is constructed at the inner boundary of the gray matter, where it meets the white matter. The vector reference provided by this surface can then be utilized in two ways: depth averaging to improve the quality of high-resolution surface topography measurements, and to resolve depth variations of cortical activity within a particular portion of the brain.

We illustrate our methods in two portions of the brain: superior colliculus (SC), a small structure in the brainstem with critical functions in eye movements and orientation of attention, and in early visual cortex, the part of cerebral cortex most immediately involved in vision.

2   Methods

2.1   High-Resolution Structural Imaging, Segmentation, and Surface Generation

Imaging was performed on human subjects using a 3-Tesla scanner (General Electric Signa Excite HD) using the product 8-channel head coil. Informed consent was obtained from all subjects based on a protocol approved by the appropriate Institutional Review Board. They were acquired using a three-dimensional (3D), inversion-prepared, radiofrequency-spoiled GRASS (SPGR) sequence (minimum TE and TR, inversion time = 450 ms, 15° flip angle, 2 excitations, ~28-min duration). MRI parameters were chosen so that the structural reference volumes were T_1-weighted with excellent gray-white contrast. We used an isometric voxel size of 0.6 or 0.7 mm so that the reference volumes would precisely delineate brain tissue boundaries.

Because all structural image volumes were obtained using surface coil arrays, they exhibited substantial spatial inhomogeneity on several scales. Therefore, volumes were preprocessed using a custom-made software application written in Matlab (Math-Works, Natick, MA). An expert user scanned through the image volume, using a graphical user interface to identify a number of points in the white matter near the gray-white interface on each slice. Intensity values in white matter were then averaged

Table 1. Neuroimaging nomenclature used in this article

Term	Meaning
GRASS	Gradient-recalled acquisition in the steady state. A common technique for creating MRI images.
T_1	Longitudinal relaxation time. The time constant for the recovery of longitudinal magnetization after excitation
T_2^*	Apparent transverse relaxation time. Lifetime of the transverse signal following excitation.
TE	Echo time: the delay between the excitation in image acquisition in MRI.
TR	Repetition time: the interval between excitation of the same tissue during MRI.
FSL	A package of neuroimaging data analysis tools created at Oxford University.
ITK-SNAP	An image processing package developed for the segmentation and rendering of brain image volumes.
FAST	Volume segmentation software based on k-means clustering.
Eccentricity	The radial coordinate from gaze center in visual space; usually measured in degrees.
Polar angle	The angular coordinate in visual space, also measured in degrees.

in a 3×3×3 neighborhood around each point, and these irregularly spaced samples were gridded onto a regular array. Points outside the hull of sampled points were filled in using nearest-neighbor extrapolation. Estimates of noise were also obtained at the sampled points, and this was combined with the interpolated white-matter intensities to create a robust normalization mask that was applied to the brain volume. We then utilized the Brain Extraction Tool (BET) provided in the FSL package [15] to remove superficial non-brain tissue from the volume.

In SC, we segmented the tissue of the midbrain, brainstem, and portions of the thalamus using a combination of automatic and manual methods provided by the ITK-SNAP application [17]. Because the superficial surface of SC exhibits a strong contrast boundary with the surrounding cerebrospinal fluid (CSF), this segmentation was straightforward.

Segmentation of visual-cortex white matter was considerably more difficult. We began by applying the FAST tool in FSL to provide an approximate segmentation [15]. However, some regions exhibited residual inhomogeneity and/or low gray-white contrast-to-noise ratio, and therefore were not accurately segmented. For these regions extensive manual adjustment was necessary to achieve a satisfactory result.

The CSF-tissue interface of the SC and the gray-white interface in visual cortex were interpolated from the corresponding segmentation using isodensity surface rendering. This initial surface was corrupted by aliasing artifacts. To obtain a smoother representation of the surface and more accurate calculation of its associated surface normal vectors, we used a deformable-surface smoothing algorithm [1, 16]. The deformable surface is based on a curvature-driven geometric evolution, which yields a family of smooth closed immersed orientable surfaces, $\{M(t): t \geq 0\}$ in $\Re^3$, according to the solution of the geometric flow,

$$\frac{\partial p}{\partial t} = N(p)V_n(k_1, k_2, p) \tag{1}$$

with $M_0 = M(0)$ defining the initial surface. Here $p(t)$ is a surface point on the $M(t)$, $V_n(k_1, k_2, p)$ denotes the normal velocity of $M(t)$ based on the principal curvatures, $k_{1,2}$ of $M(t)$, and $N(p)$ is the unit normal of $M(t)$ at $p(t)$.

There are basically two classes of solution approaches for spatial discretization of geometric flow equations (1). One approach is based on the use of finite elements (e.g., [1]) and the other on use of finite differences (e.g., [16]). The spatial discretization approach we adopt here is based on finite divided differences obtained by use of discretized differential operators (such as the Laplace-Beltrami) over simplicial (triangulated) surfaces [3]. Discretization for higher order differential operators is defined recursively from the discrete Laplace-Beltrami (see [16] for details). The time discretization of the flow equation (1) is achieved by use of a semi-implicit Euler scheme. Finally, the resulting sparse linear system is solved using an iterative Krylov subspace solver, such as GMRES [12].

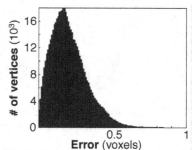

Fig. 1. Vertex errors introduced by the mesh refinement procedure

In SC, satisfactory results required three iterations of the algorithm; cortex required 6 iterations. We evaluated the accuracy of the refined surfaces by calculating nearest-neighbor distances between their vertices and the vertices of the original surfaces; mean distances were typically <0.3 voxel units, and rarely >0.7 voxels (Figure 1). These surfaces provided a means to visualize the functional data, as well as vertices and normal vectors used as a reference for the laminar calculations described below. We also approximated the Gaussian curvature of the surface at each vertex as:

$$C = \frac{R}{|R| + \sqrt{A}/4} \tag{2}$$

where R is the signed distance between each vertex and the best-fit plane containing its connected neighbors, and A is the area of all the triangles featuring that vertex. We used this metric as an intensity overlay on our surfaces: positive curvature marking protruding features (e.g., cortical gyri) appear at a light intensity and negative curvature marking intrusive features (e.g., cortical sulci) appear as a dark intensity. This binary curvature overlay improves the 3D perception of the surface, and also provides a useful indicator of aliasing artifacts.

2.2 Functional MRI

We illustrate our methods with functional image sets obtained in two brain regions: SC and early visual cortex. In SC, we again used the product head coil array to obtain time series of images on eight 1.2-mm-thick quasi-axial slices (170-mm field-of-view [FOV]) with the prescription oriented roughly perpendicular to the local neuraxis. In visual cortex we used a custom-made 7-channel surface coil array packaged in a flexible former so that it could be closely positioned against the subject's head. This array produces images with an SNR advantage of 2—4 over the product coil, depending upon depth. By choosing a tangential, quasi-coronal orientation at the back of the head, we could limit our FOV to 90—100 mm. Use of the surface coil and smaller FOV enabled imaging with 0.7 or 0.8-mm sampling. We obtained 8—12 such slices oriented approximately perpendicular to the calcarine sulcus.

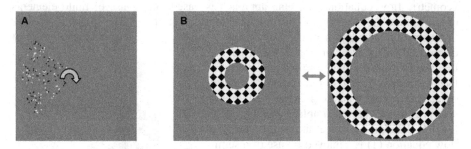

Fig. 2. Visual stimulus configurations: A) rotating wedge of moving dots to map polar angle visual-field variation in SC; B) alternating annuli to stimulate portions of early visual cortex

The SC experiments used travelling-wave techniques to map its retinotopic coordinate representation of the visual field. Stimulus was a 90° wedge of moving dots that rotated slowly (24-s period) around a fixation mark (Figure 2A). The entire stimulus rotated 9.5 times around fixation with a period of 24 seconds while subjects maintained fixation. Many MRI runs (14—18) were obtained using this stimulus presentation in each 2-hour-long scanning session.

The visual cortex experiments used a stimulus designed to activate substantial portions of posterior early visual cortex. Subjects viewed a high-contrast grating within an annular mask (Figure 2B) that alternated (18-s period) in position from small eccentricity (0.5—1.25°) to larger eccentricity (1.5—2.5°). This alternation was repeated 10.5 times to create ~3-min duration runs. Typically 8—12 runs were collected for each scanning session.

Functional images were acquired during the stimulus presentations. For excitation, we utilized a 6.4-ms windowed-sinc pulse to provide sharp slice-select resolution. For acquisition, we used a three-shot outward-spiral trajectory [5, 6] in all imaging. In SC, echo time was 40 ms, while in cortex we used 30 ms because we measured a correspondingly longer T_2^* in SC tissue (~60 ms) than typically observed in cortical gray matter (~45 ms). Acquisition bandwidth was limited to 60 kHz to reduce peak gradient current that causes unwanted heating on our scanner. We chose TR = 1 s, so that a volume was acquired every 3 s.

The multiple shots were combined together after correction by subtracting the initial value and linear trend of the phase. Image reconstruction was done by gridding with a Kaiser-Bessel kernel using 2:1 oversampling. TE was incremented by 2-ms on the first frame to estimate a field map from the first two volumes acquired, and this map was used for linear correction of off-resonance image artifacts [7]. Concomitant field effects arising during the readout gradients were corrected with a time varying phase [5]. Reconstructed images had a SNR of ~20 in both experiments.

In all imaging experiments, a set of T_1-weighted structural images was obtained on the same prescription as the functional data at the end of the session using a 3D SPGR sequence (15° flip angle, 0.7-mm pixels). These images were used to align the functional data to the segmented structural reference volume.

We estimated in-scan motion using a robust scheme [9] applied to a boxcar-smoothed (3—5 temporal frames) version of the fMRI time-series data. Between-scan motion was corrected using the same intensity-based scheme, this time applied to the temporal average intensity of the entire scan. The first scan of the session was used as the reference. After motion correction, the many runs recorded during each session were averaged together to improve SNR.

The intensity of the averaged data was spatially normalized to reduce the effects of coil inhomogeneity. The normalization used a homomorphic method, that is, dividing by a low-pass filtered version of the temporally averaged volume image intensities with an additive robust correction for estimated noise. A sinusoid at the stimulus repetition frequency was then fit to the normalized time series at each voxel, and from this fit we derived volume maps of response amplitude, coherence, and phase. The coherence value is equivalent to the correlation coefficient of the time-series data with its best-fit sinusoid. Functional data were then aligned and resampled to the reference volume [9].

2.3 Laminar Analysis

A distance map was calculated between the tissue voxels and the vertices of the associated surface. We used these distances to measure laminar position (i.e., depth, s) in the reference volume. Thus, the functional data (e.g., complex amplitudes) at each volume voxel were now associated with a depth coordinate.

These associations were used to calculate laminar profiles of functional activity within small disk-shaped regions (1.6—2.4-mm-diam) regions across the surface of the activated portion of the brain. Within these regions, we obtained the complex amplitude as a function of depth for all runs averaged together [11]. A boxcar-smoothing kernel was convolved with the average complex amplitude data as a function of depth; the magnitude of this convolution was the laminar profile.

For each profile, we define the functional thickness, s_f, from spatial moments of the laminar amplitude profile, $A(s)$:

$$\hat{A} = \int_{s_{min}}^{s_{max}} A(s)\,ds \tag{3}$$

$$\bar{s} = \frac{1}{\hat{A}} \int_{s_{min}}^{s_{max}} sA(s)\,ds \tag{4}$$

$$s_f = 2\left[\frac{1}{\hat{A}} \int_{s_{min}}^{s_{max}} (s - \bar{s})^2 A(s)\,ds\right]^{1/2} \tag{5}$$

where s_{min} and s_{max} are the boundaries of the laminar segmentation. Typically, we chose an interval of [−2, 5] mm. Note that the subtraction of the depth centroid, $\bar{s}$, makes s_f

less sensitive to alignment errors. Thus, we associate the functional thickness with every vertex on the surface, enabling the display of functional thickness as a colormap overlay on the rendered surface.

For the SC data, we also used the laminar segmentation process to enable depth averaging that improves the quality of data. For each point on the surface, the associated disk-shaped segmentation was used to average the complex amplitude data over a particular depth range. As part of our mapping process, we generally extracted the phase values from the mean complex amplitudes, and displayed these at the corresponding vertex of the surface. Coherence values were specified as the maximum value over the depth range.

3   Results

3.1   High-Resolution Structural Imaging, Segmentation, and Surface Generation

We present two examples of the high-resolution MRI data. In SC, the images clearly delineate the strong contrast boundary at its superficial dorsal surface. The segmentation, which includes nearby portions of midbrain, thalamus, and brainstem, is shown by a blue overlay (Figure 3A). The boundary of this segmentation was rendered as a surface, upon which a binary curvature map is overlaid, with a light shade indicating positive curvature, and a dark shade indicates negative curvature. The fine-scale structure evident in the curvature map is caused by aliasing artifacts in the initial surface (Figure 3B). After application of the deformable surface algorithm [16], the high spatial frequency curvature artifacts largely disappear, leaving only the actual gross features of the anatomy (Figure 3C).

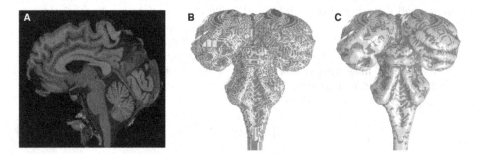

Fig. 3. Human superior colliculus: A) segmentation, including adjacent midbrain, thalamus, and brainstem structures; B) initial surface; C) refined surface

For visual cortex, we segment the entirety of the cerebral hemispheres, but pay particular attention to manual adjustment of the initial segmentation in the occipital lobe (Figure 4A). The initial isodensity surface once again shows extensive aliasing artifacts, visible as the fine stipple in the curvature overlay (Figure 4B), that are again greatly reduced by application of the deformable surface algorithm [16] (Figure 4C).

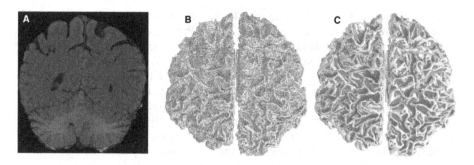

Fig. 4. Human cerebral cortex: A) segmentation; B) initial surface; C) refined surface

3.2 Functional MRI

For the SC visual field mapping experiments, we are principally interested in the phase of the sinusoidal fits. Typical data from one inplane slice, thresholded at a co-herence of 0.3, is shown as a color overlay upon their corresponding inplane anatomy images in Figure 5. The color wheel shows how the phase angle is related to visual field angle. Note the phase progression across the superficial surface of the SC, as well as in posterior visual cortex. This data is then transformed into the reference volume for that subject, so that it can be mapped onto the associated surface representations. The visual cortex data, where we are interested in the complex sinusoidal fit amplitudes, are similarly transformed from the inplane coordinates into the reference volume for that subject.

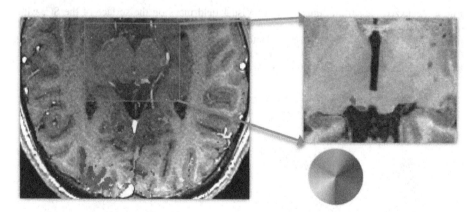

Fig. 5. Functional MRI phase data as color overlay on inplane structural MRI (*left*) and trans-formed into reference volume (*right*). Color wheel shows relationship to visual field angle.

3.3 Laminar Analysis

The SC data was analyzed in two ways. First we performed the disk-like segmenta-tion described above, averaged the complex amplitudes through a depth range of 0—1.8 mm, and then extracted the phase. This procedures produces high-quality visual field maps (Figure 6A), despite fairly low response magnitudes (~0.3% modulation with respect to the mean intensities). Phase maps prepared without the laminar segmentation and depth averaging are much noisier, as can be quantified by calculating session-to-session correlations. We also used our depth-mapping techniques to form laminar profiles of the SC activity in three regions-of-interest (ROIs) that span the surface of the SC from lateral to medial (Figure 6B). These profiles show that activity is evident principally in the superficial 2 mm of the SC tissue, which is known to correspond a preponderance of visually responsive neurons. The data also show significantly thinner profiles for the medial ROI than for the lateral and central ROIs, which is consistent with the known anatomy of human SC.

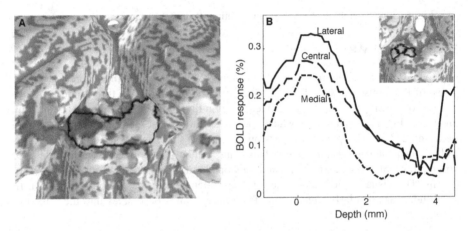

Fig. 6. Analyzed data from human SC: A) Visual field maps on the surface of the SC, with quality enhanced by depth averaging. Boundaries of SC are indicated by the black outline. B) profiles of SC activity as a function of depth within the tissue for three ROIs (*lateral: solid, central: long dashes, medial: short dashes*). Inset shows the locations of the depth-profile ROIs: lateral, central and medial (*left* to *right*).

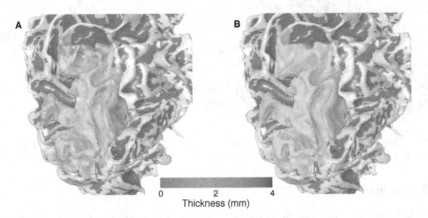

Fig. 7. Data from human visual cortex: A) functional thickness; B) structural thickness

The visual cortex data was analyzed to calculate the functional thickness metric, which was visualized as a color overlay upon surface renderings of the posterior portions of the left hemisphere of a brain (Figure 7A). This data can then be compared to structural measurements of the actual gray-matter thickness visualized in the same fashion (Figure 7B). The functional and structural thickness data are strongly and significantly correlated. Both show the characteristic pattern of gray matter thickness: thicker on crowns of the gyri and thinner in depths of the sulci.

4 Discussion

We have presented a set of surface-based methods for the analysis of high-resolution fMRI data. The analysis requires the acquisition of a high-resolution structural volume that is segmented to obtain a relevant tissue interface. This interface, in turn, is used for the generation of smooth surface that provides a geometric reference, in the form of vertices and surface. We make use of this geometry by transforming fMRI data into the reference volume. Specifically, we can construct depth profiles of the functional activity, or average the data along the surface to improve signal quality and enhance our visualization capabilities.

These procedures can essentially be viewed as a solution to a classic digital reconstruction problem: converting data sampled in one coordinate system to another. Specifically, here we take regularly sampled MRI data, and resample them into the natural coordinates of the segmented tissue boundary. This procedure is particularly useful for fMRI data, which can be subject to artifacts and mislocalization associated with superficial vascular artifacts [8, 11]. The surface based methods become particularly attractive at high spatial resolution, where the Cartesian-space sampled data begin to resolve brain function in 3D, including both the transverse extent of the brain surface as well as its laminar depth.

Acknowledgments. We thank the VISTA lab at Stanford University, particularly Bob Dougherty and Brian Wandell, for their assistance in developing some of the visualization tools and fMRI analysis methods described here. We are also grateful to Gary Glover for providing the MRI spiral-acquisition pulse sequence. Research for CB was supported in part by NIH grants R01EB00487, R01GM074258, and R01GM07308.

References

1. Bajaj, C.L., Xu, G.: Anisotropic diffusion of surfaces and functions on surfaces. ACM Trans. Graph. 22, 4–32 (2003)
2. Braitenberg, V., Schutz, A.: Anatomy of Cortex. Springer, Berlin (1991)
3. Desbrun, M., Meyer, M., Schröder, P., Barr, A.: Discrete differential-geometry operator for triangulated 2-manifolds. In: Proceedings of Visual Mathematics 2002, Berlin, Germany (2002)
4. Fischl, B., Dale, A.M.: Measuring the thickness of the human cerebral cortex from magnetic resonance images. Proc. Natl. Acad. Sci. USA 97, 11050–11055 (2000)
5. Glover, G.H.: Simple analytic spiral K-space algorithm. Magn. Reson. Med. 42, 412–415 (1999)

6. Glover, G.H., Lai, S.: Self-navigated spiral fMRI: Interleaved versus single-shot. Magn. Reson. Med. 39, 361–368 (1998)
7. Glover, G.H., Law, C.S.: Spiral-in/out BOLD fMRI for increased SNR and reduced susceptibility artifacts. Magn. Reson. Med. 46, 515–522 (2001)
8. Moon, C.H., Fukuda, M., Park, S.H., Kim, S.G.: Neural interpretation of blood oxygenation level-dependent fMRI maps at submillimeter columnar resolution. J. Neurosci. 27, 6892–6902 (2007)
9. Nestares, O., Heeger, D.J.: Robust multiresolution alignment of MRI brain volumes. Magn. Reson. Med. 43, 705–715 (2000)
10. Ogawa, S., Menon, R.S., Kim, S.G., Ugurbil, K.: On the characteristics of functional magnetic resonance imaging of the brain. Annu. Rev. Biophys. Biomol. Struct. 27, 447–474 (1998)
11. Ress, D., Glover, G.H., Liu, J., Wandell, B.: Laminar profiles of functional activity in the human brain. NeuroImage 34, 74–84 (2007)
12. Saad, Y.: Iterative Methods for Sparse Linear Systems. Society for Industrial and Applied Mathematics. SIAM, Chicago (2002)
13. Schneider, K.A., Kastner, S.: Visual responses of the human superior colliculus: a high-resolution functional magnetic resonance imaging study. J. Neurophysiol. 94, 2491–2503 (2005)
14. Schneider, K.A., Richter, M.C., Kastner, S.: Retinotopic organization and functional subdivisions of the human lateral geniculate nucleus: a high-resolution functional magnetic resonance imaging study. J. Neurosci. 24, 8975–8985 (2004)
15. Smith, S.M., Jenkinson, M., Woolrich, M.W., Beckmann, C.F., Behrens, T.E., Johansen-Berg, H., Bannister, P.R., De Luca, M., Drobnjak, I., Flitney, D.E., Niazy, R.K., Saunders, J., Vickers, J., Zhang, Y., De Stefano, N., Brady, J.M., Matthews, P.M.: Advances in functional and structural MR image analysis and implementation as FSL. NeuroImage 23(suppl.1), S208–S219 (2004)
16. Xu, G., Pan, Q., Bajaj, C.L.: Discrete surface modeling using partial differential equations. Computer Aided Geometric Design 23(2), 125–145 (2006)
17. Yushkevich, P.A., Piven, J., Hazlett, H.C., Smith, R.G., Ho, S., Gee, J.C., Gerig, G.: User-guided 3D active contour segmentation of anatomical structures: Significantly improved efficiency and reliability. NeuroImage 31, 1116–1128 (2006)

Characterization of a SimMechanics Model for a Virtual Glove Rehabilitation System

Danilo Franchi, Alfredo Maurizi, and Giuseppe Placidi

INFM, c/o AᴬVI-Lab, Department of Health Science, University of L'Aquila, Via Vetoio
Coppito II 67100 Coppito – L'Aquila, Italy
{danilo.franchi,giuseppe.placidi}@univaq.it,
alfredomaurizi@yahoo.it

Abstract. Hand rehabilitation, is a repetitive and long duration therapy that can be facilitated with the assistance of gloves based on sensors. These devices can be substituted by the Virtual Glove, a simple and low-cost system based on the images acquired by four cameras and numerical analysis. In this paper the implementation of the numerical hand model used in this system has been characterized in term of errors in joints position calculation and inverse kinematics. The first preliminary experimental data to test the proposed model have also been reported.

Keywords: numerical hand model, hand rehabilitation, virtual glove.

1 Introduction

Post stroke patients and people suffering from orthopedic hand diseases, in particular after surgery, often show residual hand impairments and need effective rehabilitation therapy: repetitive and long duration training using robots and virtual reality is helpful [6,2]. Training can be facilitated with the assistance of mechanical devices integrated with an augmented reality system. Several of these systems have been designed for rehabilitation [8,5,1,7]: they can be very expensive due to their intrinsic complexity, especially of the mechanical and haptic devices. Moreover, these devices have several force feedback terminals per finger with the forces grounded in the palm or on the back of the hand, thus making them heavy (some hundreds of grams), cumbersome and greatly limiting for the hand movements. Furthermore, the device has to be constructed specifically for each patient, taking into account the nature and extent of the patient's residual infirmities that limits the re-utilization of the mechanical device and its control system. The Virtual Glove described in [9], based on analysis of the images acquired from a set of cameras and numerical analysis, provides a non-contact solution that overcomes these limitations. The Virtual Glove idea is to analyze the hand and its fingers by using four video cameras opportunely positioned on the vertices of a cube and then use image processing and computer vision techniques to track and reconstruct the 3D pose of the patient's hand. In this way, it is possible to monitor the movements of the whole hand and of each single finger. Moreover, the forces applied by the patient's hand or fingers can be measured indirectly from the deformations

R.P. Barneva et al. (Eds.): CompIMAGE 2010, LNCS 6026, pp. 141–150, 2010.
© Springer-Verlag Berlin Heidelberg 2010

impressed on some elastic objects of known elastic coefficients (rubber balls, peg boards etc.). The deformation of the object can be recorded and the force induced by each finger can be calculated by this deformation. This is done by using a 26 DOFs (4 DOFs for each finger and 6 DOFs for the wrist) numerical model, based on the skeleton of the human hand that describes hand kinematic [4]. Such model fits the real hand on the basis of the information (position and orientation of the palm and of each finger) obtained by analyzing the images collected by the cameras. To facilitate joints and fingertips recognition, markers placed on superior part of each joint and fingertip can be used. Note that skin and other soft tissues do not influence significantly the system. In fact, markers can be placed on the back of the hand, where is present only a thin skin layer. In this way the presented numerical hand model represents, in a good approximation, the superior part of the skeleton of the hand. In what follows we characterize the Matlab/Simulink implementation of the numerical hand used in the Virtual Glove by analyzing the errors and reporting some experimental results.

2   The Virtual Glove

The main scheme of the Virtual Glove system is shown in Figure 1. It is composed by four main subsystems: the measuring system, the inverse kinematics, the hand model and the force calculation system. In the following subsections a description of such subsystems is reported and the error analysis is performed.

2.1   Measuring System

The measuring system is composed by four RGB, low-cost USB video cameras, 640x480 in resolution. The cameras are placed on the vertices of a plexiglas cube as shown in Figure 1. Each camera is oriented toward the center of the cube so that each joint or fingertip is imaged at least by two cameras. To calculate the 3D position of each marker, from the 2D data taken on the images, it is necessary to calibrate each camera. Calibration allows establishing the relationship between the 3D world coordinates and their corresponding 2D image coordinates [10]. This procedure is a fundamental step in each computer vision application. It is based on the estimation of intrinsic (focal length, principal point, skew and distortion) and extrinsic parameters (position and orientation with respect to the world coordinate system). To calibrate the cameras we used the Camera Calibration Toolbox for Matlab [3]. Once the intrinsic calibration procedure was performed for each camera, extrinsic parameters were calculated by collecting, with each pairs of cameras, the same grid of points and then computing the transformations between the reference systems. In this way each pair can be used as a measurement device. After camera calibration, it was possible to obtain, by triangulation the 2D data coming from at least a pair of cameras, the 3D coordinates of a point.

2.2   Error Analysis

To analyze the position calculation errors with different pairs of cameras it was necessary to compare the 3D coordinates of points imaged by all cameras simultaneously: the 3D coordinates were calculated by the triangulating the 2D measures taken on each pairs of views. Imaging the same points from all views simultaneously was very difficult with the configuration shown in Figure 1. For this reason, just for errors evaluation, the cameras configuration was changed by placing all cameras on the same face of the cube. This can be done just by repeating the extrinsic calibration procedure. With this new configuration we measured the coordinates of four points on a checkerboard (square dimension was about of 15.75 mm, measured with a micrometer) imaged simultaneously by the four cameras. In Figure 2 the images collected by the four cameras with the selected points (P1-P4) are reported. To take into account the picking error, we performed a series of 10 measures for each point (all points were picked 10 times). In Table 1 mean values (μ) and standard deviations (σ) of the distances between the measured points calculated with each pair of cameras are reported.

Note that the error was less than a millimeter and the maximum displacement with respect to the mean value was 0.7 mm. Figures 3-6 report for the points P1-P4 the error bar of the measured coordinates with respect to the references frame of the camera CAM1.

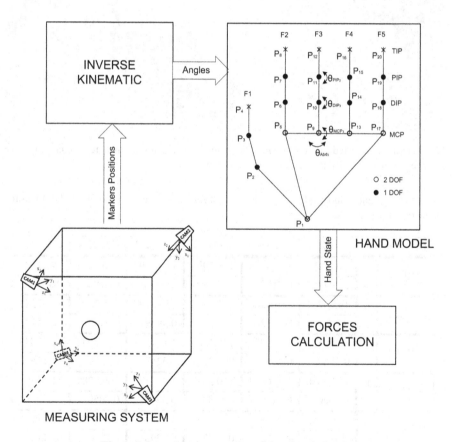

Fig. 1. Schematic representation of the virtual glove

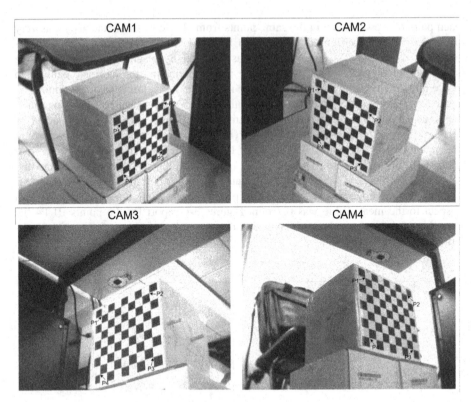

Fig. 2. Images collected by the cameras placed in the configuration used to evaluate the error. The measured points (P1-P4) are indicated by arrows.

Table 1. Mean and standard deviation on the 10 distances between the points P1-P4, measured by the 6 pairs of cameras

Distance\Pair		CAM1-2	CAM1-3	CAM1-4	CAM2-3	CAM2-4	CAM3-4
D(P1,P2)	μ	110.4465	110.9441	110.5998	110.8193	110.3223	110.7506
	σ	0.4947	0.2139	0.3864	0.3593	0.5188	0.4314
D(P1,P3)	μ	155.9741	156.3366	155.8316	156.3197	155.7503	155.7341
	σ	0.7081	0.2212	0.5614	0.5869	0.5220	0.3951
D(P1,P4)	μ	109.8522	110.1720	110.1069	109.4521	109.5932	109.7843
	σ	0.2268	0.3668	0.5629	0.5253	0.2458	0.4115
D(P2,P3)	μ	110.2430	110.6014	110.5815	110.1359	109.7789	110.1791
	σ	0.1620	0.3257	0.5383	0.3954	0.5050	0.4335
D(P2,P4)	μ	155.7153	156.4528	156.5651	155.5149	155.4485	156.1154
	σ	0.4178	0.3877	0.5227	0.3798	0.5246	0.4114
D(P3,P4)	μ	110.2614	110.6389	110.5200	110.5986	110.4145	110.3188
	σ	0.7723	0.2536	0.4299	0.3816	0.3438	0.2341

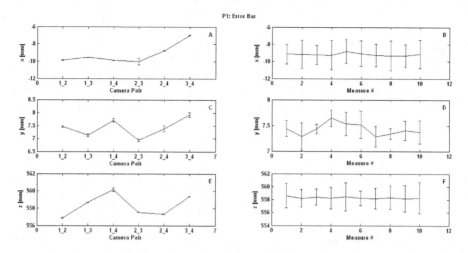

Fig. 3. Error bar plot referred to the point P1. The images A, C and D represent, for each pair of cameras, the standard deviation and the mean of the 10 measures of the coordinates of the point P1. The images B,D and E represent, for each point, the standard deviation and the mean of the 6 measures (one for each pair of cameras) of the coordinates of the point P1.

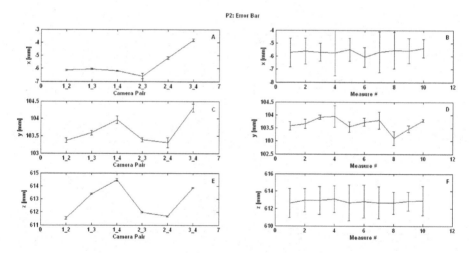

Fig. 4. Error bar plot referred to the point P2. The images A, C and D represent, for each pair of cameras, the standard deviation and the mean of the 10 measures of the coordinates of the point P2. The images B, D and E represent, for each point, the standard deviation and the mean of the 6 measures (one for each pair of cameras) of the coordinates of the point P2.

The images A, C and D of Figures 3-6 represent, for each pair of cameras, the standard deviation and the mean value of the 10 measures of the coordinates of the points P1-P4 respectively. The images B, D and E of Figures 3-6 represent, for each point, the standard deviation and the mean of 6 measures (one for each pair of cameras) of the coordinates of the points P1-P4.

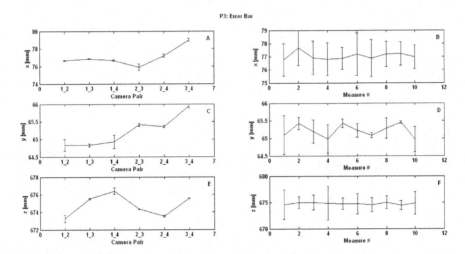

Fig. 5. Error bar plot referred to the point P3. The images A, C and D represent, for each pair of cameras, the standard deviation and the mean of the 10 measures of the coordinates of the point P3. The images B, D and E represent, for each point, the standard deviation and the mean of the 6 measures (one for each pair of cameras) of the coordinates of the point P3.

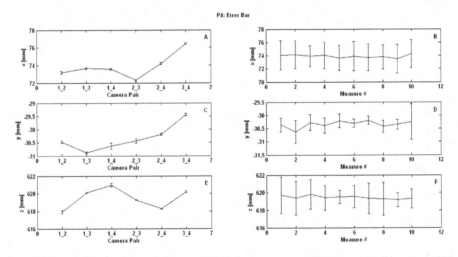

Fig. 6. Error bar plot referred to the point P4. The images A, C and D represent, for each pair of cameras, the standard deviation and the mean of the 10 measures of the coordinates of the point P4. The images B, D and E represent, for each point, the standard deviation and the mean of the 6 measures (one for each pair of cameras) of the coordinates of the point P4.

Table 1 and Figures 3-6 revealed a mismatch between the coordinate systems in which are reported the coordinates calculated by triangulating the data of each pair of cameras (we used that of camera CAM1 as a reference system). In particular, relative distances were quite accurate, less than a millimeter, while the coordinates were affected by greater errors, up to 4 mm.

This mainly depends on an inaccurate estimation of the calibration parameters. A more accurate estimation of the calibration parameters or an estimation of the transformation to align the reference systems could greatly improve the accuracy. The error in the reproduction the hand model and in its initialization (see the hand model subsection), can be reduced if the pairs with lower mismatch are used (i.e. in our configuration the pairs CAM1-2 and CAM2-3).

2.3 Inverse Kinematic

The inverse kinematic is used to calculate the joints angles knowing the position of the end points of each link: θ_{ABD}, θ_{MCP}, θ_{DIP} and θ_{PIP} (see Figure 1). For each finger it is possible to calculate θ_{DIP} and θ_{PIP} trivially by using the dot product between two vectors:

$$\cos(\vartheta) = \frac{ll' + mm' + nn'}{\sqrt{l^2 + m^2 + n^2}\sqrt{l'^2 + m'^2 + n'^2}} \tag{1}$$

where (l,m,n) and (l',m',n') are the cosine directors of the two adjacent phalanges that identify the angle; θ_{DIP} is the angle between the first and the second phalanges of each finger while θ_{PIP} is the angle between the second and third phalanges of each finger.

To calculate θ_{ABD} and θ_{MCP} a different method for the thumb, with respect to the other fingers, is required. In particular, for each finger F_i, θ_{MCPi} (i=2:5) is the angle between the first phalanx of the finger and the palm triangle identified by the points P_1, P_5 and P_{17}:

$$\cos(\vartheta_{MCPi}) = \frac{l_i A + m_i B + n_i C}{\sqrt{l_i^2 + m_i^2 + n_i^2}\sqrt{A^2 + B^2 + C^2}} \tag{2}$$

Where (l_i, m_i, n_i) are the cosine directors of the first phalanx of the finger i and (A,B,C) are the coefficient of (x,y,z) coordinates of the palm triangle plane equation. θ_{ABDi} is the angle between the projection of the first phalanx of the ith finger on the palm triangle plane and the line identified by the points P_5 and P_{17}. For the finger F_1 (the thumb), θ_{ABD1} is the angle between the projection of the line containing P_1 and P_2 (L_{12}) on the palm triangle and the line containing the points P_1 and P_5 (L_{15}); θ_{MCP1} is the angle between the line L_{15} and the projection of the line L_{12} on the plane containing the line L_{15} and perpendicular to the palm triangle.

2.4 The Hand Model

The hand model is developed by using the Simulink's SimMechanincs toolbox, by considering the hand as a mechanical system. In particular, we consider the palm triangle (indentified by the points P_1, P_5 and P_{17} in Figure 1) and each phalanx as rigid bodies connected each other with appropriate joints or composition of joints. The hand model is used to apply constrains to the angles avoiding unrealistic configurations and producing more accurate results.

This hand model was first described in [4]: here we just refine the model by relaxing the constraints among θ_{MCP}, θ_{DIP} and θ_{PIP} angles ($\theta_{MCP} = \theta_{DIP}$ and $\theta_{PIP} = 2/3*\theta_{DIP}$)

making them independent to each other. With this assumption the initial 16 DOFs hand model (6 DOFs for the rotation and translation of the wrist and 2 DOFs for each finger) becomes a 26 DOFs model with 6 DOFs for the translation and rotation of the wrist and 4 DOFs for each finger. The previous constrains are too much restrictive and can be used only if we consider a healthy hand, without any infirmity or any grasped object (without external forces). On the other hand a 26 DOFs hand model increases the system complexity and the occlusion risks (all joints and fingertips need to be measured).

The SimMechanics specification allows including in the model other parameters such as the gravity vector in the environment, the mass, the inertia and the centre of gravity of each body, making thus possible to perform a complete hand dynamic analysis. For example, it should be possible to calculate the force that each finger or the wrist applies just in the presence of gravity. This can be particularly useful in cases of patients with serious infirmities in which a little force application can be considered a big result. This feature could be particularly useful for future extensions to other human body districts (such as legs).

The SimMechanics hand model needs an initial calibration procedure to adapt the model to the user real hand.

2.5 Forces Calculation

The forces applied by each finger on a grasped object of known elastic properties can be calculated on the basis of the measure of the deformation that each finger produces on the object by using Hooke's law: $\mathbf{F} = k \cdot d \cdot \mathbf{N}$ (in Newton). In the previous formula, k is the elastic constant of the object and d is the distance between the previous and actual finger position along the vector $\mathbf{N}$ normal to the surface of the grasped object. The forces calculation can be facilitates by using pegboards which can be pressed or dragged. Furthermore, as mentioned in the previous subsection, the SimMechanics model allows performing a dynamic analysis of the problem: the forces that the whole hand or each finger can apply just in the presence of the gravity can be calculated. This last analysis can be possible by introducing in the model the mass, the inertia and the center of gravity of each part (fingers and palm triangle) of the real human hand.

3 Experimental Results

The experimental results were obtained by acquiring synchronized video streams by the four cameras. The hand model was initialized by using four synchronized starting images. The joints and fingertips were identified by picking with the mouse the marked points present on the images (crosses drown on a latex glove). Each point was visible at least by two views (without any occlusion). When possible, data were triangulated with the pairs of cameras CAM1-2 and CAM2-3 for their minor mismatching (see Figure 3-6). The first two columns in Figure 7 show four frames of the videos collected by the cameras CAM1 and CAM2, while the third shows the corresponding re-projection of the hand model, on the image plane of the camera CAM2. The visual evaluation of the results are quite satisfactory. The error was less or equal than that reported in the error analysis section.

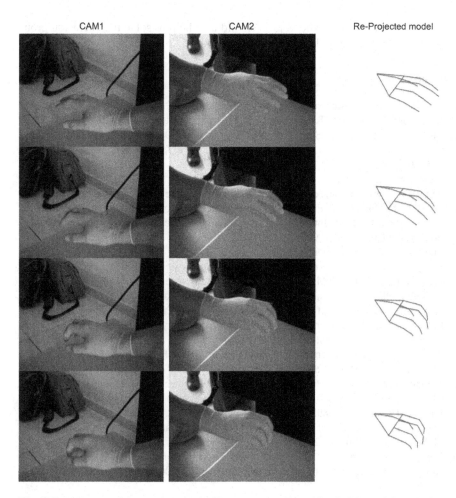

Fig. 7. Four frames of the synchronized video streams collected by CAM1 and CAM2 (first and second columns respectively) and the corresponding re-projected hand model on the image plane of CAM2 (third column)

4   Conclusions and Future Works

A characterization of a hand model for the Virtual Glove rehabilitation system has been presented. The error was below a millimeter if the reference system of each pair of cameras were aligned. The results were quite promising.

Future investigations will be devoted to automate joints and fingertips recognition. A possible solution is to use appropriate color coded markers localizable with common color segmentation algorithms. Another feasible solution is to use characters to mark joints and fingertips and OCR (Optical Character Recognition) algorithms to recognize and localize them. Furthermore major investigations will be devoted to solve the occlusion problem (utilizing for example the Kalman filter), to develop elastic objects for easy force calculation and to perform a dynamic study of the hand:

accurate development of elastic objects should also help to solve the occlusion problem. Forces calculation will be object of a future work.

References

1. Bouzit, M.: Design, Implementation and Testing of a Data Glove with Force Feedback for Virtual and Real Objects Telemanipulation. PhD Thesis, Paris, France (1996)
2. Burgar, C.G., Lum, P.S., Shor, P.C., Van der Loos, M.: Development of robots for rehabilitation therapy: the Palo Alto VA/Stanford experience. J.Rehab. Res. Develop. 37, 663–673 (2000)
3 . Camera calibration toolbox for Matlab,
   `http://www.vision.caltech.edu/bouguetj/calib_doc`
4. Franchi, D., Maurizi, A., Placidi, G.: A numerical hand model for a virtual glove rehabilitation system. In: IEEE International Workshop on Medical Measurements and Applications, vol. 00, pp. 41–44 (2009)
5 . Immersion technical support,
   `http://www.immersion.com/3d/products/cyber_grasp.php`
6. Kahn, L.E., Averbuch, M., Rimer, W.Z., Reinkensmeyer, D.J.: Comparison of robot-assisted reaching to free reaching in promoting recovery from chronic stroke. In: Int. Conf. of Assisted Tech. in the Information Age, pp. 39–44. IOS Press, Amsterdam (2001)
7. Luo, X., Kline, T., Fischer, H.C., Stubblefield, K.A., Kenyon, R.V., Kamper, D.G.: Integration of augmented reality and assistive devices for post-stroke hand opening rehabilitation. In: 27th Annual International Conference of the IEEE Engineering in Medicine and Biology Society (EMBS), Shanghai, China, pp. 6855–6858 (2005)
8. Merians, A.S., Jack, D., Boian, R., Tremaine, M., Burdea, G.C., Adamovich, S., Recce, M., Poizner, H.: Virtual reality-augmented rehabilitation for patients following stroke. Physical Therapy 82(9), 898–915 (2002)
9. Placidi, G.: A smart virtual glove for the hand telerehabilitation. Computers in Biology and Medicine 37, 1100–1107 (2007)
10. Zhang, Z.: A flexible new technique for camera calibration. IEEE Transaction on Pattern Analysis and Machine Intelligence 22(11), 1330–1334 (2000)

Numerical Methods for the Semi-automatic Analysis of Multimodal Wound Healing Images

Giuseppe Placidi, Maria Grazia Cifone, Benedetta Cinque, Danilo Franchi,
Maurizio Giuliani, Cristina La Torre, Guido Macchiarelli, Marta Maione,
Alfredo Maurizi, Gianfranca Miconi, and Antonello Sotgiu

Department of Health Sciences,
University of L'Aquila, Via Vetoio Coppito 2,
67100 L'Aquila, Italy
Giuseppe.Placidi@cc.univaq.it

Abstract. Wound healing problem requires the analysis of tens of images from different microscopic systems. We describe a set of semi-automatic algorithms to analyze a variety of microscopy images used to study the wound healing process. The proposed suite, beside the phase contrast images, allows analyzing fluorescent microscopy images, inverted light microscopy images at different magnification and staining methods, or images obtained by scanning electron microscopy. The proposed software is designed in Matlab®. It is suggested to integrate it into the CellProfiler™ software, thus introducing new functionalities without losing the CellProfiler existing capabilities. The approach is efficient, easy-to-use, and enables biologists to comprehensively and quantitatively address many questions of the wound healing problem.

Keywords: wound healing, image analysis, CellProfiler, image processing.

1 Introduction

Biologists are continuously involved in the visual analysis of a sample. While nothing can fully replace the expertise of a trained human expert, observing many samples by eye is time-consuming, subjective, and non quantitative. Certain repetitive tasks in visual analysis are suitable for automation by collecting digital images and processing them with image analysis software. This has several advantages over visual observations including speed, quantitative and reproducible results, and simultaneous measurement of many features in the image. Efforts to automate visual analysis in biology have been made, but many aspects still need improvement [7]. While numerous commercial and free software packages exist for image analysis, many of these packages are designed for a very specific purpose, such as cell counting [8]. Other packages are sold with accompanying hardware for image acquisition, but these are expensive and do not allow measurement of features beyond those that are already built-in. Most commercial software is proprietary, meaning that the underlying methods of analysis are hidden from the researcher. At the other end, some software packages are very flexible, especially for interactive analysis of individual

R.P. Barneva et al. (Eds.): CompIMAGE 2010, LNCS 6026, pp. 151–162, 2010.

images [3] or for image sequences [6]. The CellProfiler™ project was developed to provide the scientific community with an easy-to-use open source platform for automated biological image analysis [2,4,5]. It can accommodate adaptation to many biological objects and assays without requiring programming, due to its modular design; it uses the concept of pipeline, and graphical user interface. CellProfiler deals with many applications in biology, including the wound healing problem [2]. The wound healing assay is a technique to determine the migration of different cell types in different conditions. In this assay, a confluent monolayer of cells is wounded by scratching it with a pipet tip [11]. The monolayer is then imaged at time points to record the size of the wound. CellProfiler includes the study of the wound healing assays, but it is incomplete: it allows analyzing just phase contrast microscope images. Wound healing is a well orchestrated and highly coordinated process including a series of overlapping phases: inflammation, cell proliferation, matrix deposition and tissue remodeling. This involves a series of dynamic events including clotting, inflammation, granulation tissue formation, epithelialization, neovascularization, collagen synthesis, and wound contraction [9]. These effects have to be observed by using images collected from different methods. An accurate and complete observation is made more difficult when the goal is to compare the natural repair of a wound with the possible acceleration induced by a pharmacological treatment. In this case also image analysis has to become very accurate and objective. The analyzed images, beside those collected by a phase contrast microscope, are obtained by inverted light microscopy at different magnifications and staining methods, by fluorescent microscopy, and by scanning electron to observe structural and ultrastructural modifications. Samples of these images are reported in Figure 1.

In what follows, a suite of methods to analyze the above cited images and to cope completely with the articulated wound healing problem, is presented. All the proposed methods are implemented in Matlab and can be integrated in the freely available CellProfiler cell image analysis software.

2 Description of the Algorithms

The described algorithms used a series of methods which have been implemented in Matlab, by using a GUI (graphic user interface) representing a modification of the *imtool* Matlab method, release 9.2 (August 2009). This choice was made to allow the inclusion of the proposed methods into the CellProfiler software and to facilitate the role of the biologists when using the proposed suite. The user is asked to choose a method and to load the corresponding images. By using the interface, the user is able to apply the algorithms on images like those reported in Figure 1 by using the concept of pipelines, that is series of modules which can be executed singularly or in sequences (as in the CellProfiler architecture), by pressing a button on the GUI. These sequences, or pipelines, can also be saved to be re-used for following analyses. In the definition of the methods, a series of functions included into the Matlab Image Processing toolbox are used: these functions, indicated with upper-case letters in the methods descriptions, are used and included into the methods without any further specification.

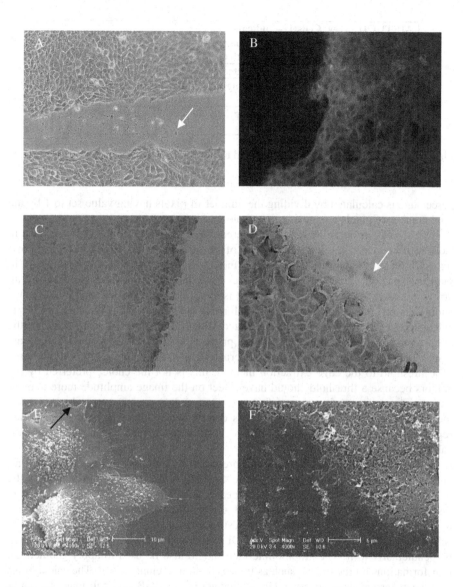

Fig. 1. Monolayer wound healing phase-contrast microscopy image (A); image by fluorescent microscopy revealing the f-actin microfilaments activation (B); light microscopy images revealing cyclin D1 (C) and Ki-67 (D); scanning electron microscopy images in wounded HaCat (E) and 3T3 (F) cells

Figure 1 shows classical images used to analyze accurately wound healing assays: the information is extracted at different times and compared. In Figure 1A, in particular, interesting information is the percentage of closure of a wound. The method used to calculate this percentage uses the function Area_Cells reported in Figure 2: the

| METHOD: Area_Cells(I) – Indicate |
pixels occupied by cells in the image I
1) Im=EDGE(I) - Edge extraction with Canny method
2) Im=elim(Im) - Discard pixels situated in low density regions
3) Im=IMCLOSE(Im) - Image closing with a disk of the dimension of a cell.
4) **Output**: Im - Binary image having 1 where cells are present and 0 elsewhere.

Fig. 2. Flow chart diagram of the method used to calculate the portion of area occupied by the cells from a phase-contrast microscopy image

percentage is calculated by dividing the number of pixels having value set to 1 by the total number of pixels composing the whole image.

Note that the proposed method is different from that reported in [10], also used in CellProfiler, concerning the introduction of step #2, necessary to exclude false positives produced by impurities or artifacts in the original image, having nothing to do with the space occupied by the cells (see, for example, the feature indicated by an arrow in Figure 1A). The method "elim", is a home-made function operating a mask sliding on the image of the edges. For each mask movement, the percentage of ones is calculated inside the mask: if the calculated value falls below a given threshold, the pixels are set to zero. For this reason, the proposed method could give more accurate results than that proposed in [10]. An alternative approach could consist in the usage of a threshold to the edge extraction method: this is not the choice preferred by the authors because a threshold should have effect on the image amplitude more than on the spatial extension of the image features. The mask, a square matrix, has normally the maximum dimension of a cell and is determined graphically on a user-defined region of the edge image. In the chosen region, the percentage threshold is automatically calculated.

In Figure 1B, useful information is represented by the green level which is correlated to the f-actin microfilament presence. Specific information is represented by the green value on the wound border with respect to the green level distribution at a given distance from it. The method is summarized in Figure 3. It uses the graphic interface to extract graphically a Region of Interest (ROI) on the image background (to be subtracted from the original image), a ROI in the wound border and a ROI extracted perpendicularly to it. The graphic interface should also be used to apply geometrical transformations on the image, such as image rotation or enlargement. The calculations have been carried out just on the Green channel of the RGB original image I. Analogous calculations are performed on images like those reported in Figures 1C and 1D: in these cases useful information is represented by the brown color, indicating the localization of cyclin D1 and Ki-67 respectively.

The input of the method is the original image: the interesting brown color range is graphically chosen by the user (all the color components of the original image are used). In a typical image such that of Figure 1C it is particularly important the background subtraction. In an image like that of Figure 1D, it is important to define exactly the region occupied by cells: spurious brown regions are also located outside the region occupied by the cells and have to be discarded (see, for example, the region indicated by the arrow in Figure 1D). In this last case, an important role is played by the presence of the blue color in the image: it is necessary to create the contrast necessary to recognize the cells presence. For this reason, the Blue channel is used to find the region occupied by the cells (this zone is characterized by a blue level above a given threshold). The brown color is mainly obtained by an approximately equal combination of the Red channel and the Green channel, e medium value, and a low value of Blue (a medium brown color is represented by R=156, G=130, and B=20): the Blue value can be high, above an expected range, due to the counterstaining used to visualize all cells. In this way, it can be possible to recognize, and discard, the brown color presence outside the region occupied by the cells. This variation can be applied to images of the type of that shown in Figure 1D.

METHOD: Green_Color (Green(I)) – Calculate the green value of the green channel of the original image I
1) I=Back_sub(I) - Background subtraction
2) A=Area_Cells(grey(I)) – Find pixels occupied by cells: the function is applied to the transformed greyscale image.
3) (m,M)=Min_Max(I,A) - Calculate the mean green value, m, and the maximum green value, M, in the region of I occupied by cells, A.
4) B=ROI(I) – Select a region on the wound border
5) (mB,MB)= Min_Max(I,B) – Calculate the mean green value, mB, and the maximum green value, MB, in the selected Region of Interest B
6) C=ROI(I) – Select a region perpendicularly to the wound border
7) (mC,MC)= Min_Max(I,C) – Calculate the mean green value, mC, and the maximum green value, MC, in the selected Region of Interest C
8) **Outputs**: (m,M), (mB,MB), (mC,MC)

Fig. 3. Flow-chart diagram of the algorithm used to calculate numerical parameters from the green component of a fluoroscopy image

Figures 1E and 1F show scanning electron microscopy images: useful information is represented by the number, the mean length and the total length of thin filopodia, cell bumps having the shape of filaments, departing from the cell surface. This information correlates with the migration of the analyzed cell type. Two images are reported, indicating two cellular lines, to highlight different complexities in extracting useful information. The proposed method, dealing with the images of Figures 1E-1F containing thin filopodia of different SNR and contrast, is based on shape recognition. It is based on the correlation of the original image with a small region selected from the cell surface: this operation serves to eliminate (through smoothing) the region occupied by the cell. The output image is then correlated with anisotropic Gaussian filters. The following of the algorithm represents a direct derivation of a segmentation method used for vessel segmentation [3]. Before the method description, it is useful to introduce some notations:

-    let P be the original grayscale image;
-    let $F_{\theta i}$ be the anisotropic Gaussian filter, oriented at an angle θ_i with respect to the horizontal axis of the image;

- let $P_{\theta i}$ be the correlation between $F_{\theta i}$ and P generated by $P_{\theta i} = F_{\theta i} * P$;
- let P_I be the 3D matrix generated by superposition of planes $P_{\theta i}$, each plane corresponding to a value θ_i (i.e. the i-th plane contains the filtered result obtained by correlating the current projection with the anisotropic Gaussian filter oriented at the angle θ_i).

We can also think of P_I as the matrix in which each pixel has associated a list of correlation intensity values, one for each angular orientation of the applied Gaussian filter. We assume that the image to be segmented contains brighter objects (the filopodia) on a dark background (this is the situation after the elimination of the region occupied by the cell body). With this assumption, the segmented image should be a binary image in which a pixel is set to 1 if it is associated with a filopodium, otherwise to 1. For each image P, the method can be summarized in Figure 4. The aim of the first three steps of the algorithm is to smooth the region occupied by the cell: the result is an image containing brighter filopodia in a dark background. Then, the resulting image is filtered with a bank of anisotropic Gaussian filters (steps 4-5) to discover short rectilinear paths (pieces of filopodia) which must belong to filopodia if their maximum is above a given value and their minimum is above another given value (step 6). This double verification serves to eliminate false positive filopodia indications where a separation of different structures is present (see, for example, the black arrow in Figure 1E indicating an edge dividing zones of different intensities). Moreover, filopodia are characterized by having low angular variations in the image plane: for this reason, pixels having a gradient below a given value (step 8), are extracted from G^2 (step 7). At the end, the matrices obtained in steps 6 and 8 are merged to obtain the final image of the filopodia paths. The two matrices are merged in logical OR because: the first matrix contains the pixels which belong to filopodia with a very high probability (they constitute rectilinear portions of filopodia); the second matrix contains pixels representing the curvilinear paths of filopodia. Very small isolated regions of connected pixels in the resulting binary image are considered to be unnatural for connected filopodia and are discarded (step 13). The skeleton calculation (step 11) serves to eliminate information about the filopodium width: useful information is considered to be their length, not their surface. Alternately, due to almost constant width of the measured filopodia, step 11 can be eliminated and length of a filopodium can be also approximated by summing the number of pixels covering it, divided by the mean width. We found that the results were approximately the same. Maybe this particular choice should result in the following advantage: skeleton extraction could produce interruptions in a thinner filopodium.

In some cases, this can produce an erroneous value for n (the number of filopodia can be higher than the real) and, consequently, an erroneous value for ml (the mean length can be lower than real). The total length should remain approximately unchanged.

METHOD: Filopodia_Meas(I) – Calculate the number of filopodia coming from a cell, their mean length and the total length.
1) Select a small region, R, on the cell surface
2) C=I*R - Calculate the correlation between I and R
3) P=Choice(I,t_r) - Assign to P the I original values where the correlation is below a threshold t_r, and the mean background intensity where the correlation goes above t_r
4) Calculate $P_{\theta i}= F_{\theta i}*P$, for each θ_i (from 0 to π radians, in steps of π/S radians), and calculate P_I
5) From P_I calculate m_{ang} and M_{ang}, the maps of angles at which minimum and maximum intensity values are obtained, respectively
6) From P_I calculate V_{ang}, the image containing one on those positions where: the maximum intensity correlation value is greater than, or equal to, a given threshold t_M and the minimum intensity value is greater than, or equal to, a given threshold t_m; zero elsewhere (one is present where a filopodium is present);
7) From M_{ang} calculate the image $G^2 = \left(\dfrac{\partial M_{ang}}{\partial x}\right)^2 + \left(\dfrac{\partial M_{ang}}{\partial y}\right)^2$
8) From G^2 calculate VI_{ang}, the image containing 1 (indicating filopodium presence) on those pixels where the square gradient is below a given threshold level, t_G, and 0 elsewhere
9) Calculate $V2_{ang}$=V_{ang} OR $V1_{ang}$
10) Recalculate $V2_{ang}$ by eliminating regions of connected pixels which are too small (only the N largest groups of regions of connected pixels are retained)
11) Find the skeleton of the result to obtain a binary image in which the filopodia are 1 pixel in width
12) Calculate the number of filopodia, n, the mean length, ml, and the total length, Tl, in pixels – It is sufficient to count the number of 1s
13) Calculate the lengths in microns
14) **Outputs**: n, ml and Tl.

Fig. 4. Flow chart used to extract the filopodia from a cell and to calculate their number, the medium and the total lengths in µm

3 Results

The described algorithms have been applied on images of the types reported in Figure 1. In particular, the Area_Cells method was applied to two sets of phase contrast microscopy images, each composed by 6 images, representing the time evolution of the wound healing repair for two cellular lines: 3T3 fibroblasts and HaCat keratinocytes.

As an example, Figure 5 reports one of these results. In particular, Figure 5A represents the original image. Figure 5B reports the intermediate image, the edge image, produced by using steps 2 and 3 of the proposed method, where low-density, lower that 10%, clusters of pixels have been eliminated (the mask used to calculate the density was 20x20). Figure 5C shows the final result: the region occupied by the cells is indicated in white. The proposed method indicated wound healing was completed at 92%. A hand-made segmentation, performed by an expert, obtained the 91%: our method produced greater results due to the closing operation performed on the image of the edges. However, our method was found to be more accurate of that used in CellProfiler (on the same image it found 95%): the higher precision was due to the use of step #2 in the proposed algorithm.

Green_Color was used on a set of 6 fluorescent microscopy wound healing images of the HaCat cellular line, at different times. A result is reported in Figure 6 as an example: from the original image, Figure 6A, the background was eliminated, Figure 6B, and the image representing the region occupied by the cells was calculated, Figure 6C (the region occupied by the cells allows the calculation of the green portion into this region). Thanks to the graphic interface, the interesting ROIs, that on the wound border and that along the perpendicular direction, can be easily extracted and numerical parameters calculated. For the reported image, the parameters had the following values: $(m,M)=(87,155)$; $(mB,MB)=(140,155)$; $(mC,MC)=(40,67)$. The calculations have been carried out just for the green channel, indicating a direct correlation with the f-actin microfilament organization. It is important to note the fundamental role of the background elimination: this operation ensures the elimination of the residual coloring substance from the image, thus allowing a very accurate calculation.

In almost the same way, 6 images collected by light microscopy to identify cycline D1 were analyzed: the images resulted brown colored and the process consisted in the extraction of the brown information inside the region occupied by the cells, once the background was eliminated. Differently for the fluoroscopy images, all the image channels, R,G and B, have been used for the calculation. In Figure 7 an example has been reported. In particular, Figure 7A shows the original image. Figure 7B shows the binary image indicating the region occupied by the cells (it has been obtained by using Area_Cells) and in Figure 7C is shown the brown color occupying the cells region. The brown separation allow to calculate the percentage of pixels occupied by brown color in the whole region occupied by the cells, in a ROI collected along the wound border and in a ROI perpendicular to the wound border. For the given image, these percentages were 85%, 100% and 65% respectively. Once the brown image has been extracted, other calculations are allowed. Light microscopy was also used to collect 6 images identifying Ki-67: the brown color revealed the presence of Ki-67. The region occupied by the cells was identified by coloring in bright blue the cells. In this case the analysis was devoted to identify the brown color in the region occupied by cells, colored in bright blue.

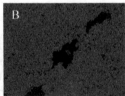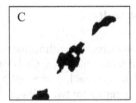

Fig. 5. Phase contrast image (A), the edge image without small isolated regions (B), and the region occupied by the cells (C)

Fig. 6. Fluoroscopy image (A), image after background elimination (B), and the region occupied by cells (C)

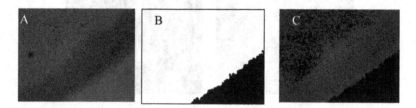

Fig. 7. Light microscopy image revealing cyclin D1 (A), the region occupied by the cells (B), the image after background elimination and brown selection (B)

A method very similar to Green_Color was used. Figure 8 reports an example of this calculation: Figure 8A shows the original image, Figure 8B indicates the region occupied by cells, Figure 8C indicates the image without the background and, finally, Figure 8D indicates the brown image in the region occupied by the cells. With this last image, calculations about the brown quantification are all possible. For biological purposes, the pixels percentage occupied by brown was the most useful: in the reported example it was 27%. As it is possible to note for image of Figure 8D, when compared with Figure 8A and figure 8C, some pixel exploiting brown coloration were discarded: this is probably due to the difficulty to separate brown from other colours. As an example, a medium brown has the following value (R=160, G=130, B=20). Blue was used for coloring cells: for this reason it was quite difficult to extract bright brown because the Blue component was increased for cells recognition purposes.

The method Filopodia_Meas was used to analyze 2 pairs of images collected by scanning electron microscopy at different time for two cellular lines. The method aimed at the extraction of the filopodia coming from a cell, counting them and calculating their total and medium lengths.

Figure 9 reports two of these images, one for each cellular line: 3T3 fibroblasts (A) and HaCat keratinocytes (D). From Figure 9D the filopodia extraction was more difficult than from Figure 9A. Figure 9B and Figure 9E report the images obtained by eliminating the zone occupied by the cell body (where 'cellular body' was found, the pixels amplitude were set to the image background). The binary images indicating filopodia presence are shown in Figure 9C and Figure 9F. These last images were cut to eliminate written information. From these last images, the number of filopodia was automatically calculated by calculating the connected regions, and the total length

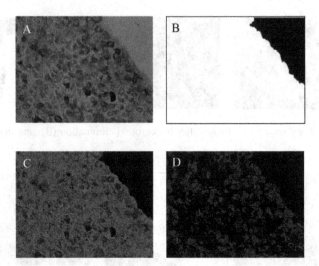

Fig. 8. Light microscopy image revealing Ki-67 (A), the region occupied by the cells (B), the image after background elimination (C) and the brown selection in the region occupied by the cells (B)

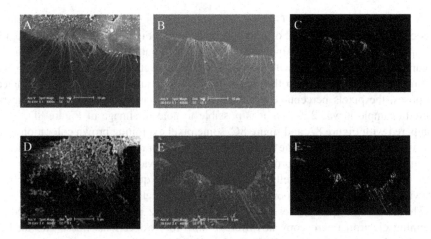

Fig. 9. Scanning Electron microscopy images of two cellular lines: 3T3 fibroblasts (A) and HaCat keratinocytes (B); images without the body cell (B, E); filopodia extraction (C, F): the lower part of the images is cut to eliminate written information

was calculated by counting the number of pixels occupied by filopodia (this number was normalized to the length occupied by a pixel). The mean length was calculated by dividing the total length by the number of filopodia. The results were n=54, Tl=520 microns and ml=9.9 microns for Figure 9A and n=53, Tl=210 microns and ml=3,61 microns for Figure 9D.

It is evident, by comparing the images of the extracted filopodia with the original images that some very thin filopodia remained out from the selection. Moreover, some filopodia were broken, thus producing an error for n and ml calculation (n was increased and ml was decreased), and some of them, being crossing each other, were considered as a single filopodium (thus tending to reduce n and to increase ml). Nevertheless, though with a very difficult image such that shown in Figure 9D, the method performed quite well and the calculations were in good agreement with a subjective control (maximum error was about 8%). The algorithm took about 3 seconds on a classical personal computer to obtain the reported results: on the contrary, a human expert took about 20 minutes to perform an accurate analysis. The proposed method allowed both quantitative and qualitative analysis.

4 Conclusion

We described a set of semi-automatic algorithms to analyze a variety of microscopy images used to study the wound healing process. The proposed suite allows analyzing different light microscopy images or images collected by scanning electron microscopy. The proposed software allows identifying objects in digital images, counting them, and recording a full spectrum of measurements for each object, including location within the image, size, shape, color intensity, textures, and various numerical parameters. It is developed in Matlab, using a graphic user interface that uses the concept of pipelines and, for these reason, it can be automatically integrated into the CellProfiler software, thus introducing new functionalities without losing the CellProfiler existing capabilities. Preliminary results revealed that the proposed software is efficient, easy-to-use, and enables biologists to comprehensively and quantitatively address many questions of the wound healing problem. Future work will be dedicated to improve the interface, introduce new functionalities, and perform a complete and accurate test of the algorithms.

References

1. Abramoff, M.D., Magalhaes, P.J., Ram, S.J.: Image processing with Image. J. Biophotonics Int. 11, 36–42 (2004)
2. Carpenter, A.E., Jones, T.R., Lamprecht, M.R., Clarke, C., Kang, I.H., Friman, O., Guertin, D.A., Chang, J.H., Lindquist, R.A., Moffat, J., Golland, P., Sabatini, D.M.: CellProfiler: image analysis software for identifying and quantifying cell phenotypes. Genome Biol. 7(R100), 1–11 (2006)
3. Franchi, D., Gallo, P., Marsili, L., Placidi, G.: A shape-based segmentation algorithm for X-ray digital subtraction angiography images. Comput. Methods Programs Biomed. 94, 267–278 (2009)
4. Jones, T.R., Kang, I.H., Wheeler, D.B., Lindquist, R.A., Papallo, A., Sabatini, D.M., Golland, P., Carpenter, A.E.: CellProfiler Analyst: data exploration and analysis software for complex image-based screens. BMC BioInf. 9, 482–497 (2008)
5. Lamprecht, M.R., Sabatini, D.M., Carpenter, A.E.: CellProfiler: free versatile software for automated biological image analysis. Biotechniques 42, 71–75 (2007)
6. Maurizi, A., Franchi, D., Placidi, G.: An optimized Java based software package for biomedical images and volumes processing. In: Proc. of the IEEE Med. Meas. & Appl., MeMeA 2009, vol. 1, pp. 219–222 (2009)

7. Murphy, R.F., Meijering, E., Danuser, G.: Special issue on molecular and cellular bioimaging. IEEE Trans. Image Process. 14, 1233–1236 (2005)
8. Selinummi, J., Seppala, J., Yli-Harja, O., Puhakka, J.A.: Software for quantification of labeled bacteria from digital microscope images by automated image analysis. BioTechniques 39, 859–863 (2005)
9. Singer, A.J., Clark, R.A.F.: Cutaneous Wound Healing. The New Engl. J. Med. 341, 738–746 (1999)
10. Skopin, M.D., Molitor, S.C.: Effects of near-infrared laser exposure in a cellular model of wound healing. Photoderm. Photoimm. & Photomed. 25, 75–80 (2009)
11. Yu, A.C., Lee, Y.L., Eng, L.F.: Astrogliosis in culture: I. The model and the effect of antisense oligonucleotides on glial fibrillary acidic protein synthesis. J. Neurosci. Res. 34, 295–303 (1993)

Customizable Visualization on Demand for Hierarchically Organized Information in Biochemical Networks

Peter Droste, Eric von Lieres, Wolfgang Wiechert, and Katharina Nöh[*]

Forschungszentrum Jülich, 52425 Jülich, Germany
{p.droste,e.von.lieres,w.wiechert,k.noeh}@fz-juelich.de

Abstract. Systems biology is concerned with systemic and integrative studies of complex interactions between molecular components within microorganisms and higher cells, and aims at generating holistic understanding of biological processes. The interactions between genes, proteins and metabolites are naturally represented by hierarchically interconnected biochemical networks on different levels. Moreover, the network topology is typically supplemented by qualitative information and quantitative data on individual mechanisms and system states, for example enzyme kinetics and flow rates. Measurement data are often combined with simulation results and knowledge from databases.

Due to constantly improving high throughput techniques we increasingly face the challenge of visualizing manifold and extensive data within large biochemical network diagrams. This issue is effectively addressed by the interactive Visualization on Demand (VoD) approach for hierarchically structured network diagrams presented in this contribution.

Keywords: Visualization on demand, scientific information visualization, hierarchical data organization, systems biology, biochemical networks.

1 Introduction

In systems biology, mathematical modeling, scientific computing and high-throughput experimental approaches are systematically combined in a closed loop cycle for iteratively improving qualitative and quantitative knowledge on biological systems. Biochemical processes within microorganisms and higher cells are typically represented by network diagrams on different levels, for example, cell metabolism, protein-protein interactions, gene regulation, and signaling networks [8]. Systems biology aims at fundamental understanding and targeted manipulation of biochemical process networks under *in-vivo* conditions, in order to improve biotechnological production, for instance, of food and feed additives, pharmaceuticals and biofuels. A system oriented and holistic approach is applied within and across different network layers that are associated with data from so called multi-omics measurement

---

[*] Corresponding author.

R.P. Barneva et al. (Eds.): CompIMAGE 2010, LNCS 6026, pp. 163–174, 2010.
© Springer-Verlag Berlin Heidelberg 2010

techniques [10]. The concise analysis of biochemical processes on these network levels, and the extraction of useful information on the studied biological systems out of
manifold and extensive data from experiments, simulations, and databases has today
become one of the most essential tasks in systems biology.

In the systems biology context information visualization is of fundamental importance not only for presenting data and discussing results in a highly interdisciplinary
community, but also for integrating heterogeneous data from various sources, as is
well-known from bioinformatics. Other important examples are the large-scale exploration of time series data, and the detection and interpretation of novel properties and
of system-level patterns within biochemical networks. Information-rich network visualization is still a challenging problem, particularly when applied to multi-layered and
hierarchically organized data. We hence propose a new and customizable Visualization on Demand approach for hierarchically organized information in biochemical
networks.

1.1 Biochemical Networks

In living cells, hundreds and thousands of different biochemical components are synthesized and degraded, activated and deactivated, imported and exported, often by
means of each other. The intracellular biochemical network is highly interconnected
and self regulated, since most metabolite conversions are catalyzed by enzymes [4].
Enzymes are themselves macromolecules that belong to the class of proteins and are
synthesized on the basis of genetic information that is encoded in specific DNA sequences. These DNA sequences are first transcribed into RNA sequences and then
translated into proteins.

Biochemical networks are regulated on several levels. For example, the expression
of individual genes, and hence the amount of synthesized enzymes, is controlled by
regulatory proteins that respond to internal system states. Signal transduction networks are based on cascaded structures of interdependent system states and control
cellular response to changes in environmental conditions. Finally, enzyme activities,
and consequently conversion rates of the catalyzed reactions, are controlled by specific binding of molecules on the metabolic network level.

The relevant components on each network layer are described by nodes, and interactions between these components are represented by links (edges) between these
nodes. We will explain our new visualization approach on the metabolic network
level. Metabolic networks are directed bipartite graphs with two types of nodes for
representing metabolites and biochemical reactions, respectively. An example is
shown in Figure 1: Blue edges between reactions and metabolites indicate flux relations or, in other words, directed metabolite conversions. The direction of each edge
classifies the corresponding metabolite as substrate or product of the connected reaction. Red edges between metabolites and reactions indicate regulatory relations. In
biochemistry, many reactions can be activated or inhibited by specific metabolites
that are not necessarily substrates or products.

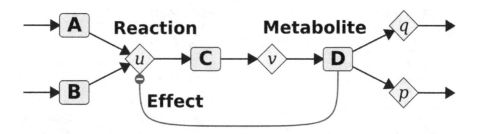

Fig. 1. Example metabolic network with metabolites (boxes), reaction nodes (diamonds), and directed edges that indicate flow (blue) and regulatory (red) relationships

1.2 Information Variety

Today, experimental high throughput techniques and computer simulations increasingly provide us with large quantities of data on various aspects of the biochemical networks within studied cells. The variety of available information includes but is not limited to: Substance concentrations, thermodynamic potentials, metabolite fluxes, reaction mechanisms, rate constants, regulatory relationships and strengths. Some computer simulations require even more detailed information: Reaction nodes are characterized by kinetic equations and parameters for each of which several values might be given in different publications. Metabolite nodes are associated with chemical structure formulas, and flux edges carry detailed information on individual atom transitions.

1.3 Customary Visualization Techniques

Visualization faces the challenge that each individual piece of information is related to a specific node or edge of the network, and that complex interactions between hundreds and thousands of different compounds must be assembled and represented even in mid-scale network models. Conventional tools usually visualize data within biochemical networks by simply annotating nodes and edges with values that are displayed by bars, plots or numbers [5-7]. Figure 2a shows a typical example. However, annotation of nodes with more than a few pieces of information causes information overload, particularly in large networks. Moreover, inherent layout problems occur when annotations are to be placed in the neighborhood of related network components without collisions with other nodes, edges or annotations.

Another straightforward way for visualizing data in networks is to map numerical values to visual properties of nodes and edges, such as color, size and filling [3,13,15,16], as illustrated by Figure 2b. This approach provides qualitative impressions, and time series can be animated. Some data types can be simultaneously visualized by different visual properties of the same nodes and edges. However, this concept is inherently limited by the human ability to capture several information types from one diagram or animation. These limitations can be overcome when hierarchical data structures are utilized for Visualization on Demand.

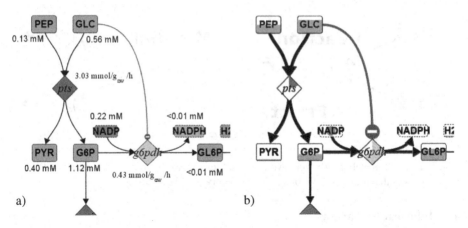

Fig. 2. Two customary techniques for data visualization in biochemical networks: a) annotations, and b) visual properties such as node fill levels and edge line widths

1.4 Hierarchical Data Structures

This contribution addresses the visualization of manifold and extensive information in association with nodes and edges of large biochemical networks, especially when the information pieces are hierarchically organized with variable depth. Such data are often presented in tables [14], which can hardly satisfy because the network context is lost. However, simultaneous visualization of comprehensive information is often not feasible, as discussed in the previous section. We hence propose a Visualization on Demand approach that solves this dilemma with interactive diagrams. Our approach is implemented in the visualization software Omix, which also provides powerful network layout features that are not in the scope of this contribution [3].

2   The Network Visualization Tool Omix

Visualization on Demand is a functional extension of the Omix software. In Omix, biochemical network diagrams are created with an integrated network editor toolbox that is designed with standard usability as known from customary graphics software. Figure 3 shows an Omix screenshot with a drawing of a small network from the central metabolism that contains several interconnected reaction and metabolite nodes. The right sidebar displays several properties of an individual network component that can be changed by the user, for instance, position and size, shape, colors and text font. Omix supports drawing of network diagrams with custom visual appearance.

Biochemical networks are manually drawn or imported from reaction databases (e.g. KEGG, PDB) or file based specifications. Network models can also be exported into various file formats and provided, for example, to simulation software packages. Omix is not only designed as integrative visualization tool for biochemical data from measurements, simulations, and databases, but also as pre and post processing tool for advanced simulation studies with large and complex biochemical network models.

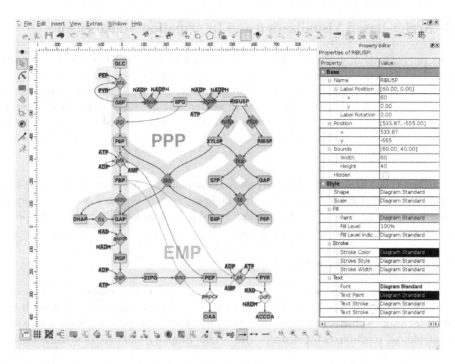

Fig. 3. Screenshot of the network editor and visualization tool Omix: A drawing area (center) is surrounded by several toolbars and a property editor (right)

2.1 Customizability and Programmability

Omix produces highly customizable biochemical network representations and is supplemented by extensive data visualization features. Customizability is very important, because biotechnological research rapidly develops new visualization demands. In recent years, many tools have been developed for visualizing data within biochemical networks [12,16]. These tools are typically designed for specific applications and contain mostly hard-coded methods for a fixed set of data types and visualization approaches [9,13]. Omix' data visualization features are, in contrast, freely and quickly reconfigurable and can, hence, be adapted to changing requirements.

Omix offers programmability for realizing most flexible and highly customizable data visualization. An object-oriented scripting engine allows free programming of network diagrams. For example, Omix enables the network modeler to define interactive elements such as buttons or input masks and to automatically change the visual attributes of graphical elements according to specific values of the associated data. In this way, data that originate from experimental studies or from computer simulations can be visualized in biochemical networks precisely according the users' requirements and preferences. This includes the customary visualization techniques from Section 1.3. The scripting language Omix is programmable which will be shortly introduced in Section 3.

3 Script-Based Visualization and Information Management

The programmability of biochemical network diagrams is implemented in Omix by the *Omix Visualization Language* (OVL). OVL is a scripting language and a modification of the object-oriented high level programming language Java. Our basic design target of OVL was to provide easy and programmable access to visual properties of network components [3]. In OVL, the appearance of nodes and edges in the diagram can be changed by simple assignments:

```
arrowSize = 2.5;
```

In this code example, a set of polynomial computations, necessary for showing the arrow in a new size, are wrapped by one single expression. Furthermore, the scripting language can not only be used to change visual properties but also to equip network components with new custom properties.

3.1 Custom Component Properties

All components in a network diagram are instances of diverse classes, for instance, `Reaction` or `Metabolite`. In OVL, these predefined classes can be extended by the user with interactive elements, functions and further properties. In the following example, all reactions are extended with a new property, the common name of the catalyzing enzyme:

```
1       extend Reaction{
2           String enzyme;
3       }
```

Applied to a network, this small script extends all reactions according to the new properties. In turn, these properties appear in the property editor when reaction items are selected (see Figure 3). More detailed information on the implementation of user interactions and functions in OVL are given elsewhere [2,3].

The syntax of the scripting language OVL is based on Java with a few modifications as shown in the code examples. Internally, OVL was implemented with an AntLR-generated parser [11]. Furthermore, normal Java classes, primitive types, and even arrays can be used in OVL scripts, a feature which is allowed by the Java Reflection API.

Biologists are usually not well-trained in programming, but the advantages of a script-based instead of a hard-coded visualization approach prevail. OVL offers a simplified syntax to access visual properties of nodes and edges and to implement interactivity. The Omix user manual contains an example in which the complex visualization task of mapping spreadsheet data to visual properties of nodes and edges is implemented in only 35 lines of OVL code [1]. Users can adapt this and other examples from the tutorial to meet their individual requirements. Exchangeability of OVL scripts among different network documents allows researchers to build their own collections of customized OVL scripts for specific tasks and visualization purposes.

3.2 Custom Data Types

With OVL scripts the user can not only extend existing component types with further functionality, but also define own class types as known from Java. OVL supports inheritance as well as information hiding. Unlike normal hard-coded Java classes, OVL classes can be created and modified dynamically at run time. Furthermore, Omix is able to inspect objects of OVL classes, display all attributes, and even respond to attribute changes. The option to define classes in OVL is new and was implemented in order to allow user-defined hierarchical information organization. Objects of any type can be assigned with properties that themselves can have own properties of various types. This feature enables the user to compose hierarchies of information in any manner and depth. Thus, custom classes are the cornerstone of our Visualization on Demand approach.

The following code example shows how to use OVL for equipping biochemical networks with various hierarchically organized data types. The previously mentioned extension of reactions by names of the catalyzing enzymes is here replaced by more complex and custom defined information types. For example, the following class En-zyme encapsulates not only the enzyme name, but also a structural image of the molecule shape, a MathML formula of the enzyme kinetics, the atomic mass, the Enzyme Commission (EC) number, the enzyme ID in a reference database, and a list of sub units that are stored in an array:

```
4       class Enzyme{
5           String name;
6           Image image;
7           MML kinetics;           // as MathML formula
8           double mass;
9           String ecNumber;
10          String databaseID;
11          SubUnit[] subUnits;
12      }
```

When the variable type in line 2 is changed from String to Enzyme this custom information type associates all reactions with the corresponding properties. The variable types String (line 5), Image (6) and MML (7) used for defining the example Enzyme class are native Java classes, and provided by the Java runtime library and other sources. However, the data type for describing enzyme sub units in line 11 is an OVL class that combines information on the activity of the sub unit with information on the expressing gene sequence that could be a further custom data type.

```
13      class SubUnit{
14          boolean catalyticalActive;
15          Gene expressingGeneSequence;
16          //...further properties
17      }
```

The example illustrates how programmability of the network visualization software Omix enables user defined organization of large data amounts in hierarchies, relations and aggregations along the nodes and edges of biochemical networks. Individual networks components can be augmented with many different information types that evolve from or refer to experiments, simulations and databases. Depending on the nature of the supplementary information the definition of composed OVL class types can help to subclassify complex data into different levels of detail.

3.3 Meta-information

Variables in OVL scripts are not only visualized in the network but are also visible and editable in the property editor sidebar (see Figure 3) and in other window components of Omix. The presentation of these variables in window components can be supplemented with meta-information using an annotation concept as known from the Java programming language. In OVL, annotations can be applied on variables and other programming constructs. The following example provides meta-information for two variables of the Enzyme class, mass and ecNumber:

```
8        @Unit("Da") double mass;
9        @Label("EC Number") String ecNumber;
```

The mass property (line 8) is supplemented with a physical unit (Dalton) in order to be correctly interpreted. The annotation type Unit causes suffixing of the displayed value with the unit symbol. Line 9 changes the label of the variable ecNumber. Usually OVL defined properties are labeled with the variable name. However, variable names are restricted to a limited character set. The Label annotation type is hence useful for overriding variable names with more general labels. Omix provides several other annotation types that represent meta-information on displaying or on editing information, as presented elsewhere [2].

3.4 Information Management

Custom properties of network objects are initially empty or set to default values. In order to insert data into network diagrams Omix offers two ways by loading property variables with information: First, OVL can import data from files or databases and assign these data to properties of network components. Omix offers several Java classes in a simple programming interface that are specialized for extracting information from CSV files and Excel spreadsheets [2]. Second, data can be inserted into networks by manually changing the properties of all network components. This is implemented in the previously mentioned property editor. Omix provides editor components for a multitude of Java types which are frequently used in OVL, for example, floating point numbers, boolean values, plain text, colors, lists and arrays or file references, and many more. Generally, objects of all kinds of Java classes can be constructed via dynamic access to their class definitions in a set of dialog windows as shown in Figure 4.

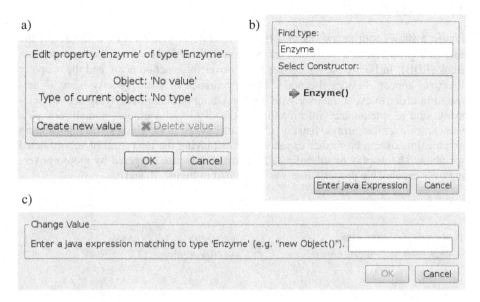

Fig. 4. Dialog windows in Omix that offer dynamic access for constructing objects from arbitrary Java classes: a) object creation and deletion, b) constructor selection for creating objects of unspecific type, c) input of Java expressions for dynamic object construction

4 Visualization on Demand

In Section 1.3 we have already discussed the practical impossibility of simultaneously visualizing manifold and extensive information over entire diagrams of realistically sized biochemical networks, and proposed an interactive approach. Hence, we have implemented Visualization on Demand (VoD) as an optional network viewing mode in the Omix software. The VoD mode facilitates user controlled displaying of supplementary information that is related to metabolite and reaction nodes, and to their interconnecting edges in arbitrary levels of detail. In VoD mode, simple mouse hovering over network elements activates displaying of all associated properties of the respective node or edge. The user can open further levels of detail by hovering over the respective displayed property. Layout problems and information-overload are effectively avoided by showing properties of only one network component and zooming in the details of only one property at a time.

Global representation of the network is hardly affected by the details of single components, because user perception is temporarily directed to individual pieces of information in their local context. The nodes and edges of the biochemical network are globally arranged in a macro layout, whereas the hierarchically organized details are locally arranged in a dynamic tree-structured micro layout at the corresponding network components. When the mouse hovers over a node or edge, the associated properties are itemized to the left and right of this network component. In addition, the individual items are connected with the corresponding node or edge by a dashed line.

4.1 Worked Example

Figure 5 shows four snapshots of a typical interactive visualization example for the Enzyme property of a reaction (see Section 3.2) with data from the Protein Data Bank (PDB): In Figure 5a, the mouse hovers over the reaction node, and the property Enzyme appears besides the node. The appearance of such property items is animated in order to assist the user with distinguishing between underlying network elements and supplementary information. If the displayed variables contain complex values, for example arrays, lists, or objects of custom OVL classes, the representing graphical items can be further expanded for displaying the next level of subordinated variables. The display of subordinated information is also triggered by mouse hovering over expandable property items as illustrated in Figure 5b and c.

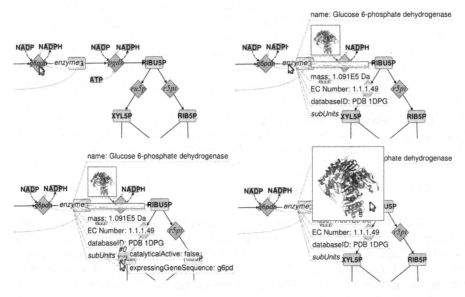

Fig. 5. Visualization of the Enzyme property in several levels of detail

In Figure 5b the mouse hovers over the Enzyme property causing its expansion. The name, image representation, kinetic equation, mass, EC number, database ID and sub units of the enzyme become visible. In Figure 5c the SubUnit property of the enzyme is additionally unfolded. Images that are elements of itemized properties are initially displayed with a rather small default size, in order to avoid overloading of the network diagram. On demand, such images can be magnified up to their original size by mouse wheel interaction as illustrated in Figure 5d. This way, the user can visualize arbitrary levels of detail on demand.

5 Conclusions

Systems biology aims at generating holistic understanding of complex biochemical networks in living cells. Experiments, simulations and databases provide vast amounts of multilayered data that are associated with nodes and edges of the studied intracellular biochemical networks. Integrated visualization of these data is particularly challenging due to apparently incompatible goals, such as completeness of large network representations, accessibility of all available information, and clearness of the displayed diagrams. Visualization on Demand (VoD) effectively solves this dilemma by dynamically and interactively displaying individual pieces of hierarchically organized information at network nodes and edges in subordinated levels of detail. The mouse controlled adaption of selective information display to user perception stands in stark contrast to customary static visualization approaches which simultaneously display all available information.

We have implemented VoD for biochemical networks as functional extension of the visualization software Omix. The implementation of VoD in Omix is technically realized by programmability of network components in a script language, the Omix Visualization Language (OVL). OVL facilitates the definition of new information types and the extension of network components with custom properties. By design, the VoD extension of Omix provides free and easy customization of information management and visualization in biochemical network diagrams.

Acknowledgments. The authors are thankful to Stephan Noack and Tina Kubitzki for scientific discussions and providing data as well as Evonik Industries for financial support within the BMBF co-funded project SysMAP (project no. 0313704).

References

1. Droste, P.: Omix – Editor and Visualization Tool for Biochemical Networks – User Manual. Institute of Biotechnology 2, Forschungszentrum Jülich, Jülich (2008)
2. Droste, P.: Omix Visualization Language – Technical Manual. Institute of Biotechnology 2, Forschungszentrum Jülich, Jülich (2008)
3. Droste, P., Nöh, K., Noack, S., Wiechert, W.: Customizable visualization of Multi-Omics data in the context of biochemical networks. In: Banissi, E., et al. (eds.) Int. Conference on Visualization, Visualization in Built and Rural Environments, BioMedical Visualization, Geometric Modeling and Imaging, pp. 21–25. IEEE, Inc., Los Alamitos (2009)
4. Gottschalk, G.: Bacterial Metabolism. Cambridge University Press, Cambridge (1986)
5. Junker, B.H., Klukas, C., Schreiber, F.: VANTED: A system for advanced data analysis and visualization in the context of biological networks. BMC Bioinformatics 7 (2006)
6. Klamt, S., Stelling, J., Ginkel, M., Gilles, E.D.: FluxAnalyzer: exploring structure, pathways, and flux distributions in metabolic networks on interactive flux maps. Bioinformatics 19, 261–269 (2003)
7. Klamt, S., Saez-Rodriguez, J., Gilles, E.D.: Structural and functional analysis of cellular networks with CellNetAnalyzer. BMC Systems Biology 1(2) (2007)
8. Kremling, A., Jahreis, K., Lengeler, J.W., Gilles, E.D.: The organization of metabolic reaction networks: A signal-oriented approach to cellular models. Metabolic Engineering 2, 190–200 (2000)
9. Neuweger, H., Persicke, M., Albaum, S.P., Bekel, T., Dondrup, M., Huser, A.T., Winnebald, J., Schneider, J., Kalinowski, J., Goesmann, A.: Visualizing post genomics data-sets on customized pathway maps by ProMeTra - aeration-dependent gene expression and metabolism of Corynebacterium glutamicum as an example. BMC Systems Biology 3 (2009)

10. Palsson, B.O.: Systems Biology: Properties of Reconstructed Networks. Cambridge (2006)
11. Parr, T.J., Quong, R.W.: ANTLR: A Predicated-LL(k) Parser Generator. Software – Practice and Experience 25 (1995)
12. Pavlopoulos, G.A., Wegener, A.-L., Schneider, R.: A survey of visualization tools for biological network analysis. BioData Mining 1(12) (2008)
13. Qeli, E., Wahl, A., Degenring, D., Wiechert, W., Freisleben, B.: MetVis: A tool for designing and animating metabolic networks. In: Proceedings of the 2003 European Simulation and Modelling Conference, pp. 333–338. Eurosis Press, Naples (2003)
14. Reuss, M., Aguilera-Vázquez, L., Mauch, K.: Reconstruction of dynamic network models from metabolite measurements. In: Nielsen, J., Jewett, M.C. (eds.) Metabolomics. Topics in Current Genetics, vol. 18, pp. 97–127. Springer, Heidelberg (2007)
15. Rost, U., Kummer, U.: Visualisation of biochemical network simulations with SimWiz. IEE Systems Biology 1, 184–189 (2004)
16. Sudermann, M., Hallett, M.: Tools for visually exploring biological networks. BMC Bioinformatics 23, 2651–2659 (2007)

Improved Kernel Common Vector Method for Face Recognition Varying in Background Conditions

C. Lakshmi[1], M. Ponnavaikko[2], and M. Sundararajan[3]

[1] School of Computer Science & Engg. SRM University, India
slva90@yahoo.co.in
[2] Bharathidasan University, India
[3] Sri Lakshmi Ammal Engineering College, Chennai, India

Abstract. The Common Vector (CV) method is a linear subspace classifier for datasets, such as those arising in image and word recognition. In this approach, a class subspace is modeled from the common features of all samples in the corresponding class. Since the class subspace are modeled as a separate subspace for each class in feature domain, there is overlapping between these subspaces and also loss of information in the common vector of a class. This reduces the recognition performance. In multi-class problems, within-class and between-class scatter should be considered in classification criterion. Since the within class scatter S_W and between class scatter S_B followed in Discriminative Common Vector method (DCV) are based on the assumption that all classes have similar covariance structures, these class scatters cannot be followed in CV method. Generally a linear subspace classifier fails to extract the non-linear features of samples which describe the complexity of face image due to illumination, facial expressions and pose variations. In this paper, we propose a new method called "Improved kernel common vector method" which solves the above problems by means of its appealing properties. First the inclusion of boosting parameters in the proposed between-class and within-class scatters consider the neighboring class subspaces and also consider a sample of a class with samples of other classes. This increases the recognition performance. Second the obtained common vector by using the above proposed scatter spaces has more significant discriminative information which also increases the recognition performance. Third like all kernel methods, it handles non-linearity in a disciplined manner which extracts the non-linear features of samples representing the complexity of face images. Experimental results on Yale B face database demonstrate the promising performance of the proposed methodology.

Keywords: subspace classifiers, kernel common vector, pair wise class discriminant criterion, mislabel distribution, boosting parameter, scatter spaces.

R.P. Barneva et al. (Eds.): CompIMAGE 2010, LNCS 6026, pp. 175–186, 2010.
© Springer-Verlag Berlin Heidelberg 2010

1   Introduction

In the last two decades, face recognition technology has become one of the most wanted technologies for its potential applications in personal identification, security access control, surveillance, telecommunications, digital libraries, human-computer interaction, military and so on [1,4,28]. Face recognition can be described as the identification process of a given input face image using a stored face database [4].

The extraction of best representative features from the face images significantly improves the performance of any face recognition system. Thus the feature extraction is a critical issue in face recognition tasks. Numerous approaches have been proposed in recent years. Among them linear subspace analysis is one of the most popular feature extraction methods, which aims to project face images into a low-dimensional subspace with a linear transformation. This linear subspace classifier uses a linear subspace for each class [18]. In this method, it is assumed that the vector distribution of each class corresponds to a lower dimensional subspace of the original sample space. The subspaces representing classes are defined in terms of basis vectors that are linear combinations of the sample vector of each class. Also, determining the dimension of each subspace is a major issue since subspace dimensions have a strong influence on the performance of the subspace classifier. In particular, large subspace dimensions lead a low recognition performance due to the overlapping regions among classes whereas small subspace dimensions increase the error rates because of a poor resulting approximation [15,16].

The first subspace method [12] is the class-featuring information processing (CCAFIC) for pattern classification. This method employs the principal component analysis (PCA) to compute the basis vectors spanning the subspace of each class. However, the subspaces may sometimes have a large overlapping region in common, which causes poor classification of data samples. Therefore, the method of orthogonal subspace was proposed which attempts to remove the common regions of the classes and makes the class subspaces mutually orthogonal [22]. Another new method proposed in [14] selects the basis vectors in such a way that the projections onto the so-called rival subspaces are minimized.

In some classification tasks, the dimensionality of the sample space can be larger than the number of training samples in each class. The computations that carried out at full dimensionality may not deliver the advantages of high dimensional sample space when the number of training samples is insufficient. Therefore the dimensionality of the sample space is usually reduced before applying a classifier to data samples in the original sample space. The Eigen face method [24] and Fisher's linear discriminant analysis [9] are two popular feature extraction methods that are used for dimension reduction. However, dimensionality reduction through feature extraction may cause loss of important discriminatory information. Therefore [13] proposed the common vector subspace classifier method that models subspaces in such a way that their basis vectors span the null space of the co-variance matrix of each class, assuming that the number of samples in each class is smaller than or equal to the dimensionality of the sample space [13,14]. This method has been successfully applied in the isolated word recognition and face recognition problems [5,13]. However, the linear subspaces may not extract non-linear features of classes since each class is associated with a linear subspace [2,23]. The kernel-based non-linear subspace method, which is called the kernel class featuring information compression, was developed to overcome this limitation [2,23]. In this, it is assumed that all samples in each class lie in some non-linear subspace. Therefore, all data samples in each class are mapped to a high dimensional feature space through a non-linear kernel mapping function and the kernel PCA [20] has been employed to compute the principal components of the correlation matrices of classes in the mapped space. This process spreads the data over a greater volume which in turn reduces overlapping regions among the classes. In this, the mapped function or the mapped samples are not used explicitly, which makes this method feasible.

Another new non-linear method, the Kernel Common Vector method was developed in [6]. In this method, the training set samples are mapped into an implicit higher dimensional space using a non-linear kernel mapping function and then applying the linear CV method in the mapped space. In this the kernel functions are used to compute the dot products of the mapped samples. As a result the mapping function and the mapped samples are not used explicitly which makes the method feasible. However, in this method, the followed discriminant criterion considers the within-class scatter only. Within-class scatter may cause the overlapping between the class subspaces. This makes the followed criterion neglecting the overlapping between the classes and thus reduces the recognition performance. This shows the importance of consideration of between-class scatters also. Rifat Edizkan et al. [8] proposed an improvement in common vector method by introducing two different optimization criteria in their study report. In this, the first optimization criterion maximizes the distances of inter-class scatter in the indifference subspace and the second optimization criterion minimizes the distances of intra-class scatter in the difference subspace. The obtained class subspace dimension is less as compared to the class subspace obtained in KCV method. The results in [8] show among these two criteria, the first criterion provides advantages in designing recognizer in terms of processing time and memory space utilization. However, in first criterion, the methods followed in the distances of inter-class scatter are measured in the indifference subspace leads to overlapping between the class subspaces. The within-class scatter criteria of [6] consider only the class co-variance and neglecting the neighboring class co-variances. Thus the within-class scatter fails to estimate the correct value for recognition.

In this paper, we propose a new method called "Improved Kernel Common Vector" (IKCV) method which integrates the boosting parameters with scatter spaces and then applying KCV which works based on our proposed scatter spaces. These boosting parameters have been applied to LDA, KDA, and its recognition performance are showed in [3,7]. The remainder of this paper is organized as follows: In Section 2, a brief review of the KCV method is presented; Section 3 describes the proposed within-class and between-class scatter spaces. In Section 4 we describe our proposed method "Improved Kernel Common Vector" method. We discuss our experimental results in Section 5 and our conclusions are given in Section 6.

2   A Brief Review of KCV Method

Let the training set be composed of C classes, where the ith class contains N_i samples and let x_m^i be a d-dimensional column vector, which denotes the mth sample from the ith class. There is a total of $M = \sum_{i=1}^{C} N_i$ samples in the training set.

In this method, the training set samples are mapped into an implicit higher dimensional space using a non-linear kernel mapping function and then applying the linear CV method in the mapped space. In high dimensional space, let $\phi = [\phi^{(1)}, \phi^{(2)}, ..., \phi^{(c)}]$ represents the matrix whose columns are the mapped training samples where $\phi^i = [\phi(x_1^i), \phi(x_2^i), ..., \phi(x_{N_i}^i)]$ is the matrix class.

The scatter matrix S_i^ϕ of each class is defined as

$$S_i^\phi = \sum_{m=1}^{N_i} \left(\phi\left(x_m^i\right) - \mu_i^\phi \right) \left(\phi\left(x_m^i\right) - \mu_i^\phi \right)^T \tag{1}$$

$$i = 1, \dots, C,$$

where μ_i^ϕ is the mean of samples of the ith class. The total scatter matrix is defined as,

$$S_T^\phi = \sum_{i=1}^{C} \sum_{m=1}^{N_i} \left(\phi\left(x_m^i\right) - \mu^\phi \right) \left(\phi\left(x_m^i\right) - \mu^\phi \right) \tag{2}$$

where μ^ϕ is mean of all samples. The kernel matrix of the mapped data is given as $K = \phi^T \phi = (K^{ij}), i = 1, \dots, C, j = 1, \dots, C$, where each submatrix K^{ij} is defined as

$$(K_{mn}^{ij}) \leq \phi\left(x_m^i\right), \phi\left(x_n^j\right) > m = 1, \dots, N_i, \quad n = 1, \dots, N_i \tag{3}$$

The following class subspace is the intersection of the null space of that class scatter matrix and the range space of the total scatter matrix, i.e., $N\left(S_i^\phi\right) \cap R\left(S_T^\phi\right), i = 1, \dots, C$. The basis vectors spanning these spaces represent optimal class subspaces. Since the projection matrices of above spaces are commuted as shown in Theorem 1 in [6], the projection matrix $P_{int}^{(i)}$ of the intersection subspace

$$P_{int}^{(i)} = P_{NS}^{(i)} P = P P_{NS}^{(i)}, i = 1, \dots, C \tag{4}$$

Where $P_{NS}^{(i)}$ is the projection matrix of the null spaces of class i and P is the projection matrix of the subspace of the total scatter matrix. The basis vectors spanning each intersection subspace $P_{int}^{(i)}, i = 1, \dots, C$, can be found by transferring the training set samples onto $R\left(S_T^\phi\right)$ using the kernel PCA and then compute the null space of the scatter matrix of each class in the transformed space by using Eigen decomposition method.

The result of the above method gives the basis vectors for all the class projections intersection subspaces i.e., the column vector $W^{(i)}$ represent the basis vectors of the intersection subspaces of class i. The transformation of samples onto their corresponding intersection subspace gives the feature vector of the class. This vector is called as CV of the class. The transformation of all other samples in this intersection subspace gives the same vector shows the CV is independent of m. The CV of class i is defined as

$$\Omega^i_{com} = W^{(i)^T} \phi\left(x^i_m\right), \quad i = 1, \ldots, C, \quad m = 1, \ldots, N_i \tag{5}$$

In this method, the given test image sample x_{test} is recognized by comparing the feature vector of a test sample with the CV of all the classes using Euclidean distance method. Thus the test sample is assigned to the class that minimizes the distance.

3   Proposed Within-class and Between-class Scatter Spaces

In multi-class problems, the samples are grouped in the form of classes and the sample space consists of classes. Thus the within-class and between-class scatters should be considered in classification criterion. The common vector is a unique vector which represents the common properties of each class. These common properties represent features that are common to all samples in each class. This vector is used in the recognition of classes in CV method. In this paper, we propose an enhanced within-class and between-class scatter spaces in order to address the problems mentioned in Section 1.

The within-class scatter of the class will be close to the average of that class. The within-class scatter represents the distance between a sample and other samples in the class. Based on the above concept the within-class scatter matrix is defined as $S^{i_\phi}_w$

$$S^{i_\phi}_w = \sum_{m=1}^{N_i} \left(\phi\left(x^i_m\right) - \mu^\phi_i\right)\left(\phi\left(x^i_m\right) - \mu^\phi_i\right)^T \tag{6}$$

In high dimensional feature space, the distances between the classes are represented by between-class scatter S^ϕ_b. The between-class scatter of class i,$S^{i_\phi}_b$ is defined as

$$S^{i_\phi}_b = \sum_{i=1}^{C-1} \sum_{j=i+1}^{C} \left(\mu^\phi_i - \mu^\phi_j\right)\left(\mu^\phi_i - \mu^\phi_j\right)^T \tag{7}$$

For a better discrimination the criterion should have the significant discriminant information in it. However in the above the between-class scatter is computed at the expense of classes that are close to each other, leading to significant overlap between them. Thus the required modification in between-class scatter is that it has to consider the separability parameter of a sample with other classes. Guangoai et al. proposed some boosting parameters which enhance the performance of scatter spaces [12]. The pair wise class discriminant distribution parameter measures the distance between the classes in terms of the separability parameter. The value of the pair wise class discriminant distribution is based on the mislabel distribution of samples in the classes [10]. The pair wise class discriminant distribution $d_{i,j}$ between classes X_i and X_j can be calculated as follows:

$$d_{i,j} = \{\tfrac{1}{2} \sum_{m=1}^{N_i} \Gamma\left(x_m^i, j\right) + \sum_{n=1}^{N_j} \Gamma\left(x_n^j, i\right)\}$$
$$i \neq j$$
$$0, otherwise$$
(8)

Here the mislabel distribution $\Gamma\left(*, \bullet\right)$ measures the extent of the difficulty of discriminating the sample * from the improper label ?. Obviously, a larger value of $d_{i,j}$ indicates the worse separability between two classes X_i and X_j. Therefore this parameter is used to compute the between class scatter$S_b^{i\phi}$. Thus the modified between-class scatter $S_B^{i\phi}$ is defined as

$$S_B^{i\phi} = \sum_{i=1}^{C-1} \sum_{j=I+1}^{C} \frac{N_i N_j}{N^2} w\left(d_{i,j}\right) \left(\mu_i^\phi - \mu_j^\phi\right) \left(\mu_i^\phi - \mu_j^\phi\right)^T$$
(9)

Where the weighting function w(*) is generally chosen to be monotonically increasing function of *. For simplicity, we let w (*) =* in this paper. Based on the above processing, it can be seen that classes that are not well separated in high dimensional space and thus can potentially impair the classification performance should be more heavily weighted in this space.

Another scatter space, the within-class scatter $S_w^{i\phi}$ computation procedure considers only the distance between the samples in that class. This will fail to estimate the correct value for improved classification, due to minimizing the spread of the outlier classes while neglecting the minimization of other co-variances. In order to solve this problem the parameter r_i measures the relevance based weight for class i and the other parameter q_{im} which measures the hardest samples in class i are considered in the computation procedure of within-class scatter $S_w^{i\phi}$. The modified within-class scatter $S_W^{i\phi}$ is defined as

$$S_W^{i\phi} = \sum_{m=1}^{N_i} r_i q_{im} \left(\phi\left(x_m^i\right) - \mu_i^\phi\right) \left(\phi\left(x_m^i\right) - \mu_i^\phi\right)^T,$$
(10)

$$m = 1, \ldots, N_i, i = 1, \ldots C,$$

where $r_i = \sum_{j \neq i} w\left(d_{i,j}\right)$ is the relevance-based weight for class i and it shows the influence of class i in the estimation of $S_W^{i\phi}$ [19]. The parameter

$q_{im} = w \left(\sum_{j \neq i} \Gamma \left(x_m^i, j \right) \right)$ indicates a greater difficulty of classifying a sample of class i. Thus the parameter q_{im} shows the hardest samples in the class i.

From the above, the parameters $d_{i,j}, r_i$ and q_{im} enhance the computation of within-class and between-class scatter spaces. Thus these parameters are called boosting parameters. These modified scatter spaces $S_W^{i\phi}, S_B^{i\phi}$ are called as boosted scatter spaces. In this paper, we use these boosted scatter spaces in the calculation of common vector of each class in the transformed space.

4   Proposed Improved Kernel Common Vector Method: IKCV

Based on the boosted scatter spaces $S_W^{i\phi}$, $S_B^{i\phi}$ we propose the modified IKCV algorithm called Improved KCV algorithm. In IKCV algorithm, the KCV technique with modified scatter spaces is used to extract the common vector of a class in feature space F. In general, some sampling procedures are employed to artificially weaken the discriminant technique and in IKCV, we choose some examples in each class based on q_{im} to focus hardest samples in each class. Then the improved KCV technique is applied on these classes for feature extraction. The kernel common vector of each class can be computed by using our proposed algorithm.

Thus IKCV method classifies a new test image x test to class C by finding the minimum Euclidean distance between Ω_{test}^{ϕ} and Ω_i^{ϕ}, i.e.,

$$\hat{C} = \min_i \left\| \Omega_i^{\phi} - \Omega_{test}^{\phi} \right\|, i = 1, \dots, C \tag{11}$$

Algorithm:
Assuming that in a set

$$X = \left\{ \left\{ x_1^1, x_2^1, \dots, x_N^1 \right\}, \left\{ x_1^2, x_2^2, \dots, x_N^2 \right\}, \dots, \left\{ x_1^c, x_2^c, \dots, x_N^c \right\} \right\}$$

there are C classes and each class contains N samples. Let X_m^i be the mth sample in ith class. There are a total of $M = N * C$ samples in the training set X.

In kernel method [17] and [21], the training samples in X are transformed into an implicit higher dimensional feature space F through a non linear mapping $\phi(x)$. Let the sample matrix be $X = [x_1, x_2, \dots, x_n]$ which becomes $X_\phi = [\phi(x_1), \phi(x_2), \dots, \phi(x_n)]$ after samples are mapped into feature space F through a non-linear mapping.

The modified within class scatter $S_W^{i\phi}$, the modified between class scatter $S_B^{i\phi}$ and the total scatter matrix of a class are defined by using the boosting parameters as,

$$S_W^{i\phi} = \sum_{m=1}^{N_i} r_i q_{im} \left(\phi \left(x_m^i \right) - \mu_i^\phi \right) \left(\phi \left(x_m^i \right) - \mu_i^\phi \right)^T \tag{12}$$

$$S_B^{i\phi} = \sum_{i=1}^{C-1} \sum_{j=I+1}^{C} \frac{N_i N_j}{N^2} w\left(d_{i,j}\right) \left(\mu_i^\phi - \mu_j^\phi\right) \left(\mu_i^\phi - \mu_j^\phi\right)^T \tag{13}$$

$$S_T^{i\phi} = S_B^{i\phi} + S_W^{i\phi} \tag{14}$$

The total scatter matrix of all classes is defined as

$$S_T^\phi = \sum_{i=1}^{C} S_T^{i\phi}, \tag{15}$$

where μ^ϕ is mean of all samples and μ_i^ϕ is the mean of samples of the ith class in F. The $d_{i,j}$, r_i and q_{im} are boosting parameters which are described above.

The algorithm for IKCV based on subspace methods is summarized as follows.

Step 1: In transformed feature space F, the training set samples of class i is transformed on to R (S_T^ϕ) using the kernel PCA.

Step 2: Compute the new within-class scatter matrix $\tilde{S}_W^{i\phi}$ as

$$\tilde{S}_W^{i\phi} = \sum_{m=1}^{N_i} r_i q_{im} \left(\phi\left(x_m^i\right) - \tilde{\mu}_i^\phi\right) \left(\phi\left(x_m^i\right) - \tilde{\mu}_i^\phi\right)^T \tag{16}$$

in the reduced space.

Step 3: Compute the new between-class scatter matrix $\tilde{S}_B^{i\phi}$ as

$$\tilde{S}_B^{i\phi} = \sum_{i=1}^{C-1} \sum_{j=I+1}^{C} \frac{N_i N_j}{N^2} w\left(d_{i,j}\right) \left(\tilde{\mu}_i^\phi - \tilde{\mu}_j^\phi\right) \left(\tilde{\mu}_i^\phi - \tilde{\mu}_j^\phi\right)^T \tag{17}$$

in the reduced space.

Step 4: For each class, find a basis of the null space of $\tilde{S}_W^{i\phi}$. This can be done by Eigen decomposition. The normalized Eigen vectors corresponding to the zero Eigen values of $\tilde{S}_W^{i\phi}$ form an orthonormal basis for the null space of$\tilde{S}_W^{i\phi}$.

Step 5: The basis vectors $W^{(i)}$, whose columns span the intersection subspace of the ith class. The number of basis vectors spanning the intersection subspace is determined by the dimensionality of $N(\tilde{S}_W^{i\phi})$ for each class.

Step 6: The extracted features all classes are available in the matrix W. The feature of class i is available in $W^{(i)}$. Thus the common feature of class i is obtained by projecting any sample of a class on to its projection matrix. This is defined as

$$\Omega_{com}^{(i)} = W^{(i)^T} \Phi(x_m^i), \quad i = 1, \ldots, C, \quad m = 1, \ldots, N_i \tag{18}$$

Note that the above step independent of m that is the common vector of a class is independent of samples of a class.

Step 7: To recognize a given test sample, we compute the feature vector of a test sample by

$$\Omega_{test}^{(i)} = W^{(i)^T} \phi(x_{test}^i) \tag{19}$$

Step 8: This method classifies a new test image x test to class C by finding the minimum Euclidean distance between Ω_{test}^{ϕ} and Ω_i^{ϕ}, i.e.,

$$\hat{C} = \min_i \left\| \Omega_i^{\phi} - \Omega_{test}^{\phi} \right\|, i = 1, \ldots, C$$

5 Experimental Results

The face images of Yale B university database [12] was used to test our proposed method. The sample training images are shown in Figure 1. In this portion of the face database were retrieved for our training and testing purpose. The retrieved face database consists of images from $C=12$ different people, using 10 images from each person, for a total of 120 images. The image contains variations with the following facial expression as center-light, left-light, and normal, right-light, happy, sad and surprised. First these images were converted to grayscale images. Second we preprocessed these images by aligning and scaling them so that the distance between the eyes was the same for all images and also ensuring that the eyes occurred in the same co-ordinates of the image. The resulting images were then cropped. The final size of the image was 92 × 112.

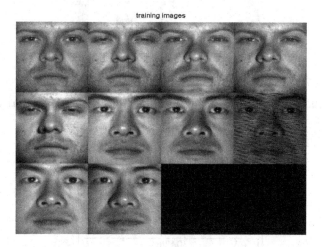

Fig. 1. The sample images from Yale B database. The training set consists of seven images that were randomly selected from each subject, and the rest of the images were used for constructing test set. Thus a training set of 84 images and a test set of 36 images were created. This recognition process was repeated 5 times and 5 different training and test sets were created. These 5 training set and testing set were created by randomly selecting samples from classes at each trial.

The final recognition rates for the experiment were found by averaging these rates that were obtained in each trial. An appropriate selection of kernel functions give rise to different constructions of the implicit feature space [19] we have experimented with polynomial kernels $k(x, y) = (< x, y >)^n$ of degree $n = 2$.

The sample test result is shown in Figure 2. The Figure 2 shows that the proposed method identified the given test image varying in different lighting conditions and also varying in facial expression. The top few matches of a given test image is found and displayed along with its label. The IKCV method significantly outperformed the KCV method and Modified CV method in all cases, i.e., in terms of accuracy and in recognition time.

We can apply both the Modified CV and KCV methods also here since the dimensionality of the sample space, which is 10304, is much larger than the total number of samples in the training set. The computed recognition rates on Yale B face database of KCV, Modified CV and IKCV are given in Table 1.

In terms of classification accuracy, the IKCV method achieved the highest recognition rate than other non-linear methods. The recognition result in Table 1 shows that the IKCV method outperformed the other CV methods for Yale B face database. The reason for this is that the classes were better represented by the unique subspace that were obtained using all the data samples in the training set by the IKCV method. Among subspace classifiers, improved kernel common vector method (IKCV) outperforms other methods in the case of classes having different co-variance structures in a high dimensional sample space.

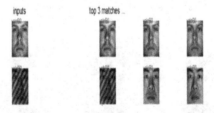

Fig. 2. Sample test result identified the given test image in a trial

Table 1. Comparison of average recognition rates (%)

Linear &Non-linear classifiers	Recognition rates (%)
Kernel CV	91.71
Modified CV	92.26
IKCV	94.26

6   Conclusion

In this paper, we have proposed a new algorithm for face recognition which addresses the non balanced problems in KCV. We have shown that the modified between class scatter and weighted within class scatter solves the problems of KCV. These spaces are calculated by using the pair wise class discriminant information which improves the classification accuracy. The hardest samples for training are selected based on the mislabel distribution; it also increases the recognition performance in testing time. Our proposed algorithm gives an ensemble-based KCV framework with strong nonlinear feature extraction capability, and simultaneously overcomes the non-balanced and small sample size problems commonly encountered by KCV based methods. The experimental results show that the proposed IKCV enhances the recognition performance of the KCV.

References

1. Abate, A.F., Nappi, M., Riccio, D., Sabatino, G.: 2D and 3D face recognition: A Survey. Pattern Recognition Letters 28, 1885–1906 (2007)
2. Balachander, T., Kothari, R.: Kernel based subspace pattern classification. Proc. Int. Joint Conf. Neural Netw. 5, 3119–3122 (1999)
3. Baudat, G., Anouar, F.: Generalized discriminant analysis using a kernel approach. Neural Computation 12, 2385–2404 (2000)
4. Chellappa, R., Wilson, C.L., Sirohey, S.: Human and machine recognition of faces: A Survey. Proc. IEEE 83, 705–740 (1995)
5. Cevikalp, H., Barkana, B., Barkana, A.: A comparison of the common vector and the discriminative common vector methods for face recognition. In: Proc. 9th World Multi-Conf. Systemics, Cybern. and Inf., Orlando (2005)
6. Cevikalp, H., Neamtu, M., Barkana, A.: The kernel common vector method: A novel nonliear subspace classifier for pattern recognition. IEEE Trans. Systems, Man, and Cybernetics 37(4), 937–951 (2007)
7. Dai, G., Yeung, D.-Y.: Boosting kernel discriminant analysis and its application to tissue classification of gene expression data. In: IJCAI 2007, pp. 744–749 (2007)
8. Edizkan, R., Gulmezoglu, M.B., Ergin, S., Barkana, A.: Improvements on common vector approach for multi class problems. Study report of the project (200315053) supported by the Research Fund of Osmangazi University
9. Fisher, R.A.: The use of multiple measurements in taxonomic problems. Ann. Eugen. 7(2), 179–188 (1936)
10. Freund, Y., Schapire, R.E.: A decision therotic generalization of online learning and an application to boosting. Journal of Computer and System Sciences 55(1), 119–139 (1997)
11. Fukunaga, K., Koonz, W.L.: Application of the Karhuenn-Loeve expansion to feature selection and ordering. IEEE Trans. Comput. C-19(4), 311–318 (1970)
12. Georghiades, A.S., Behumeur, P.N., Kriegman., D.J.: From few to many: illumination cone models for face recognition under variable lighting and pose. IEEE Trans. Pattern Analysis & machine Intelligence 23(6), 643–660 (2001)
13. Gulmezoglu, M.B., Dzhafarov, V., Bakana, A.: The common vector approach and its relation to principle component analysis. IEEE Trans. Speech Audio Process 9(6), 655–662 (2001)
14. Gulmezoglu, M.B., Dzhafarov, V., Keskin, M., Bakana, A.: A novel approach to isolated word recognition. IEEE Trans. Speech Audio Process. 7(6), 620–628 (1999)

15. Kim, S.-W., Oommen, B.J.: On utilizing search methods to select subspace dimensions for kernel-based nonlinear subspace classifiers. IEEE Trans. Pattern Anal. Mach. Intell. 27(1), 136–141 (2005)
16. Laaksonen, J.: Subspace classifiers in recognition of handwritten digits. Ph.D. Dissertion, Helsinki Univ. Technol., Finland (1997)
17. Mller, K.-R., Mika, S., Rtsch, G., Tsuda, K., Schlkopf, B.: An introduction to kernel-based learning algorithms. IEEE Transactions on Neural Networks 12(2), 181–201 (2001)
18. Oja, E.: Subspace Methods of Pattern Recognition. Res. Stud. Press, New York (1983)
19. Perez–Cruz, F., Bousquet, O.: Kernel methods and their potential use in signal processing. IEEE Signal Process. Mag. 21(3), 57–65 (2004)
20. Scholkopf, B., Smola, A.J., Muller, K.R.: Nonlinear component analysis as a kernel Eigen value problem. Neural Comput. 10(5), 1299–1319 (1998)
21. Shawe-Taylor, J., Cristianini, N.: Kernel Methods for Pattern Analysis. Cambridge Univ. Press, England (2004)
22. Tang, E.K., Suganathan, P.N., Yao, X., Qin, A.K.: Linear dimensionality reduction using relevance weighted lda. Pattern Recognition 38(4), 485–493 (2005)
23. Tsuda, K.: Subspace classifier in reproducing kernel Hilbert space. In: Proc. Int. Joint Conf. Neural Netw., vol. 5, pp. 3454–3457 (1999)
24. Turk, M., Pentland, A.P.: Eigenfaces for recognition. J. Cogn. Neurosci. 3(1), 71–86 (1991)
25. Watanabe, S., Lambert, P.F., Kulikowski, C.A., Buxton, J.L., Walker, R.: Evaluation and selection of variables in pattern recognition. In: Compter and Information Sciences II, p. 91. Academic Press, New York (1967)
26. Watanabe, S., Pakvasa, N.: Subspace method in pattern recognition. In: Proc. 1st Int. Conf. Pattern Recog., Washington, DC, pp. 25–32 (1973)
27. Zhao, W., Chellappa, R., Krishnaswamy, A.: Discriminant analysis of principal components for face recognition. In: Proc. Third IEEE Int'l Conf. Automatic Face and Gesture Recognition, pp. 336–341 (1998)
28. Zhao, W., Chellappa, R., Rosenfeld, A., Phillips, P.J.: Face Recognition: A Literature Survey. Technical Report CAR-TR-948, Univ. of Maryland, College Park (2000)

Compact Binary Patterns (CBP) with Multiple Patch Classifiers for Fast and Accurate Face Recognition

Hieu V. Nguyen and Li Bai

School of Computer Science, University of Nottingham,
Jubilee Campus, Wollaton Road, Nottingham, NG8 1BB, UK
{vhn,bai}@cs.nott.ac.uk
http://www.nottingham.ac.uk/cs/

Abstract. Face recognition is one of the most active research areas in pattern recognition for the last decades because of its potential applications as well as scientific challenges. Although numerous methods for face recognition have been developed, recognition accuracy and speed still remain a problem. In this paper, we propose a novel method for fast and accurate face recognition. The contribution of the paper is three folds: 1) we propose a new method for facial feature extraction named the Compact Binary Patterns (CBP), which is a more compact and efficient generalization of Local Binary Patterns. 2) We show that Whitened Principal Component Analysis (WPCA) is a simple but very efficient way to enhance CBP features. 3) To further improve the recognition rate, we divide a face into patches and perform recognition using multiple classifiers, whose weights are estimated by a Memetic Algorithm. Our method is tested thoroughly on the FERET dataset and achieves promising results.

Keywords: compact binary patterns, face recognition, multiple patch classifiers, whitened PCA, memetic algorithm.

1 Introduction

Face recognition is the identification of individuals from a database of labeled face images. The applications of face recognition can be found in surveillance, security, telecommunication, and smart environments [5]. Major difficulties in face recognition arise from image variations due to illumination and facial expression. A robust face recognition system should recognize a face regardless of these variations [1].

Many face recognition systems emphasize facial features that are robust to both intrapersonal and extrapersonal variations in images. Popular feature extraction methods include the Discrete Cosine Transform, Wavelet Transform, etc. Among these, the Gabor Filter is one of the most effective. Gabor features are robust to the imprecision of facial feature localization methods [18]. Gabor filters were first used for face recognition by Lades et al. in [9]. They proposed

R.P. Barneva et al. (Eds.): CompIMAGE 2010, LNCS 6026, pp. 187–198, 2010.
© Springer-Verlag Berlin Heidelberg 2010

the Dynamic Link Architecture (DLA), which recognizes faces by extracting Gabor jets at each node of a rectangular grid over the face image. In [25], Wiskott et al. extended DLA and proposed the Elastic Bunch Graph Matching (EBGM) method. The EBGM algorithm was the top performer in the FERET evaluation contest. However, both DLA and EBGM require extensive amount of computation - 30s on a SPARC station 10- 512 [25]. Many systems based on Gabor Filters have been developed since then [4], [21], [20]. In [19], Shen and Bai introduced an improved version of Adaboost called MutualBoost to select a small number of highly discriminant Gabor features which are then passed to Generalized Discriminant Analysis (GDA) for classification.

Although MutualBoost+GDA achieved very high recognition accuracy, Gabor feature extraction is computationally expensive. Recently, the local binary patterns (LBP) operator has been successfully used for face detection and recognition. LBP encodes both local and global information using a histogram [2]. Facial feature extracted by the LBP operator is robust to illuminating variations because LBP features are invariant to gray-scale changes. Moreover, because of its simplicity, LBP is extremely fast to extract [3]. However, under varying lighting and aging effects, LBP performance is still not satisfactory [27] and requires further improvements. More recently, LBP is enhanced by Gabor Filters to create so called Local Gabor Binary Pattern Features which achieve excellent results on FERET database [26,7]. The problem with LGBP is that it is computationally expensive. Hence, the development of a fast and accurate face recognition system remains a challenge.

In the paper, we introduce a novel method for facial feature extraction, named Compact Binary Patterns (CBP) which is a generalization of Local Binary Patterns but more compact and discriminant. CBP features are then enhanced by Whitened Principal Component Analysis. Finally, the accuracy is further improved by Multiple Patch Classifiers (MPC) trained by a Memetic Algorithm. With experimental results, we will show that if classifiers are ordered in descending order of their weights, recognition rate can be improved significantly with a small speed overhead compared to the single classifier.

2   Face Recognition with CBP and WPCA

2.1   Facial Feature Extraction

Local Binary Patterns. The original LBP operator, introduced by Ojala et al. in [14], is a powerful method for texture description. The operator labels the pixels of an image by thresholding the 3×3-neighborhood of each pixel with the center value and representing the result as a binary number. The histogram of the labels can then be used as a texture descriptor. An illustration of the basic LBP operator is shown in Figure 1.

An extension to the original operator is to use the so called uniform patterns [13]. A Local Binary Pattern is called uniform if it contains at most two bitwise transitions from 0 to 1 or vice versa when the binary string is considered circular. Ojala noticed that in their experiments with texture images, uniform patterns

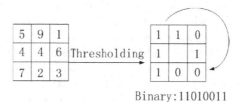

Binary:11010011

Fig. 1. Local Binary Patterns

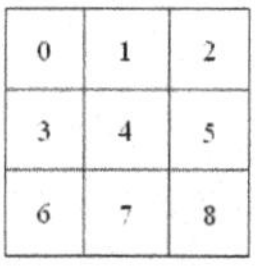

0	1	2
3	4	5
6	7	8

Fig. 2. 3×3 block indexing

account for a little less than 90% of all patterns. As a result, only uniform patterns are often used for Face Recognition [3]. In the next section, we will generalize the LBP by generalizing uniform notion.

Compact Binary Patterns. There are two important properties of LBP which make it efficient: local and uniform. The locality property means that each pixel is compared only to its close neighbors. This is essential for recognition since discriminant structures on the face tend not to change a lot over a local region. The uniformness reduces the dimension of the feature vector. It not only reduces the runtime complexity but also increases the representativeness and robustness of the features. We propose an improved version of LBP by preserving the locality property and generalizing the uniform property. The locality property is preserved by limiting all the binary comparison within 3×3 windows and the uniform property is generalized by the introduction of dominant patterns. Specifically, if we number each pixel in a 3×3 block as shown in Figure 2 and consider each pixel a node in a 9-node tree, LBP will be the concatenation of 8 bits computed from edges of the LBP tree in Figure 3. From this angle, we can see that LBP corresponds to only one tree among many possible trees and it is not clear if LBP tree is the best one to represent faces. The tree in the middle of Figure 3 is a random tree (RDT) and we will show that in terms of compactness, LBP is the same as RDT. Inspired by the notion of uniform patterns, we define compactness as the minimum number of distinct patterns which account for at least 90% of all patterns. We call these distinct patterns dominant patterns. In the feature extraction step, only dominant patterns are used. As a result, there are a total of 22+1 (for all non-dominant patterns) used patterns. In Table 1, compactnesses of LBP, RDT and CBP are computed from all faces in FERET gallery. The idea behind compactness is similar to the idea behind PCA, aiming to find the most compact representation of the input data.

From Cayley's formula, we know that the total number of trees is $9^7 = 4782969$ (generally n^{n-2} with n nodes [22]). Our goal is to find the most compact tree in the hope that it is also the most discriminant one. CBP Tree in Figure 3 is the most compact tree found by exhaustive search method (we can do so because the number of trees is tractable). Intuitively, we can see from Figure 4 that edges in CBP face are enhanced compared to LBP and RDT faces.

It is not difficult to see that the order of edges in the tree to compute a pattern is not important. We use the order corresponding to numbers on edges of CBP Tree in Figure 3.

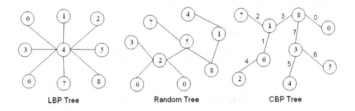

LBP Tree   Random Tree   CBP Tree

Fig. 3. LBP, Random and CBP Tree

Table 1. Compactnesses of LBP, RDT and CBP estimated from 1196 images in FERET gallery

Pattern	Compactness
Local Binary Patterns	52.99
Random Tree Patterns	51.96
Compact Binary Patterns	21.96

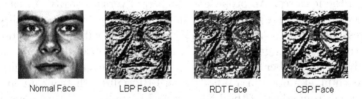

Normal Face   LBP Face   RDT Face   CBP Face

Fig. 4. Normal Face, LBP Face, RTD Face and CBP Face

Face Description with CBP. We divide the face image into a grid then slide a 8×8 window over the edges of the grid as shown in Figure 5. From each 8×8 window, we can extract histograms of 23 CBP patterns. Hence, the total number of features is $\left(\frac{H}{4} - 1\right) * \left(\frac{W}{4} - 1\right) * 23$ where H and W are height and width of the face image respectively. Our method is somewhat different from the method used in [3] where the grid unit is of a different size and the windows are non-overlap.

After facial features have been extracted, we use Whitened PCA for classification.

Fig. 5. Face Grid to extract CBP Features

2.2 Whitened PCA as Classifier

Standard PCA. A classical technique for dimensionality reduction, particularly in face recognition, is principal component analysis (PCA). In order to produce a compact representation, the feature vector is projected into a lower dimensional feature space found by PCA

$$\mathbf{u} = \mathbf{W_{pca}x} \tag{1}$$

The input vectors are first transformed by subtracting the mean: $\Phi_i = x_i - m$. The principal components of the training data set are given by the eigenvectors of its covariance matrix $\sum = \frac{1}{n} \sum_{i=1}^{n} \Phi_i \Phi_i^T$. In practice, only $M(M < n - 1)$ eigenvectors having the largest eigenvalues (and, hence, the largest variance in the data set) are kept empirically to form the projection matrix W_{PCA}.

The PCA technique is optimal in maximizing the scatter of all the projected training samples, which means it maximizes both intrinsic difference and intrapersonal variations in the training set. However, the latter has adverse effect on classification. We resolve this problem through the whitening process.

Whitening Process. PCA based features have two obvious shortcomings: (1) the eigenvectors corresponding to large eigenvalues encode mostly illumination and facial expression, rather than discriminating information [15]; and (2) Mean-Square-Error (MSE) principle underlying PCA favors low frequencies [24,11,10] and thus loses the discriminating information contained in the high frequency components. The whitening process normalizing the PCA based feature can directly counteract these disadvantages. Specifically, the PCA based feature u is subjected to the whitening transformation and yields yet another feature set w:

$$\mathbf{w} = \mathbf{\Lambda_M^{-1/2} u} \tag{2}$$

where $\Lambda_M^{-1/2} = diag\{\lambda_1^{-1/2}, \lambda_2^{-1/2}, \ldots, \lambda_M^{-1/2}\}$. The integrated projection matrix $\Lambda_M^{-1/2} W_{PCA}$ treats variance along all principal component axes as equally significant by weighting components corresponding to smaller eigenvalues more heavily and is arguably appropriate for discrimination. Consequently, the influence of the eigenvectors corresponding to large eigenvalues is reduced while the discriminating details encoded in other eigenvectors are enhanced [6].

We use cosine similarity measure for classification. Although WPCA is very robust to variations, it does not have the ability to distinguish intrapersonal variations from extrapersonal variations. In the next section, we propose Multiple Patch Classifiers to solve this problem.

3   Multiple Patch Classifiers

3.1   Multiple Patches

The CBP+WPCA method uses holistic representation of images, which has three disadvantages. Firstly, in holistic representation the spatial information of facial features is not utilized. Secondly, facial features are used indiscriminately of their capacity for discrimination. Generally speaking, facial features such as eyes, nose, and mouth are considered to be more discriminative for face recognition. Thirdly, image variation due to pose and illumination changes within the whole image space is sometimes too large to be modeled by linear subspace methods such as PCA [23]. To solve these problems, we propose a multiple classifier system in which each classifier is responsible for a local region of the face. We use a simple way to select facial patches (more advanced patch selection methods such as Adaboost can also be used to further improve the accuracy of the system). The face is divided into equal sized patches of varying resolution to obtain a total of 25 patches as shown in Figure 6. From each patch, CBP feature vector is extracted then WPCA is used as the classifier. Consequently, we have a system of 25 classifiers. The next step is to combine these classifiers in an efficient way.

Fig. 6. Multiple Patches from an example face

3.2   Multiple Classifier System

It is widely accepted that the classification accuracy can be improved by combining outputs of multiple classifiers [8]. However, how to combine multiple classifiers with various (potentially conflicting) decisions is still an open research topic. Because the contributions of patches to the classification are different, it is essential to compute a weight value for each patch. While Boosting is a popular method to determine weights for multiple classifiers, it is more suitable in situations where there are a number of weak classifiers which are slightly better than random guessing. Logistic Regression is another popular method to combine multiple classifiers [8].

Assuming we have p classifiers, the goal is to estimate p parameters $(\beta_0, \beta_1, ..., \beta_{p-1})$ in the linear form of the ensemble:

$$\beta_0 x_0 + \beta_1 x_1 + ... + \beta_{p-1} x_{p-1} \tag{3}$$

where β_i is the marginal contribution of the classifier i to the ensemble and x_i is the similarity score between a testing face and a face in gallery estimated by the classifier i. In this paper, we propose a Memetic Algorithm to estimate β_i.

3.3   Memetic Algorithm

The Memetic Algorithm (MA) [12] is a combination of Genetic Algorithm (GA) and Local Search. We propose MA instead of GA because it has been known that in many optimization problems, MA converges much quicker than GA. In algorithm 1, Memetic Algorithm pseudocode used to train classifiers is presented.

Algorithm 1. Memetic Algorithm for training Multiple Patch Classifiers

```
Memetic_Algorithm() {
    initialize population P;
    repeat {
        for i = 1 to k {
            select two parents p₁ and p₂ from P;
            offspringᵢ = crossover(p₁, p₂);
            offspringᵢ = mutation(offspringᵢ);
            Hill_Climbing(offspringᵢ);
        }
        replace offspring₁,... and offspringₖ in P;
    } until (stopping_condition);
    return the best solution;
}
```

Chromosomes and Fitness Function. Each chromosome is represented by an array of real numbers between 0 and 1 $(\beta_0, \beta_1, ..., \beta_{p-1})$. The i-th position of the array corresponds to the weight of the i-th classifier of the ensemble. The number of elements in the array is equal to the number of classifiers p. The fitness of a chromosome is defined as the recognition rate of the ensemble with the weights represented by the chromosome. Note that by using the performance of the whole ensemble as fitness the diversity of the individual classifiers is also taken into account.

Initialization. A population of 20 is used in the algorithm. All positions of the chromosomes are set to random values between 0 and 1 at the beginning of the algorithm. If the fitness values of the ten best chromosomes are similar the algorithm is terminated. Otherwise the algorithm is terminated after 100 generations (time limit can also be used as the stopping condition). The weights of the chromosome with the highest fitness value during all generations (not only the last one) are the final result and are used for the weighted voting combination.

Algorithm 2. Hill Climbing algorithm

```
Hill_Climbing(startSolution) {
    currentSolution = startSolution;
    loop {
        L = NEIGHBORS(currentSolution);
        nextFitness = - INF;
        nextSolution = NULL;
        for all x in L
            if Fitness(x)>nextFitness {
                nextSolution = x;
                nextFitness = Fitness(x);
            }
        if nextFitness<=Fitness(currentSolution) {
            return currentSolution;
        }
        currentSolution = nextSolution;
    }
}
NEIGHBORS(current) {
    resultSet = [];
    for i=1 to p {
        neighbor = current;
        change chromosome i of neighbor to a random number in [0, 1];
        resultSet = resultSet + [neighbor];
    }
    return resultSet;
}
```

Crossover and Mutation. Each position in chromosome of the child A copies value randomly from either parents with equal probability or 50%. To encourage the diversity of the population, the mutation operator is applied to all new chromosomes produced by the crossover operator. This operator first changes the value of one random position of the array to a random number from 0 to 1. Then that position and another random position are swapped with probability of 20%. Normally, the mutation rate is set to be smaller than 10%. In practice, however, higher mutation rate sometimes can help the algorithm converge much more quickly and through experiments we found out that this is true in our application.

Hill Climbing. Genetic Algorithms are able to find global optimum by exploring a large search space when the selection pressure is properly controlled. However, the algorithms are weak with regard to fine-tuning near local optimum points, resulting in a long running time. That explains why Local Search is used in the Memetic Algorithms. Here, we use the popular Hill Climbing algorithm as the Local Search as shown in Algorithm 2.

4   Experimental Results

4.1   Results on FERET Dataset

A large data set from The FacE REcognition Technology (FERET) database is used to assess the effectiveness and robustness of our proposed method. Please refer to [16,17] for details about the FERET evaluation protocol. In our experiments, we strictly evaluate all the methods using the standard gallery images (1196 images of 1196 subjects)and four probe sets, fb (1195 images), fc (194 images), dup I (722 images), and dup II (234 images). 736 frontal images of 314 subjects are used as the training set for methods that need a training stage. The FERET images displays diversity across gender, ethnicity, and age. To obtain a precise performance assessment, we evaluate our method against different images with varying lighting conditions, facial expression, and acquisition times. In the preprocessing stage, face images are all cropped and resized to 128×128 pixels, and aligned using the locations of the eyes given in FERET database. Histogram equalization is then applied to reduce the illumination effect. Finally, all faces are normalized to zero mean and unit variance.

To illustrate the effectiveness of the proposed Memetic Algorithm, we compare it with the Logistic Regression as mentioned in [8]. In Table 2, our original method is named CBP+WPCA+MA and the method using Logistic Regression is named CBP+WPCA+LR. As the experimental results show, CBP is consistently better than LBP as a face descriptor and MA is consistently better than LR as a classifier combination method. Best results for datasets are highlighted as bold numbers. Our method achieves the best results for all sets with only one exception: fc set. In fact, the main performance difference between fb and fc is that in fc, the illumination changes a lot, and in some cases the change is global which is too much for CBP (or LBP) to deal with. The best method for fc is Weighted LGBPHS because Gabor filter has proven to be robust to large illumination variation [18]. WPCA doesn't help much in this case because it maximizes both types of variations: intrapersonal which is bad for recognition and extrapersonal which is good for recognition [7]. In fc, intrapersonal (mainly illumination variation) is sometimes even larger than extrapersonal variation. Although the final classifier can deal with illumination to some extend through classifier combination, there is not so much large illumination variation in the training data to train the final classifier. In short, the difference in fc between the proposed method and Weighted LGBPHS is mainly because of the robustness of the facial descriptor to illumination. This may be a potential direction for further research.

4.2   Speed of the Multiple Patch Classifiers

We order patches (classifiers) in descending order of their weights. For first i patches, we use MA to estimate their weights which may be different from their weights in the ensemble of p classifiers. Figure 7 shows the curve with the number of patches in x-axis and the recognition rate in y-axis. As we can see, the

Table 2. Rank-1 recognition rates of different algorithms on the FERET probe sets

Methods	fb	fc	dup I	dup II
Fisherface	94.0	73.0	55.0	31.0
Best Results of [16]	96.0	82.0	59.0	52.0
Results of [2]	97.0	79.0	66.0	64.0
MutualBoost+GDA[19]	96.7	85.6	59.3	62.4
Weighted LGBPHS [26]	98.0	**97.0**	74.0	71.0
LBP+WPCA	95.0	72.0	68.0	56.0
CBP+WPCA	96.0	79.2	74.8	65.0
CBP+WPCA+LR	97.5	85.1	76.2	72.6
CBP+WPCA+MA	**98.1**	88.7	**78.5**	**74.8**

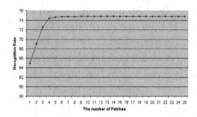

Fig. 7. (Number of Patches, Recognition Rate) Curve for Dup II

recognition rate stabilizes very quickly when the number of patches increases. We can use only 2 or 3 patches to get very good result. In practice, a good strategy is to use as many patches as possible within the time limit. This is still true in fb, fc and dup I probe sets.

5   Discussion and Conclusion

In this paper, we show that CBP feature and WPCA are a perfect combination for fast face recognition. CBP has the same complexity as LBP but has more discriminant power. In addition, some regions of a face have less intrapersonal variations than others and for this reason we have proposed a patch-based approach for face recognition. The weight of each patch is computed by a Memetic Algorithm. Although the final classifier is the combination of CBP, WPCA and MA, the contributions of these components are independent. As a result, other techniques can also be considered at each stage. Experiments show that CBP, WPCA and MA work effectively together. The proposed method is not only accurate but also very fast because when patches are arranged in descending order of their weights, and only a few patches are needed to achieve the near optimal recognition result. The final classifier CBP+WPCA+MA is tested thoroughly on the FERET database. The results are comparable to the state of the art methods based on Gabor Filters.

References

1. Adini, Y., Moses, Y., Ullman, S.: Face Recognition: The Problem of Compensating for Changes in Illumination Direction. IEEE Transactions PAMI 19(7), 721–732 (1997)
2. Ahonen, T., Hadid, A., Pietikainen, M.: Face Recognition with Local Binary Patterns. In: Pajdla, T., Matas, J(G.) (eds.) ECCV 2004. LNCS, vol. 3021, pp. 469–481. Springer, Heidelberg (2004)
3. Ahonen, T., Hadid, A., Pietikäinen, M.: Face Description with Local Binary Patterns: Application to Face Recognition. IEEE Transactions PAMI 28(12), 2037–2041 (2006)
4. Bai, L., Shen, L.: InfoBoost for Selecting Discriminative Gabor Features. In: Gagalowicz, A., Philips, W. (eds.) CAIP 2005. LNCS, vol. 3691, pp. 423–432. Springer, Heidelberg (2005)
5. Chellappa, R., Wilson, C., Sirohey, S., et al.: Human and machine recognition of faces: a survey. Proceedings of the IEEE 83(5), 705–740 (1995)
6. Deng, W., Hu, J., Guo, J.: Gabor-Eigen-Whiten-Cosine: A Robust Scheme for Face Recognition. In: Zhao, W., Gong, S., Tang, X. (eds.) AMFG 2005. LNCS, vol. 3723, pp. 336–349. Springer, Heidelberg (2005)
7. Hieu, N., Bai, L., Shen, L.: Local Gabor binary pattern whitened pca: A novel approach for face recognition from single image per person. In: Tistarelli, M., Nixon, M.S. (eds.) ICB 2009. LNCS, vol. 5558, pp. 269–278. Springer, Heidelberg (2009)
8. Ho, T.K., Hull, J.J., Srihari, S.N.: Decision combination in multiple classifier systems. IEEE Transactions PAMI 16(1), 66–75 (1994)
9. Lades, M., Vorbruggen, J., Buhmann, J., Lange, J., von der Malsburg, C., Wurtz, R., Konen, W.: Distortion invariant object recognition in the dynamic link architecture. IEEE Transactions on Computers 42(3), 300–311 (1993)
10. Liu, C.: Gabor-based kernel PCA with fractional power polynomial models for face recognition. IEEE Transactions PAMI 26(5), 572–581 (2004)
11. Moghaddam, B., Pentland, A.: Probabilistic visual learning for object representation. IEEE Transactions PAMI 19(7), 696–710 (1997)
12. Moscato, P.: On evolution, search, optimization, genetic algorithms and martial arts: Towards memetic algorithms. Caltech Concurrent Computation Program, C3P Report (1989)
13. Ojala, T., Pietikäinen, M., Mäenpää, T.: Multiresolution gray-scale and rotation invariant texture classification with local binary patterns. IEEE Transactions PAMI 24(7), 971–987 (2002)
14. Ojala, T., Pietikinen, M., Harwood, D.: A comparative study of texture measures with classification based on featured distributions. Pattern Recognition 29(1), 51–59 (1996)
15. Pentland, A., Starner, T., Etcoff, N., Masoiu, N., Oliyide, O., Turk, M.: Experiments with eigenfaces. In: Looking at People Workshop, IJCAI 1993, Chamberry, France (1993)
16. Phillips, P., Moon, H., Rizvi, S., Rauss, P.: The FERET evaluation methodology for face-recognition algorithms. IEEE Transactions PAMI 2(10), 1090–1104 (2000)
17. Phillips, P., Wechsler, H., Huang, J., Rauss, P.: The FERET database and evaluation procedure for face-recognition algorithms. Image and Vision Computing 16(5), 295–306 (1998)
18. Shan, S., Gao, W., Chang, Y., Cao, B., Yang, P.: Review the strength of Gabor features for face recognition from the angle of its robustness to mis-alignment. In: 17th International Conference on Pattern Recognition (ICPR 2004), vol. 1, pp. 338–341 (2004)

19. Shen, L., Bai, L.: MutualBoost learning for selecting Gabor features for face recognition. Pattern Recognition Letters 27(15), 1758–1767 (2006)
20. Shen, L., Bai, L.: A SVM face recognition method based on optimized Gabor features. In: Qiu, G., Leung, C., Xue, X.-Y., Laurini, R. (eds.) VISUAL 2007. LNCS, vol. 4781, pp. 165–174. Springer, Heidelberg (2007)
21. Shen, L., Bai, L., Fairhurst, M.: Gabor wavelets and general discriminant analysis for face identification and verification. Image and Vision Computing 27, 1758–1767 (2006)
22. Shor, P.W.: A new proof of Cayley's formula for counting labeled trees. J. Comb. Theory Ser. A 71(1), 154–158 (1995)
23. Su, Y., Shan, S., Chen, X., Gao, W.: Patch-based gabor fisher classifier for face recognition. In: Proceedings of the 18th International Conference on Pattern Recognition, pp. 528–531 (2006)
24. Sung, K., Poggio, T.: Example-based learning for view-based human face detection. IEEE Transactions PAMI 20(1), 39–51 (1998)
25. Wiskott, L., Fellous, J., Krüger, N., von der Malsburg, C.: Face recognition by elastic bunch graph matching. IEEE Transactions PAMI 19(7), 775–779 (1997)
26. Zhang, W., Shan, S., Gao, W., Chen, X., Zhang, H.: Local Gabor binary pattern histogram sequence (LGBPHS): A novel non-statistical model for face representation and recognition. In: Tenth IEEE International Conference on Computer Vision (ICCV 2005), vol. 1, pp. 786–791 (2005)
27. Zou, J., Ji, Q., Member, S., Nagy, G.: A comparative study of local matching approach for face recognition. IEEE Transactions PAMI 16, 2617–2628 (2007)

Graph-Theoretic Image Alignment Using Topological Features

Waleed Mohamed[1], A. Ben Hamza[1], and Khaled Gharaibeh[2]

[1] Concordia Institute for Information Systems Engineering
Concordia University, Montréal, QC, Canada
[2] Telecommunication Engineering Department
Hijawi Faculty of Engineering Technology
Yarmouk University, Irbid, Jordan

Abstract. In this paper, we introduce a feature-based image alignment method using topological singularities. The main idea behind our proposed framework is to encode a medical image into a set of Morse critical points. Then an entropic dissimilarity measure between the Morse features of the target and the reference images is maximized to bring the data into alignment. We also show that maximizing this divergence measure leads to minimizing the total length of the joint minimal spanning tree between the features of the misaligned medical images. Illustrative experimental results clearly show the much improved performance and the registration accuracy of the proposed technique.

Keywords: Image alignment, Morse theory, Tsallis entropy.

1 Introduction

Image registration refers to the process of aligning images so that their details overlap accurately [6, 8, 14]. Images are usually registered for the purpose of combining or comparing them. Image registration is indispensable for such tasks as data fusion, navigation, clinic studies, and motion detection. A wide range of registration techniques has been developed for many different types of applications and data, such as mean squared alignment, correlation registration, and moment invariant matching. Inspired by the successful application of the mutual information measure [8, 14], and looking to address its limitations in often difficult imagery, a generalized information-theoretic measure for medical image registration was proposed in [5]. This entropic measure enjoys appealing mathematical properties affording a great flexibility in a number of applications [2, 7].

Multisensor data fusion technology combines data and information from multiple sensors to achieve improved accuracies and better inference about the environment that could be achieved by the use of a single sensor alone. In this paper, we introduce a nonparametric multisensor data fusion algorithm for the registration of magnetic resonance images (MRIs). The goal of registration is to align a target MRI to the location of a reference MRI using global or feature-based techniques. Our proposed method falls into the category of feature-based techniques

R.P. Barneva et al. (Eds.): CompIMAGE 2010, LNCS 6026, pp. 199–209, 2010.
© Springer-Verlag Berlin Heidelberg 2010

which require that features be extracted and described before two MRIs can be registered. The proposed approach consists of two major steps. The first step involves extracting Morse singularity features [3, 9, 12] from the MRIs represented as 3D surfaces. Inspired by the mutual information based approaches for image registration, we propose in the second step the use of an information-theoretic divergence based on Tsallis entropy as a dissimilarity measure between Morse features of the target and reference MRIs. Tsallis entropy can be estimated using the length of the minimal spanning tree (MST) over Morse feature vectors of a MRI. Then, the registration is performed by minimizing the length of a joint MST which spans the graph generated from the overlapping target and reference MRIs [6].

The rest of the paper is organized as follows. The next section is devoted to the problem formulation, followed by a brief review of Morse singular points, and the minimal spanning tree. In Section 3, we describe the proposed method, and discuss in more detail its most important algorithmic steps. In Section 4, we provide experimental results to show the robustness and the registration accuracy of the proposed method. And finally, we conclude in Section 5.

2   Problem Formulation

Most medical imaging methods produce full 3D volumes. Traditionally, the medical scans are viewed as a series of superposed 2D slices of the full 3D volume as depicted in Figure 1. These 2D slices are often misaligned. Medical image registration refers to the process of aligning such images so that their details overlap accurately. The goal of medical image registration is to find a spatial transformation such that a dissimilarity metric between two or more images taken at different times, from different sensors, or from different viewpoints achieves its maximum. Given two misaligned MRIs I_1 and I_2 as shown in Figure 2, the goal of medical image registration is to align the target I_1 to the reference I_2 by maximizing a dissimilarity measure D between I_1 and $\mathcal{T}_{(t_x,t_y,\theta)}I_2$

$$(t_x^\star, t_y^\star, \theta^\star) = \arg \max_{(t_x,t_y,\theta)} D(I_1, \mathcal{T}_{(t_x,t_y,\theta)}I_2), \qquad (1)$$

or equivalently

$$(t_x^\star, t_y^\star, \theta^\star) = \arg \max_{(t_x,t_y,\theta)} D(\mathcal{U}, \mathcal{T}_{(t_x,t_y,\theta)}\mathcal{V}), \qquad (2)$$

where $\mathcal{U}$ and $\mathcal{V}$ are two sets of feature vectors extracted from I_1 and I_2, and $\mathcal{T}_{(t_x,t_y,\theta)}$ is a Euclidean transformation with translation parameters t_x and t_y, and a rotation angle θ.

In this paper, we propose a feature-based algorithm for medical image registration. The main idea behind our proposed framework is to encode an MRI into a set of feature points extracted from the surface of the MRI. Then an entropic dissimilarity measure between the features of the target MRI and the reference MRI is maximized to bring both MRIs into alignment. We also show that maximizing this divergence measure leads to minimizing the total length of the joint minimal spanning tree between the features of the misaligned images.

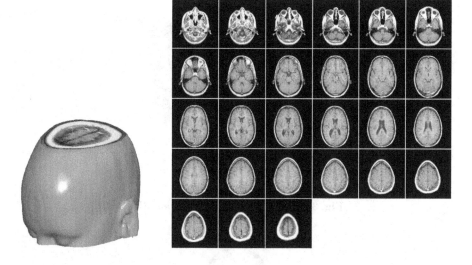

Fig. 1. 2D slices of a 3D volumetric medical image

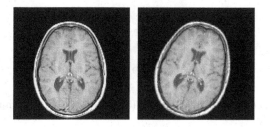

Fig. 2. Misaligned target and reference images

2.1 Morse Singular Points

An image I may be viewed as a 3D surface $\mathbb{M} \subseteq \mathbb{R}^3$ defined as $\mathbb{M} = \{(x, y, z) : z = I(x, y)\}$ as illustrated in Figure 3, where $z = I(x, y)$ is the pixel value viewed as the height value. The nondegenerate singular points of an image are the minimum, maximum and saddle points as depicted in Figure 4. We say that an image is a Morse function if all its singular points are nondegenerate.

2.2 Minimal Spanning Tree

Let $\mathcal{V} = \{v_1, v_2, \ldots, v_n\}$ be a set of feature vectors (e.g. Morse singularities), where $v_i \in \mathbb{R}^d$ (e.g. $d = 3$ for 3D data). A spanning tree $\mathcal{E}$ is a connected acyclic graph that passes through all features and it is specified by an ordered list of edges e_{ij} connecting certain pairs $(v_i, v_j), i \neq j$, along with a list of edge

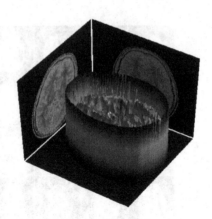

Fig. 3. Surface representation of an MRI

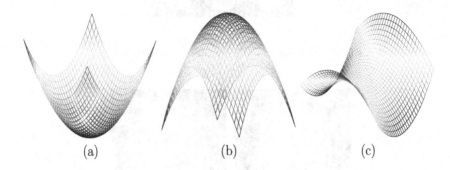

(a)   (b)   (c)

Fig. 4. Nondegenerate singular points: (a) minimum, (b) maximum, (c) saddle

adjacency relations. The edges e_{ij} connect all n features such that there are no paths in the graph that lead back to any given feature vector. The total length $L_\mathcal{E}(\mathcal{V})$ of a tree is given by

$$L_\mathcal{E}(\mathcal{V}) = \sum_{e_{ij} \in \mathcal{E}} \|e_{ij}\|. \tag{3}$$

The minimal spanning tree $\mathcal{E}^\star$ is the spanning tree that minimizes the total edge length $L_\mathcal{E}(\mathcal{V})$ among all possible spanning trees over the given features

$$L^\star(\mathcal{V}) = \sum_{e_{ij} \in \mathcal{E}^\star} \|e_{ij}\| = \min_\mathcal{E} L_\mathcal{E}(\mathcal{V}). \tag{4}$$

Figure 5 depicts an example of an MST with 2D and 3D feature vectors respectively.

We define Tsallis entropy as

$$\widehat{H}_\alpha(\mathcal{V}) = \frac{1}{1-\alpha} \left[\frac{L^\star(\mathcal{V})}{\beta\, n^\alpha} - 1 \right], \tag{5}$$

Random data: 128 Samples   Minimal spanning tree

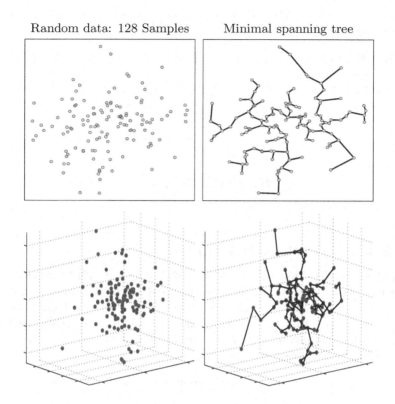

Fig. 5. Illustration of a MST in 2D and 3D

where $L^\star(\mathcal{V})$ the total length of the MST, and α is a nonnegative parameter. It can be easily shown that Shannon entropy is the limiting case of Tsallis entropy when $\alpha \to 1$.

3 Proposed Method

The goal of our proposed approach may be described as follows: Given two MRIs to be registered, we first extract their Morse singularity features, and we compute a joint MST connecting their Morse features, then we optimize the Jensen-Tsallis divergence to bring these MRIs into alignment. Without loss of generality, we consider the transformation $\mathcal{T}_{\ell}$, where $\ell = (t, \theta)$, that is a Euclidean transformation with translation parameter vector $t = (t_x, t_y)$, and a rotation parameter θ. In other words, for $x = (x, y)$ we have $\mathcal{T}_{\ell}(x) = Rx + t$, where R is a rotation matrix given by

$$R = \begin{pmatrix} \cos\theta & \sin\theta \\ -\sin\theta & \cos\theta \end{pmatrix}. \tag{6}$$

Let I_1 and I_2 be two MRIs to be registered. The proposed methodology may now be concisely described as follows:

(i)   Find the Morse singularity features $\mathcal{U} = \{u_1, \ldots, u_k\}$ and $\mathcal{V} = \{v_1, \ldots, v_m\}$ of I_1 and I_2 respectively.

(ii) Transform $\mathcal{V}$ to a new set $\mathcal{W} = T_\ell \mathcal{V} = \{w_1, \ldots, w_m\}$

(iii) Find the optimal parameter vector $\ell^\star = (t^\star, \theta)$ of the Jensen-Tsallis divergence

$$\ell^\star = \arg \max_\ell D(\mathcal{U}, \mathcal{W}), \tag{7}$$

where

$$D(\mathcal{U}, \mathcal{W}) = \widehat{H}_\alpha(\mathcal{U} \cup \mathcal{W}) - \lambda \widehat{H}_\alpha(\mathcal{U}) - (1 - \lambda)\widehat{H}_\alpha(\mathcal{W}), \tag{8}$$

and $\lambda = k/(k + m)$.

3.1   Extraction of Morse Singularities

We applied the algorithm introduced by Takahashi *et al.* [12] to extract Morse singular points from the target and reference MRIs. The algorithm extracts the singularity points while preserving the topological integrity of the surface of a MRI. This means that the extracted singular points must satisfy the Euler-Poincaré formula, which states that the number of maxima, minima, and saddles satisfy the topological relation given by

$$\chi = \#\text{minima} - \#\text{saddlepoints} + \#\text{maxima} = 2. \tag{9}$$

The extraction algorithm is based on the 8-neighbor method, which compares a point v with its 8-adjacent neighbors by computing the height difference between v and each of its neighbors as illustrated in Figure 6.

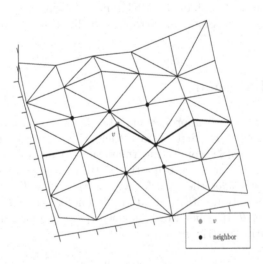

Fig. 6. Illustration of the 8-neighborhood method

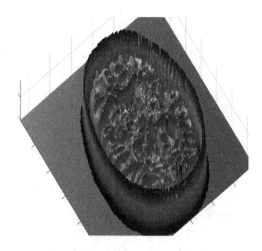

Fig. 7. MRI maxima features and minimal spanning tree

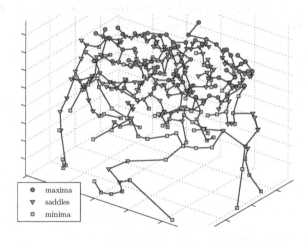

Fig. 8. Morse singular points of an MRI and its corresponding MST

In addition, to ensure that the potential singular points satisfy the Euler-Poincaré formula, it is necessary to study the changes on the contours considering their heights. The classification of a feature point is based on the topological variations between the cross-sectional contours. According to this criterion, a feature point v is classified as a maximum point if a new contour appears at v. Therefore, a peak is given by a point that is higher than all other points in its neighborhood. A feature point v is classified as a minimum point if an existing contour disappears at v. Therefore, a pit is given by a point that is lower than all other points in its neighborhood. A pass occurs when a contour is divided or two contours are merged at v.

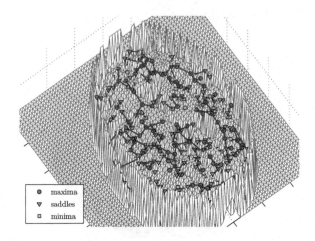

Fig. 9. Morse singular points of an MRI and its corresponding MST

The Morse singular points of an MRI and the corresponding MST connecting all these features are displayed in Figure 7 through Figure 9.

3.2   Optimization of the Dissimilarity Measure

Using and Eq. (5) and Eq. (7), it is clear that solving

$$\ell^\star = \arg\max_\ell D(\mathcal{U}, \mathcal{T}_\ell \mathcal{V}), \tag{10}$$

may be reduced to solving

$$\ell^\star = \arg\max_\ell \widehat{H}_\alpha(\mathcal{U} \cup \mathcal{T}_\ell \mathcal{V})$$

$$= \arg\max_\ell \frac{1}{1-\alpha} \left[\frac{L^\star(\mathcal{U} \cup \mathcal{T}_\ell \mathcal{V})}{\beta\,(k+m)^\alpha} - 1 \right], \tag{11}$$

or equivalently solving the minimization problem

$$\ell^\star = \arg\min_\ell L^\star(\mathcal{U} \cup \mathcal{T}_\ell \mathcal{V})$$

$$= \arg\min_\ell \sum_{e_{ij} \in \mathcal{E}^\star} \|e_{ij}\|, \tag{12}$$

where $\mathcal{E}^\star$ is the MST of $\mathcal{U} \cup \mathcal{T}_\ell \mathcal{V}$, and $\|e_{ij}\|$ is the edge length which depends on the transformation parameter ℓ and is given by

$$\|e_{ij}\| = \sqrt{(I_1(\boldsymbol{x}_i) - I_1(\boldsymbol{x}_j))^2 + (\mathcal{T}_\ell I_2(\boldsymbol{x}_i) - \mathcal{T}_\ell I_2(\boldsymbol{x}_j))^2}$$

$$= \sqrt{(I_1(\boldsymbol{x}_i) - I_1(\boldsymbol{x}_j))^2 + (I_2(R\boldsymbol{x}_i + \boldsymbol{t}) - I_2(R\boldsymbol{x}_j + \boldsymbol{t}))^2}, \tag{13}$$

where $\boldsymbol{x}_i = (x_i, y_i) \in \Omega$, and $\boldsymbol{x}_j = (x_j, y_j) \in \Omega$.

Hence, the MRI registration is performed by minimizing the total length of the minimum spanning tree which spans the joint MST generated from the overlapping feature vectors of the target and the reference MRIs. The minimization problem given by Eq. (12) may be solved using the method of steepest descent [11]. Let ℓ^r be the value of the objective function given by Eq. (12) at the r-th iteration. At each iteration, the update rule is given by

$$\ell^{r+1} = \ell^r + \alpha\, d^r = \ell^r - \alpha \sum_{e_{ij} \in \mathcal{E}^*} \nabla \|e_{ij}\|, \qquad (14)$$

where $d^r = -\sum_{e_{ij} \in \mathcal{E}^*} \nabla \|e_{ij}\|$ is the direction vector of steepest descent that is the direction for which the objective function will decrease the fastest, and α is a scalar which determines the step size taken in that direction. Taking the gradient of the edge length with respect to ℓ yields

$$\nabla \|e_{ij}\| = \frac{1}{\|e_{ij}\|} \Big(I_2(R x_i + t) - I_2(R x_j + t) \Big)$$
$$\times \Big(\nabla I_2(R x_i + t) \cdot J_{R x_i + t} - \nabla I_2(R x_j + t) \cdot J_{R x_j + t} \Big), \qquad (15)$$

where $J_{R x + t}$ is the Jacobian matrix given by

$$J_{R x + t} = \begin{pmatrix} 1 & 0 & -x \sin\theta + y \cos\theta \\ 0 & 1 & -x \cos\theta - y \sin\theta \end{pmatrix}. \qquad (16)$$

4 Experimental Results

In this section we present some experimental results to show the much improved performance of the proposed method in MRI registration. In the first set of experiments, we calculated the total length of the joint MST and we estimated Tsallis entropy for two misaligned MRIs I_1 and I_2. Tsallis entropy estimator for the feature sets of the target and the reference is given by

$$\widehat{H}_\alpha(\mathcal{U} \cup T_\ell \mathcal{V}) = \frac{1}{1-\alpha} \left[\frac{L^*(\mathcal{U} \cup T_\ell \mathcal{V})}{\beta\,(k+m)^\alpha} - 1 \right], \qquad (17)$$

where k and m are the numbers of Morse singular points of I_1 and I_2 respectively.

The numerical results are depicted in Table 1. As expected, note that both the length of the joint MST and Tsallis entropy increase as the rotation angle between the reference and the target increases.

In the second set of experiments, we estimated the parameters corresponding to the spatial transformation between the target and the reference MRIs. We applied a Euclidean transformation to the reference MRI, with known parameters (t_x, t_y, θ). To register these two MRIs, we then applied the iterative gradient descent algorithm described in Section 3 to find the optimal parameters $t_x^\star$, $t_x^\star$ and $\theta^\star$. The registration results are provided in Table 2, where the errors between the original and the estimated transformation parameters are also listed.

Table 1. Total length and Tsallis entropy estimator of the joint MST

θ	$L^*(\mathcal{U} \cup \mathcal{T}_\ell \mathcal{V})$	$\hat{H}_\alpha(\mathcal{U} \cup \mathcal{T}_\ell \mathcal{V})$
$0°$	696.22	7.85
$15°$	1018.39	8.62
$30°$	1104.28	8.78
$45°$	1146.83	8.85

Table 2. Registration results

ℓ			ℓ^*			error $= \ell - \ell^*$		
t_x	t_y	θ	$t_x^\star$	$t_y^\star$	$\theta^\star$	t_x^e	t_y^e	θ^e
5	4	0	5.09	4.03	0.15	0.09	0.03	0.15
5	4	5	3.97	3.98	4.87	1.03	0.02	0.13
4	8	15	2.14	8.75	14.66	1.86	0.75	0.34
8	5	15	7.75	5.59	14.98	0.25	0.59	0.02

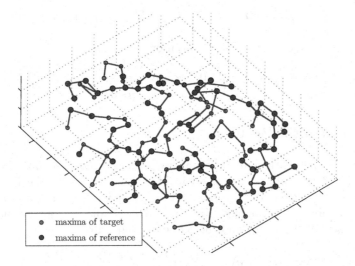

- ○ maxima of target
- ● maxima of reference

Fig. 10. Joint MST of target and reference MRIs (only maxima features are displayed)

The estimated values clearly indicate the effectiveness and the accuracy of the proposed algorithm in registering MRI data. The joint MST of the target and reference is displayed in Figure 10. Note that for ease of visualization, only the maxima features are displayed.

5   Conclusions

We proposed a graph-theoretic technique for registration of MRIs using Morse singularities and an entropic dissimilarity measure. The registration is achieved by minimizing the total length of the joint minimal spanning tree of the target and the reference MRIs. The main advantages of the proposed approach are: (i) Tsallis entropy provides a reliable data estimator, (ii) the proposed approach is simple and computationally fast, and (iii) the experimental results provide accurate registration results and clearly indicate the suitability of the proposed method for MRI registration.

References

1. Burbea, J., Rao, C.R.: On the convexity of some divergence measures based on entropy functions. IEEE Trans. on Information Theory 28, 489–495 (1982)
2. Corici, D., Astola, J.: Information divergence measures-for detection of borders between coding and noncoding DNA regions using recursive entropic segmentation. In: Proc. IEEE Workshop Statistical Signal Processing, pp. 577–580 (2003)
3. Fomenco, A.T., Kunii, T.L.: Topological Modeling for Visualization. Springer, Tokyo (1997)
4. Havrda, M.E., Charvát, F.: Quantification method of classification processes: concept of structural α-entropy. Kybernitica 3, 30–35 (1967)
5. He, Y., Ben Hamza, A., Krim, H.: A generalized divergence measure for robust image registration. IEEE Trans. on Signal Processing 51, 1211–1220 (2003)
6. Hero, A.O., Ma, B., Michel, O., Gorman, J.: Applications of entropic spanning graphs. IEEE Signal Processing Magazine 19, 85–95 (2002)
7. Hibbard, L.S.: Region segmentation using information divergence measures. Medical Image Analysis 8, 233–244 (2004)
8. Maes, F., Collignon, A., Vandermeulen, D., Marchal, G., Suetens, P.: Multimodality image registration by maximization of mutual information. IEEE Trans. on Medical Imaging 16, 187–198 (1998)
9. Milnor, J.: Morse Theory. Princeton University Press, Princeton (1963)
10. Rényi, A.: On measures of entropy and information. In: Selected Papers of Alfréd Rényi, vol. 2, pp. 525–580. Akademiai Kiado, Budapest (1961)
11. Sabuncu, M.R., Ramadge, P.J.: Using spanning graphs for efficient image registration. IEEE Trans. on Image Processing 17, 788–797 (2008)
12. Takahashi, S., Ikeda, T., Shinagawa, Y., Kunii, T.L., Ueda, M.: Algorithms for extracting correct critical points and constructing topological graphs from discrete geographical elevation data. Computer Graphics Forum 14, 181–192 (1995)
13. Tsallis, C.: Possible generalization of Boltzmann-Gibbs statistics. Journal of Statistical Physics 52, 479–487 (1988)
14. Viola, P., Wells, W.M.: Alignment by maximization of mutual information. International Journal of Computer Vision 24, 173–154 (1997)

Fast Automatic Microstructural Segmentation of Ferrous Alloy Samples Using Optimum-Path Forest

João Paulo Papa[1], Victor Hugo C. de Albuquerque[2], Alexandre Xavier Falcão[3], and João Manuel R.S. Tavares[4]

[1] São Paulo State University, Computer Science Department, Bauru, Brazil
[2] University of Fortaleza, Technological Research Center, Fortaleza, Brazil
[3] University of Campinas, Institute of Computing, Campinas, Brazil
[4] University of Porto, Faculty of Engineering, Porto, Portugal

Abstract. In this work we propose a novel automatic cast iron segmentation approach based on the Optimum-Path Forest classifier (OPF). Microscopic images from nodular, gray and malleable cast irons are segmented using OPF, and Support Vector Machines (SVM) with Radial Basis Function and SVM without kernel mapping. Results show accurate and fast segmented images, in which OPF outperformed SVMs. Our work is the first into applying OPF for automatic cast iron segmentation.

Keywords: supervised classification, image segmentation, cast irons, microstructural evaluation, materials science.

1 Introduction

Cast irons are an iron-carbon-silicon alloy that have been used in numerous industrial applications, such as the base structures of manufacturing machines, rollers, valves, pump bodies and mechanical gears, among others. The main families of cast irons are: nodular cast iron, malleable cast iron, gray cast iron and white cast iron [3]. Their properties, as of all materials, are influenced by their microstructure and therefore, the correct characterization of their microstructure is highly important. Thus, metallographic evaluation of materials is commonly used to determine the quantity, appearance, size and distribution of the phases and constituents of materials. To carry this analysis, segmentation and quantification of the microstructure of cast irons from metallographic images is usually done.

Manual microstructural characterization, i.e., characterization based on human visual inspection, is an exhausting task, because the specialists spend much time exposed to high luminosities in the microscope device, which can produce fatigue and, consequently, increase the probability of measurement errors.

Several works for automatic microstructural image analysis have been developed based on computer vision techniques [2,6,11,15]. Scozzafava et al. [15] presented an approach for graphite nodules shape characterization, in which spheroidal cast irons were evaluated aiming to obtain quantitative analysis of their constitutive elements. Images of the metallographic sections acquired by means of a light optical microscope were processed in order to obtain a simpler image representation, in which the

R.P. Barneva et al. (Eds.): CompIMAGE 2010, LNCS 6026, pp. 210–220, 2010.

nodules are black regions over a white background, and a method for automatic classification of the graphite's shape particles in cast iron was proposed by De Santis et al. [6]. Shape and size parameters for discriminating cast iron are commonly used features, but Gomes et al. [9] have proposed a new parameter, the average internal angle, and shown its relevance for accurate classification. However, such techniques consider image segmentation based on global threshold binarization, which are frequently defined by manual adjustment in function of the image to be analyzed, or even so in local measurements. These approaches are proposed to errors, mainly because of the amount of the noise in the images to be analyzed.

Other works are based on artificial intelligence for the evaluation of cast iron microstructures. Jiang et al. [11] used six types of gray cast iron and an Artificial Neural Network (ANN) [6] for their categorization. Zhibin et al. [17] have presented a nodular cast iron recognition system based on fuzzy approach. Albuquerque et al. [1, 2] addressed the segmentation and quantification of the cast iron microstructures obtained from metallographic images by means of an ANN using multilayer perceptron (ANN-MLP) and Self-Organizing Maps (SOM) [6]. However, as an unstable classifier, collections of ANN-MLP can improve its performance up to some unknown limit of classifiers [10]. SOM networks suffer from the high computational burden, in which its parameters choice, i. e., neural network architecture, is a hard task, and strongly depends on each application. Artificial neural networks with Radial Basis Function (RBF) also have their limitations. Different from ANN-MLP, which find hyperplanes to separate elements from different classes, ANN-RBF make use of hyperellipsoids to best cluster data into groups [6]. The main problem relies on the parameters that need to be estimated for these geometrical polygons, i. e., the hyperellipsoids' center and standard deviation.

Support Vector Machines (SVM) is another pattern recognition technique that have been extremely used in several applications, which assume linearly separable classes in a higher-dimensional feature space [5]. However, its computational cost rapidly increases with the training set size and the number of support vectors. As a binary classifier, multiple SVM are required to solve a multi-class problem. Tang and Mazzoni [16] proposed a method to reduce the number of support vectors in the multi-class problem. Their approach suffers from slow convergence and high computational cost, because they first minimize the number of support vectors in several binary SVM, and then share these vectors among the machines. However, in all SVM approaches, the assumption of separability may also not be valid in any space of finite dimension [14].

Therefore, the commonly used pattern recognition techniques cannot handle both efficiency and effectiveness in the overall process, i.e., training and test phases. Another question that needed to be pointed out is that there is a need for fast automatic cast iron microstructures identification given that, usually, the metallographic images are obtained from high-resolution sensors, which generate images with millions of pixels. This context makes unviable the use of artificial neural networks and SVM due to their high computational burden in the training phase. Although the training step can be performed in a separated manner, such techniques cannot handle real time and iterative segmentation systems for cast iron microstructures. Imagine that you have a system in which the technician can mark some samples from each kind of cast iron in a given high resolution image. After that, the system needs to be trained in order to classify the remaining image pixels. After that, the user can modify the classified image in order to make this process more accurate, marking some misclassified pixels with their correct labels. In this context, the system needs to be retrained for further classification. This overall process can be executed until some criteria (e.g., the user compliance with the final result). As aforementioned, a simple selection of some pixels by user in such kind of images can involve several hundreds of pixels. In such a way, it is reasonable to assume that the user can wait for a just few seconds for the cast iron microstructures classification.

Recently, a novel graph-based classifier that reduce the pattern recognition problem as an optimum-path forest (OPF) computation in the feature space induced by a graph was presented [12]. The OPF classifier does not interprets the classification task as a hyperplanes optimization problem, but as a polynomial combinatorial optimum-path computation from some key samples (prototypes) to the remaining nodes. Each prototype becomes a root from its optimum-path tree and each node is classified according to its strongly connected prototype. This process defines a discrete optimal partition (influence region) of the feature space. The OPF classifier has some advantages with respect to the aforementioned classifiers: (i) is free of parameters, (ii) do not assume any shape/separability of the feature space, (iii) run training phase faster and (iv) make decisions based on a global criteria. Results in several applications, such that fingerprint and face recognition, remote sensing image classification, biomedical signal processing and many other works, have been demonstrated that OPF is superior than ANN-MLP, SOM and k-Nearest Neighbors (k-NN), and similar to SVM, but much faster [12].

This paper presents an innovative computational tool based on OPF classifier for the analysis of images of ferrous alloys, which optimizes the process of segmentation and quantification of their microstructures. We are the first into applying the optimum-path forest classifier in this research field, usually called by quantitative metallography. In order to accomplish comparisons about computational cost, accuracy, and speed in the segmentation and quantification process with other classifiers, images from nodular, gray and malleable cast irons were analyzed using OPF and SVM using Radial Basis Function kernel and SVM without kernel mapping. Additionally, visual and analytical comparisons were also addressed. This paper is organized as follows. The next section presented the OPF classifier theory. Section 3 discusses the experimental results. Finally, the Section 4 states conclusions and future works.

2   Optimum-Path Forest Classifier

Let Z_1 and Z_2 be training and test sets with $|Z_1|$ and $|Z_2|$ samples of a given dataset. Here, we use samples as pixels of images. Let $\lambda(s)$ be the function that assigns the correct label i, $i = 1, 2, \ldots, c$, to any sample $s \in Z_1 \cup Z_2$, $S \subseteq Z_1$ be a set of prototypes from all classes, and v be an algorithm that extracts n features (Red, Blue and Green values from each pixel) from any sample $s \in Z_1 \cup Z_2$ and returns a vector $\vec{v}(s)$. The distance $d(s,t) > 0$ between two samples, s and t, is the one between their corresponding feature vectors $\vec{v}(s)$ and $\vec{v}(t)$. One can use any distance function suitable for the extracted features, been the most common the Euclidean norm [12].

Our problem consists of projecting a classifier that can predict the correct label $\lambda(s)$ of any sample $s \in Z_2$. Training consists of finding a special set $S^* \subseteq Z_1$ of prototypes and a discrete optimal partition of Z_1 in the feature space (i.e., an optimum-path forest rooted in S^*). The classification of a sample $s \in Z_2$ is done by evaluating the optimum paths incrementally, as though it were part of the forest, and assigning to it the label of the most strongly connected prototype.

2.1 Training

Let (Z_1, A) be a complete graph whose nodes are the training samples and any pair of samples defines an arc in $A = Z_1 x Z_1$ (Figure 1a). The arcs do not need to be stored and so the graph does not need to be explicitly represented. A path is a sequence of distinct samples $\pi_t = \langle s_1, s_2, \ldots, t \rangle$ with terminus at a sample t. A path is said trivial if $\pi_t = \langle t \rangle$. We assign to each path π_t a cost $f(\pi_t)$ given by a connectivity function f. A path π_t is said optimum if $f(\pi_t) \leq f(\pi_\tau)$ for any other path π_τ. We also denote by $\pi_s \cdot \langle s, t \rangle$ the concatenation of a path π_s and an arc (s, t).

We will address the connectivity function $f_{\max}$:

$$f_{\max}(\langle s \rangle) = \begin{cases} 0 \ \textit{if} \ s \in S \\ +\infty \ \textit{otherwise,} \end{cases} \tag{1}$$

$$f_{\max}(\pi_s \cdot \langle s, t \rangle) = \max\{f_{\max}(\pi_s), d(s, t)\},$$

such that $f_{\max}(\pi_s \cdot \langle s, t \rangle)$ computes the maximum distance between adjacent samples along the path $\pi_s \cdot \langle s, t \rangle$. The minimization of $f_{\max}$ assigns to every sample $t \in Z_1$ an optimum path $P^*(t)$ from the set $S \in Z_1$ of prototypes, whose minimum cost $C(t)$ is:

$$C(t) = \min_{\forall \pi_t \in (Z_1, A)}\{f_{\max}(\pi_t)\}. \tag{2}$$

The minimization of $f_{\max}$ is computed by *Algorithm 1*, called OPF algorithm, which is an extension of the general image foresting transform (IFT) algorithm [7] from the image domain to the feature space, here specialized for $f_{\max}$. This process assigns one optimum path from S to each training sample t in a non-decreasing order of minimum cost, such that the graph is partitioned into an optimum-path forest P (a function with no cycles which assigns to each $t \in Z_1 \setminus S$ its predecessor $P(t)$

in $P^*(t)$ or a marker *nil* when $t \in S$, as shown in Figure 1b). The root $R(t) \in S$ of $P^*(t)$ can be obtained from $P(t)$ by following the predecessors backwards along the path, but its label is propagated during the algorithm by setting $L(t) = \lambda(R(t))$.

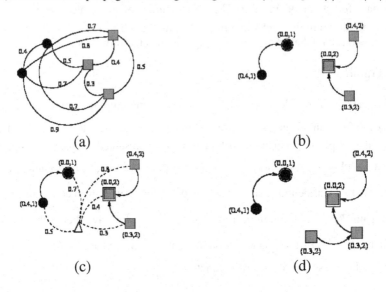

Fig. 1. (a) Complete weighted graph for a simple training set. (b) Resulting optimum-path forest for f_{max} and two given prototypes (circled nodes). The entries (x, y) over the nodes are, respectively, the cost and the label of the samples. The directed arcs indicate the predecessor nodes in the optimum path. (c) Test sample (white triangle) and its connections (dashed lines) with the training nodes. (d) The optimum path from the most strongly connected prototype, its label 2, and classification cost *0.3* are assigned to the test sample.

Follow, bellow, the OPF classifier algorithm. Lines 1-3 initialize maps and insert prototypes in Q. The main loop computes an optimum path from S to every sample s in a non-decreasing order of minimum cost (Lines 4-11). At each iteration, a path of minimum cost $C(s)$ is obtained in P when we remove its last node s from Q (Line 5). Ties are broken in Q using first-in-first-out policy. That is, when two optimum paths reach an ambiguous sample s with the same minimum cost, s is assigned to the first path that reached it. Note that $C(t) > C(s)$ in Line 6 is false when t has been removed from Q and, therefore, $C(t) \neq \infty$ in Line 9 is true only when $t \in Q$. Lines 8-11 evaluate if the path that reaches an adjacent node t through s has a cost lower than the current path with terminus t and update the position of t in Q, $C(t)$, $L(t)$ and $P(t)$ accordingly.

OPF Algorithm

Input: A training set Z_1, λ-labeled prototypes $S \subseteq Z_1$ and the pair (v, d) for feature vector and distance computations.

Output: Optimum-path forest P, cost map C and label map L.

Auxiliary: Priority queue Q and cost variable cst.

1. For each $s \in Z_1 \setminus S$, set $C(s) = +\infty$.
2. For each $s \in S$, do
   2.1. $C(s) = 0$, $P(s) = nil$, $L(s) = \lambda(s)$, and insert s in Q.
3. While Q is not empty, do
   3.1. Remove from Q a sample s such that $C(s)$ is minimum.
   3.2. For each $t \in Z_1$ such that $t \neq s$ and $C(t) > C(s)$, do
      3.2.1. Compute $cst = \max\{C(s), d(s, t)\}$.
      3.2.2. If $cst < C(t)$, then
         3.2.2.1. If $C(t) \neq +\infty$, then remove t from Q.
         3.2.2.2. $P(t) = s$, $L(t) = L(s)$ and $C(t) = cst$.
         3.2.2.3. Insert t in Q.

2.2 Classification

For any sample $t \in Z_2$, one consider all arcs connecting t with samples $s \in Z_1$, as though t were part of the training graph (Figure 1c). Considering all possible paths from S^* to t, one find the optimum path $P^*(t)$ from S^* and label t with the class $\lambda(R(t))$ of its most strongly connected prototype $R(t) \in S^*$. This path can be identified incrementally, by evaluating the optimum cost $C(t)$ as:

$$C(t) = \min_{\forall s \in Z_1} \{\max\{C(s), d(s, t)\}\}. \tag{3}$$

Let the node $s^* \in Z_1$ be the one that satisfies Equation 3 (i.e., the predecessor $P(t)$ in the optimum path $P^*(t)$). Given that $L(s^*) = \lambda(R(t))$, the classification simply assigns $L(s^*)$ as the class of t (Figure 1d). An error occurs when $L(s^*) \neq \lambda(t)$.

3 Experimental Results

In this section we will describe the dataset used, as well as the evaluation methodology for the microstructural characterization of the computational methods used.

3.1 Dataset

For the application of the computational methods used here, it was necessary to perform, firstly, the metallographic preparation of the cast iron samples to be analyzed. Then, the samples were microscopically analyzed, accomplishing with a brightness and contrast adjustment, and acquired the correspondent images. Figure 2 displays some examples of the cast iron images used.

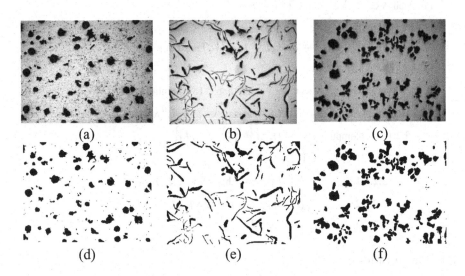

Fig. 2. Microstructure images of cast irons: (a) nodular, (b) gray and (c) malleable and their respective labeled images in (d), (e) and (f). All images shown in this paper have 320x240 pixels and, for visualization purposes, a magnification of 100x was applied on them.

3.2 Classifiers

We evaluated the cast iron segmentation by means of three supervised classifiers: Support Vector Machines using Radial Basis Function (SVM-RBF) for kernel mapping, Support Vector Machines without kernel mapping (SVM-LINEAR), and Optimum-Path Forest (OPF). We used as features, for each pixel, its RGB values.

For SVM-RBF, we used the latest version of the LibSVM package [4] with Radial Basis Function (RBF) kernel, parameter optimization and the one-versus-one strategy for the multi-class problem. With respect to SVM-LINEAR, we used the LibLINEAR package [8] with C parameter optimized using cross validation. Regarding OPF we used the LibOPF [13], which is a library for the design of optimum-path forest-based classifiers.

3.3 Results from Experiments

We performed two series of experiments: in the former (Section 3.3.1) we used one image from each cast iron type (nodular, gray, and malleable in Figure 2) to evaluate the effectiveness of the classifiers. For training classifiers, we used 1% of the whole image and the remaining 99% for testing, and in the last experiment (Section 3.3.2) we used the classifiers trained in previous images to segment new ones (Figure 3).

3.3.1 Robustness of the Classifiers

We used 1% (768 samples) of the whole image (one for each cast iron) for training classifiers and 99% (69120 samples) to test them (the images were labeled by a technician – see Figures 2d, 2e and 2f). Notice that here the SVM-RBF, SVM-LINEAR, and OPF algorithms were executed 10 times with randomly generated training and test sets, to compute the mean accuracy and its standard deviation, and the mean training and test execution times in seconds. The accuracy was computed by taking into account that the classes may have different sizes using a methodology proposed by Papa et al. [12]. Tables 1, 2 and 3 display the results for the different cast irons.

Table 1. Evaluation of the classifiers into classifying nodular cast iron with respect to the mean accuracy and mean execution times

Classifier	Mean accuracy	Mean training execution time [s]	Mean test execution time [s]
OPF	96.26 % ± 5.58	0.478548	4.097354
SVM-RBF	73.75 % ± 23.94	124.929431	2.029066
SVM-LINEAR	81.16 % ± 22.64	114.229541	0.055253

Table 2. Evaluation of the classifiers into classifying gray cast iron with respect to the mean accuracy and mean execution times

Classifier	Mean accuracy	Mean training execution time [s]	Mean test execution time [s]
OPF	99.83 % ± 0.24	0.048117	5.434169
SVM-RBF	99.62 % ± 0.32	23.883542	1.746221
SVM-LINEAR	93.70 % ± 3.68	24.924486	0.163015

Table 3. Evaluation of the classifiers into classifying malleable cast iron with respect to the mean accuracy and mean execution times

Classifier	Mean accuracy	Mean training execution time [s]	Mean test execution time [s]
OPF	99.86 % ± 0.19	0.051487	5.737038
SVM-RBF	99.59 % ± 0.37	20.336996	1.059828
SVM-LINEAR	98.69 % ± 0.83	10.927093	0.163563

From Tables 1, 2 and 3, we can see that OPF classifier outperformed SVM-RBF, and SVM-LINEAR for nodular cast iron. Although the results were similar for gray and malleable cast iron, OPF was 497.5 times and 392.68 times faster than SVM-RBF in the training phase for gray and malleable cast iron, respectively. Finally, for malleable cast iron, OPF and SVM-RBF achieved similar results, being OPF and SVM-LINEAR faster in the training and test phases, respectively.

3.3.2 Cast Iron Segmentation Analysis

In this section we show the experiment results for automatic cast iron segmentation. We used 1% of the images used in the previous experiment (Figure 2), from each cast iron, to train the classifiers. Further, we evaluated them in another collection of images, whose segmentation results are displayed in Figure 3.

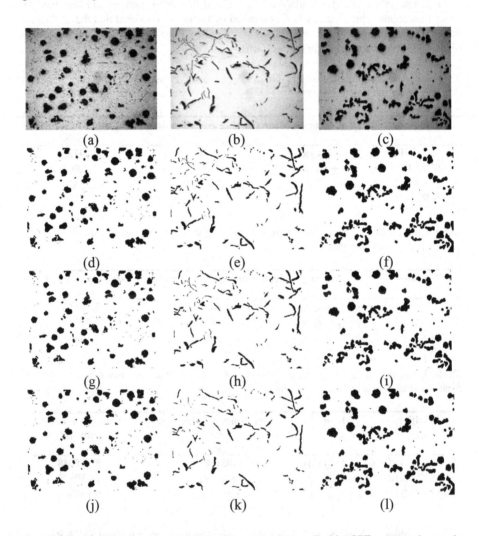

Fig. 3. Original cast iron images: (a) nodular, (b) gray, and (c) malleable; OPF segmentation results in (d)-(f), SVM-RBF results in (g)-(i) and, finally, SVM-LINEAR segmentation ones in (j)-(l)

The results appear to be similar for all cast iron images, in which the classifiers performed good segmentation results. For gray cast iron, one can see that SVM_RBF and SVM-LINEAR methods lose some graphite particles (see the top left region of Figure 3b, 3e, 3h and 3k), which modify completely the results of quantification of microstructure of the samples used. However, when we used the OPF classifier these particles are totally preserved. Thus, regarding SVM classifiers, this method presents better segmentation results, is faster, is lesser computational demanded, and principally more accurate.

4 Conclusions

We have presented a new methodology for fast automatic cast iron segmentation using the Optimum-Path Forest classifier, which is characterized by its extremely efficiency allied with goof effectiveness.

In the experimental evaluation we performed two rounds of experiments. In the former, we compared OPF against SVM-RBF and SVM-LINEAR by using 1% of the input image for training and the remaining 99% for testing. The OPF outperformed SVM-RBF and SVM-LINEAR in both efficiency (overall execution time, i.e., training + testing) and effectiveness. Only for the malleable cast iron that the classifiers achieved similar results. In the last round of experiments, we used the classifiers trained in the previous one to segment another collection of cast iron images. The classifiers achieved similar segmentation results, except for the gray cast iron, in which the OPF segmented successfully more structures than SVM-RBF and SVM-LINEAR. With the work reported, we are the first ones into applying the OPF classifier for cast iron image segmentation, and also in the microstructural analysis of microstructures of metallic materials.

For future works, we are interested into segment white cast irons, as well as on comparing the methods here considered with others computational techniques as Artificial Neural Network using multilayer perceptron (ANN-MLP), and self-organized maps (ANN-SOM) training algorithms.

Acknowledgments

This work was partially done in the scope of the project with reference PTDC/EEA-CRO/103320/2008, financially supported by FCT – Fundação para Ciência e Tecnologia of Portugal.

References

1. Albuquerque, V.H.C., Alexandria, A.R., Cortez, P.C., Tavares, J.M.R.S.: Evaluation of multilayer perceptron and self-organizing map neural network topologies applied on microstructure segmentation from metallographic images. NDT & E International 42(7), 644–651 (2009)
2. Albuquerque, V.H.C., Cortez, P.C., Alexandria, A.R., Tavares, J.M.R.S.: A new solution for automatic microstructures analysis from images based on a backpropagation artificial neural network. Non-destructive Testing and Evaluation 23(4), 273–283 (2008)

3. Callister, W.D.: Materials Science and Engineering: An Introduction. John Wiley & Sons Inc., New York (2006)
4. Chang, C.C., Lin, C.J.: LIBSVM: A Library for Support Vector Machines (2001), http://www.csie.ntu.edu.tw/~cjlin/libSVM
5. Cortes, C., Vapnik, V.: Support-vector networks. Machine Learning 20(3), 273–297 (1995)
6. De Santis, A., Di Bartolomeo, O., Iacoviello, D., Iacoviello, F.: Quantitative shape evaluation of graphite particles in ductile iron. Journal of Materials Processing Technology 196, 292–302 (2008)
7. Falcão, A.X., Stolfi, J., Lotufo, R.A.: The image foresting transform: Theory, algorithm and applications. IEEE Transactions on Pattern Analysis and Machine Intelligence 26(1), 19–29 (2004)
8. Fan, R.-E., Chang, K.-W., Hsieh, C.-J., Wang, X.-R., Lin, C.-J.: LIBLINEAR: A library for large linear classification. Journal of Machine Learning Research 9, 1871–1874 (2008)
9. Gomes, O.F.M., Paciornik, S.: Automatic classification of graphite in cast iron. Microscopy and Microanalysis 11, 363–371 (2005)
10. Haykin, S.: Neural Networks: A Comprehensive Foundation. Prentice-Hall, Englewood Cliffs (1998)
11. Jiang, H., Tan, Y., Lei, J., Zeng, L., Zhang, Z., Hu1, J.: Auto-analysis system for graphite morphology of grey cast iron. Journal of Automated Methods & Management in Chemistry 25(4), 87–92 (2003)
12. Papa, J.P., Falcão, A.X., Suzuki, C.T.N.: Supervised pattern classification based on optimum-path forest. International Journal of Imaging Systems and Technology 19(2), 120–131 (2009)
13. Papa, J.P., Suzuki, C.T.N., Falcão, A.X.: LibOPF: A library for the design of optimum-path forest classifiers (2008), http://www.ic.unicamp.br/~afalcao/LibOPF
14. Reyzin, L., Schapire, R.E.: How boosting the margin can also boost classifier complexity. In: Proceedings of the 23rd International Conference on Machine Learning, vol. 8, pp. 753–760 (2006)
15. Scozzafava, A., Tomesani, L., Zucchelli, A.: Image analysis automation of spheroidal cast iron. Journal of Materials Processing Technology 153-154, 853–859 (2004)
16. Tang, B., Mazzoni, D.: Multiclass Reduced-set Support Vector Machines. In: Proceedings of the 23rd International Conference on Machine Learning, pp. 921–928 (2006)
17. Zhibin, C., Yongquan, Y., Heqing, C., Shaomin, Y.: Fuzzy recognition of graphite morphology in nodular cast iron based on evolution strategy. In: Proceedings of 2005 International Conference on Machine Learning and Cybernetics, vol. 8, pp. 4930–4935 (2005)

Numerical Simulations of Hypoeutectoid Steels under Loading Conditions, Based on Image Processing and Digital Material Representation

Łukasz Rauch, Łukasz Madej, and Bogdan Pawłowski

AGH- University of Science and Technology, al. Mickiewicza 30,
30-059 Kraków, Poland
{lrauch,lmadej,bpawlow}@agh.edu.pl

Abstract. Numerical simulations of material behavior under loading conditions play crucial role in determination of final properties of material, design of production technology, lifecycle modeling, etc. Special interest in this area is devoted to simulations of microstructures with precisely described grains, inclusions or crystallographic orientation, according to the idea of the Digital Material Representation (DMR). The DMR is applied in the present work to simulate the hypoeutectoid steel, which due to presence of Widmannstätten ferrite is characterized by specific properties. The 2D microstructure model is prepared on the basis of the optical microscopy image as a result of image segmentation algorithm. Specific material properties are attached to each microstructure component. Furthermore, the model is equipped with homogenic mesh and processed with the Finite Element (FE) Forge2 software. The results obtained from the simulations are discussed and presented in the paper as well.

Keywords: digital material representation, finite element, image segmentation, hypoeutectoid steel.

1 Introduction

The software dedicated to simulation of advanced metal forming processes and exploitation conditions became highly sophisticated and accurate in recent years. The developed solutions allow describing in details the behavior of material under deformation. Therefore, they contribute to the general knowledge about the microstructural phenomena occurring during metal processing and under exploitation conditions. The majority of existing approaches is based on the multi scale models, which combine various numerical methods (e.g. FE, Boundary Element (BE), Extended Finite Element (XFE), Cellular Automata (CA), Molecular Dynamics (MD)), connected together in one complex solution [11,12]. However, the methods still suffer from lack of common numerical representation of material. Therefore, the concept of DMR was proposed and is dynamically evolving [1]. The main objective of the DMR is creation of the digital representation of microstructure with its features (e.g. grains, grain orientations, inclusions, cracks, and different phases) represented explicitly.

R.P. Barneva et al. (Eds.): CompIMAGE 2010, LNCS 6026, pp. 221–230, 2010.
© Springer-Verlag Berlin Heidelberg 2010

Generation of material microstructure with specific properties is one of the most important algorithmic parts of the methodology based on the DMR. As mentioned, such DMR is further used in numerical simulations of processing conditions or simulation of material behavior under exploitation conditions. The more accurate the digital representation is, the more accurate results can be obtained. The Voronoi Tessellation is the most commonly used method to create the digital representation of grains. However other method like Cellular Automata, Monte Carlo, Sphere Growth or Image Processing can also be found in the literature [4]. The image segmentation algorithms offer the highest reliability in creation of microstructure representation. Nevertheless, final quality of created structures depends on quality of input images, while most of them are noised, corrupted or blurred. These visible picture distortions highly affect performance of the segmentation algorithms as well as reliability of the numerical simulations.

An approach to segmentation of microscopic pictures of hypoeutectoid steels is presented in the paper. The proposed approach based on the Feed-Back Pulse Coupled Neural Network (FBPCNN) combined with the Watershed algorithm is followed by post-processing of the objects detected inside images. Remaining steps of the procedure such as FE mesh generation, assigning material properties and finally numerical simulations are presented in the next sections.

2 Review of the Image Segmentation Methods

The image segmentation algorithms are one of the most explored methods in the literature. For the last two decades hundreds of papers have been published in this research area. Existing approaches can be divided into several subgroups depending on the type of the algorithms e.g. template matching, edge detection, tracing; or depending on the type of implemented numerical techniques e.g. matrices convolution, artificial intelligence or nature inspired (neural networks, content-based processing, cognitive recognition), clustering, statistical approaches, nonlinear diffusion analysis. Such algorithms play very important role not only in the analysis of the 2D pictures, but also in the 1D signals, 3D images processing, and in the multidimensional calculations. However their complexity increases respectively to with increasing data dimensionality. In the case of microstructure image processing all of the mentioned methods can be more or less successfully applied. Thus, the review of the most recent papers regarding this field of research can be enumerated as follows:

- Convolution – in practice, well-known and widely applied methods based on the derivative operators. The methods are very flexible and simple in implementation by using special kernel matrices e.g. Prewitt or Sobel to obtain effect of edge detection [14].

- Nature inspired – one of the most popular methods is the Watershed algorithm, which originates from natural solution of landscape and watersheds [2,21]. The idea of this method is based on the initial segmentation of data into disjoint areas, which in the next steps are filled successively with water puddles until two of them meet. The authors also proposed the application of special type of the

Watershed method implemented by using CA [16]. This offers high flexibility in case of various images, their shapes, colors, etc.

- Nonlinear diffusion – technique of image processing based on the nonlinear diffusion and popularized by Perona and Malik [15]. This method was further modified and improved for applications in the area of the texture-based segmentation. The example of the approach is presented in [20], where the author proposed to measure the scale of texture by using nonlinear diffusion followed by the multi-channel statistical region active contour adaptation. The method can be seen as a kind of unsupervised segmentation, because parameters are not sensitive to different texture images.

- Clustering-based – these approaches are sufficient mainly for images without additional distortions, however their efficiency in case of even slightly noised data is very poor [9]. Thus, the combination of these methods with other computational techniques like optimization procedures are often proposed [22]. The main advantage of the solution is higher insensibility for distortions, which offers much more reliable results.

The process of segmentation is very sophisticated and obtained results can be highly diversified even for the same input data and algorithm. This phenomenon depends mainly on the parameters established for the selected algorithm. Moreover, the automated assessment of the results is very difficult, thus it is hard to design the universal segmentation method able to work with various types of images. The proposition of a method dedicated to assess segmentation results is presented in [18]. This approach consists of a framework based on the Bayesian network, which determines optimal segmentation algorithm through a specific learning process. Another assessment method was proposed by the authors in [16]. The calculation of fractal dimension offer higher efficiency and slightly different quality measure of the results. Wider review of similar evaluation techniques, which offers objective comparison of different segmentation methods, is presented in [20].

3 The Method Based on the FBPCNN and the Watershed Algorithm

The method proposed in this paper (Figure 1) is composed of two approaches based on the FBPCNN and the Watershed Algorithm implemented using the Cellular Automaton (WCA). Composition of these two methods offers interesting capabilities of generalization and flexibility. Application of the neural network in the first step of calculations is responsible for generalization. The FBPCNNs are characterized by unique architecture, where neurons are organized as 2D matrix. Each neuron is connected with the set of neighboring neurons, therefore the whole network can be easily mapped on the structure of images containing neighboring pixels. In that case, amount of neurons reflects the amount of pixels inside an input image. Flexibility is offered by WCA, which can be applied with various transition rules, types of neighborhood and internal states.

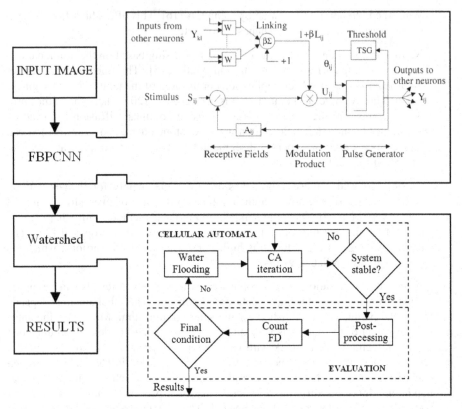

Fig. 1. Main scheme of the proposed image processing algorithm

FBPCNN

The FBPCNN architecture originates directly from the PCNN proposed by Eckhorn, who observed oscillatory activities stimulated by an external stimulus in the cat's primary visual cortex [6]. Some of those signals caused synchronous oscillations in distant regions of the cortex, characterized by local similarities. The main result of this research was creation of the neural model able to simulate mechanism of visual cortex. The model has a significant application potential in the image processing area and was finally adapted for the purposes of sophisticated approaches based on neural networks architecture. Each neuron is made of three fundamental elements i.e. Linking Field, Feeding Field (Stimulus) and Pulse Generator, which are related to specific weight parameters. The basic challenge in application of the FBPCNN is the preprocessing stage, aiming to establish proper values of weight parameters. The sensitivity analysis of the networks on variation of weight parameters was presented by the authors in [10]. As the result of this work optimal coefficients were determined for the FBPCNN dedicated to processing of pictures of material microstructures. This final network was applied in the paper as a first step of the image analysis algorithm to produce input data for the watershed approach.

Watershed

The Watershed Algorithm is the second phase of the proposed image processing approach and was presented by the authors in [16]. It is a complex method realized on a basis of the Cellular Automata framework followed by the Fractal Dimension calculation to evaluate segmentation results.

The results obtained by the FBPCNN are used further as an input data for the CA algorithm, which runs procedure of flooding iteratively. It uses a terrain originating from 3D plot of image, where Z-axis (grayscale value) is related to the terrain altitude. The CA algorithm runs until the space of cells remains stable and then the fractal dimension of obtained image is calculated. If it does not satisfy the requirement of the stop condition (1), the whole procedure is repeated. The stop criterion is defined as follows:

$$\frac{FD(I_k)-FD(I_{k-1})}{FD(I_{k-1})} \le Th \,, \tag{1}$$

where Th is the main threshold, I_k is an image in k^{th} iteration, and FD is a function that calculates 3D fractal dimension. Otherwise, if the obtained fractal dimension is close enough to its predecessor, the algorithm finishes and the final result is synthesized from images segmented in each step. Th may be established depending on image complexity.

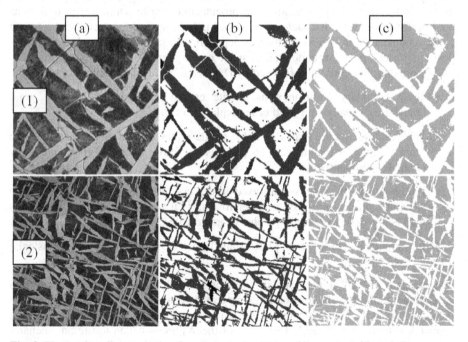

Fig. 2. The results of segmentation for microscopic picture of hypoeutectoid steel. Rows: magnification x200 (1) and x500 (2), Columns: original (a), separated Widmannstätten ferrite (b) and pearlite (c).

The calculations of all of the steps described above are very time consuming when implemented directly. Nevertheless, the solution based on the CA can usually be easily parallelized. The previous work of the authors was focused on creation of such parallelized CA framework, designed to run fast and be as universal as possible, allowing definitions of new algorithms based on the CA techniques [17]. The developed architecture of the Cellular Automata framework is equipped with the modified approach based on the splitting of information packages to small parts that fit into L2 cache memory. The approach improved the final efficiency 6-7 times allowing construction of much larger CA spaces.

Post processing

According to the requirements of the FEM and DMR, segmented images of microstructures (Figure 2) are meshed with the homogenic or heterogenic FE mesh. Each element is characterized by specific material properties dependently on the type of real microstructural component. The obtained digital microstructure is further applied in the numerical calculations of the compression test.

4   Material Description

The hypoeutectoid steels have a microstructure consisting of pearlite, being a mixture of two phases i.e. ferrite-cementite and proeutectoid ferrite. During the continuous cooling from the austenitic state to eutectoid transformation temperature the ferrite forms a number of growth morphologies depending on factors such as chemical composition of steel, prior austenite grain size and cooling rate. Classification of proeutectoid ferrite morphologies was proposed by Dubé et al. and Honeycombe [5,7]:

- Grain boundary allotriomorphs: ferrite crystals nucleate at austenite grain boundaries, usually equi-axed or lenticular in form.

- Widmannstätten side plates or laths: ferrite plates (laths) nucleate at austenite grain boundaries (or nucleate on pre-existing ferrite allotriomorphs) and grow along defined matrix planes.

- Intragranular idiomorphs: equi-axed ferrite crystals which nucleate within the austenitic grains and possess either irregular curved boundaries or boundaries with better-defined crystallographic characteristics.

- Intragranular plates: ferrite plates (laths) nucleate entirely within the austenite grains.

The presence of the Widmannstätten ferrite is favored by large austenite grains and accelerated cooling in the temperatures range between Ar_3 and Ar_1, and depends on the carbon content [8]. Widmannstätten ferrite is not necessarily detrimental to the mechanical properties of steel. The effect of the Widmannstätten ferrite on mechanical properties depends mostly on the prior austenite grain size and on the ferrite grain size [3]. Both strength and toughness increase with decreasing prior austenite grain size and increasing cooling rate, which is caused by refinement of the polygonal ferrite and the Widmannstätten ferrite.

Table 1. Mechanical properties of ferrite and pearlite [7,19]

Component	Yield strength [MPa]	Ultimate tensile strength [MPa]	Hardness [HB]	Elongation A, [pct]
Ferrite	150	300	80	40
Pearlite	400[*]	700÷900[*]	180÷220[*]	8÷10[*]

[*] Properties of pearlite strongly depend on spacing between ferrite–cementite plates

The mechanical properties of microstructural components (ferrite and pearlite) of the plain carbon hypoeutectoid steels are presented in Table 1. For purposes of this work, both ferrite and pearlite are treated as separated phases.

5 Modeling and Simulations

Numerical simulations of the phenomena occurring at the scale of single grains, is crucial to solve various problems that occur during the processing and exploitation of modern steel grades e.g. DP (Dual Phase) or TRIP (Transformation Induced Plasticity). The digital representation of the dual phase microstructure obtained in this work by an automatic image processing can be a valuable input for this micro scale analysis. The major advantage of the approach is that it realistically describes the shape of the grains in the considered microstructure, without any significant geometrical simplifications. This is important because when micro scale behavior of the DP or TRIP steels is considered, any variation in grains shape can play important role and can influence the final properties.

In the present work the digital microstructure obtained in the previous section is incorporated into the commercial FE Forge2 software using the user defined subroutines. This procedure is described in details in other authors' work [11]. The algorithm is as follows:

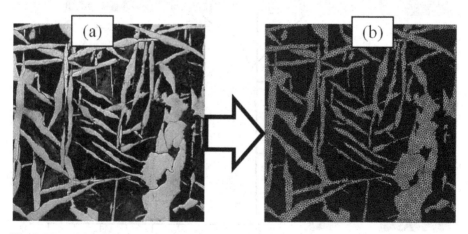

Fig. 3. The original image (a) transformed to digital material representations with finite element mesh (b)

1. Based on the input data from the FBPCNN image processing, the generation of the triangular mesh is performed. Particular groups of mesh nodes are located inside separated phases as seen in Figure 3;
2. The flow curves describing ferrite and pearlite phases are assigned to the particular phases, respectively.
3. Starting the FE simulation is the final step.

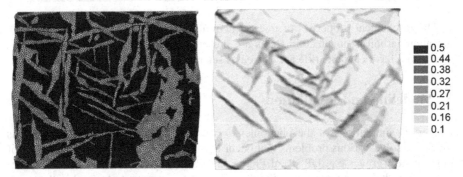

Fig. 4. Final geometry of the microstructure and corresponding strain distribution

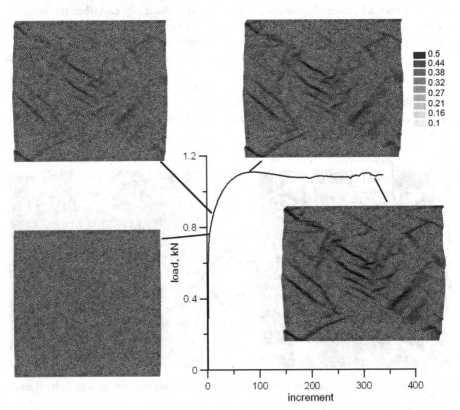

Fig. 5. Strain evolution and its influence on load values during subsequent stages of deformation

This FE model based on the digital material representation can be applied to simulate the behavior of micro scale samples used in e.g. micro forging, but also to simulate local material behavior of the larger structures under conditions of manufacturing and exploitation. The main advantage of the developed approach is simplicity. It gives the possibility of fast and efficient transfer of the optical microscopy image to the FE software and to analyze the microstructure behavior during deformation. Examples of application of this approach to simulate behavior of the hypoeutectoid steels under loading are presented in Figure 4. As seen in this figure, due to large differences in properties of ferrite and pearlite phases, the material flow is highly inhomogeneous. Regions with large strain localization that are forming characteristic bands are observed. This behavior in reality will lead to fracture initiation and will damage the sample. The strain evolution and its influence on loads during the subsequent stages of deformation can also be analyzed as seen in Figure 5.

In the present approach the FE simulation was performed with the homogenous FE mesh and it provided very interesting results of inhomogeneous deformation at the micro scale level. There is also a possibility to obtain even more accurate results with the heterogeneous FE meshes. This problem was the subject of other authors' work [11].

6 Conclusions

The idea of the image processing methods combined with digital representation of microstructure and the obtained advantages are presented in the paper. Particular attention was put on development of the FBPCNN image processing algorithm. The algorithm gives the possibility to obtain a realistic digital microstructure based on the easily accessible optical microscopy images. As presented, the algorithm can be applied to very sophisticated microstructures. The FE simulations based on the DMR show the large capabilities of the developed methodology in interpretation of inhomogeneous material behavior at the micro scale level.

The presented approach combined with the sophisticated optimization methods can provide a powerful tool able to support the designing process of initial microstructure, which will be the main subject of the future work.

Acknowledgments. The financial support of Polish Ministry of Science and Higher Education project no. R15 012 03 is acknowledged.

One of the authors (Łukasz Madej) is grateful for the financial support of the Foundation for Polish Science within the Start Programme.

References

1. Bernacki, M., Chastel, Y., Digonnet, H., Resk, H., Coupez, T., Logé, R.E.: Development of numerical tools for the multiscale modeling of recrystallisation in metals, based on a digital material framework. Computer Methods in Materials Science 7(1), 142–149 (2007)
2. Bleau, A., Leon, L.J.: Watershed-Based segmentation and region merging. Computer Vision and Image Understanding 77, 317–370 (2000)

3. Bodnar, R.L., Hansen, S.S.: Effects of Widmannstätten ferrite on the mechanical properties of a 0.2 Pct C – 0.7 Pct Mn Steel. Metallurgical and Materials Transactions A 25A, 763–773 (1994)
4. Cybułka, G., Jamrozik, P., Wejrzanowski, T., Rauch, L., Madej, L.: Digital representation of microstructure. In: Proc. CMS Conf., Krakow, pp. 379–384 (2007)
5. Dubé, C.A., Aaronson, H.I., Mehl, R.F.: La formation de la ferrite proeutectoide dans les aciers au carbone. Revue de Métallurgie 55(3), 201–210 (1958)
6. Eckhorn, R.: Oscillatory and non-oscillatory synchronizations in the visual cortex and their possible roles in associations of visual features. Progress in Brain Research 102, 405–426 (1994)
7. Honeycombe, R., Bhadeshia, H.K.D.H.: Steels. Microstructure and Properties, 2nd edn. published by Edward Arnold, a division of Hodder Headline PLC, London (1995)
8. Leontiev, B.A., Kosenko, A.P.: Formation of Widmannstätten structure in carbon steels. Metallovedenie i Termicheskaya Obrabotka Metallov 6, 59–60 (1973)
9. Liew, A.W., Yan, H., Law, N.F.: Image segmentation based on adaptive cluster prototype estimation. J. IEEE Transactions on Fuzzy Systems 13(4), 444–449 (2005)
10. Lukasik, L., Rauch, L.: Estimation of parameters of Feed-Back Pulse Coupled Neural Networks (FBPCNN) for purposes of microstructure images segmentation. Computer Methods in Materials Science (2009) (in review)
11. Madej, L., Hodgson, P.D., Pietrzyk, M.: Development of the multi-scale analysis model to simulate strain localization occurring during material processing. Archive of Computer Methods in Engineering 16, 287–318 (2009)
12. Madej, L., Mrozek, A., Kuś, W., Burczyński, T., Pietrzyk, M.: Multi scale modeling, multi-physics phenomena and evolving discontinuities in metal forming. Computer Methods in Materials Science 8(1), 1–10 (2008)
13. Madej, L., Rauch, L., Yang, C.: Strain distribution analysis based on the digital material representation. Archives of Metallurgy and Materials 54(3), 499–507 (2009)
14. Nixon, M.S., Aguado, A.S.: Feature Extraction and Image Processing, 1st edn. Newnes (2002)
15. Perona, P., Malik, J.: Scale space and edge detection using anisotropic diffusion. J. IEEE Transactions on Pattern Analysis and Machine Intelligence 12, 629–639 (1990)
16. Rauch, L., Straus, M.: Implementation of watershed algorithm based on cellular automata combined with estimation of 2D fractal dimension. In: Proc. of SEECCM 2009 European Conf. on Computational Mechanics, pp. 89–96 (2009)
17. Spytkowski, P., Klimek, T., Rauch, L., Madej, L.: Implementation of cellular automata framework dedicated to digital material representation. Computer Methods in Materials Science 9(2), 283–288 (2009)
18. Shah, S.K.: Performance modeling and algorithm characterization for robust image segmentation. International Journal of Computer Vision 80, 92–103 (2008)
19. Tisza, M.: Physical Metallurgy for Engineers. ASM International, Materials Park Ohio. USA and Freund Publishing House Ltd., London-Tel Aviv (2001)
20. Zhang, Y.: Texture image segmentation based on nonlinear diffusion. Geo-spatial Information Science 11(1), 38–42 (2008)
21. Zhao, C.G., Zhuang, T.G.: A hybrid boundary detection algorithm based on watershed and snake. Pattern Recognition Letters 26, 1256–1265 (2005)
22. Zhou, X.C., Shen, Q.T., Liu., L.M.: New two-dimensional fuzzy C-means clustering algorithm for image segmentation. Journal of Central South University of Technology 15, 882–887 (2008)

Surface Finish Control in Machining Processes Using Haralick Descriptors and Neuronal Networks

Enrique Alegre*, Rocío Alaiz-Rodríguez, Joaquín Barreiro,
Eduardo Fidalgo, and Laura Fernández

Dept. of Electrical, Automatic and Systems Engineering,
University of León, 24071 León, Spain
Phone: 0034 987 291989,
Fax: 0034 987 291970
enrique.alegre@unileon.es

Abstract. This paper presents a method to perform a surface finish control using a computer vision system. The goal pursued was to design an acceptance criterion for the control of surface roughness of steel parts, dividing them in those with low roughness acceptable class and those with high roughness defective class. We have used 143 images obtained from AISI 303 stainless steel machining. Images were described using three different methods texture local filters, the first four Haralick descriptors from the gray-level co-occurrence matrix and a 20 features vector obtained from the first subband of a wavelet transform of the original image and also the gray-level original image. Classification was conducted using K-nn and Neuronal Networks. The best error rate - 4.0% - with k-nn was achieved using texture descriptors. With the neuronal network, an eight node hidden layer network using Haralick descriptors leads to the optimal configuration - 0.0% error rate.

Keywords: roughness control, textural descriptors, gray level co-occurrence matrix, k-nn, neuronal network, classification.

1 Introduction

Surface measurement has been an important topic in the research during the last decades. The reason is that it constitutes an important property of parts and products with high significance in their functionality. In many situations, it is required to qualify and quantify diverse aspects of the surfaces: geometry, topography, texture, roughness and defects [18]. When the quality control point of view is considered, the necessity of evaluate the surface roughness is obvious, since it represents an important requirement in many engineering applications [1,2,19].

The measurement of surface roughness started a few decades ago with the advent of tactile profilometers. These drag a stylus along a line segment and

---

* Corresponding author.

R.P. Barneva et al. (Eds.): CompIMAGE 2010, LNCS 6026, pp. 231–241, 2010.
© Springer-Verlag Berlin Heidelberg 2010

record the vertical deflection of the stylus as it moves over the surface, thus recording the height of the surface at the sampling points. Using this traditional technology, the surface finish can be estimated by means of some roughness parameters defined in international standards [6]. Development of these standards is basically oriented to tactile measuring devices that provide twodimensional records of part profile.

However, even though the stylus instrument is still considered to be the accepted standard for measurement of surface roughness, the method has several disadvantages [15,18]: a) the stylus has to stay in permanent contact with the surface and is therefore easily damaged or soiled; b) the single profile line covers only a small part of the surface, possibly missing important areas; c) surface damage in some instances by the stylus force; d) low efficiency due to scanning. More disadvantages of stylus-based method can be found in [19].

These numerous disadvantages of contact methods have forced to surface measurement technologies to evolve significantly during last years [1] towards non-contact methods. A large research has been done in order to characterize 3D measurements of surface without contact at once. Among the common techniques are white-light interferometry, fringe projection, microscopy, speckle, light scattering and others.

Among these modern techniques, those based on computer vision can be remarked in terms of speed and accuracy. The advantages this technology provides are diverse. Whereas tactile techniques characterize a linear track over the part surface, computer vision techniques allow characterizing wide areas of the part surface providing more information [3,11,15,16]. Also, computer vision techniques take measures faster, since images are captured in a very short time, and they can be in-machine implemented. In addition, the application of exhaustive validity checking to each part is also possible. This aspect would be very difficult to achieve with traditional tactile porfilometers, which are slow and delicate.

Continuous advances have been made in sensor technologies. Particularly, vision sensors have been greatly enhanced in capabilities and cost reduction. Additionally, advances in image processing technology provide more reliable conclusions than before.

In all, computer vision is a very interesting technology for industrial environment. The use of these systems for the monitoring of machining operations has proved [4,12] an important reduction in the cycle time and the required resources. In particular, the modeling and prediction of surface roughness by computer vision have received a great deal of attention [2,3,4,5,6,8,9,10,11,12,15,16,17,19].

As far as the traditional contact techniques are concerned, computer vision techniques use other parameters to measure the surface finish. In the view of this consideration, the current standards developed for tactile devices do not reflect the current state of technology. New procedures are necessary to correlate the results obtained with tactile instruments with those obtained using other devices, as those based on computer vision. In this context, two lines should be remarked: the study on the spatial domain and the study in the frequency domain. This work tackles the measurement of surface quality from the point of view of the spatial domain.

Tarng and Lee [9] and Lee et al. [13] analyze the use of artificial vision and image analysis to quantify the roughness in different turning operations. Methods based on image analysis capture an image of the surface and analyze its pixels to obtain a diffuse light pattern. Later on, roughness parameters are calculated by means of statistical descriptors. One of the most used parameters is the standard deviation of gray levels. Kumar et al. [8] focus on milling, turning and molding processes. They make zoom over original images to obtain the Ga parameter (the image gray level average), finding a high correlation amongst the Ga parameter and the surface roughness. Kiran et al. [7] used a measure called texture unit, calculated from the gray scale values of the image, in order to describe the local texture of a pixel. Al-Kindi et al. [3] proposed a method named intensitytopography compatibility (ITC), characterizing the image data by three components: lightning, reflectance and surface characteristics. They calculate the value of conventional roughness parameters combining statistical such as mean value and standard deviation. Ramana and Ramamoothy [14] proposed a method based on the gray-level difference matrix for texture analysis. Tasan et al. [17] proposed a method for the comparison of local heights from the image data using successive surface images. Lee et al. [12] developed a computer vision system that measures the roughness in turning processes automatically.

In this work we propose a new method that can be used as an acceptance criterion in a quality control process. We have classified the roughness of carbon steel parts into two classes without error using texture descriptors.

The rest of the paper is organized as follows: Section 2 describes the image acquisition process. A description of the features used is included in Section 3 and the classification stage in Section 4. Finally, conclusions are summarized in Section 5.

2 Samples and Image Acquisition

2.1 Test Parts and Machining Characteristics

Test parts were made of AISI 303 X8CrNiS189 stainless steel. This material was chosen due to its common use in the small part mass-manufacturing industry. A MUPEM CNC multiturret parallel lathe ICIAR/1/42 model was used for the machining of parts.

Figure 1 shows the test part used. Several part operations were carried out, all of them representative of massive precision machining. However, only the cylindrical shape was used for surface finish measurement. Cutting tools were coated carbide inserts from Sandvik. The machining parameters used for the tests were fixed at the following values: cutting speed 250 m/min, feed rate 0.27 mm/rev and cutting depth 2 mm, considered as reference values. A surface finish control was performed on a HOMMELWELKE class 1 perfilometer. It was evident that the evolution of surface finish Ra values was far worse when increasing the machining time.

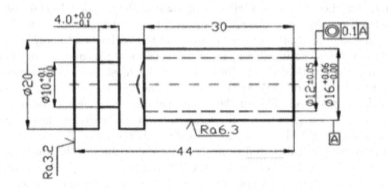

Fig. 1. Test parts used to measure the surface roughness

2.2   Image Acquisition

Images of the parts were captured using a specific location fixture which had attached a camera and a diffuse lighting system (Figure 2). The part was positioned onto a V shape bracket. The lighting system comprised a FOSTEC regulated light source DCR RIII. A NER SCDI-25-F0 diffuse illumination SCDI system was used to avoid shines. The system provided diffuse illumination in the camera axis.

The images were obtained using a Pulnix PE2015 B/W camera with 1/3 CCD. A Matrox Meteor II frame grabber card was used to digitize the images.

The optic assembly was composed of an OPTEM industrial zoom 70XL, with an extension tube of 1X and 0.5X/0,75X/1.5X/2.0X OPTEM lens. We used the maximum magnification of the system.

2.3   Experimental Image Set

Using such system, 143 images were captured (see Figure 3) with the same z scale. Each of the images was labeled with its R_a roughness parameter, obtained using the median of three repeated R_a measuring. The roughness values were in the range 2.40 to 4.33 m.

Several experiments were carried out and the images were divided in two sets: the first class corresponds to low roughness (satisfactory) and the second class to high roughness (unacceptable). Images of both classes are shown in Figure 3.

Three different cases were considered. In the first case, the first thirty images (ordered by R_a values) were separated from the last thirty and labeled as class 1 and class 2 respectively. In the second case, one class was composed by the first fifty images and the second one by the last fifty. In the third case, seventy of them were assigned to class 1 while the other seventy to class 2. Images of both classes will be included in train and test subgroups as explained in Section 4.

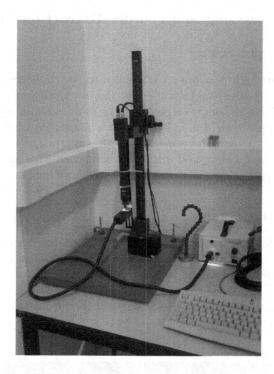

Fig. 2. Camera and lighting system used in the image acquisition

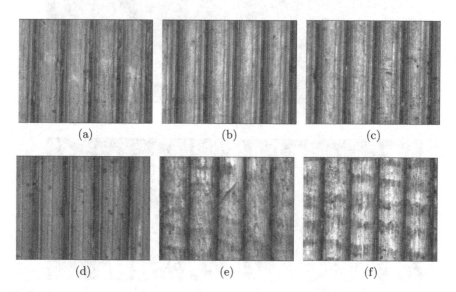

Fig. 3. Images of both classes 1 and 2. a, b and c with low roughness (R_a of 2.66, 2.77 and 2.82 μm respectively) and d, e and f with high roughness (R_a of 3.65, 4.03 and 4.03 μm).

3   Image Processing and Feature Extraction Methods

3.1   Image Preprocessing

A vertical Prewitt high pass filter was applied to the complete set of images in order to enhance contrast and make easier the description of roughness. Later on, three sets of descriptors were obtained for the original images and also for the filtered images. Figure 4 a and b show two images with different Ra before filtering and c and d show the same images after filtering, all of them have the same z scale. Since a better performance was reached with filtered images, we only show values obtained when classifying with those images.

3.2   Texture Descriptors

Three different feature vectors were obtained by computing some texture descriptors: three texture local features (entropy, range, and standard deviation), the four main Haralick features (Contrast, Correlation, Energy, Homogeneity) from the Gray Level Co-occurrence Matrix and twenty features from the Haralick descriptors applied over the original image and the first sub band of a Wavelet Transform of the original image.

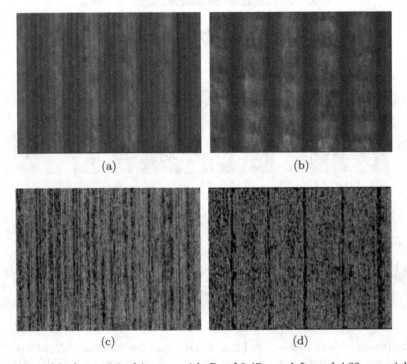

(a)   (b)

(c)   (d)

Fig. 4. a and b show original images with R_a of 2.47 μm -left- and 4.33 μm -right-. c and d show the same images after filtering.

4   Classification Methods

The former feature vectors were classified by means of k-nn using the random sampling validation method. This let us to compare the results of classification with those obtained by means of neural networks. The neural network used was a multilayer Perceptron (MLP) with sigmoidal transfer functions. The learning algorithm belongs to the group of backpropagation algorithms, in particular the Levenberg-Marquadt optimized version.

The feature vector values were normalized, in such a way that a translation and a scaling were applied to each random sampling extracted from the training set. The translation of the group of vectors was applied from its own centroid to the origin of the space in order to achieve a medium value of cero. The scaling was done dividing each vector by the medium energy of the group, calculated as the root mean square. This operation leads to a standard deviation value of one.

The optimum number of nodes in the hidden layer and the number of training cycles have been selected empirically. The validation method is a random sampling type. This method divided the available set of images in subgroups randomly, 70% for training and 30% for test. Performance is evaluated computing the mean error rate over ten runs. Also, the effect of data normalization over the classification error was analyzed.

4.1   k-Nearest Neighbors

The best results have been achieved with the texture local features descriptors.

The lower error is 4.0% for the case of fifty images by class. The error increases up to 10% and 9% when using thirty and seventy images respectively and the error distribution is fairly uniform among the classes. Table 1 shows the minimum errors in each class for the three descriptors used in this work.

4.2   Neural Network

The error rates obtained with the neural network are similar, lower than 10% for several descriptors. The error rate was 0.0% with fifty images in each class and using the Haralick descriptors obtained over the Wavelet transform. Only

Table 1. Minimal errors in each case. First column with local filters, second columns with GLCM (GrayLevelCooccurrenceMatrix) and first four Haralick descriptors and third column with the 20 features vector using wavelet.

Images	Local Texture	GLCM Descriptors	Haralick and Wavelet
30	10.56	6.11	8.33
50	**4.00**	5.00	5.00
70	9.05	6.90	8.33

the Haralick descriptors enhance their results when using the vertical Prewitt filtering, the rest of them achieve significant better results when the filter is not applied.

All descriptors were used for this test, and the results obtained from them are acceptable, in most of the cases with error rates below 10.0%.

Table 2 shows the global error rate for the case of thirty images in each class, used filtered images in Haralick descriptors, and non filtered images with the other two descriptors. Minimum error rate equals 0,69%. The values in the first row and first column are the number of cycles and the number of nodes in the hidden layer, respectively.

Table 3 and 4 show the global error rate for the other cases, that is, fifty and seventy images in each class. It is observed that the lower error rates correspond to the fifty image case, even better than those obtained with thirty images. The best error rate obtained reaches the 0.0%.

The reason of this behavior may be that, in the case of thirty images, the training set is not large enough for optimum network learning and a reliable classification. In the case of seventy images the error rates increase up to 5,65% as expected, since values near to the decision border in both classes are very close, but even in this case, the Haralick descriptors achieve acceptable error rates.

Table 2. Error rates in %. Classes with 30 images filtered with Prewitt in case of Local Texture and GLCM Descriptors. Number of cycles is shown in rows and number of nodes in the hidden layer in columns.

	Local Texture				GLCM Descriptors				Haralick Wavelet			
	25	100	200	1000	25	100	200	1000	25	100	200	1000
2	11.11	10.42	*9.03*	*9.03*	7.64	*6.94*	10.42	11.11	3.47	*2.78*	3.47	3.47
4	*9.03*	*9.03*	15.28	18.06	8.33	10.42	*7.64*	*7.64*	3.47	5.56	*2.78*	5.56
6	10.42	11.11	*8.33*	9.03	11.11	9.03	*7.64*	8.33	6.94	*1.39*	*1.39*	2.78
8	9.03	*7.64*	9.72	8.33	9.03	9.72	9.03	*7.64*	9.03	**0.69**	2.78	2.78
10	12.5	9.03	*6.25*	6.94	11.81	*8.33*	*8.33*	9.03	1.39	1.39	*0.69*	1.39
14	10.42	8.33	9.72	*6.94*	10.42	8.33	*7.64*	*7.64*	*1.39*	*1.39*	*1.39*	2.08

Table 3. Error rates in %. Classes with 50 images filtered with Prewitt in case of Local Texture and GLCM Descriptors. Number of cycles is shown in rows and number of nodes in the hidden layer in columns.

	Local Texture				GLCM Descriptors				Haralick Wavelet			
	25	100	200	1000	25	100	200	1000	25	100	200	1000
2	*6.67*	7.5	7.5	*6.67*	*7.5*	8.75	*7.5*	*7.5*	*0.42*	*0.42*	0.83	1.67
4	13.33	*6.25*	7.08	7.92	*7.92*	10.83	10.42	8.75	*0.83*	*0.83*	6.67	2.08
6	9.17	7.5	7.08	*5.83*	10.83	10.83	*7.5*	8.33	1.25	0.42	0.42	**0.00**
8	8.33	*7.92*	17.08	*7.92*	10.42	*7.92*	9.17	9.58	0.83	*0.42*	6.67	2.08
10	7.5	*6.25*	7.5	10.83	8.33	*7.5*	16.67	8.75	1.25	*0.42*	*0.42*	2.08
14	5.83	7.08	5	5.42	10	9.58	*7.5*	9.17	0.83	2.92	0.42	**0.00**

Table 4. Error rates in %. Classes with 70 images filtered with Prewitt in case of Local Texture and GLCM Descriptors. Number of cycles is shown in rows and number of nodes in the hidden layer in columns.

	Local Texture				GLCM Descriptors				Haralick Wavelet			
	25	**100**	**200**	**1000**	**25**	**100**	**200**	**1000**	**25**	**100**	**200**	**1000**
2	11.31	11.01	10.12	*9.82*	*8.33*	8.63	8.93	10.42	*5.95*	8.04	9.52	9.23
4	16.96	*10.42*	16.37	11.9	10.42	*8.63*	9.52	9.52	***5.65***	7.44	7.74	6.55
6	*10.71*	11.01	*10.71*	12.2	*10.71*	16.96	11.31	*10.71*	6.25	7.44	6.85	7.14
8	10.12	11.01	10.71	*9.82*	10.71	11.31	13.69	*9.82*	7.44	8.04	*6.85*	7.14
10	*9.52*	16.07	11.01	13.69	12.2	12.8	*11.31*	*11.31*	9.82	*6.25*	7.74	7.74
14	16.07	12.5	15.77	*10.42*	*10.42*	10.71	12.5	12.5	7.74	*6.55*	*6.55*	7.44

4.3 Minimum Errors

Table 5 shows the minimum errors obtained with each descriptor and with both classification methods. The n parameter indicates that feature vectors are normalized. It can be observed that the MLP classifier gives better results in most of the cases, reaching its best result in the case of 50 images.

Table 5. Minimum errors with Local Texture Descriptors, Gray Level Co-occurrence Matrix Descriptors and Haralick Descriptors

Class	30 images			50 images			70 images		
	LText	**GLCM**	**Har.W**	**LText**	**GLCM**	**Har.W**	**LText**	**GLCM**	**Har.W**
KNN	8.33	*6.65*	8.33	*5.00*	*5.00*	*5.00*	*7.86*	*7.86*	8.57
KNN n.	11.11	*6.11*	8.33	*4.00*	5.00	5.00	9.29	*6.90*	8.33
MLP	16.67	*1.39*	7.41	10.00	*3.33*	4.44	8.33	*7.14*	*7.14*
MLP n.	6.25	6.25	*0.69*	5.00	7.08	**0.00**	9.23	8.04	*5.65*

5 Conclusions

This paper proposes a method based on computer vision to measure the surface finish quality of machined metallic parts. The performance of three different sets of descriptors was analyzed, applied on both filtered and unfiltered images. With k-nn classification filtered images showed a better performance, but with the neuronal network the non filtered images lead to lower error rates in the case of Haralick with wavelet descriptors.

The best results were achieved using neuronal network classification, with Haralick descriptors applied to the first subband of the wavelet transform and to the original image. This configuration leads to a classification accuracy of 100% when the first 50 and last 50 images were used. The results show that the use of texture descriptors is a feasible method to evaluate the roughness of metallic parts in the context of product quality and future research will focus on this line.

Acknowledgments. This work has been partially supported by the research projects DPI2006-02550 supported by the Spanish Ministry of Education and Science, ULE2005-01 by the University of León and LE018B06 by the Junta de Castilla y León.

References

1. Al-Kindi, G.A., Shirinzadeh, B.: An evaluation of surface roughness parameters measurement using vision-based data. Intl. J. of Mach. Tools & Manuf. 47, 697–708 (2007)
2. Al-Kindi, G.A., Shirinzadeh, B.: Feasibility assessment of vision-based surface roughness parameters acquisition for different types of machined specimens. Image and Vision Computing 27, 444–458 (2009)
3. Al-Kindi, G.A., Baul, R., Gill, K.: An application of machine vision in the automated inspection of engineering surfaces. Intl. J. of Production Research 30(2), 241–253 (1992)
4. Castejón, M., Alegre, E., Barreiro, J., Hernández, L.K.: On-line tool wear monitoring using geometric descriptors from digital images. Intl. J. of Machine Tools & Manufacture 47, 1847–1853 (2007)
5. Gadelmawla, E.: A vision system for surface roughness characterization using the gray level co-occurrence matrix. NDT& E Int. 37, 577–588 (2004)
6. ISO4288:1996. Geometrical product specification (GPS) Surface texture: Profile method
7. Kiran, M., Ramamoorthy, B., Radhakrishan, V.: Evaluation of surface roughness by vision system. Intl. J. of Machine Tools and Manufacture 38, 685–690 (1998)
8. Kumar, R., Kulashekar, P., Dhansekar, B., Ramamoorthy, B.: Application of digital image magnification for surface roughness evaluation using machine vision. Intl. J. of Machine Tools and Manufacture 45, 228–234 (2005)
9. Lee, B., Tarng, Y.: Surface roughness inspection by computer vision in turning operations. Intl. J. of Machine Tools and Manufacture 41, 1251–1263 (2001)
10. Lee, B., Hoa, S., Hob, S.: Accurate estimation of surface roughness from texture features of the surface image using an adaptative neuro-fuzzy inference system. Precision Engineering 29, 95–100 (2005)
11. Lee, B., Yu, S., Juan, H.: The model of surface roughness inspection by vision system in turning. Mechatronics 14(1), 129–141 (2004)
12. Lee, B., Juan, H., Yu, S.: A study of computer vision for measuring surface roughness in the turning process. Intl. J. of Advanced Manufacturing Technology 19, 295–301 (2002)
13. Lee, S., Chen, C.: On-line surface roughness recognition system using artificial neural networks system in turning operations. The International Journal of Advanced Manufacturing Technology 22(7-8), 498–509 (2003)
14. Ramana, K., Ramamoorthy, B.: Statistical methods to compare texture features of machined surfaces. Pattern Recognition 29, 1447–1459 (1996)
15. Schmähling, F.A., Hamprecht, F.A., Hoffmann, D.M.P.: A three-dimensional measure of surface roughness based on mathematical morphology. Intl. J. of Machine Tools and Manufacture 46, 1764–1769 (2006)

16. Senin, N., Ziliotti, M., Groppetti, R.: Three-dimensional surface topography segmentation through clustering. Wear 262, 395–410 (2007)
17. Tasan, Y., De Rooij, M., Schipper, D.: Measurement of wear on asperity level using image-processing techniques. Wear 258, 83–91 (2005)
18. Tian, G.Y., Lu, R.S., Gledhill, D.: Surface measurement using active vision and light scattering. Optics and Lasers in Engineering 45, 131–139 (2007)
19. Whitehouse, D.J.: Handbook of Surface and Nanometrology. Institute of Physics Publishing (IOP) (2003)

Direction-Dependency of a Binary Tomographic Reconstruction Algorithm

László Varga, Péter Balázs*, and Antal Nagy

Department of Image Processing and Computer Graphics
University of Szeged
Árpád tér 2, H-6720 Szeged, Hungary
{vargalg,pbalazs,nagya}@inf.u-szeged.hu

Abstract. We study how the quality of an image reconstructed by a binary tomographic algorithm depends on the direction of the observed object in the scanner, if only a few projections are available. To do so we conduct experiments on a set of software phantoms by reconstructing them form different projection sets using an algorithm based on D.C. programming (a method for minimizing the difference of convex functions), and compare the accuracy of the corresponding reconstructions by two suitable approaches. Based on the experiments, we discuss consequences on applications arising from the field of non-destructive testing, as well.

Keywords: discrete tomography, reconstruction, non-destructive testing, D.C. programming; GPU-accelerated computing.

1 Introduction

The goal of *tomography* is to reconstruct an image from its projections. In the general case this problem can be solved, e.g., by the filtered backprojection method that can reconstruct the image when a sufficiently great number of projections - usually a few hundreds - are available [9]. However, in certain applications of tomography it is not possible to make so many projections of the observed objects. *Discrete tomography* deals with the case when the objects to be reconstructed consist of just a few different materials, with known attenuation coefficients [7,8]. With this prior information, algorithms were developed capable of reconstructing the original image (or a similar one) from just a few – usually 2-10 – projections. Several works have been done to investigate how small perturbations in the projection data can affect the result of discrete tomographic reconstruction, and how the original and the reconstructed image can differ from each other in such cases (see, e.g., [1,4]). However, having so few projections, defined by very differing angles brings up additional questions. Does

---

* Corresponding author. This research was partially supported by the TÁMOP-4.2.2/08/1/2008-0008 program of the Hungarian National Development Agency and by the János Bolyai Research Scholarship of the Hungarian Academy of Sciences.

R.P. Barneva et al. (Eds.): CompIMAGE 2010, LNCS 6026, pp. 242–253, 2010.

the result of the reconstruction depend on how we choose these angles? How should we choose the angles of the projections to obtain the best result possible for a given number of projections?

Such studies are motivated by practical applications. For example, in non-destructive testing (NDT) of objects made of homogeneous materials, the acquisition of the projections may be very expensive, so it is important to keep the number of projections as small as possible. In NDT often a blueprint image is available, and the task is to determine how much the object of interest differs from the given blueprint. Usually, the object studied might be placed with some rotation into the scanner, which may affect the accuracy of the reconstruction, and make the comparison to the blueprint impossible. Even if the effect of rotation is somehow eliminated, projections of a given object from certain directions can be more informative than other ones, which makes sense to use the blueprint image to determine how to put the objects into the scanner to get better results without making additional projections.

The aim of this paper is to determine – at least empirically – how dependent a discrete tomographic reconstruction can be, on the angles chosen for the projections. We do this by performing experimental tests on a set of software phantoms, trying to reconstruct them from different projection sets. Such results have been briefly mentioned before in [10], but to our knowledge no detailed research in this topic has been done so far.

The paper is structured as follows. We start out by stating the reconstruction problem in Section 2. Then, in Section 3 we go into more details to specify the test framework. Section 4 describes the experiments we conducted, while we give our experimental results in Section 5. In Section 6 we discuss how our results are related to applications of non-destructive testing. Finally, Section 7 is for the conclusion.

2   The Reconstruction Problem

We study the reconstruction of binary images of size $n \times n$ from their projections. The projection data is measured by line integrals taken from a set of directions defined by different angles, using parallel beam geometry. In this case, the binary reconstruction problem can be represented as a system of equations

$$\mathbf{Ax} = \mathbf{b}, \quad \mathbf{A} = (a_{i,j})_{n^2 \times m} \in \mathbb{R}^{n^2 \times m}, \; \mathbf{x} \in \{0,1\}^{n^2}, \; \mathbf{b} \in \mathbb{R}^m , \tag{1}$$

where m is the total number of projection rays used, $a_{i,j}$ gives the length of the line segment of the i-th ray through the j-th pixel, and b_i gives the projection of the image along the i-th projection ray as illustrated in Figure 1.

Although this gives an exact formulation of the reconstruction problem, solving the related equation system is usually not the best approach. As mentioned before, in discrete tomography just a handful of projections are available, therefore the corresponding system of equations is usually underdetermined, and due to errors in the measured projection data, it can be inconsistent as well. There

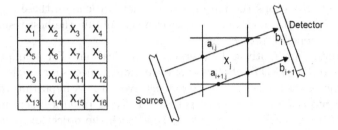

Fig. 1. Representation of the parallel beam geometry used

are two main approaches to overcome these problems. First, one can apply iterative algorithms for finding an approximate solution. These methods are the different versions of the so-called algebraic reconstruction technique [2,6,9]. The other main approach is based on defining a function

$$f(\mathbf{x}) = \|\mathbf{A}\mathbf{x} - \mathbf{b}\|_2^2 + \lambda \cdot g(\mathbf{x}) \, , \tag{2}$$

where $\mathbf{A}$, $\mathbf{b}$, and $\mathbf{x}$ are the same as defined in (1) and $g(\mathbf{x})$ is a function representing prior information about the image to be reconstructed, with a given λ weight. After this reformulation, the reconstruction problem can be redefined as finding the minimum of the function $f(\mathbf{x})$ by some optimization strategies, like genetic algorithms, simulated annealing, or other numerical methods. Examples for this kind of algorithms can be found in [5,13,14].

For our experiments we were using the numerical method specified in [13] (in the following referred to as DC algorithm where the abbreviation DC stands for the difference of convex functions), which performs the reconstruction by minimizing the function

$$J_\mu(\mathbf{x}) := \|\mathbf{A}\mathbf{x} - \mathbf{b}\|_2^2 + \frac{\gamma}{2} \sum_{j=1}^{n^2} \sum_{l \in N_4(j)} (\mathbf{x}_j - \mathbf{x}_l)^2 - \mu \frac{1}{2} \langle \mathbf{x}, \mathbf{e} - \mathbf{x} \rangle \, , \quad \mathbf{x} \in [0,1]^{n^2} \, , \tag{3}$$

where γ is a given constant controlling the weight of the smoothness term on the image, $N_4(j)$ is the set of pixels 4-connected to the j-th pixel, and $\mathbf{e}$ denotes the vector with all n^2 coordinates equal to 1. In the beginning of the optimization process $\mu = 0$, so the best continuous solution is found. In the sequel, μ is iteratively increased by μ_Δ, to force binary results. This algorithm is suitable to our task for several reasons:

- luck must not have an influence on the results, so a deterministic algorithm is needed,
- DC is proved to be an accurate algorithm that can work with a small number of projections, and
- its parallel implementation for a GPU makes the algorithm capable of performing a large number of tests required, in a relatively short time.

3   Technical Specification of the Reconstructions

The parameters of the DC reconstruction algorithm were mostly set as specified in [14], for example we used $\gamma = 0.25$. Though, instead of calculating μ_Δ from the first continuous reconstruction and the projection matrix $\mathbf{A}$, we explicitly set $\mu_\Delta = 0.1$, to avoid performing a large number of computation, and keep the running time of the algorithm as low as possible.

Reconstruction of the test objects were done from projection sets with different numbers of angles. Each time the angles were uniformly placed on the half circle as follows

$$S(\alpha, p) = \left\{ 90° + \alpha + i \frac{180°}{p} \mid i = 0, \ldots, p-1 \right\}, \tag{4}$$

where p (the number of angles) and α (the starting offset) are given values. Figure 2 gives an example using 4 projection angles. For each image the number of projections p ranged form 2 to 16, and for each such projection sets the starting angle α ranged from $0°$ to $\left(\left\lceil \frac{180}{p} \right\rceil - 1 \right)°$ with a step of $1°$ as illustrated in Figure 3. That makes a total of $\sum_{i=2}^{16} \left\lceil \frac{180}{i} \right\rceil = 431$ different reconstruction tasks for each image. For each projection the rays were placed at equal distances,

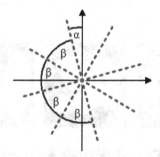

Fig. 2. The projection sets $S(\alpha, 4)$ used in the tests (α is predefined, $\beta = 45°$)

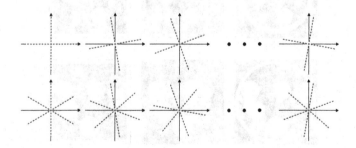

Fig. 3. The projection sets used for testing the DC algorithm with 2 (top row) and 3 (bottom row) projections. Dashed red lines represent the direction of the projections.

and covered the whole image. The distance between the detector elements was set to 1/2 pixels to ensure that we have information of all the pixels in every projection.

4   Test Data and Experiments

We conducted several experiments using software phantoms from three different sources: three phantoms used for testing the algorithm in [14], two phantoms used in [2], and – in addition – 10 newly generated software phantoms, each containing five randomly positioned disks of random sizes. Where it was possible (in the case of the 10 new software phantoms and one taken from [14]) two altered versions of the phantoms were also generated: one with a ring, and one with a rectangular stripe around the original objects. All the 37 phantoms had the same size of 256 by 256 pixels. Some of the phantoms used in our tests can be seen in Figure 4.

The algorithm was implemented with GPU acceleration on the NVIDIA CUDA programming toolkit (detailed description of CUDA can be found in [11]). For the computation we used a 2.5 GHz Core 2 Quad CPU, and an NVIDIA GeForce 8800 GT GPU. The time required to perform the total 431 reconstruction tasks for each phantom was about 1-2 hours, depending on the phantom processed.

During the experiments we used two approaches to evaluate the results. The first one was to measure the accuracy of the reconstruction by counting the

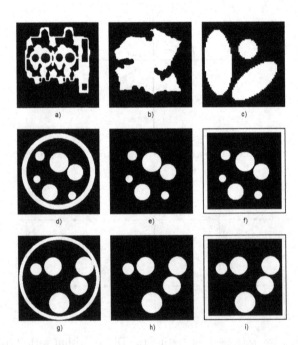

Fig. 4. Some of the software phantoms used for testing

number of pixels differing in the original phantoms and the result images for each given set $S(\alpha, p)$ of projections by

$$E(\mathbf{x}^*, S(\alpha, p)) := \|\mathbf{x}^* - \mathbf{x}_{S(\alpha, p)}\|_2^2, \tag{5}$$

where $\mathbf{x}^*$ is the original software phantom and $\mathbf{x}_{S(\alpha, p)}$ denotes the result reconstructed from the set of directions $S(\alpha, p)$ defined in (4).

The other kind of evaluation was performed by computing the direction-dependency for each software phantom and for every number of projections with the formula

$$D_t(\mathbf{x}^*, p) := \frac{(E_{max}(\mathbf{x}^*, p) - E_{min}(\mathbf{x}^*, p))}{n^2} \left(\frac{\cos\left(\pi \frac{E_{min}(\mathbf{x}^*, p)}{n^2}\right) + 1}{2} \right)^q, \tag{6}$$

where

$$E_{min}(\mathbf{x}^*, p) := \min_{\alpha = 0°, \ldots, \left(\left\lceil \frac{180}{p} \right\rceil - 1\right)°} E\left(\mathbf{x}^*, S\left(\alpha, p\right)\right), \tag{7}$$

$$E_{max}(\mathbf{x}^*, p) := \max_{\alpha = 0°, \ldots, \left(\left\lceil \frac{180}{p} \right\rceil - 1\right)°} E\left(\mathbf{x}^*, S\left(\alpha, p\right)\right), \tag{8}$$

and q is determined as the root of the equation

$$\left(\frac{\cos(\pi t) + 1}{2} \right)^q = 1 - t, \tag{9}$$

with a given $t \in (0, 1)$ value.

The function (6) simply gets the ratio of the missed pixels in the result and multiplies it with a correction function. The task of the correction function is to guarantee that the value of $D_t(\mathbf{x}^*, p)$ will not be too large, if the ratio of the missed pixels on the best result is much greater than t, therefore we can set an approximate threshold of accuracy we are interested in, with the parameter t. It is obvious, that the larger value means that the quality of the reconstruction is more dependent on the choice of the directions.

5   Experimental Results

We used the function defined in (6) to find the "software phantom-projection number" pairs which are the most sensitive to rotation, and to compare the best and worst reconstruction results. Of course, in a real application only accurate results would be acceptable, so we were interested in the cases when the results had only small errors, therefore we set the parameter $t = 0.001$. Figure 5 shows the values of our direction-dependency measurement $D_t(\mathbf{x}^*, p)$ for Figures 4d-f.

First, we examined the simple phantoms, where there was no ring or rectangular stripe around the objects. In this case, for most of the phantoms we found that the direction-dependency is the largest when about 3-5 projections are available for the reconstruction. More precisely, for most of the phantoms, there is a

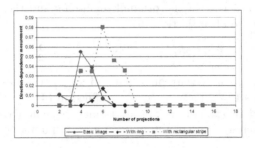

Fig. 5. Direction-dependency of the software phantoms of Figures 4d-f (the higher the values are the more dependent the phantom is to the choice of directions)

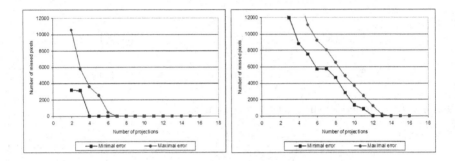

Fig. 6. Minimal and maximal number of missed pixels as it depends on the number of projections, for software phantoms of Figure 4e (left) and Figure 4a (right)

certain minimal number of projections where the algorithm can reconstruct the original objects almost perfectly, if there is a proper set of projections available, but we might need more projections when we take the wrong angles. For example, on the left of Figure 6 we can see that with the right angles we can get the original phantom from 4 projections, but if we have the worst possible angles we need 7 projections for the same results. Figures 8a-c give another example of a greatly direction-dependent software phantom, with the original phantom, and the best and worst reconstructions from 3 projections, respectively.

Although all the software phantoms showed this kind of sensitivity to the rotation of the projection sets, such great differences did not always occur. For example, on the right-hand side of Figure 6, we can see that there is no significant difference between the minimal and maximal error independently on the number of projections, so we can not get a much better result by finding the best angles. The results of this phantom reconstructed from 10 projections can be seen on Figures 8d-f, representing the original phantom, the best, and the worst results, respectively.

It is also useful to have a look at the exact errors for some of the phantoms, and projection numbers, according to the starting angles. Figure 7 shows the

number of missed pixels for the software phantoms shown in Figure 4g-i reconstructed from 3 and 4 projections. It immediately becomes visible that there is
a big difference between the minimal and maximal values on each curve, which
coincides with the previous statements, and proves that the choice of the projection angles can significantly influence the quality of the reconstruction. We can
also observe that the curves depicted in Figure 7 are relatively smooth which
suggests that it is not necessary to find the optimal angles for the projections
to obtain a good reconstruction. Any angles close to the optimal ones can give
acceptable results.

Comparing the curves of Figure 7 belonging to the different versions of the
phantoms we can see that the original objects give the smallest errors. If we add
a ring around the original objects then the curve looks similar but with greater
error values. The explanation of this could be that the ring brings more instability
into the equation-system of the reconstruction problem, but this symptom is
still a subject to our further studies. We can also realize that the ring makes
the relative difference between the best and worst results smaller compared to
the total number of misreconstructed pixels, therefore the phantom becomes less
dependent on the choice of the angles of the projections. Figures 8g-i give an
example for this case, with the original software phantom, and the best and worst
reconstructions from 6 projections. The situation is quite different when we add
a rectangular stripe to the objects. An example is given in Figures 8j-l, with the
original phantom, the best and, the worst results from 4 projections. In this case
we can see that the error functions shown in Figure 7 can take extremely large
values related to their global minima. The rectangle stripe added to the objects
can be entirely reconstructed if two projection angles are aligned to its sides,
and in this case the stripe does not effect the reconstruction, and the result is
the same (or at least very close to that) as if there were no rectangular stripe.
Furthermore, the farther the projection angles are from the proper alignment,
the less accurate the reconstruction is (similarly as in the case of adding a ring to
the objects). This means that adding such objects to the phantom can greatly
increase the direction dependency of the reconstruction. We used equiangular

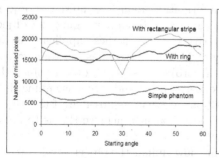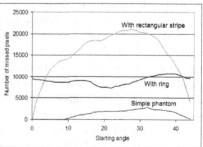

Fig. 7. Example for the number of missed pixels, for the software phantoms of Figures 4g-i, reconstructed from 3 (left) and 4 (right) projections

projection geometries, so we have two minima on the curves in the case when we had an odd number of projections, because only one projection can be aligned to the side of the rectangular stripe at once. In case of the ring we can not observe such minimal values because the ring is invariant to the rotation.

As a summation Table 1 shows the minimal number of projections required for a reconstruction with a ratio of missed pixels less than $t = 0.001$, for the best and worst projection sets of the phantoms. Again we can see that it is important to find the right angles, if we want to reduce the number of projections required for an acceptable reconstruction.

Finally, we had the assumption that the accuracy of the reconstruction is the best if the projections are taken from the direction defined by the first or second principal components of the objects. Although reconstructions using the projections from the directions including the principal components usually give good results, our tests revealed that - at least empirically - there is no straightforward connection between the best projection directions and the principal components.

Table 1. Minimal number of projections required for a reconstruction with a ratio of missed pixels less than $t = 0.001$, for the best and worst projection sets of the images, each column representing the results of a software phantom (s.p. - simple phantom; w.r. - phantom with ring; r.s. - phantom with rectangular stripe)

	1.	2.	3.	4.	5.	6.	7.	8.	9.	10.	11.	12.	13.	14.	15.
s.p. - best	4	5	12	5	4	4	4	4	4	4	4	4	4	4	4
s.p. - worst	5	6	14	6	7	5	5	5	5	5	5	5	5	6	5
w.r. - best	-	-	-	-	6	6	7	6	6	6	7	6	7	7	7
w.r. - worst	-	-	-	-	7	7	7	7	7	6	7	7	7	7	7
r.s. - best	-	-	-	-	6	6	6	6	4	6	6	6	4	6	6
r.s. - worst	-	-	-	-	9	9	9	9	9	9	9	9	9	9	9

6   Direction-Dependency in Non-Destructive Testing

In industry, there is often a need to get information about the interior of objects (industrial parts) in a non-destructive way, i.e. without damaging the object itself. This process is called non-destructive testing. In these applications the information about the object is usually collected by transmission tomography using X-rays or neutron rays to form the projections of the object. Since the acquisition of such projections can be very expensive and time-consuming, it is important to keep the number of projections as small as possible. If the object is made of homogeneous material then an approach to achieve this is to apply binary tomography for the reconstruction [3].

A frequent task in NDT is to determine how similar the object studied to the given blueprint image is. The way to do it is the following. One places the object into the scanner, forms its projections from a few directions, and applies some (binary) reconstruction method to obtain an image from the object. Finally, the

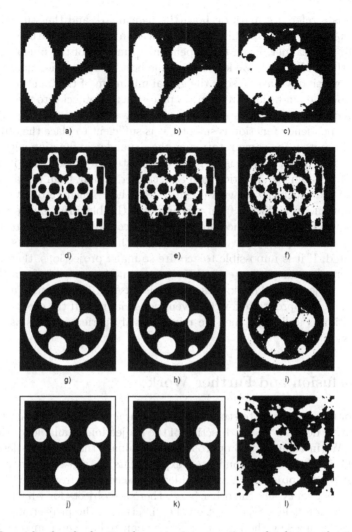

Fig. 8. Examples for the best and worst reconstructions of software phantoms, with given projection numbers. The original phantoms (first column), and the best and worst results (second and third column, respectively) for the same number of projections but different starting angles (b, c: 3 projections with starting angles 5° and 36°; e, f: 10 projections with 0° and 5°; h, i: 6 projections with 6° and 25°; k, l: 4 projections with 0° and 27°).

difference of the blueprint and the reconstructed images is measured according to an arbitrary similarity metric. Since the blueprint image is available in advance, we can simulate its projections in arbitrary directions, and perform all the tests of Section 5 in order to characterize the blueprint image from the viewpoint of direction-dependency. This information turns out to be especially useful in several scenarios of NDT.

If there is a reference mark on both the benchmark and the studied objects then it is possible to place this latter one with a rotation of arbitrary known degree into the scanner. From the dependency function of the blueprint image, similar to that of Figure 7, we know when the best reconstruction quality can be achieved – we simply have to seek the global minimum of the function. This determines how (i.e., in which direction) to place the test object into the scanner to have the most accurate reconstruction from the available number of projections. Since the dependency function is smooth, it is sufficient to place the object with only approximately the same rotation as the dependency function suggests.

On the other hand, if there is no mark on the studied object, then it might be placed with an unknown rotation into the scanner. Again, from the dependency function of the blueprint image we can predict how sensitive our test will be to this rotation. In addition, from the graph of the blueprint image similar to that of Figure 6 we can deduce how many projections are needed to keep the maximal error acceptably low, i.e., to be sure that the effect of rotation will be eliminated. If it is impossible to acquire so many projections, then from the minimal error we can estimate the best reconstruction possible from the given number of projections. This knowledge is also useful, since it tells us whether DC algorithm is appropriate for the given industrial test. If the error of the best reconstruction is still high, then we might classify perfect objects as damaged ones and vice versa.

7   Conclusion and Further Work

The aim of this paper was to study how the accuracy of the DC binary tomography algorithm depends on the direction of the projections available for the reconstruction. We introduced two approaches to evaluate the direction-dependency of the DC algorithm, and conducted experiments on software phantoms. We found that certain objects behave considerably sensitively from the viewpoint of direction-dependency. On the other hand, there are objects for which the result of reconstruction is less dependent on the direction of the projections, but even in those cases choosing the proper directions can reduce the number of projections needed for an accurate reconstruction. Our investigations can be essentially useful in the non-destructive testing of industrial objects made of homogeneous materials.

The presented results can be extended in many different ways. In our future work we intend to perform similar studies on other reconstruction algorithms, and – in the same time – investigate the effect of noise added to the projections. We also want to examine whether the observations of this paper still hold if the projections are non-equiangularly acquired or if the investigated objects consist of more than one materials.

Finally, we are planing to extend the investigation on adaptive projection acquisition (like in [12]), i.e., to determine the the best angles half way through the data acquisition, by using information gathered from projections already made, when a blueprint image is not available.

Acknowledgments

The authors would like to thank Joost Batenburg and Christoph Schnörr for providing test images to the studies.

References

1. Alpers, A.: Instability and Stability in Discrete Tomography. Ph.D. Thesis, Technische Universität München. Shaker Verlag, Aachen (2003)
2. Batenburg, K.J., Sijbers, J.: DART: a fast heuristic algebraic reconstruction algorithm for discrete tomography. In: IEEE Conference on Image Processing IV, pp. 133–136 (2007)
3. Baumann, J., Kiss, Z., Krimmel, S., Kuba, A., Nagy, A., Rodek, L., Schillinger, B., Stephan, J.: Discrete Tomography Methods for Nondestructive Testing. In: [8], ch. 14, pp. 303–331 (2007)
4. van Dalen, B.E.: Stability results for two directions in discrete tomography. arXiv:0804.0316 [math.CO] (2008)
5. Di Gesu, V., Lo Bosco, G., Millonzi, F., Valenti, C.: A memetic algorithm for binary image reconstruction. In: Brimkov, V.E., Barneva, R.P., Hauptman, H.A. (eds.) IWCIA 2008. LNCS, vol. 4958, pp. 384–395. Springer, Heidelberg (2008)
6. Herman, G.T.: Fundamentals of Computerized Tomography, Image Reconstruction from Projections, 2nd edn. Springer, London (2009)
7. Herman, G.T., Kuba, A. (eds.): Discrete Tomography: Foundations, Algorithms and Applications. Birkhäuser, Boston (1999)
8. Herman, G.T., Kuba, A. (eds.): Advances in Discrete Tomography and Its Applications. Birkhäuser, Boston (2007)
9. Kak, A.C., Slaney, M.: Principles of Computerized Tomographic Imaging. IEEE Press, New York (1999)
10. Nagy, A., Kuba, A.: Reconstruction of binary matrices from fan-beam projections. Acta Cybernetica 17(2), 359–385 (2005)
11. NVIDIA CUDA Programming Guide, Version 2.0, http://developer.download.nvidia.com/compute/cuda/2_0/docs/ NVIDIA_CUDA_Programming_Guide_2.0.pdf
12. Placidi, G., Alecci, M., Sotgiu, A.: Theory of adaptive acquisition method for image reconstruction from projections and application to EPR imaging. Journal of Magnetic Resonance, Series B, 50–57 (1995)
13. Schüle, T., Schnörr, C., Weber, S., Hornegger, J.: Discrete tomography by convex-concave regularization and D.C. programming. Discrete Applied Mathematics 151, 229–243 (2005)
14. Weber, S., Nagy, A., Schüle, T., Schnörr, C., Kuba, A.: A benchmark evaluation of large-scale optimization approaches to binary tomography. In: Kuba, A., Nyúl, L.G., Palágyi, K. (eds.) DGCI 2006. LNCS, vol. 4245, pp. 146–156. Springer, Heidelberg (2006)

Circular Acquisition to Define the Minimal Set of Projections for Optimal MRI Reconstruction

Giuseppe Placidi

A^VI-Lab, c/o Department of Health Sciences,
University of L'Aquila, Via Vetoio Coppito 2,
67100 L'Aquila, Italy
Giuseppe.Placidi@cc.univaq.it

Abstract. An acquisition technique for optimal MRI reconstruction from projections is presented. It consists of the acquisition of two circular paths which are used to calculate the most informative directions to be acquired. The selection of the acquisition angles is performed where the information content is maximal. The information content is directly evaluated using the power spectra of the k-space samples acquired by the circular paths. The method makes it possible to reduce the total acquisition time without degradation of the reconstructed image and it adapts to the arbitrary shape of the sample. For these reasons, it is particularly useful in those applications where acquisition from projections is strongly recommended for saving acquisition time, in particular for fMRI. The method has been tested on experimental data collected by a commercial MRI apparatus and compared with other adaptive acquisition sampling schemes.

Keywords: sparse MRI, adaptive acquisition, fMRI, rapid imaging, sparse imaging.

1 Introduction

Reconstruction from projections, RP [6], has been revaluated for MRI applications, especially for real time and functional MRI (fMRI), with respect to Cartesian acquisition methods [2,5,10,11,13]. In fact, RP methods reduce the effects due to motion because the center of k-space is over-sampled and it is sampled at the start of the reading time, thus eliminating the movement occurring in the last period of the reading interval. Another advantage of RP methods is the improvement of signal to noise ratio (SNR) in the reconstructed image as the result of over-sampling of the central region of the k-space.

For these reasons, RP methods are beginning to be widely used in angiography, where speed is important to reduce artifacts due to blood flow [10,13], in brain functional imaging [2,5,11,18], in cardiac and lung imaging [3,4,8,17], in functional imaging of muscles [7], in imaging of moving joints [12] and of abdominal regions where it is important to reduce artifacts due to peristaltic and breathing movements [9,16]. In the described applications, the gain in the reconstruction images, both in artifacts reduction and in improvement of functional information, is proportional to the time

R.P. Barneva et al. (Eds.): CompIMAGE 2010, LNCS 6026, pp. 254–262, 2010.
© Springer-Verlag Berlin Heidelberg 2010

saved. It has been demonstrated elsewhere [15] that it may be possible to reduce the number of collected projections, below the minimum required to obtain an image of a given dimension without artifacts [1], if information about sample internal symmetries and shape can be collected during acquisition.

In fact, the adaptive MRI acquisition from projections [15] is able to collect a near optimal set of projections without any a-priori information about the sample, by calculating the information content of the projections through an entropy function, during the progress of the acquisition process (for this reason, we refer to it as the blind adaptive method). This method, though very effective in reducing the acquisition time and under-sampling artifacts, suffers from two limitations: some important projections are excluded from the acquired set, especially in the proximity of entropy function minima or maxima; it is necessary to use efficient software (dedicated hardware is also to be recommended) to calculate the information content of the collected projections during the sequence repetition time, without wasting time.

In the present work we want to overcome these limitations. For this reason, we consider the problem of measuring exactly the most informative set of projections by collecting a-priori information about the sample through the preliminary measurement of two circular paths at different distances from the k-space center. The directions of the most informative projections can then be set using information acquired from the power spectra of these paths of coefficients.

In what follows, a full method description is given and some experimental results are reported; a comparison between the proposed technique and other adaptive acquisition techniques is shown.

2 The Proposed Method

2.1 Reconstruction from Projections: Background

We suppose that the function $f(x,y)$, defined in a limited two-dimensional (2-D) domain D, represents an image. The projection $P_\varphi(r)$ of $f(x,y)$ along the r direction is given by:

$$P_\varphi(r) = \int_{-\infty}^{\infty} f(r,s)\,ds \tag{1}$$

where $r = x\cos(\varphi) + y\sin(\varphi)$ and $s = x\sin(\varphi) - y\cos(\varphi)$.

Let

$$P_\varphi(\omega) = \int_{-\infty}^{\infty} p_\varphi(r)\,e^{-2\pi i \omega r}\,dr \tag{2}$$

be the Fourier transform of the projection taken at an angle φ. The Fourier terms of the image $f(x,y)$, in polar coordinates, are described by:

$$F_\varphi(\omega) = \int_{-\infty}^{\infty}\int_{-\infty}^{\infty} f(r,s)\,e^{-2\pi i \omega r}\,drds = \int_{-\infty}^{\infty} p_\varphi(r)\,e^{-2\pi i \omega r}\,dr = p_\varphi(\omega) \tag{3}$$

MR imaging from projections consists of the following steps: acquire the real and imaginary parts of a limited set of radial projections (collected in the k-space); position them at the correct angles in the plane, according to Eq.[3]; interpolate to obtain a rectangular grid of Fourier coefficients; calculate the 2-D Fourier transform to obtain the final image.

2.2 The Proposed Algorithm

The idea behind the algorithm is that the power spectrum of a standard MR image, for example that shown in Figure 1A, is mainly distributed along particular radial directions, as shown in Figure 1B. These directions often terminate before the k-space border has been reached (see for example the direction labeled 1 in Figure 1B). Some of them do not start from the k-space center and extend to the k-space border (see, as an example, the direction labeled 2 in Figure 1B). In order to take into account these opposite situations, a set of preliminary circular trajectories has to be collected. The preliminary collection of these circular trajectories allows the interception of these projections. By analyzing the collected data, it is possible to establish the desired set of projections before the image acquisition starts. The individuation of the most informative directions allows both time acquisition reduction and image quality maximization. The acquisition algorithm consists of the preliminarily collection of two circular trajectories having the center in the image k-space center and radii of s_1R and s_2R (where R is the image radius in pixels). The choice of these values is quite arbitrary but it is necessary to take into account the previously described effects. The value of s_1 must not be too close to the k-space center in order to collect the start of "star-like" differentiation (near the center the star effect has not yet been highlighted), as shown in Figure 1B. The value of the s_2 must be chosen not too close to the k-space border to avoid noise effects, mainly evident at high frequencies, as shown in Figure 1B, and more clearly in Figure 2. Figure 2, in fact, shows the power spectrum configurations related to the circular paths highlighted in Figure 1B, with $s_1=0.2$ and $s_2=0.9$. As it is evident from the two plots (amplitudes have been normalized for graphical reasons), the upper plot (related to the internal circle) has a smoother distribution than the lower: this effect is due to noise.

From the logarithm (used to reduce differences in scale) of the power spectra of the collected trajectories, the mean values are calculated and maxima above the mean value, in both curves, are used to indicate the presence of the most informative radial directions. The set of these angular directions is considered as the optimal, most informative, set of projections to be collected in a standard way. The flow chart of the algorithm is shown in Figure 3. In particular, A represents the matrix where the S circular paths are stored in columns (all circular paths have the same number of samples).

The first two columns of A are used to contain the Boolean values of the chosen angles (initially, all the values are placed to zero and, at the end of the process, the values for the chosen angles are set to 1) and the values of the measured angular values respectively. The number of rows of A is N, one angular value for each measured coefficient. The coefficients in the whole set of circular paths are always measured at the same angles. N is calculated to consider as minimum angular separation that indicating the width of a pixel situated on the circle of maximum radius, that is $\Delta\alpha=1/(Rs_{max})$ where Rs_{max} is the radius of the maximum circle. In this case, Nyquist

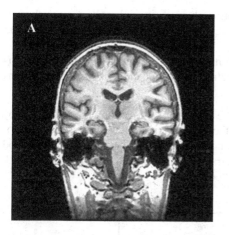
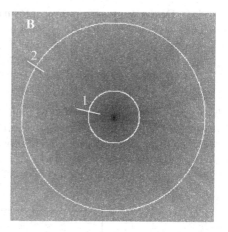

Fig. 1. MRI image of a brain used as a test (A) and its power spectrum (B). In B are also indicated the circular paths of power spectrum coefficients used to estimate the most informative radial directions and two of these directions are labeled (with the number 1 and 2 respectively). For commodity Figure 1B is shown inverted in amplitude (darker values correspond to greater values).

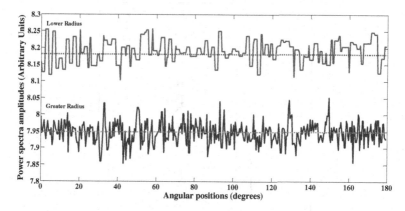

Fig. 2. Plot of the power spectrum coefficients collected in the two circular paths labeled in Figure 1B and the corresponding mean values (represented by dotted lines)

criterion is maintained also for the external circular path. The first two columns of A represent the output of the described algorithm. The chosen angles will have 1 in the first column. The vector M contains the mean values of the logarithm of the power spectra of the measured circular paths (it has length S) and is set at step 2 of the algorithm. The output of the algorithm, namely the set of the chosen angles, is used by a standard acquisition sequence from projections to collect the necessary data set. It is important to note that:

1)   Data measured to collect information about the sample (allowing to the circular trajectories) can also be used to reconstruct the final image, thus improving its quality;

2)   Our algorithm requires some preliminary time to collect the necessary information about the optimal angle set, before the acquisition of radial projections starts.

The termination parameter used to limit the number of projections is represented by the mean values of the collected data: all the local maxima above this value are chosen; the others are discarded. In the following section, we apply the presented method to experimental data in order to demonstrate its effectiveness. Comparisons with others acquisition techniques are also reported.

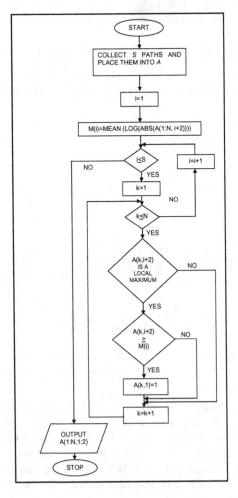

Fig. 3. Flow chart summarizing the algorithm used to select the most informative projections

3   Experimental Results

The presented algorithm has been tested on k-space data obtained by inverse Fourier Transform of a complete coronal MRI 256*256 spin density image of a head obtained with a commercial 1.5 T apparatus, shown in Figure 1A. A completely sampled image has been chosen to allow a numerical calculation of a complete set of radial projections. The optimal subset of different projections was extracted using the proposed method: the collection of two circular trajectories of coefficients taken at 0.2R and 0.9R, those indicated in Figure 1B, was first done (Figure 2 shows the power spectra of the two paths, with the corresponding mean values). Subsets of the projections were extracted using either the proposed method or the blind adaptive criterion reported elsewhere [15], whose results are the best actually obtainable with non-uniform acquisition from projections. A modified Fourier Reconstruction algorithm [14], including an interpolation method, has been used to obtain the reconstructed images with a low number of projections. The images have been compared both visually and numerically by using the mean square error, MSE, calculated between the image to be tested and the image reconstructed by using the whole set of projections. The comparison with the image obtained with the whole set of projections, and not with the theoretical starting image, was made to eliminate the effects of the reconstruction method from the calculated error of the image under inspection. The reference image, obtained by using the whole set of projections, is shown in Figure 4. The images obtained by using a set of 89 projections, obtained by the application of the proposed method, and by using a set of 106 FIDs whose orientations have been calculated by applying the adaptive acquisition method, are shown in Figures 5A and 5B respectively. The number of projections obtained with the blind method, 106, depends

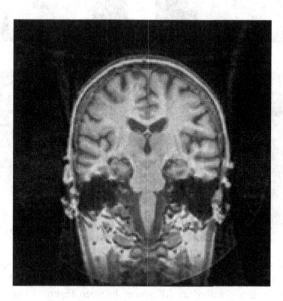

Fig. 4. Image reconstructed by collecting a complete set of 500 radial projections from the test image

on the shape of the original test image. It is important to note that the numbers obtained by the two methods are not so different, but the blind adaptive acquisition method collects a greater number of projections because it acts without any *a-priori* information about the sample.

The estimated number of projections is 40% and 53% of the minimum number of projections, 201, necessary to reconstruct an image having dimensions and resolution of the given test image. The images obtained by the two methods are quite similar. In fact, they do not show noticeable artifacts because of the optimal and near optimal choice of the angular positions of the collected projections. The similarities between the two images are also demonstrated by the values of the MSE function (MSE=0.070 for Figure 5A and MSE=0.080 for Figure 5B). Difference images between Figure 4 (image reconstructed by a complete set of projections) and Figures 5A and 5B are shown in Figures 5C and 5D respectively, in an expanded grey scale, demonstrating the similarities and the lack of under-sampling artifacts (in the bottom region, Figure 5D shows a low residual of the original image profile). It is important to note that the sets of projections obtained by the two methods differ by 22 projections which are

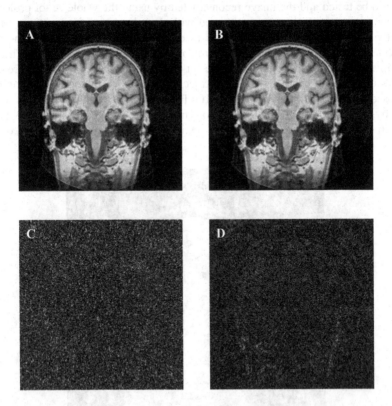

Fig. 5. Images reconstructed by collecting a set of 89 projections by using the proposed method (A) and a set of 106 projections collected by using the blind adaptive method (B). Figures 5C and 5D report the images obtained as differences between Figure 4 and figures 5A and 5B respectively: the grey scale has been expanded to highlight lower details.

situated near the starting projections used by the blind adaptive method (the blind adaptive method collects 17 more projections than the proposed method).

The proposed method produces a further 20% reduction in the number of collected projections with respect to the blind method. Obviously, the proposed method requires the collection of the two circular paths before data acquisition. In spite of this, the proposed method allows saving acquisition time with respect to blind method, it is completely deterministic and follows the shape of the imaged object whatever it is. Conversely, the blind method has two main drawbacks: some information maxima cannot be collected; optimal calculation hardware/software are required for a real time implementation. The proposed method maximizes the image information content while reducing the number of collected projections. We did not compare our method to the regular acquisition method, in which the projections are collected at constant angular distances, because this comparison was made when the blind adaptive method was presented [15] and it was in favor of the blind method.

4 Conclusion

In the present work, the information content of an MRI projection directly in the k-space has been defined. An optimal RP adaptive acquisition method has been described that makes it possible to reduce the total acquisition time, with minimum loss of resolution and the introduction of negligible distortion in the resulting image. The method has been tested on experimental data. As shown in the preliminary reported tests, the use of the adaptive technique reduces the number of projections to about 60% of the theoretical number of projections required to obtain an image of given dimensions and resolution, saving 40% of the acquisition time. For the experimental test reported, only 29% of the theoretical number of projections was required, saving more than 70% in acquisition time. The results of the presented method have also been compared to those of the blind adaptive acquisition method reported in [15]: MSE is reduced and 17 projections are saved with respect to the blind method (though some time has been spent to collect the two circular acquisitions).

It is important to note that the radii of the two circular paths have been chosen arbitrarily. The lower does not represent a real problem, but the higher can be source of oscillation effects due to noise (see the lower plot of Figure 2). The evaluation of the noise level in the power spectrum would allow a better selection of the maximum radius, the maximum value for which the signal level overcomes the noise level. This should allow a further reduction of the number of acquired projections by eliminating the "false important" produced by spurious oscillations due to noise.

Moreover, further investigation should be dedicated to the definition of "importance" of the projections: here we decided to select, as most important, the projections whose power spectrum represented a local maximum above the mean value. An alternative choice could be the choice of the projections whose power spectrum has a maximum in variation (by collecting the maxima of the power spectrum derivate). Because these choices are all reasonable and are strictly dependent on the interpolation algorithm used to resample a full Cartesian grid, this argument will be the subject of a future paper.

References

1. Brooks, R.A., di Chiro, G.: Principles of computer assisted tomography (CAT) in radiographic and radioisotopic imaging. Phys. Med. Biol. 21, 689–732 (1976)
2. DeYoe, E.A., Bandettini, P., Miller, D., Winans, P.: Functional magnetic resonance imaging (FMRI) of the human brain. J. Neurosci. Methods 54(2), 171–187 (1994)
3. Fischer, M.C., Spector, Z.Z., Ishii, M., Yu, J., Emami, K., Itkin, M., Rizi, R.: Single acquisition sequence for the measurement of oxygen partial pressure by hyperpolarized gas MRI. Magn. Reson. Med. 52, 766–773 (2004)
4. Kim, R.J., Fieno, D.S., Parrish, R.B., Harris, K., Simonetti, O., Bundy, J., Finn, J.P., Klocke, F.J., Judd, R.M.: Relationship of MRI delayed contrast enhancement to irreversible injury, infarct age, and contractile function. Circulation 100, 1992–2002 (1999)
5. Kwong, K.K., Belliveau, J.W., Chesler, D.A., Goldberg, I.E., Weisskoff, R.M., Poncelet, D.N., Kennedy, B.P., Hoppel, B.E., Cohen, M.S., Turner, R., Cheng, H., Brady, T.J., Rosen, B.R.: Dynamic magnetic resonance imaging of human brain activity during primary sensory stimulation. Proc. Nat. Acad. Sci. 89, 5675–5679 (1992)
6. Lauterbur, P.C.: Image formation by induced local interactions: examples employing nuclear magnetic resonance. Nature 242, 190–191 (1973)
7. Ledermann, H.P., Heidecker, H.G., Schulte, A.C., Thalhammer, C., Aschwanden, M., Jaeger, K.A., Scheffler, K., Bilecen, D.: Calf muscles imaged at BOLD MR: correlation with TcPO2 and flowmetry measurements during ischemia and reactive hyperemia—initial experience. Radiology 241(2), 477–484 (2006)
8. Lima, J.A.C., Judd, R.M., Bazille, A., Schulman, S.P., Atalar, E., Zerhouni, E.A.: Regional heterogeneity of human myocardial infarcts demonstrated by contrast-enhanced MRI: Potential Mechanisms. Circulation 92, 1117–1125 (1995)
9. Mitchell, D.G.: Fast MR imaging techniques: impact in the abdomen. J. Magn. Reson. Imag. 6, 812–821 (1996)
10. Nishimura, D., Macovski, A., Jackson, J.I., Hu, R.S., Stevick, C.A., Axel, L.: Magnetic resonance angiography by selective inversion recovery using a compact gradient echo sequence. Magn. Reson. Med. 8, 96–103 (1988)
11. Ogawa, S., Lee, T.M., Kay, A.R., Tank, D.W.: Brain Magnetic resonance imaging with contrast, dependent on blood oxygenation. Proc. Nat. Acad. Sci. 87, 9868–9872 (1990)
12. Ordidge, R.J., Coxon, R., Howseman, A., Chapman, B., Turner, R., Stehling, M., Mansfield, P.: Snapshot head imaging at 0.5 T using the echo planar technique. Magn. Reson. Med. 8, 110–115 (1988)
13. Pauli, J.M., Conolly, S., Nishimura, D., Macovski, A.: A Slice-selective excitation for very short T2 species. In: Proc. Eighth Annual Meeting, Society of Magnetic Resonance in Medicine, vol. 28 (1989)
14. Placidi, G., Alecci, M., Colacicchi, S., Sotgiu, A.: Fourier reconstruction as a valid alternative to filtered back projection in iterative applications: implementation of Fourier spectral spatial EPR imaging. J. Magn. Reson. 134, 280–286 (1998)
15. Placidi, G., Alecci, M., Sotgiu, A.: ω-space adaptive acquisition technique for magnetic resonance imaging from projections. J. Magn. Reson. 143(1), 197–207 (2000)
16. Riederer, S.J.: Recent technical advances in MR imaging of the abdomen. J. Magn. Reson. Imag. 6, 822–832 (1996)
17. Roberts, D.A., Gefter, W.B., Hirsch, J.A., Rizi, R.R., Dougherty, L., Lenkinski, R.E., Leigh Jr., J.S., Schnall, M.D.: Pulmonary perfusion: respiratory-triggered three-dimensional MR imaging with arterial spin tagging—preliminary results in healthy volunteers. Radiology 212(3), 890–895 (1999)
18. Smits, M., Visch-Brink, E., Schraa-Tam, C.K., Koudstaal, P.J., van der Lugt, A.: Functional MR imaging of language processing: an overview of easy-to-implement paradigms for patient care and clinical research. RadioGr. 26(suppl.1), S145–S158 (2006)

Surface Reconstruction with an Interactive Modification of Point Normals

Taku Itoh

Faculty of Science and Technology, Seikei University,
Musashino, Tokyo 180-8633, Japan
taku@st.seikei.ac.jp

Abstract. A surface reconstruction method without point normals as input data is proposed. In the proposed method, point normals are first estimated as the gradient vectors of a roughly-determined implicit function. An initial surface is generated by the Delaunay tetrahedralization with the estimated point normals. In addition, an interactive modification algorithm of the estimated point normals is also proposed. The algorithm are repeated until redundant triangles do not exist on a surface. Experiments demonstrated that the redundant triangles were gradually decreased by repeating the algorithm. In addition, the accuracy of point normals was better by repeating the algorithm.

Keywords: 3D reconstruction, Delaunay tetrahedralization, implicit function, point normals.

1 Introduction

The surface reconstruction problem for three-dimensional (3D) scattered point data derived from 3D range scanners has been investigated in fields such as computer graphics (CG) and computer-aided design (CAD) [6,1,5,8,9].

The implicit surface reconstruction has been one of the methods for solving the above problem. For generation of an implicit function in general domain, normal data on each of given points may be required. For example, the Multilevel Partition of Unity implicits (MPU) method [5], the Sparse Low-degree Implicit Surfaces (SLIM) method [4], and the method of Turk and O'Brien with the normal constraints [10] require the normal data. However point data does not always contain normal data.

On the other hand, Itoh has proposed the surface estimation method without normals as input data [3]. However some dents were found on the estimated surface by the method. In the method, although point normals were estimated as gradient vectors of a scalar-valued function, accuracy of the estimated normals was insufficient. It was a reason why some dents were found on the surface.

The purpose of the present study is to propose a method of surface reconstruction without point normals as input data. The proposed method is based on [3]. Namely a roughly-determined implicit function is first generated. By using the implicit function, the point normals are estimated as the gradient vectors.

R.P. Barneva et al. (Eds.): CompIMAGE 2010, LNCS 6026, pp. 263–274, 2010.

An initial surface is generated by the Delaunay tetrahedralization with the estimated point normals [6,11]. In addition, it is also the purpose of the present study to propose an interactive modification algorithm for point normals. By repeating the algorithm, accuracy of a reconstructed surface with the modified normals will gradually be better than that of a previous surface.

2   Roughly-Determined Implicit Function

In this section, we consider the generation of a scalar-valued function $f(p)$ from 3D scattered point data. The point data is given as a set of coordinate values without point normals.

First, it is well known that the gradient vector is normal to the surface, for a constant data value surface. Therefore we can estimate point normals from given point data if a scalar-valued function is generated. An implicit function is one of the scalar-valued functions, hence we consider generation of an implicit function. For generating an implicit function, positioning of constraint points and setting of height values on each of constraint points are important. Point normals can be solved the positioning and the setting since the geometrical feature of given points is easily extracted, therefore a generated implicit function with point normals tends to be accurate. However, given point data does not have point normals, hence we use the method of Itoh [3] for positioning of constraint points and for setting of height values. Although the accuracy of a generated implicit function by the method is less than that by other method with point normals, a roughly-determined implicit function will be obtained.

For placing constraint points appropriately, the method first employed the Delaunay tetrahedralization [6]. In next subsection, we briefly describe about the Delaunay tetrahedralization.

2.1   Delaunay Tetrahedralization

Given a collection of n points that are scattered in a domain, $\mathcal{P} = \{p_1, p_2, \ldots, p_n\}$, where $p_i = [x_i, y_i, z_i]^T \in \mathbf{R}^3$. Figure 1a is an example of $\mathcal{P}$. The reconstructed result from only $\mathcal{P}$ that is obtained by the Delaunay tetrahedralization is composed of tetrahedra, that is, the result is a solid object, whose shape is a convex polyhedron [6] (see Figure 1b). Therefore, even if the original shape of $\mathcal{P}$ has concave aspects, the shape of the reconstructed result obtained by the Delaunay tetrahedralization does not retain these aspects since it is impossible for both the inside and outside of an expected surface to be identified from only $\mathcal{P}$. It is an important property that the outside of the convex polyhedron is exactly outside of the expected surface.

By the way, for generating an implicit function $f(p)$, we place m constraint points $\hat{\mathcal{P}} = \{p_{n+1}, p_{n+2}, \ldots, p_{n+m}\}$ on the domain, together with scalar height values $\mathcal{H} = \{h_{n+1}, h_{n+2}, \ldots, h_{n+m}\}$ at each of the constraint points. These constraint points $\hat{\mathcal{P}}$ with scalar height values $\mathcal{H}$ are appropriately generated by using the above property. In next subsection, we describe about a method of placing the constraint points $\hat{\mathcal{P}}$ that is based on the property.

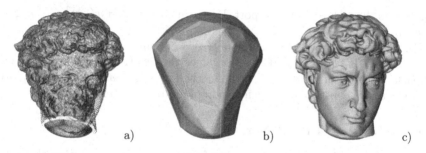

Fig. 1. Demonstration of surface reconstruction by the Delaunay tetrahedralization. a) Data points (The Head of David model, number of points: $n = 73205$). b) Generated convex polyhedron. The surface of convex polyhedron is constructed by triangles. c) Result of surface reconstruction from both given points $\mathcal{P}$ and additional points $\tilde{\mathcal{P}}$.

2.2 Positioning of Constraint Points

As has already been mentioned, the outside of the convex polyhedron is exactly outside of the expected surface. Note that the surface of convex polyhedron is constructed by triangles. On the surface of the ith triangle, the outward-directed normal vector $\boldsymbol{n}_i^{\mathrm{s}}$ is easily determined by the outer product. Using the outward-directed normal vector $\boldsymbol{n}_i^{\mathrm{s}}$, the ith constraint points $\boldsymbol{p}_{n+i}$ is placed as follows:

$$\boldsymbol{p}_{n+i} = \boldsymbol{p}_i^{\mathrm{g}} + \beta_{\mathrm{c}} \boldsymbol{n}_i^{\mathrm{s}}, \quad \text{for } 1 \le i \le n_{\mathrm{tri}}, \tag{1}$$

where $\boldsymbol{p}_i^{\mathrm{g}}$ is the gravity point of the ith triangle, β_{c} is a small positive value, and n_{tri} is the number of triangles. The constraint points generated by eq. (1) are positioned slightly outside of the surface of the convex polyhedron. Therefore constraint points are easily placed on the outside of the expected surface.

2.3 Setting of Height Values

On the outside of an expected surface, an implicit function $f(\boldsymbol{p})$ is negative [1,5]. In addition, the implicit function $f(\boldsymbol{p})$ may be considered as a signed distance function from the expected surface [1,5]. Therefore the $(n + i)$-th height value h_{n+i} on $\boldsymbol{p}_{n+i}$ is determined by using a weighted distance average as follows:

$$h_{n+i} = -\frac{\sum_{j=1}^{N_{\mathrm{np}}} w_j(\boldsymbol{p}_{n+i}) d_{ij}}{\sum_{j=1}^{N_{\mathrm{np}}} w_j(\boldsymbol{p}_{n+i})}, \quad \text{for } 1 \le i \le n_{\mathrm{tri}}, \tag{2}$$

where $d_{ij} = \|\boldsymbol{p}_{n+i} - \boldsymbol{p}_j^{(n+i)}\|_2$, for $1 \le j \le N_{\mathrm{np}}$, the collection of the N_{np} nearest points from $\boldsymbol{p}_{n+i}$ are $\{\boldsymbol{p}_1^{(n+i)}, \boldsymbol{p}_2^{(n+i)}, \ldots, \boldsymbol{p}_{N_{\mathrm{np}}}^{(n+i)}\}$, and the weight function is

$$w(r) = \begin{cases} 1 - 6\left(\dfrac{r}{R}\right)^2 + 8\left(\dfrac{r}{R}\right)^3 - 3\left(\dfrac{r}{R}\right)^4, & \text{for } r \le R, \\ 0, & \text{for } r > R, \end{cases} \tag{3}$$

where R is the radius of the support. Here, we abbreviated $w(\|\boldsymbol{p}_j^{(n+i)} - \boldsymbol{p}_{n+i}\|_2)$ to $w_j(\boldsymbol{p}_{n+i})$.

For generating an implicit function $f(\boldsymbol{p})$, we assume $f(\boldsymbol{p}_i) = h_i$, for $1 \leq i \leq n + m$. Note that $h_i = 0$ for $1 \leq i \leq n$, since the function $f(\boldsymbol{p})$ is equal to zero on each of the given points. In [3], the method of Tobor et al. [8] was employed with the above constraints for generation of an implicit function.

2.4   Estimation of Point Normals

An implicit function can be generated from given points by using the above constraint points and height values (see [3] and [8] for more detail). For a constant data value surface, it is well known that the gradient vector is normal to the surface. The outward-directed unit normals $\boldsymbol{n}_i$ on the ith given point $\boldsymbol{p}_i$, for $1 \leq i \leq n$, are evaluated as the following normalized gradient vector.

$$\boldsymbol{n}_i = -\frac{\nabla f(\boldsymbol{p}_i)}{\|\nabla f(\boldsymbol{p}_i)\|_2}, \quad \text{for } 1 \leq i \leq n. \tag{4}$$

If normal vectors are obtained on each of given points, the Delaunay tetrahedralization with the method of Yamashita et al. [11] can be employed for generation of surface. In next section, the method is described briefly.

3   Delaunay Tetrahedralization with Normals

Reference [11] indicates that the inside and outside of an expected surface can be identified in a result that is reconstructed from $\mathcal{P}$ together with appropriate additional nodes that are positioned slightly inside the expected surface. The additional nodes are generated by projecting from the given nodes $\mathcal{P}$ along normals $\mathcal{N}$ positioned at β away from the given nodes. The additional nodes $\tilde{\mathcal{P}} = \{\tilde{\boldsymbol{p}}_1, \tilde{\boldsymbol{p}}_2, \ldots, \tilde{\boldsymbol{p}}_n\}$ are generated as follows:

$$\tilde{\boldsymbol{p}}_i = \boldsymbol{p}_i - \beta \boldsymbol{n}_i, \quad i = 1, 2, \ldots, n, \tag{5}$$

where β is a small positive value. Additional nodes are positioned slightly inside the expected surface by assigning an appropriate value of β in eq. (5), since it is assumed that the given nodes $\mathcal{P}$ are on the original surface. Figure 2 shows a reconstructed result from $\mathcal{P}$ and $\tilde{\mathcal{P}}$ in two dimensions (2D). In Figure 2, tetrahedra are labeled as one of three types [11]:

(a) Tetrahedra that consist of only $\mathcal{P}$,
(b) Tetrahedra that consist of both $\mathcal{P}$ and $\tilde{\mathcal{P}}$,
(c) Tetrahedra that consist of only $\tilde{\mathcal{P}}$.

Note that triangles are drawn instead of tetrahedra in Figure 2 since the reconstructed result is shown in 2D. Triangles and tetrahedra are similarly labeled in accordance with the three above types. Tetrahedra of types (a) and (c) can be deleted since these tetrahedra are redundant for reconstruction of the surface.

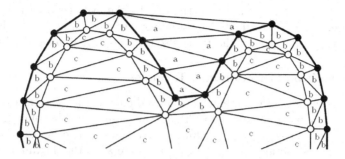

Fig. 2. Reconstructed result from given nodes $\mathcal{P}$ and additional nodes $\tilde{\mathcal{P}}$ obtained by the Delaunay tetrahedralization (●: Given nodes $\mathcal{P}$, ○: Additional nodes $\tilde{\mathcal{P}}$). "a", "b" and "c" denote tetrahedra as follows: a) Tetrahedra that consist of only $\mathcal{P}$, b) Tetrahedra that consist of both $\mathcal{P}$ and $\tilde{\mathcal{P}}$, c) Tetrahedra that consist of only $\tilde{\mathcal{P}}$.

After deleting tetrahedra of types (a) and (c), an expected surface can be constructed by extracting triangles that consist of only $\mathcal{P}$ from tetrahedra of type (b) (see Figure 1c).

However, if point normals are not accurate, some redundant triangles may be generated since the position of some additional nodes is not appropriate. Accuracy of a generated implicit function by the method of Itoh tends to be less than that by other method with point normals, therefore accuracy of some estimated normals by eq. (4) may be insufficient. Hence, we propose a method for modification of the estimated normals in next section.

4 Modification of Estimated Normals

A generated surface by the Delaunay tetrahedralization with the estimated normals occasionally has redundant triangles. The redundant triangles can be decreased by re-execution of the Delaunay tetrahedralization with more accurate normals. In this section, we present a method for modification of the estimated normals. The method and the Delaunay tetrahedralization are interactively repeated, depending on a generated surface.

4.1 Estimated Point Normals by the Average of Surface Normals

The top of Figure 3 shows that a flow chart of the method. As indicated in the flow chart, triangles around $\boldsymbol{p}_k$ are first found for modification of the kth normal $\boldsymbol{n}_k$. Let these triangles be $\{T_1^k, T_2^k, \ldots, T_{m_k}^k\}$, where m_k is the number of triangles around $\boldsymbol{p}_k$. After that, the sum of angles $\{\theta_1^k, \theta_2^k, \ldots, \theta_{m_k}^k\}$ that are corner of T_i^k around $\boldsymbol{p}_k$ is calculated. Ideally, the sum of angles equals to 2π. An ideal case is illustrated in the bottom left of Figure 3. In this case, the kth point normals $\boldsymbol{n}_k$ is estimated as the average of $\{\boldsymbol{n}_1^s, \boldsymbol{n}_2^s, \ldots, \boldsymbol{n}_{m_k}^s\}$, where $\boldsymbol{n}_i^s$ is the surface normal of T_i^k. However, in case that the sum of $\{\boldsymbol{n}_1^s, \boldsymbol{n}_2^s, \ldots, \boldsymbol{n}_{m_k}^s\}$ nearly equals to zero, the n_k can not be estimated by the average of surface normals. In this case, the n_k is estimated by other procedures. In addition, the sum of angles does not equal to 2π, the n_k is also estimated by other procedures.

4.2   Recognition of Redundant Triangles

If the sum of angles is greater than 2π, some redundant triangles may exist around p_k (see the bottom right of Figure 3). In this case, the kth point normals n_k is estimated after recognition of redundant triangles. For recognizing redundant triangles, we first obtain $\{s_1^k, s_2^k, \ldots, s_{m_k}^k\}$, where s_i^k is the maximum length of three sides of T_i^k, since redundant triangles tend to have large sides in comparison with other triangles (see experimental results of Figs. 5a and 6a). After that, $\{T_1^k, T_2^k, \ldots, T_{m_k}^k\}$ are renumbered in ascending order of $\{s_1^k, s_2^k, \ldots, s_{m_k}^k\}$. After renumbering, the sum of the angles $\{\theta_1^k, \theta_2^k, \ldots, \theta_j^k\}$ and the sum of $\{n_1^s, n_2^s, \ldots, n_j^s\}$ are calculated, where j is the number that satisfies $\sum_{i=1}^{j} \theta_i^k = 2\pi$, therefore j occasionally does not exist. Here, we scout out j by a C-like pseudo code in the flow chart of Figure 3. If j is found, we consider $\{T_{j+1}^k, T_{j+2}^k, \ldots, T_{m_k}^k\}$ as redundant triangles, and n_k will be estimated by the average of $\{n_1^s, n_2^s, \ldots, n_j^s\}$. If j is not found, we consider that recognition of redundant triangles is difficult, therefore n_k will be estimated by a weighted average of other point normals. Note that, even if j is found, $\sum_{i=1}^{j} n_i^s$ is nearly equal to zero infrequently. In this case, n_k will also be estimated by the weighted average.

4.3   Estimated Point Normals by a Weighted Average

After the above procedures are finished, some point normals do not estimated. For this case, we employ a weighted average of other point normals as follows:

$$\hat{n}_k = \frac{\sum_{i=1}^{N_{np}^k} w(r_{ki}) n_i^k}{\sum_{i=1}^{N_{np}^k} w(r_{ki})}, \quad n_k = \frac{\hat{n}_k}{\|\hat{n}_k\|_2}, \quad r_{ki} = \|p_i^k - p_k\|_2, \tag{6}$$

where $w(r)$ is the weight function same as eq. (3), and the collection of the N_{np}^k nearest points from p_k are $\{p_1^k, p_2^k, \ldots, p_{N_{np}^k}^k\}$, together with estimated point normals $\{n_1^k, n_2^k, \ldots, n_{N_{np}^k}^k\}$ at each of the points. Note that $\{p_1^k, p_2^k, \ldots, p_{N_{np}^k}^k\}$ are selected from the points that already have the estimated point normals after finishing the flow chart of Figure 3. Here, N_{np}^k is determined as the number of points that are contained in the kth radius of the support R^k, where R^k is obtained by $R^k = R^k + \alpha R_{ini}$ that is iterated until $N_{np}^k \geq N_{min}$. We usually set $\alpha = 0.1$ and $N_{min} = 40$. In addition, $R_{ini} = \beta_R \max(x_{max} - x_{min}, y_{max} - y_{min}, z_{max} - z_{min})$, where β_R is a small positive value like 0.05.

4.4   Delete Large Triangles

Accuracy of the estimated point normals by the above procedures tends to be better than that of the previous point normals, therefore redundant triangles of a reconstructed result with the current point normals will be decreased in comparison with that with the previous point normals. However, redundant triangles sometimes keep existing, even if the above procedures for modification of point normals and the Delaunay tetrahedralization with current point normals are repeated. In this case, we delete large triangles since redundant triangles tend to have large sides. Here, we define s_{ave} as the average of $\{s_1, s_2, \ldots, s_{n_{tri}}\}$, where s_i is the maximum length of three sides of T_i. We consider triangles T_i that satisfy $s_i > \gamma s_{ave}$ as large triangles. Here, γ is a positive value. We usually set γ as 3.0. After deleting large triangles, the modification of point normals and the Delaunay tetrahedralization with current point normals are repeated again. Note that some large triangles that satisfy $s_i > \gamma s_{ave}$ may not be redundant. Although the large triangles are deleted with redundant triangles, the large triangles will be obtained by the Delaunay tetrahedralization with current point normals.

4.5 Algorithm of Modification of Point Normals

In this subsection, we assemble an algorithm of the modification of point normals. Note that the initial surface is first generated by the procedures of Section 2 and Section 3. The algorithm is as follows:

Step 1: Estimate point normals by the flow chart of Figure 3 (see Section 4.1 and Section 4.2).

Step 2: Estimate point normals using eq. (6) on the points that do not have the estimated normals after the Step 1 (see Section 4.3).

Step 3: Generate a new surface by the Delaunay tetrahedralization with the current point normals (see Section 3).

The above algorithm is interactively repeated until redundant triangles do not exist on a new surface. In case that redundant triangles keep existing even if the above algorithm is repeated, we delete large triangles by using the procedure that described in Section 4.4. After deleting large triangles, the above algorithm is repeated again.

5   Experiments

In this section, some experiments are conducted to demonstrate the proposed method by using the data illustrated in Figs. 4a and 4b. The original data of Figs. 4a and 4b were obtained from the web pages [7] and [2], respectively. These original data include triangle mesh connectivity that consists of surface points. Figs. 4a and 4b consist of only the point coordinates. Note that the original data of Figure 4a has some points that are not used as the triangle mesh connectivity. Figure 4a does not contain these points.

In the following section, let Figs. 4a and 4b be Cases A and B, respectively.

5.1 Parameters and Computation Environment

The given points $\mathcal{P}$ were first rescaled so that an axis-aligned bounding cube has a unit-length main diagonal.

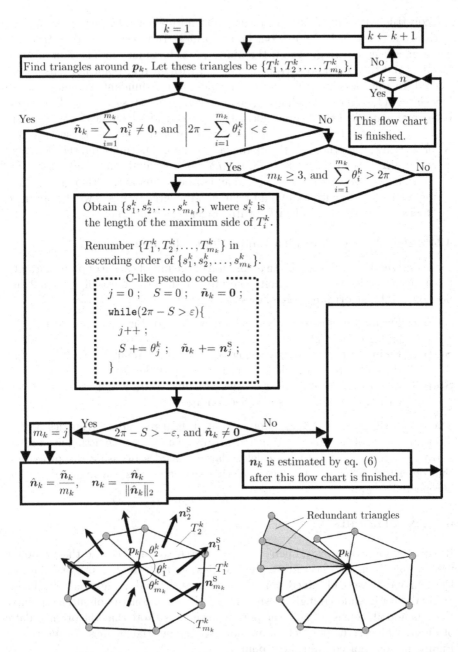

Fig. 3. Top: A flow chart for estimation of point normals. Note that n_k is a estimated point normal on p_k. In addition, ε is a small positive value like 0.1. Bottom Left: Triangles around p_k in an ideal case. Here, n_i^s is a surface normal of T_i^k, where T_i^k is the ith triangle around p_k, and θ_i^k is the angle of corner of T_i^k. In additon, m_k is the number of triangles around p_k. Bottom right: Triangles around p_k in case containing redundant triangles.

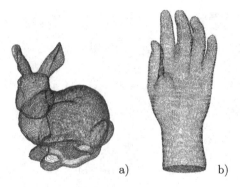

Fig. 4. Data points for experiments. a) Bunny model ($n = 34834$), and b) Hand model ($n = 38219$), where n is the number of points.

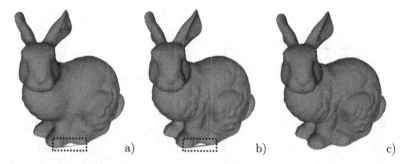

Fig. 5. Results of surface reconstruction from Figure 4a. Obvious redundant triangles are boxed. a) An initial surface ($\ell = 0$). b) and c) are reconstructed results with $\ell = 1$ and 2 respectively. Here, ℓ is the number of repetitions of the algorithm that is described in Section 4.5.

For generating an implicit function, we employed the method of Tobor et al. [8]. For the method, we set parameters same as [3]. For placing constraint points, we set β_c as 10^{-2} in eq. (1). In addition, for setting height value, we set N_{np} as 15 in eq. (2). For searching the collection of the N_{np} nearest points from p_{n+i}, the octree-based search technique was employed. The radius of the support in eq. (3) was set same as the radius that used for finding neighbor points.

Computations were performed on a computer equipped with dual 2.8 GHz Quad-Core Intel Xeon processors, 24 GB RAM, Mac OS X ver. 10.5.8 and g++ ver. 4.4.0.

5.2 Demonstration

First, let the number of repetitions of the above algorithm be ℓ. The initial surfaces for Cases A and B are shown in Figs. 5a and 6a. For the initial surfaces, we set $\ell = 0$.

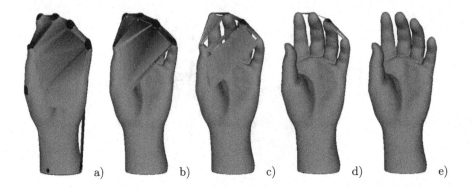

a)   b)   c)   d)   e)

Fig. 6. Results of surface reconstruction from Figure 4b. a) An initial surface ($\ell = 0$). Obvious redundant triangles cover an expected surface. b), c), d) and e) are reconstructed results with $\ell = 4, 8, 9$ and 11 respectively.

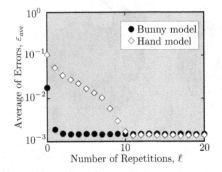

Fig. 7. Relation between the number of repetitions ℓ and the average of errors ε_{ave}

Table 1. Memory and computational time measurements

Model	Before Step 1		Step 1 to 3	
	Peak RAM	Comp. Time	Peak RAM	Comp. Time
Bunny	118(MB)	30.0(s)	154(MB)	1.7(s)
Hand	133(MB)	32.3(s)	187(MB)	1.7(s)

In Figure 5a, obvious redundant triangles are found in the dotted box. Figs. 5b and 5c show that the reconstructed results with $\ell = 1$ and 2, respectively. From Figure 5b, we see that redundant triangles keep existing in the dotted box. However, the redundant triangles do not exist in Figure 5c.

On the other hand, in Figure 6a, obvious redundant triangles cover an expected surface. Figs. 6b, 6c, 6d, and 6e show that the reconstructed results with $\ell = 4, 8, 9$ and 11, respectively. From Figs. 6b, 6c, 6d and 6e, we see that the redundant triangles of Figure 6a are gradually decreased.

For some data points, the current experiments demonstrates that the redundant triangles were decreased by the proposed method.

5.3   Numerical Evaluation

Let us first investigate the accuracy of point normals estimated by the proposed method. Figure 7 illustrates a relation between the number of repetitions ℓ and the average of errors ε_{ave}. Here, we defined the average of errors as

$$\varepsilon_{\text{ave}} = \frac{1}{N} \sum_{i=1}^{N} |1 - (\boldsymbol{n}_i, \boldsymbol{n}_i^{\text{e}})| , \tag{7}$$

where $(\cdot, \cdot)$ is the inner product and $\boldsymbol{n}_i^{\text{e}}$ is the exact point normal on $\boldsymbol{p}_i$. Note that $\boldsymbol{n}_i^{\text{e}}$, for $1 \leq i \leq N$, were obtained from the original data of Figs. 4a and 4b as the average of surface normals of triangles around $\boldsymbol{p}_i$. From Figure 7, we see that the accuracy of point normals are gradually better until $\ell = 2$ for Case A and $\ell = 11$ for Case B. The accuracy of normals in $\ell \geq 3$ for Case A is almost constant, hence reconstructed results are almost same as Figure 5c. For Case B in $\ell \geq 12$, the accuracy of normals is almost same behavior as Case A in $\ell \geq 3$.

Next, we investigate the memory and computational time measurements. Table 1 shows that the peak RAM before Step 1, and that of Step 1 to 3. Computational time before Step 1 and that of Step 1 to 3 are also shown in Table 1. Note that each repetition requires the computational time of Step 1 to 3. From Table 1, the proposed method may not have advantages for the memory utilization and those for the computational time, in comparison with the state-of-the-art method as typified by the MPU method [5]. However, the proposed method has an advantage that point normals are not required as input data. Namely, point coordinates are only required as input data. It is particularly worth noting that input data is very simple. Although the method of [3] also has the same advantage, the method of [3] did not have a normal modification algorithm. Hence we consider the proposed method as an extended method of [3].

6   Conclusion

A surface reconstruction method without point normals as input data has proposed. In the method, point normals first estimated as the gradient vectors of a roughly-determined implicit function. An initial surface was generated by the Delaunay tetrahedralization with the estimated normals. In addition, the method had an interactive modification algorithm of the estimated point normals. The algorithm and the Delaunay tetrahedralization with the estimated point normals were repeated until redundant triangles do not exist on a surface. Experiments have demonstrated the surface reconstruction with the proposed method. Conclusions obtained in the present study are summarized as follows:

1. In the experiments, the redundant triangles were gradually decreased by repeating the proposed method. In addition, the accuracy of the estimated point normals was better by the repetition.

2. From the results of the experiments, the proposed method did not have advantages for the memory utilization and those for the computational time, however it is particularly worth noting that some reconstruction results were obtained from only point coordinates as input data.

By writing down the estimated point normals with given point coordinates to a data file, the data file may be utilized as a data set for the MPU method and so on. Namely, the proposed method may also be used as a preprocessing for a method that requires point normals.

It is a future work that the proposed method is applied to more complicated models. In addition, theoretical analysis is a future investigation.

Acknowledgments. We would like to thank the Stanford 3D Scanning Repository for the David model and for the Stanford Bunny model. We would also like to thank the FarField Technology Ltd for the Hand model. This work was supported by a Grant-in-Aid for Scientific Research (No. 20700098) from the Ministry of Education, Culture, Sports, Science and Technology of Japan.

References

1. Bloomenthal, J., Bajaj, C., Blinn, J., Cani-Gascuel, M.P., Rockwood, A., Wyvill, B., Wyvill, G.: Introduction to Implicit Surfaces. Morgan Kaufmann Publishers, Inc., San Francisco (1997)
2. FarField Technology: Farfield: Downloads,
   http://www.farfieldtechnology.com/download/
3. Itoh, T.: A method of boundary estimation from 3D scattered point data without normals by implicit function and Delaunay tetrahedralization. In: Proceedings of Asia Simulation Conference 2009 (CD-ROM), Paper ID: 064. Kusatsu (2009)
4. Ohtake, Y., Belyaev, A., Alexa, M.: Sparse low-degree implicit surfaces with applications to high quality rendering, feature extraction, and smoothing. In: Eurographics Symposium on Geometry Processing (SGP 2005), pp. 145–158 (2005)
5. Ohtake, Y., Belyaev, A., Alexa, M., Turk, G., Seidel, H.P.: Multi-level partition of unity implicits. ACM Transactions on Graphics 22(3), 463–470 (2003)
6. Taniguchi, T., Moriwaki, K.: Automatic Mesh Generation for 3D FEM - Robust Delaunay Triangulation (in Japanese). Morikita, Tokyo (2006)
7. The Stanford 3D Scanning Repository,
   http://www.graphics.stanford.edu/data/3Dscanrep/
8. Tobor, I., Reuter, P., Schlick, C.: Efficient reconstruction of large scattered geometric datasets using the partition of unity and radial basis functions. WSCG 12(3), 467–474 (2004)
9. Turk, G., O'Brien, J.F.: Shape transformation using variational implicit functions. In: Proceedings of ACM SIGGRAPH 1999, Los Angeles, pp. 335–342 (1999)
10. Turk, G., O'Brien, J.F.: Modelling with implicit surfaces that interpolate. ACM Transactions on Graphics 21(4), 855–873 (2002)
11. Yamashita, Y., Moriwaki, K., Taniguchi, T.: Surface generation of arbitrary 3-dimensional domain by using nodes on its surface (in Japanese). Transactions of JSCES 2001(20010032) (2001),
    http://www.jstage.jst.go.jp/article/jsces/
    2001/0/2001_20010032/_article/-char/ja/

On the Effects of Normalization
in Adaptive MRF Hierarchies

Albert Y.C. Chen and Jason J. Corso

Dept. of Computer Science and Engineering
University at Buffalo, SUNY
aychen@buffalo.edu

Abstract. In this paper, we analyze the effects of energy normalization in adaptive-hierarchy-based energy minimization methods. Adaptive hierarchies provide a convenient multi-level abstraction of the underlying MRF. They have been shown to both accelerate computation and help avoid local minima. However, the standard recursive way of accumulating energy throughout the hierarchy causes energy terms to grow at different rates. Consequently, the faster-growing term, typically the unary term, dominates the overall energy at coarser level nodes, which hinders larger-scale energy/label change from happening. To solve the problem, we first investigate the theory and construction of adaptive hierarchies, then we analyze the theoretical bounds and expected values of its energy terms. Based on these analyses, we design and experimentally analyze three different energy-normalizing schemes. Our experiments show that properly normalized energies facilitate better use of the hierarchies during optimization: we observe an average improvement in the speed by 15% with the same accuracy.

1 Introduction

Markov random fields (MRF) provide a convenient and consistent way of modeling contextual constraints and stochastic interaction among variables, and have been shown useful in solving both low-level vision (e.g. restoration, stereo matching) and high-level vision problems (e.g. semantic image labeling). These problems are formulated as *labeling* tasks, where each site μ in the lattice G^0 is assigned a label $\mathcal{L}$ that can represent either low- or high-level features. The optimal solution is pursued by searching for the labeling configuration with the highest posterior probability, or equivalently, by minimizing the corresponding Gibbs energy function. Achieving the global optimum, however, is typically intractable, since the solution space is combinatorial in the number of labels. Therefore, a variety of approximation algorithms have been proposed to accelerate computation [2,5,8,15]; hierarchical approaches [3,4,9,10,12], such as multiscale/multi-resolution methods, multigrid relaxation, or renormalization group theory/transformation, are among the popularly studied ones.

Traditional hierarchies, where finer-level nodes are grouped into coarser-level nodes by their spatial coordinates instead of their intrinsic similarity, contain incoherent nodes around boundary regions at coarser levels. An incoherent node at layer $n+1$ (e.g., μ^{n+1} in Figure 1) is a mixture of multiple intrinsically different nodes at level n, denoted $\{\mu_j^n\}$. Incoherent nodes not only blur the boundaries of the finer-level graph (e.g., the

R.P. Barneva et al. (Eds.): CompIMAGE 2010, LNCS 6026, pp. 275–286, 2010.

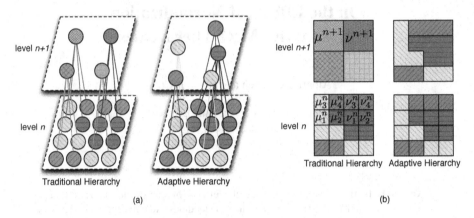

Fig. 1. Traditional versus Adaptive Hierarchies. The hierarchies in (a) are projected onto 4×4 images (b) for the ease of visualization. The coherent node at level $n+1$ of the adaptive hierarchy can accumulate the energies of belonging to the red, yellow, or blue labels (textured with slashes, backslashes, and horizontal lines respectively for monochrome prints) directly from their child nodes, whereas the incoherent nodes in the traditional hierarchy requires a re-computation.

edges between μ_3^n, μ_4^n, and μ_2^n, μ_4^n) but also make the direct reutilization of energies from the original graph difficult. For example, the energy between μ_2^n, ν_1^n and μ_4^n, ν_3^n are 0 while using the Potts model, yet the energy between μ^{n+1} and ν^{n+1} is 1, which cannot be derived from its children μ_j^n's directly and hence must be recalculated at level $n+1$. Conversely, it is difficult for a label/energy change at μ^{n+1} to propagate effectively to its children on level n: $\{\mu_j^n\}$. Therefore, traditional hierarchy-based approaches require an costly overhead of recalculating the energies and weights for every coarser level. Adaptive hierarchies, such as [7,11,1], produce coherent nodes because the methods coarsen based on the similarity of the node attributes (e.g., color) rather than spatial coordinates alone. These coherent nodes can be treated as a union of their underlying finer-level nodes, and the energy can be directly accumulated from level n to $n+1$. A label change at a coarser-level node is equivalent to altering all its underlying finest-level nodes, which triggers a large yet reasonable change in the overall energy.

Adaptive-hierarchy based energy minimization algorithms, such as [7,6], modify the hierarchy dynamically to reflect the change in labels and energies. Experiments on a wide range of vision problems have demonstrated the aptness of adaptive hierarchy-based energy minimization methods, and have consistently reported convergence time within a few seconds on typically-sized images. These methods, although efficient, give rise to a new class of *normalization* problems that were nonexistent or insignificant on flat MRFs and traditional hierarchies. Nodes on any given level of a traditional hierarchy/flat MRF are of the same size, therefore, a constant set of weights (at each level) suffices to balance the influence of different energy terms. However, nodes in adaptive hierarchies grow at different speeds as the hierarchy is coarsened; therefore, different weights need to be learned for nodes of different sizes/shapes. Directly learning all of these weights is not possible. In this paper, we theoretically analyze the effects of these normalization problems. To overcome them, we experimentally design three normalization schemes and analyze them. Our analysis indicates that a further speedup of 15% on average is possible when properly normalized hierarchies are used.

The remainder of the paper is organized as follows. We discuss the mechanism of an adaptive hierarchy-based energy minimization method—Graph-Shifts—in Section 2. We then analyze the theoretical upper and lower bounds and expected value of the energy terms, investigate the effects of having energy terms growing at different rates, and propose our normalization solution in Section 3. Experiments and results are presented in Section 4, and we conclude in Section 5.

2 Review of Adaptive-Hierarchy-Based Energy Minimization

Our discussion on adaptive hierarchy-based energy minimization is focused on the recently proposed graph-shifts algorithm [7], due to its efficiency and its inseparable relation with adaptive-hierarchies. In short, the graph-shifts algorithm is composed of two steps: (a) *coarsening*, i.e. the construction of the adaptive hierarchy, and (b) *shifting*, i.e. the dynamic modification of the hierarchical structure for energy minimization.

2.1 The Energy Model

Given an input image $\mathbf{I}$, each pixel corresponds to a node μ^0 in a regular lattice G^0. The superscript 0 indicates that we are at the lowest level of a to-be-defined hierarchy. Associate with each node a label variable m_{μ^0} that takes values from a fixed set of labels $\{\mathcal{L}_1, \mathcal{L}_2, ..., \mathcal{L}_K\}$. The task is to find the assignment of all label variables $\{m_{\mu^0}\}$ that yields the highest posterior probability (MAP-MRF), or equivalently, minimizes the following energy function:

$$E\left[\{m_{\mu^0} : \mu^0 \in G^0\}\right] = \lambda_1 \sum_{\mu^0 \in G^0} E_1\left(\mathbf{I}\left(S\left[\mu^0\right]\right), m_{\mu^0}\right) + \lambda_2 \sum_{\langle \mu^0, \nu^0 \rangle} E_2\left(m_{\mu^0}, m_{\nu^0}\right) . \quad (1)$$

E_1 (unary energy) is the potential of each node being assigned a certain label, defined on the local sub-image $S\left[\mu^0\right]$ surrounding μ^0. E_2 (binary energy) is induced by the interaction between neighboring nodes, where $\langle \mu^0, \nu^0 \rangle$ denotes all neighbor pairs μ^0 and ν^0; λ_i's are the weights of the different energy terms, where $\sum_i \lambda_i = 1$.

We use the same energy model for E_1 as in [7] to ease direct comparison between unnormalized and normalized energies in adaptive hierarchies. In short, the E_1 term is the negative log probability on the local subimage surrounding μ trained via boosting in a supervised manner:

$$E_1\left(\mathbf{I}\left(S\left[\mu^0\right]\right), m_{\mu^0}\right) = -\log \Pr\left(m_{\mu^0} \mid \mathbf{I}\left(S\left[\mu^0\right]\right)\right) . \quad (2)$$

A pairwise smoothness measurement is used for the E_2 term:

$$E_2\left(m_{\mu^0}, m_{\nu^0}\right) = 1 - \delta\left(m_{\mu^0}, m_{\nu^0}\right) . \quad (3)$$

For evaluating normalization effects, these choices for the energy terms are largely arbitrary. As we will show in the remainder of the paper, the normalization problems are a function of the graph structure and not the form of the energy terms. For this paper, we choose high-level semantic image labeling as the main comparative problem.

2.2   Coarsening the Adaptive Hierarchy

The adaptive hierarchy is defined as a graph G with a set of nodes and a set of edges stratified on multiple levels of an hierarchy. All nodes and edges in level n can be viewed as a separate graph, denoted as G^n, and a node at level n is denoted as μ^n. As above, the lowest level of the hierarchy is essentially a lattice G^0 of regular sites (nodes) μ^0, and two nodes are linked with an edge if they are neighbors on the lattice.

Coarser-level nodes are computed recursively and stochastically as follows. Edges on G^0 are randomly turned on or off based on the local affinity. The *on* edges induce a connected components clustering; the clusters become nodes in the next coarse layer in the hierarchy. The structure of the coarsened adaptive hierarchy is constrained by a coarsening threshold τ_1 that limits the maximum number of nodes in a group, and an affinity threshold τ_2 that restricts un-similar nodes from joining. Any two nodes μ^{n+1}, ν^{n+1} (at level $n+1$) are connected by an edge if any two of their children (at level n) are connected. The nodes are recursively coarsened until the size of graph G^n at level n is within a pre-specified range of the number of labels.

A label layer $G^{\mathcal{L}}$ that contains a single node per label is attached on top of the highest layer of the current hierarchy G^T. Each node in G^T becomes a child of a node in $G^{\mathcal{L}}$ which it best fits (based on E_1), then takes the label it represents; each node in $G^{\mathcal{L}}$ has at least one child in G^T. The nodes in G are constrained to have a single parent except the nodes in $G^{\mathcal{L}}$ (which have no parents), and to have at least one child except for the ones in G^0 (which have no children). Since each node in $G \setminus G^{\mathcal{L}}$ has only one parent and can trace its ancestry back to a single node in $G^{\mathcal{L}}$, it will take the same label as its parent and ancestors (a.k.a. *parent-label constraint*), and an instance of the graph G is equivalent to a labeled segmentation $\{m_{\mu^0} : \mu^0 \in G^0\}$ of the image.

2.3   Recursive Computation of the Energy

For any node μ^n, let $P(\mu^n)$ be its parent, $C(\mu^n)$ be the set of its children, $A^l(\mu^n)$ denote its ancestor at level l, and $D^l(\mu^n)$ be the set of its descendants at level l. By construction, any coarser-level node μ^n's pixel-level descendants all belong to the same label. Therefore, μ^n is treated as a union of $\mu_i^0 \in D^0(\mu^n)$, and the overall energy is accumulated recursively throughout the hierarchy.

The unary term for assigning a label m_μ to a node μ is defined recursively as

$$E_1\left(\mu^n, m_{\mu^n}\right) = \begin{cases} E_1\left(\mathbf{I}\left(S\left[\mu^n\right]\right), m_{\mu^n}\right) & \text{if } n = 0 \\ \sum_{\mu^{n-1} \in C(\mu^n)} E_1\left(\mu^{n-1}, m_{\mu^{n-1}}\right) & \text{otherwise} \end{cases} \quad (4)$$

where $E_1\left(\mathbf{I}\left(S\left[\mu^n\right]\right), m_{\mu^n}\right)$ is defined in (2). The binary energy between two neighboring nodes μ, ν at the same level n, with labels m_μ and m_ν is defined as:

$$E_2\left(\mu^n, \nu^n, m_{\mu^n}, m_{\nu^n}\right) =$$

$$\begin{cases} E_2\left(m_{\mu^n}, m_{\nu^n}\right) & \text{if } n = 0 \\ \sum_{\substack{\mu^{n-1} \in C(\mu^n) \\ \nu^{n-1} \in C(\nu^n) \\ \langle \mu^{n-1}, \nu^{n-1} \rangle}} E_2\left(\mu^{n-1}, \nu^{n-1}, m_{\mu^{n-1}}, m_{\nu^{n-1}}\right) & \text{otherwise} \end{cases} \quad (5)$$

where $E_2(m_{\mu^n}, m_{\nu^n})$ is defined in (3). The overall energy specified in (1) is for level 0 of the hierarchy, however, it can be computed at any level n as:

$$E[\{m_{\mu^n} : \mu^n \in G^n\}] = \sum_{\mu^n \in G^n} E_1(\mu^n, m_{\mu^n}) + \sum_{\langle \mu^n, \nu^n \rangle} E_2(\mu^n, \nu^n, m_{\mu^n}, m_{\nu^n}) . \quad (6)$$

Note that we've intentionally dropped the weights on the terms to avoid confusion since they will take different forms depending on our normalization scheme (Section 3).

2.4 Graph-Shifts

Graph-Shifts minimizes the energy by using a mechanism called a *shift*, which dynamically alters the adaptive hierarchy during energy minimization. A basic *shift* is the process of a node μ^n changing its parent to ν^n's parent, where $\langle \mu^n, \nu^n \rangle$. Due to the *parent-label constraint*, μ^n and all its descendants $D^{l<n}(\mu^n)$ will change their label to $P(\nu^n)$'s, thus cause a relabeling at G^0 and a change in total energy. Refer to [7] for more details regarding all types of *shifts* a node can perform.

Potential shifts are evaluated by their *shift-gradients*, which are computed efficiently using the recursive formulae in (4), (5). For a node μ^n shifting from label m_{μ^n} to label $\hat{m}_{\mu^n}$, the shift-gradient is

$$\Delta E(m_{\mu^n} \to \hat{m}_{\mu^n}) = E_1(\mu^n, \hat{m}_{\mu^n}) - E_1(\mu^n, m_{\mu^n})$$
$$+ \sum_{\langle \mu^n, \nu^n \rangle} [E_2(\mu^n, \nu^n, \hat{m}_{\mu^n}, m_{\nu^n}) - E_2(\mu^n, \nu^n, m_{\mu^n}, m_{\nu^n})] . \quad (7)$$

We go through all nodes in $G \setminus G^{\mathcal{L}}$, calculate possible shifts, and only those with $\Delta E < 0$ are added to our list of potential shifts S.

At each round, Graph-Shifts chooses the shift with the steepest shift-gradient in S and makes the corresponding shift in the hierarchy. For the nodes affected by the shift, not only are their labels changed, but also their energies re-computed, possible shifts and shift-gradients re-calculated, and S updated. The algorithm is repeated until convergence, when no further shift will reduce the overall energy anymore (i.e. S becomes empty). Notice that, although higher-level shifts tend to induce larger energy changes, lower-level shifts might as well cause large energy changes and be executed before higher-level shifts.

3 Proper Energy Normalization in Adaptive Hierarchies

Usually, in MRFs, there is no need to normalize E_1 and E_2 individually in (1), since the weights λ_1, λ_2 are learned to optimize the labeling result. Traditional hierarchy's coarser-level nodes are also exempt from this concern, because the nodes are incoherent and requires a recalculation of E_1 and E_2 (i.e. they cannot accumulate finer-level energies for their own use). Adaptive hierarchies overcome the need of energy recalculation at coarser levels, yet the way it accumulates energies from finer-level nodes gives rise to a normalization problem caused by the different growth rates of E_1 and E_2. In the upcoming subsections, we prove the theoretical bounds and expected values of the two energy terms, discuss the effect of having unnormalized energies during the energy minimization process, and describe our proposed ways of normalizing the energy terms in the adaptive hierarchy.

3.1 E_1 Term Growth Rate Analysis

Due to the way energies are accumulated throughout the adaptive hierarchy (as in (4)), a coarser-level node μ^n's E_1 term is primarily determined by the number of pixel-level (level 0) nodes it represents; let $\mathcal{M}(\mu^n) = |D^0(\mu^n)|$ denote this number. The theoretical upper/lower bound and the expected value of $\mathcal{M}(\mu^n)$, and therefore its E_1, is mainly decided by the coarsening threshold τ_1. Let Ψ_1^n and Φ_1^n denote the maximum and minimum possible E_1 energy μ^n can possess, and let $\mathcal{E}_1^0$ be an unknown constant that represents the average E_1 energy at $\mu^0 \in D^0(\mu^n)$. $\mathcal{E}_1^0$ is constrained on the energy model we use, e.g. the implementation of (2) using a discrete set of probability values $P(\cdot) = \{0, \frac{1}{255}, ..., \frac{254}{255}, 1\}$ with $\log(0)$ set to a finite number larger than $\log(\frac{1}{255})$ defines $\Psi_1^0 = 0 \le \mathcal{E}_1^0 \le 5.6 = \Phi_1^0$. For levels other than the lowest one, the upper bound of μ^n's E_1 energy, Ψ_1^n, grows exponentially as we go up the hierarchy:

$$\Psi_1^n = \max_{\mu^n} E_1(\mu^n, m_{\mu^n}) = \max_{\mu^n} \Psi_1^0 \cdot \mathcal{M}(\mu^n) = \Psi_1^0 \cdot (\tau_1)^n \ . \tag{8}$$

The lower bound of μ^n's E_1 energy, Φ_1, is

$$\Phi_1^n = \min_{\mu^n} E_1(\mu^n, m_{\mu^n}) = \min_{\mu^n} \Phi_1^0 \cdot \mathcal{M}(\mu^n) = \Phi_1^0 \cdot (1)^n = \Phi_1^0 \ . \tag{9}$$

As for the expected value of E_1 (denoted as $\mathbb{E}(\cdot)$), we treat the number of finer-level nodes that form a coarser-level node as a random variable $X \in \{1, 2, ..., \tau_1\}$ with probability $P_X(x) = 1/\tau_1$ for all x:

$$\mathbb{E}(X) = \sum_{X=1}^{\tau_1} \frac{1}{\tau_1} X = \frac{1}{\tau_1} \sum_{X=1}^{\tau_1} X = \frac{1}{\tau_1} \cdot \frac{(\tau_1 + 1)\tau_1}{2} = \frac{\tau_1 + 1}{2} \ . \tag{10}$$

Therefore, for any node μ^n, its expected E_1 energy is:

$$\mathbb{E}(E_1(\mu^n, m_{\mu^n})) = \mathbb{E}(\mathcal{E}_1^0 \cdot \mathcal{M}(\mu^n)) = \mathcal{E}_1^0 \cdot \left(\frac{\tau_1 + 1}{2}\right)^n \ , \tag{11}$$

which still grows exponentially as we go up the hierarchy.

3.2 E_2 Term Growth Rate Analysis

The upper/lower bound and expected value of a node's *local E_2 energy* (sum of all E_2 on μ^n's edges, denoted as $E_2'(\mu^n)$), are conditioned not only on the number of pixel-layer nodes $\mathcal{M}$, but also on how the nodes are distributed. For any two neighboring nodes μ^0 and ν^0, the energy on their common edge is neglected after they are grouped into a coarser-level node μ^n, as defined in (5). Thus, $E_2'(\mu^n)$ is not determined by all edges of all $\mu^0 \in D^0(\mu^n)$, but only on edges of all $\mu^0 \in D^0(\mu^n)$ where $\langle \mu^0, \nu^0 \rangle$, $\nu^0 \notin D^0(\mu^n)$. We define the size of this set as $\mathcal{N}$:

$$\mathcal{N}(\mu^n) = \sum_{\substack{\mu^0 \in D^0(\mu^n) \\ s.t. \, \langle \mu^0, \nu^0 \rangle, \, \nu^0 \notin D^0(\mu^n)}} \left(1 - \delta(m_{\mu^0}, m_{\nu^0})\right) . \tag{12}$$

$\mathcal{N}(\mu^n)$ is analogous to the perimeter of the object formed by all $\mu^0 \in D^0(\mu^n)$, while $\mathcal{M}(\mu^n)$ is analogous to the area it occupies (on a 2D lattice). Therefore, $E_2'(\mu^n)$ is constrained on $\mathcal{N}(\mu^n)$, while the relationship between $\mathcal{N}(\mu^n)$ and $\mathcal{M}(\mu^n)$ is dependent on the object's shape. This definition allows us to discover, when given a coarser-level node μ^n with a fixed $\mathcal{M}(\mu^n)$, the possible values of $\mathcal{N}(\mu^n)$ and therefore derive the upper/lower bound and expected value of a node's E_2' from $\mathcal{M}(\mu^n)$.

Let Ψ_2^n and Φ_2^n denote the upper and lower bound of $E_2'(\mu^n)$ at level n, and let $\mathcal{E}_2^0$ be the average E_2 energy of a single edge at level 0: $\langle \mu^0, \nu^0 \rangle$, where $\mu^0 \in D^0(\mu^n)$ and $\nu^0 \notin D^0(\mu^n)$. The bounds of $\mathcal{E}_2^0$ are dependent on the energy model used, e.g. (3) would yield $\mathcal{E}_2^0 = \{0, 1\}$, and are again denoted Ψ_2^0 and Φ_2^0. From basic geometry, given any $\mathcal{M}(\mu^n)$, $\mathcal{N}(\mu^n)$ is largest when its $D^0(\mu^n)$ are aligned linearly as in Figure 2.(a), where $\mathcal{N}(\mu^n) = 2\mathcal{M}(\mu^n) + 2$. Therefore, in theory, Ψ_2^n can increase exponentially at the same speed of Ψ_1^n.

$$\Psi_2^n = \max_{\mu^n} E_2'(\mu^n) = \max_{\mu^n} \sum_{\langle \mu^n, \nu^n \rangle} E_2(\mu^n, \nu^n, m_{\mu^n}, m_{\nu^n})$$

$$= \max_{\mu^n} \Psi_2^0 \cdot \mathcal{N}(\mu^n) = \max_{\mu^n} \Psi_2^0 \cdot 2\mathcal{M}(\mu^n) + 2 = \Psi_2^0 \cdot 2(\tau_1)^n + 2 . \tag{13}$$

$\mathcal{N}(\mu^n)$ is smallest when the shape formed by all its $D^0(\mu^n)$ is near circle/square (depending on the neighborhood system used), as in Figure 2.(b)-(d). Although $\mathcal{N}(\mu^n) = 4(\mathcal{M}(\mu^n))^{1/2}$, i.e. $\mathcal{N}$ grows only at a fraction of $\mathcal{M}$'s speed, notice that $\mathcal{N}(\mu^n) > \mathcal{M}(\mu^n)$ while $\mathcal{M}(\mu^n) < 16$.

$$\Phi_2^n = \min_{\mu^n} E_2'(\mu^n) = \min_{\mu^n} \sum_{\langle \mu^n, \nu^n \rangle} E_2(\mu^n, \nu^n, m_{\mu^n}, m_{\nu^n})$$

$$= \min_{\mu^n} \Phi_2^0 \cdot \mathcal{N}(\mu^n) = \min_{\mu^n} \Phi_2^0 \cdot 4(\mathcal{M}(\mu^n))^{\frac{1}{2}} = \Phi_2^0 \cdot 4(1)^{\frac{n}{2}} = 4\Phi_2^0 . \tag{14}$$

The expected value of $E_2'(\mu^n)$ requires the knowledge of the mean shape of all nodes at G^n. We estimate E_2' by using a rectangular-shaped node with variable length l and width αl ($\alpha \in \mathbb{R}^+$) to approximate any shape a nodes can possess. Therefore, for any node, $\mathcal{M} = \alpha l^2$, $\mathcal{N} = 2(\alpha l + l)$, $\mathcal{N} = 2(\alpha + 1)(\mathcal{M}/2)^{1/2}$, and its expected E_2':

$$\mathbb{E}(E_2'(\mu^n)) = \mathbb{E}\left(\sum_{\langle \mu^n, \nu^n \rangle} E_2(\mu^n, \nu^n, m_{\mu^n}, m_{\nu^n})\right) = \mathbb{E}(\mathcal{E}_2^0 \cdot \mathcal{N})$$

$$= \mathcal{E}_2^0 \cdot 2(\alpha + 1)\left(\frac{\mathcal{M}}{2}\right)^{\frac{1}{2}} = \mathcal{E}_2^0 \cdot \sqrt{2}(\alpha + 1)\left(\frac{\tau_1 + 1}{2}\right)^{\frac{n}{2}} . \tag{15}$$

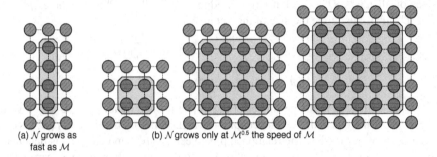

(a) $\mathcal{N}$ grows as   (b) $\mathcal{N}$ grows only at $\mathcal{M}^{0.5}$ the speed of $\mathcal{M}$
fast as $\mathcal{M}$

Fig. 2. $\mathcal{N}(\mu^n)$ versus $\mathcal{M}(\mu^n)$ under different shapes. Each node is a pixel-level node, the gray bevelled rectangle represents the range of the coarser-level node μ^n, and blue nodes (textured with horizontal lines for monochrome prints) indicate $\mu^0 \in D^0(\mu^n)$. Solid lines are the edges between nodes of different labels.

Empirically, α is a relatively small constant. Therefore, $\mathbb{E}(E'_2(\cdot))$ is only a fraction of $\mathbb{E}(E_1(\cdot))$ at the same level of the adaptive hierarchy.

3.3   The Effects of Un-Normalized Energies in Adaptive Hierarchies

As we have shown in 3.1 and 3.2, for any node μ^n, the relationship between its expected E_1 and E'_2 is

$$\mathbb{E}\left(E_1\left(\mu^n, m_{\mu^n}\right)\right) \approx \mathbb{E}\left(E'_2\left(\mu^n\right)\right)^2 \approx \left(\left(\tau_1 + 1\right)/2\right)^n \ . \tag{16}$$

In other words, μ^n's E_1 is expected to be $\left(\left(\tau_1 + 1\right)/2\right)^{n/2}$ times as large as its E'_2 energy. Let $E'(\mu^n)$ be the local energy cached at node: μ^n, $E'(\mu^n) = E_1(\mu^n, m_{\mu^n}) + E'_2(\mu^n))$. The difference between $\mathbb{E}(E_1(\mu^n, m_{\mu^n}))$ and $\mathbb{E}(E'_2(\mu^n))$ becomes much more significant at coarser-level nodes, which would eventually cause the E_1 term to dominate $E'(\mu^n)$. While considered with their respected weights λ_1, λ_2 learned from the pixel-layer standard MRF

$$\mathbb{E}\left(E'\left(\mu^n\right)\right) = \lambda_1 \mathbb{E}\left(E_1\left(\mu^n, m_{\mu^n}\right)\right) + \lambda_2 \mathbb{E}\left(E'_2\left(\mu^n\right)\right)$$
$$\approx \lambda_1 \mathbb{E}\left(E_1\left(\mu^n, m_{\mu^n}\right)\right) + \lambda_2 \mathbb{E}\left(E_1\left(\mu^n, m_{\mu^n}\right)\right)^{1/2} \tag{17}$$

$\lambda_2 \mathbb{E}(E'_2(\mu^n))$ becomes negligible as n increase. In other words, no matter what value λ_2 is assigned while it is learned, it has little effect on the final local energy of a coarser-level node.

The effects of this phenomenon are two-fold: (a) coarser-level nodes in the hierarchy are less likely to change their labels even when they are spatially inconsistent with their neighboring nodes, and therefore (b) *shifts* are more likely to happen at finer-level nodes. One might argue that the first effect is desirable, due to the intuition that coarser-level nodes are more likely to represent individual objects such as a ball or a box, thus being able to easily change their labels would be unreasonable. However, there is no guarantee that the likelihood term is reliable (i.e. we might have bad coarser-label nodes at the beginning). Furthermore, even if we were to design an adaptive hierarchy with different weights λ_1, λ_2 for different levels, it should be learned instead of being adjusted by the coarsening factor. One notable drawback of the first effect is that the algorithm is more likely to be trapped in local minima, which contradicts with one of the original design goal of the Graph-Shifts algorithm. The second effect tends to increase the total number of shifts, since more finer-level shifts are needed to accomplish the same energy-change as one coarser-level shift.

3.4   Normalizing the Energy Terms

We experimentally design three strategies for normalizing E_1 and E_2' for nodes in the Graph-Shifts hierarchy: (a) energies normalized only at level 0 of the hierarchy, denoted as EN0, (b) energies normalized by a constant, denoted as ENC, and (c) energies normalized with the node mass ($\mathcal{M}$), denoted as ENM. We will experimentally analyze them, along with the unnormalized version, denoted as UNE, in 4.

The only difference between version (a) (EN0) and unnormalized energies (UNE) is that: at level 0 of the hierarchy, the output of E_1 and E_2 are normalized to the interval $[0, 1]$

$$\Omega_1 \left(\mathbf{I} \left(S \left[\mu^0 \right] \right), m_{\mu^0} \right) = E_1 \left(\mathbf{I} \left(S \left[\mu^0 \right] \right), m_{\mu^0} \right) / \Psi_1^0 \ ,$$
$$\Omega_2 \left(m_{\mu^0}, m_{\nu^0} \right) = E_2(m_{\mu^0}, m_{\nu^0}) / \Psi_2^0 \ . \tag{18}$$

For comparison, high-level energies defined in (2), (3) causes E_1 to output discrete values in the interval $[0, 5.6]$, and $E_2 \in \{0, 1\}$. Note that coarser-level nodes are still unnormalized. Since the optimum values for λ_1, λ_2 are learned for different energies, we show in 4 that this normalization have no effect on convergence speed or labeling accuracy. Proving this equivalence facilitates the normalization of coarser-level energies.

Version (b) (ENC) normalizes all nodes' E_1 and E_2' to the interval $[0, 1]$ as

$$\Omega_1 \left(\mu^n, m_{\mu^n} \right) = E_1 \left(\mu^n, m_{\mu^n} \right) / \left(\Psi_1^0 \cdot \mathcal{M} \left(\mu^n \right) \right) \ ,$$
$$\Omega_2 \left(\mu^n \right) = E_2' \left(\mu^n \right) / \left(\Psi_2^0 \cdot \mathcal{N} \left(\mu^n \right) \right) \ . \tag{19}$$

The unnormalized energies E_1, E_2 are still used for the recursive computation of coarser-level energies. This is because normalizing the terms to $[0, 1]$ is just for balancing their effects on the final E, not for reweighting all finer-level nodes when they are grouped into a coarser-level one. Notice that, since all nodes in the hierarchy are normalized to the same interval $[0, 1]$, a coarser-level label-change no longer tends to cause a larger energy change. In other words, instead of favoring coarser-level shifts at the early rounds of the Graph-Shifts algorithm, it will give equal preference to finer- and coarser-level shifts. This characteristic is both an advantage and disadvantage, in the sense that local minima have a higher chance of being avoided, yet it is expected to take a much longer time to converge.

The third and final normalizing scheme, (c), (ENM) overcomes the unreasonable fairness between finer- and coarser-level shifts induced by version (b). The energies

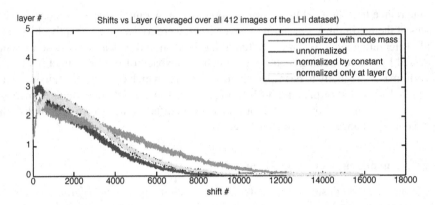

Fig. 3. Shifts versus the layer it occurred. For every labeling task, if it takes z shifts to converge, the layer at which the shift number (shift #) $y \leq z$ takes place is averaged over all labeling tasks where y occurred.

Ω_1 and Ω_2' are normalized to the same interval, so that the final energy term Ω is not dominated by a single energy term, yet higher-level nodes preserve their original tendency of causing a larger energy change.

$$\Omega_1 \left(\mu^n, m_{\mu^n} \right) = E_1 \left(\mu^n, m_{\mu^n} \right) / \Psi_1^0 \ ,$$

$$\Omega_2 \left(\mu^n \right) = \frac{E_2' \left(\mu^n \right)}{\Psi_2^0 \cdot \left(\mathcal{N} \left(\mu^n \right) / \mathcal{M} \left(\mu^n \right) \right)} \ . \tag{20}$$

4   Experiments and Results

Our experiments are conducted on an 11-label, 412-image subset of the LHI dataset [14]. We randomly split the data into training and testing sets, where 170 of them were used for training and 242 of them for testing. We trained the PBT classifier [13] to select and fuse features from a set of 10^5 features, consisting of color, intensity, position, histograms, and Gabor filter responses. The pair-wise contextual relationships between different labels are also learned to construct the PBT classifier. For a test image, the probability of each pixel belonging to one of the 11 labels are computed from the PBT classifier, then formulated into the E_1 term using (2). We then compare the energy-minimization effects of the Graph-Shifts algorithm using unnormlized energies (UNE) versus the three versions of normalized energies (EN0, ENC, ENM defined in (18), (19), and (20) respectively). The hierarchy coarsening parameters are empirically set to $\tau_1 = 20$ and $\tau_2 = 0.5$ in all experiments. The optimum weights are learned, where UNE's $\lambda_1 = 0.1, \lambda_1 = 0.9$, EN0's $\lambda_1 = 0.3, \lambda_2 = 0.7$, ENC and ENM's $\lambda_1 = 0.6, \lambda_2 = 0.4$.

Our results show a significant improvement in convergence speed when coarser-level energies are normalized properly (using ENM). The average number of *shifts* required while using ENM is 3774, versus 4110 shifts for UNE; the average convergence time is 3.17 seconds versus 3.71 seconds, which is a 15% speedup. This result is expected, because unnormalized energy causes the E_1 term to dominate E, which discourages

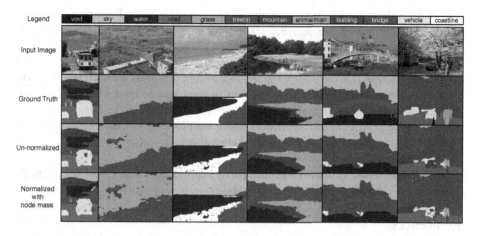

Fig. 4. Randomly selected labeling results. ENM converges to results similar to those of UNE in only 85% of time. The details are slightly different due to the different orders *shifts* take place while approximating the global minimum.

higher-level shifts from taking place. Our analysis in Figure 3 shows that, the properly normalized version (red line) not only converges faster, but also induces more coarser-level shifts (which tend to cause larger energy change) at earlier stages of the energy minimization process. Energies normalized only at level 0 (EN0, yellow line), exhibits almost the same characteristic as the unnormalized version (UNE, blue line). One interesting point is, while equally weighting all nodes at different levels of the hierarchy (ENC, green line), finer-level shifts are more likely to happen early during the energy minimization process, causing the algorithm to require more shifts (5740) and take 1.5 times as long (4.31 seconds) to converge.

Interestingly, however, UNE, EN0, ENC, ENM achieves almost the same labeling accuracy of $70\% \pm 0.5\%$. This is because the pixel-level MRF energy models are essentially the same for UNE, EN0, ENC, and ENM, as shown in 3.4, therefore should converge to similar energy-minimized results. Their difference in coarser-level energy accumulation only affects the level and order at which *shifts* takes place (Figure 4). In ENM, coarser-level shifts happen more frequently at earlier stages of the energy minimization process, thus in some sense optimizes the shifting sequence. In UNE, since coarser-level shifts are unreasonably oppressed, groups of finer-level shifts have to be performed to achieve the same pixel-level label change.

5   Conclusion

In summary, this paper has investigated the theory and construction of adaptive hierarchies, then has examined the potential problems of using it to perform energy minimization without proper normalization. The recursive energy accumulation of adaptive hierarchies causes unnormalized energy terms to grow at different speeds, thus resulting in the faster growing terms to dominate the final energy in coarser-level nodes. Empirically, the unary energy outweighs the binary energy at coarser-level nodes, which makes coarser-level shifts less likely to occur, therefore increasing the total number of shifts required for minimization. We designed three different methods for normalizing coarser-level energies, and experimentally confirmed that the best results are achieved when *the different energy terms of a node are normalized to the same interval, while coarser-level nodes still possess relatively larger energies compared to finer-level nodes.* Properly normalized energies triggers a 15% speedup in convergence time while maintaining the same accuracy rate. We plan to further justify our findings in the future by experimenting on other types of energy models, along with looking into the effects of proper normalization in other types of hierarchical algorithms.

Acknowledgements. This work has been partly supported by NSF CAREER grant IIS 0845282 and DARPA grant HR0011-09-1-0022.

References

1. Ahuja, N.: A transform for multiscale image segmentation by integrated edge and region detection. IEEE Trans. on Pattern Analysis and Machine Intelligence 18(12), 1211–1235 (1996)
2. Besag, J.: Spatial interaction and the statistical analysis of lattice systems (with discussion). Journal of the Royal Statistical Society, B 36, 192–236 (1974)
3. Bouman, C., Liu, B.: Multiple resolution segmentation of textured images. IEEE Trans. on Pattern Analysis and Machine Intelligence 13(2), 99–113 (1991)
4. Bouman, C., Shapiro, M.: A multiscale random field model for Bayesian image segmentation. IEEE Trans. on Image Processing 3(2), 162–177 (1994)
5. Boykov, Y., Veksler, O., Zabih, R.: Fast Approximate Energy Minimization via Graph Cuts. IEEE Trans. Pattern Analysis and Machine Learning 23(11), 1222–1239 (2001)
6. Chen, A.Y.C., Corso, J.J., Wang, L.: HOPS: Efficient region labeling using higher order proxy neighborhoods. In: Proc. of International Conference on Pattern Recognition (2008)
7. Corso, J.J., Yuille, A., Tu, Z.: Graph-Shifts: Natural Image Labeling by Dynamic Hierarchical Computing. In: Proc. of IEEE Conf. on Computer Vision and Pattern Recognition (2008)
8. Geman, S., Geman, D.: Stochastic Relaxation, Gibbs Distributions, and Bayesian Restoration of Images. IEEE Trans. on Pattern Analysis and Machine Intelligence 6, 721–741 (1984)
9. Gidas, B.: A renormalization group approach to image processing problems. IEEE Trans. on Pattern Analysis and Machine Intelligence 11(2), 164–180 (1989)
10. Kato, Z., Berthod, M., Zerubia, J.: Multiscale Markov random field models for parallel imageclassification. In: Proc. of Fourth International Conference on Computer Vision (1993)
11. Sharon, E., Brandt, A., Basri, R.: Fast Multiscale Image Segmentation. In: Proc. of IEEE Conf. on Computer Vision and Pattern Recognition, vol. I, pp. 70–77 (2000)
12. Terzopoulos, D.: Image analysis using multigrid relaxation methods. IEEE Trans. on Pattern Analysis and Machine Intelligence 8(2), 129–139 (1986)
13. Tu, Z.: Probabilistic Boosting-Tree: Learning Discriminative Models for Classification, Recognition, and Clustering. In: Proc. of the Tenth IEEE Int'l Conf. on Computer Vision, vol. 2 (2005)
14. Yao, Z., Yang, X., Zhu, S.C.: Introduction to a Large Scale General Purpose Ground Truth Dataset: Methodology, Annotation Tool, and Benchmarks. In: Yuille, A.L., Zhu, S.-C., Cremers, D., Wang, Y. (eds.) EMMCVPR 2007. LNCS, vol. 4679, pp. 169–183. Springer, Heidelberg (2007)
15. Yedidia, J., Freeman, W., Weiss, Y.: Generalized Belief Propagation. Advances in Neural Information Processing Systems 13, 689–695 (2000)

Topology Preserving Parallel Smoothing
for 3D Binary Images

Gábor Németh, Péter Kardos, and Kálmán Palágyi

Department of Image Processing and Computer Graphics,
University of Szeged, Hungary
{gnemeth,pkardos,palagyi}@inf.u-szeged.hu

Abstract. This paper presents a new algorithm for smoothing 3D binary images in a topology preserving way. Our algorithm is a reduction operator: some border points that are considered as extremities are
removed. The proposed method is composed of two parallel reduction
operators. We are to apply our smoothing algorithm as an iteration-
by-iteration pruning for reducing the noise sensitivity of 3D parallel
surface-thinning algorithms. An efficient implementation of our algorithm is sketched and its topological correctness for (26,6) pictures is
proved.

1 Introduction

Contour smoothing is a frequently required pre-processing step in image processing, image understanding, pattern recognition, and visualization. There exist
numerous approaches for smoothing curves and surfaces [1,2,10,11].

Yu and Yan developed a 2D sequential boundary smoothing algorithm that
uses operations on chain codes [11]. It removes some noisy pixels along a contour, decomposes the contour into a set of straight lines, and detects structural
feature points which correspond to convex and concave segments along the contour. Based on this work, Hu and Yan proposed an improved algorithm [2]. The
method that is introduced by Taubin is suitable for smoothing piecewise linear
shapes of arbitrary dimensions [10]. This method is a linear low-pass filter that
removes high curvature variations. In [1], Couprie and Bertrand assumed binary
images that are composed of several objects. They introduced the homotopic
alternating sequence filter (HASF), a topology preserving operator which is controlled by a constraint set. Their HASF is a composition of homotopic cuttings
and fillings by spheres of various radii. In these works (with the exception of
[1]), a single object was considered (i.e., just one closed curve or surface was
smoothed).

This paper presents a new 3D smoothing algorithm for 3D binary images that
may contain arbitrary number of objects. Our algorithm is a reduction operator:
some border points that are considered as extremities are removed from the input
image. It is composed of two topology preserving parallel reduction operators,
hence the entire algorithm is topology preserving too. The support (i.e., the

R.P. Barneva et al. (Eds.): CompIMAGE 2010, LNCS 6026, pp. 287–298, 2010.

minimal set of points whose values determine whether a point is deletable) of these two operators is $3 \times 3 \times 3$ that makes an efficient implementation possible.

It is well-known that skeletonization algorithms are rather sensitive to coarse object boundaries and surfaces, hence the produced false skeletal segments must be removed by a pruning process as a post-processing step [9]. We are to apply our smoothing algorithm for reducing the noise sensitivity of 3D parallel surface-thinning algorithms [7].

2   Basic Notions and Results

Let p be a point in the 3D digital space denoted by $\mathbb{Z}^3$. Let us denote $N_j(p)$ (for $j = 6, 18, 26$) the set of points that are j-adjacent to point p (see Figure 1a).

The sequence of distinct points $\langle x_0, x_1, \ldots, x_n \rangle$ is called a j-path (for $j = 6, 18, 26$) of length n from point x_0 to point x_n in a non-empty set of points X if each point of the sequence is in X and x_i is j-adjacent to x_{i-1} for each $1 \leq i \leq n$ (see Figure 1a). Note that a single point is a j-path of length 0. Two points are said to be j-connected in the set X if there is a j-path in X between them.

The 3D binary $(26, 6)$ digital picture $\mathcal{P}$ is a quadruple $\mathcal{P} = (\mathbb{Z}^3, 26, 6, B)$ [4]. Each element of $\mathbb{Z}^3$ is called a point of $\mathcal{P}$. Each point in $B \subseteq \mathbb{Z}^3$ is called a black point and has a value of 1. Each point in $\mathbb{Z}^3 \backslash B$ is called a white point and has a value of 0. 26-adjacency is associated with the black points and 6-adjacency is assigned to the white ones. A black component is a maximal 26-connected set of points in B, while a white component is a maximal 6-connected set of points in $\mathbb{Z}^3 \backslash B$. A black point is called a border point in a $(26, 6)$ picture if it is 6-adjacent to at least one white point.

A reduction operator transforms a binary picture only by changing some black points to white ones (which is referred to as the deletion of 1's). A parallel reduction operator deletes all points satisfying its condition simultaneously. A

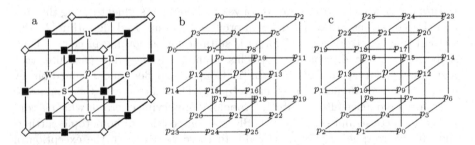

Fig. 1. Frequently used adjacencies in $\mathbb{Z}^3$ (a). The set $N_6(p)$ of the central point $p \in \mathbb{Z}^3$ contains p and the 6 points marked $u=u(p)$, $n=n(p)$, $e=e(p)$, $s=s(p)$, $w=w(p)$, and $d=d(p)$. The set $N_{18}(p)$ contains the set $N_6(p)$ and the 12 points marked "■". The set $N_{26}(p)$ contains $N_{18}(p)$ and the 8 points marked "◇".

Indexing schemes to encode all possible $3 \times 3 \times 3$ configurations (b-c). They are assigned to the first (b) and the second (c) parallel reduction operators of the proposed method.

3D reduction operator does *not* preserve topology [3] if any black component is split or is completely deleted, any white component is merged with another white component, a new white component is created, or a hole (that donuts have) is eliminated or created.

A *simple* point is a black point whose deletion is a topology preserving reduction [4]. Now we will make use the following result:

Theorem 1. [5] *A black point p is simple in picture $(\mathbb{Z}^3, 26, 6, B)$ if and only if all of the following conditions hold:*

1. *The set $(B\backslash\{p\}) \cap N_{26}(p)$ contains exactly one 26–component.*
2. *The set $(\mathbb{Z}^3\backslash B) \cap N_6(p)$ is not empty.*
3. *Any two points in $(\mathbb{Z}^3\backslash B) \cap N_6(p)$ are 6–connected in the set $(\mathbb{Z}^3\backslash B) \cap N_{18}(p)$.*

Based on Theorem 1, simple points can be locally characterized; the support of an operator which deletes $(26, 6)$–simple points is $3 \times 3 \times 3$.

Parallel reduction operators delete a set of black points and not just a single simple point. Hence we need to consider what is meant by topology preservation when a number of black points are deleted simultaneously. The following theorem provides *sufficient conditions* for 3D parallel reduction operators to preserve topology.

Definition 1. *A unit square is a $2 \times 2 \times 1$, a $2 \times 1 \times 2$, or a $1 \times 2 \times 2$ subset of $\mathbb{Z}^3$.*

Theorem 2. [6] *Let $\mathcal{O}$ be a parallel reduction operator. Let p be any black point in any picture $\mathcal{P} = (\mathbb{Z}^3, 26, 6, B)$ such that p is deleted by $\mathcal{O}$. Let $\mathcal{Q}$ be the family of all the sets of $Q \subseteq (N_{18}(p)\backslash\{p\}) \cap B$ contained in a unit square. The operator $\mathcal{O}$ is topology preserving if all of the following conditions hold:*

1. *p is simple in the picture $(\mathbb{Z}^3, 26, 6, B\backslash Q)$ for any Q in $\mathcal{Q}$.*
2. *No black component contained in a $2 \times 2 \times 2$ cube can be deleted completely by $\mathcal{O}$.*

3 The New Smoothing Algorithm

The proposed algorithm for smoothing 3D binary pictures are composed of two parallel reduction operators denoted by R_1 and R_2. Deletable points (i.e., black points to be deleted simultaneously by R_1 and R_2) are given by a set of matching templates. A point is deletable by R_1 if at least one template in the set of 13 templates

$$\mathcal{T}_{R_1} = \{U, N, W, UN, UE, US, UW, NW, NE, UNW, UNE, USE, USW\}$$

shown in Figures 2-4 matches it. In these figures, we use the following notations: each element marked "p" or "$\bullet$" matches a black point; each element marked "$\circ$" matches a white point; each "$\cdot$" (don't care) matches either a black or a white point. Deletable points by operator R_2 are defined by matching templates too. Templates in Figures 2-4 reflected to the point p are taken into consideration.

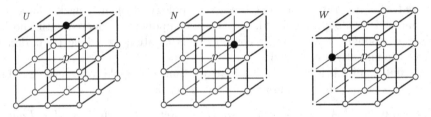

Fig. 2. Templates assigned to the first three faces

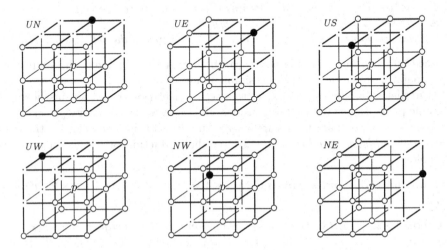

Fig. 3. Templates assigned to the first six edges

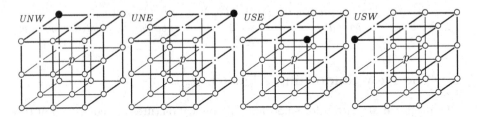

Fig. 4. Templates assigned to the first four nodes

Our algorithm is sketched by the following program:

Input: picture $(\mathbb{Z}^3, 26, 6, X)$
Output: picture $(\mathbb{Z}^3, 26, 6, Y)$

begin
    $Y = X$;
    $Y = Y \setminus \{\, p \mid p$ is deletable by R_1 in $(\mathbb{Z}^3, 26, 6, Y)\,\}$;
    $Y = Y \setminus \{\, p \mid p$ is deletable by R_2 in $(\mathbb{Z}^3, 26, 6, Y)\,\}$;
end

If the 13+13 templates of operators R_1 and R_2 are considered, then one may think that the proposed algorithm is time consuming and it is rather difficult to implement it on conventional sequential computers. Thus we sketch here an efficient and fairly general implementation method. It can be used for various reduction operators (e.g., parallel thinning algorithms) as well [7,8].

The proposed implementation uses just one pre-calculated look-up-table to encode deletable points. Since the $3 \times 3 \times 3$ support of our operators contains 26 points with the exception of the central point p in question (see Figures 2-3), the look-up-table has 2^{26} entries of 1 bit in size. It is not hard to see that it requires just 8 MB of storage space in memory.

An integer in $[0, 2^{26})$ can be assigned to each $3 \times 3 \times 3$ configuration. This index is calculated as $\sum_{k=0}^{25} 2^k p_k$. Operator R_1 uses the indexing scheme depicted in Figure 1b, and R_2 takes the reflected scheme (see Figure 1c) into consideration. Then the calculated index is to address the look-up-table.

In addition, two lists are used to speed up the process: one for storing the border points in the current picture (since operators R_1 and R_2 can only delete border points, thus the repeated scans of the entire image array are avoided); the second list is to store all deletable points in the current phase of the process.

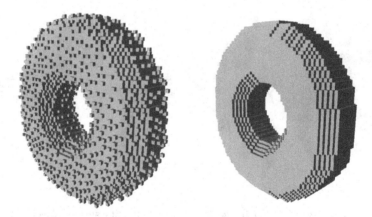

Fig. 5. A $64 \times 64 \times 19$ 3D image of a noisy torus (left) and the smoothed image produced by the proposed algorithm

Fig. 6. A $103 \times 47 \times 75$ 3D image of a noisy bird (left) and the smoothed image produced by our algorithm

Fig. 7. A $100 \times 100 \times 40$ 3D image of a noisy character "A" (left) and its smoothed version. Note that the smooth boundary segments are not altered.

       92 534   9 037   7 146

Fig. 8. A $300 \times 239 \times 83$ 3D image of a horse (left); its surface-skeleton produced by a parallel surface-thinning algorithm (middle); and the produced skeleton with iteration-by-iteration smoothing (right). Numbers mean the count of black points. We can state that the thinning with smoothing produces much less skeletal points without overshrinking.

    In experiments the proposed smoothing algorithm was tested on objects of various images. Here we present three illustrative examples below (Figures 5-7). It is illustrated in Figure 7 that our algorithm is a proper smoothing one: it does not alter the smooth boundary segments of the original image.

    We are to apply our smoothing algorithm for reducing the noise sensitivity of 3D parallel surface-thinning algorithms. In Figure 8 we present an example in which the proposed smoothing is applied before each iteration step of the 3D parallel surface-thinning algorithm described in [8].

4 Verification

Now we will show that the proposed smoothing algorithm is topology preserving for (26,6) pictures. We are to prove that the first operator R_1 given by the set of matching templates T_{R_1} fulfills both conditions of Theorem 2. It can be proved for the second operator R_2 in a similar way. Hence the entire smoothing algorithm is topology preserving, since it is composed of topology preserving reductions.

Let us classify the elements of the templates in the set of templates T_{R_1} (see Figures 2-4). The element in the centre of a template (marked "p") is called *central*. A noncentral template element is called *black* if it is marked "●". A noncentral template element is called *white* if it is marked "○". Any other non-central template element which is neither white nor black, is called *potentially black* (marked "·"). A black or a potentially black noncentral template element is called *nonwhite*.

A black point p is *deletable* if at least one template in the set of 13 templates in T_{R_1} matches it (i.e., if it is deletable by R_1).

Now let us state some properties of the set of templates T_{R_1}.

Proposition 1. *Element $d(p)$ is white in each template in T_{R_1}.*

Proposition 2. *Element $s(d(p))$ is white in each template in T_{R_1}.*

Proposition 3. *If element $s(p)$ is nonwhite in a template in T_{R_1}, then $u(s(p))$, $e(u(s(p)))$, or $w(u(s(p)))$ is black.*

Lemma 1. *Each deletable point is simple.*

Proof. The first thing we need to verify is that there exists a 26-path between any two potentially black elements (condition 1 of Theorem 1). Here it is sufficient to show that any potentially black element is 26-adjacent to a black element and any black element is 26-adjacent to another black element. This is really apparent from a careful examination of the templates in T_{R_1}.

To prove that conditions 2 and 3 of Theorem 1 hold, it is sufficient to show that, for each template,

- there exists a white element 6-adjacent to the central element,
- for any potentially black or white element 6-adjacent to the central element p, there exists a 6-adjacent white 18-neighbor which is 6-adjacent to a white element 6-adjacent to p.

These two points are obvious by Proposition 1 and a careful examination of the set of templates T_{R_1}.   □

Lemma 2. *The simplicity of a deletable point does not depend on any black point coinciding with a potentially black template element. (In other words, a deletable point remains simple after the deletion of any (sub)set of points coinciding with template elements marked "·".)*

It can be proved similarly as Lemma 1.

Lemma 3. *Let p and q be any two black points in a picture $(\mathbb{Z}^3, 26, 6, B)$ such that $q \in N_{18}(p)$. If both points p and q are deletable, then p is simple in picture $(\mathbb{Z}^3, 26, 6, B\backslash\{q\})$.*

Proof. Since point p is deletable, by Lemma 1 it is simple. To prove this lemma, we must show that p remains simple after the deletion of q.

If q coincides with a potentially black template element, then this lemma holds by Lemma 2. Hence it is sufficient to deal with the deletable points coinciding with template elements marked "●" in templates U, N, W, UN, UE, US, UW, NW, and NE (see Figures 2-3). We do not have to take templates UNW, UNE, USE, and USW into consideration since elements marked "●" in these four templates are not 18-adjacent to their central elements marked "p" (see Figure 4).

Let us see the 9 templates in question:

- If p is deleted by U, then $q = u(p)$ is not deletable by Proposition 1.
- If p is deleted by N, then $q = n(p)$ may be deleted by templates US, USE, or USW since element $s(p)$ is nonwhite in these three templates. The three possible configurations are depicted in Figure 9. Consequently, point q is not deletable.
- If p is deleted by W, then $q = w(p)$ may be deleted by templates UE, NE, UNE, or USE since element $e(p)$ is nonwhite in these four templates. The four possible configurations are depicted in Figure 10. Consequently, point q is not deletable.
- If p is deleted by UN, then $q = n(u(p))$ is not deletable by Proposition 2.
- If p is deleted by UE, then $q = e(u(p))$ may be deleted by templates W and NW since element $w(d(p))$ is nonwhite in these two templates. The two possible configurations are depicted in Figure 11. Black point r (see Figure 11a) is not deletable by Proposition 1, and the set of black points $\{p, q, s\}$ is not contained in a unit square (see Figure 11b). It is easy to see that p remains simple after the deletion of q in both configurations.
- If p is deleted by US, then point $q = s(u(p))$ may be deleted by templates N, NW, and NE since element $n(d(p))$ is nonwhite in these three templates. The three possible configurations are depicted in Figure 12. Black point r (see Figure 12a) is not deletable by Proposition 1, and the sets of black points $\{p, q, s\}$ and $\{p, q, t\}$ are not contained in a unit square (see Figures 12b-c). It is not hard to see that p remains simple after the deletion of q in all the three configurations.
- If p is deleted by UW, then point $q = w(u(p))$ may only be deleted by template NE since it is the only template in which element $e(d(p))$ is nonwhite. The possible configuration is depicted in Figure 11c in which the set of black points $\{p, q, r\}$ is not contained in a unit square. It is not hard to see that p remains simple after the deletion of q.
- If p is deleted by NW, then point $q = w(n(p))$ may be deleted by templates UE, US, and USE since element $e(s(p))$ is nonwhite in these three templates. The three possible configurations are depicted in Figure 13. The sets of black points $\{p, q, r\}$ and $\{p, q, s\}$ are not contained in a unit square (see

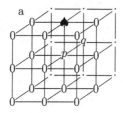 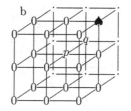 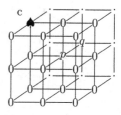

Fig. 9. Possible configurations in which point p is deleted by template N and q is to be deleted by templates US (a), USE (b), and USW (c). Each point marked "♠" coincides a white template element in N, but it coincides with a black element if q coincides with the central element of templates US, USE, and USW.

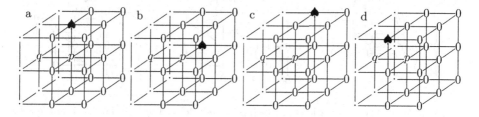

Fig. 10. Possible configurations in which point p is deleted by template W and q is to be deleted by templates UE (a), NE (b), UNE (c), and USE (d). Each point marked "♠" coincides a white template element in W, but it coincides with a black element if q coincides with the central element of templates UE, NE, UNE, and USE.

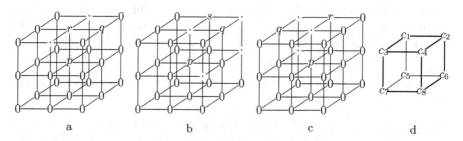

Fig. 11. Possible configurations in which point p is deleted by template UE and q is to be deleted by templates W (a) and NW (b), where r and s are black points. The possible configuration in which point p is deleted by template UW and q is to be deleted by template NE (c). The $2 \times 2 \times 2$ cube that contains a black component C (d).

Figures 13a-b). It is easy to see that p remains simple after the deletion of q in these configurations. Black point q in the last configuration (see Figure 13c) is not deletable.

- If p is deleted by NE, then $q = e(n(p))$ may be deleted by templates W, US, UW, or USW since element $w(s(p))$ is nonwhite in these four templates. The

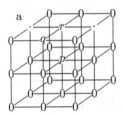 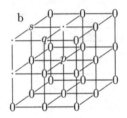 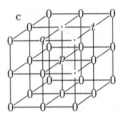

Fig. 12. Possible configurations in which point p is deleted by template US and q is to be deleted by templates N (a), NW (b), and NE (c), where r, s, and t are black points

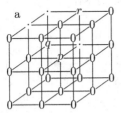 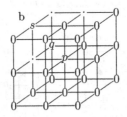 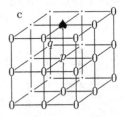

Fig. 13. Possible configurations in which point p is deleted by template NW and q is to be deleted by templates UE (a), US (b), and USE (c), where r and s are black points. The point marked "♠" coincides a white template element in NW, but it coincides with a black element if q coincides with the central element of USE.

four possible configurations are depicted in Figure 14. Black point r (see Figure 14a) is not deletable by Proposition 3, and the sets of black points $\{p, q, s\}$ and $\{p, q, t\}$ are not contained in a unit square (see Figure 14b-c). It is easy to see that p remains simple after the deletion of q in all these three configurations. Black point q in the last configuration (see Figure 14d) is not deletable. □

Lemma 4. *No black component C contained in a $2 \times 2 \times 2$ cube can be deleted completely by the operator R_1.*

Proof. Let us examine the $2 \times 2 \times 2$ cube depicted in Figure 11d.

It is easy to check that if $c_1 \in C$, then c_1 is not deletable by R_1, and if $c_k \in C$ ($k = 2, \ldots, 8$), then there exists a $c_j \in C$ ($j = 1, \ldots, k - 1$) that is not deletable by R_1. Thus C cannot be deleted completely. □

We are now ready to state our main theorem.

Theorem 3. *Operator R_1 is topology preserving for $(26, 6)$ pictures.*

Proof. We need to show that both conditions of Theorem 2 are satisfied:

1. Let us examine the simplicity of a deletable point p in picture $(\mathbb{Z}^3, 26, 6, B \backslash Q)$, where the set of deletable points $Q \subseteq (N_{18}(p) \backslash \{p\}) \cap B$ is contained in a unit square. It is clear that the number of elements in Q (denoted by $\#(Q)$) is less than or equal to 3.

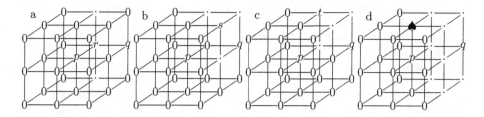

Fig. 14. Possible configurations in which point p is deleted by template NE and q is to be deleted by templates W (a), US (b), UW (c), or USW (d), where r, s, and t are black points. The point marked "♠" (d) coincides a white element in NE, but it coincides with a black element if q coincides with the central element of template USW.

The following points have to be checked:
- $\#(Q) = 0$ $(Q = \emptyset)$:
  Condition 1 of Theorem 2 is satisfied by Lemma 1.
- $\#(Q) = 1$ $(Q = \{q\})$:
  Condition 1 of Theorem 2 is satisfied by Lemma 3.
- $\#(Q) = 2, 3$:
  Each template in $\mathcal{T}_{R_1}$ contains just one black element and the simplicity of p does not depend on any black point coinciding with a potentially black template element by Lemma 2. Hence these cases are to be ignored.
2. Condition 2 of Theorem 2 (i.e., no black component contained in a $2 \times 2 \times 2$ cube can be deleted completely) is satisfied by Lemma 4. □

Acknowledgements

This research was supported by the TÁMOP-4.2.2/08/1/2008-0008 program of the Hungarian National Development Agency and the NKTH-OTKA-CNK80370 Grant.

References

1. Couprie, M., Bertrand, G.: Topology preserving alternating sequential filter for smoothing two-dimensional and three-dimensional objects. Journal of Electronic Imaging 13, 720–730 (2004)
2. Hu, J., Yu, D., Yan, H.: A multiple point boundary smoothing algorithm. Pattern Recognition Letters 19, 657–668 (1998)
3. Kong, T.Y.: On topology preservation in 2-d and 3-d thinning. Int. Journal of Pattern Recognition and Artificial Intelligence 9, 813–844 (1995)
4. Kong, T.Y., Rosenfeld, A.: Digital topology: Introduction and survey. Computer Vision, Graphics, and Image Processing 48, 357–393 (1989)
5. Malandain, G., Bertrand, G.: Fast characterization of 3D simple points. In: Proc. 11th IEEE Internat. Conf. on Pattern Recognition, ICPR 1992, pp. 232–235 (1992)

6. Palágyi, K., Kuba, A.: A parallel 3D 12-subiteration thinning algorithm. Graphical Models and Image Processing 61, 199–221 (1999)
7. Palágyi, K.: A 3D fully parallel surface-thinning algorithm. Theoretical Computer Science 406, 119–135 (2008)
8. Palágyi, K., Németh, G.: Fully parallel 3D thinning algorithms based on sufficient conditions for topology preservation. In: Brlek, S., Reutenauer, C., Provençal, X. (eds.) DGCI 2009. LNCS, vol. 5810, pp. 481–492. Springer, Heidelberg (2009)
9. Shaked, D., Bruckstein, A.: Pruning medial axes. Computer Vision and Image Understanding 69, 156–169 (1998)
10. Taubin, G.: Curve and surface smoothing without shrinkage. In: Proc. 5th Int. Conf. Computer Vision, ICCV 1995, pp. 852–857 (1995)
11. Yu, D., Yan, H.: An efficient algorithm for smoothing, linearization and detection of structural feature points of binary image contours. Pattern Recognition 30, 57–69 (1997)

Coding a Simulation Model of the
3D Structure of Paper

Eduardo L.T. Conceição[1], Joana M.R. Curto[2],
Rogério M.S. Simões[2], and António A.T.G. Portugal[1]

[1] CEM Group, Department of Chemical Engineering, University of Coimbra,
Rua Sílvio Lima – Pólo II, 3030-790 COIMBRA, Portugal
{etc,atp}@eq.uc.pt

[2] Science and Technology Paper Department, University of Beira Interior,
Rua Marquês d'Ávila e Bolama, 6201-001 COVILHÃ, Portugal
{jmrc,rmss}@ubi.pt

Abstract. Almost everyone agrees on the central role that simulation plays in the understanding of complex systems such as the 3D network formed by stacking millions of fibers on top of each other in a paper sheet. Clearly, the computational implementation of the few models which describe the microstructure of paper is far from trivial. Unfortunately, to our knowledge, there is no description in the literature of the methodology used for programming these algorithms. As a contribution towards overcoming this gap, the present article explains the software implementation of key features of a 3D random fiber deposition model into a high-level MATLAB computer code.

Keywords: 3D modeling, paper structure, cellular automata.

1 Introduction

The formation of a paper sheet involves the drainage of a suspension of cellulosic fibers in water leading to a network structure in which the fibers lie roughly horizontal and their agglomeration is stochastic in nature. It turns out that even for a thin material as paper it appears necessary to develop a 3D structure model to be able to predict various of its properties consistent with experimental data [2]. Simulation models which grow networks by random deposition of fibers are traced to the work of [6], which featured a 3D stacking of bendable fibers resembling real paper. Certainly, the KCL-PAKKA simulation model [5] ranks as one of the most successful and mature of these approaches.

Although the fundamentals of the KCL-PAKKA paper model have been published in the literature for over one decade, lack of availability of an open source implementation on which we could base our studies led to the decision to design and develop a prototype system from scratch.

In this context, this paper serves to illustrate and discuss the concepts and techniques used in translating the KCL-PAKKA model, by describing key building blocks of our MATLAB implementation. Throughout this work we assume the reader to be familiar with the MATLAB language.

R.P. Barneva et al. (Eds.): CompIMAGE 2010, LNCS 6026, pp. 299–310, 2010.

In the next section we briefly review the basics for the sedimentation-like process of forming a paper web. Besides the standard KCL-PAKKA we also discuss an extension of this model to incorporate a formation control parameter. Section 3 is the core of the paper. There we present the prominent design features and discuss its MATLAB-specific implementation. Calculation of physical properties is briefly considered in Section 4. Section 5 gives some conclusions.

2   Brief Description of the Handsheet Formation Model

In order to grow a paper web, *flexible* straight fibers are laid down, one at a time, onto a flat substrate. Fibers are positioned and oriented at random in the in-plane (x and y) directions and placed parallel to the substrate on top of the underlying network. Thereafter the parts of the fiber that do not touch the network underneath them undergo bending in the vertical (z) direction (or thickness direction) such that they either do contact with previously deposited fibers or the largest deflection allowed by the bending stiffness of fibers is reached. In the latter case, free space arises in the thickness direction between the fiber and the entangled network of fibers located just below because its stiffness prevents it from adjusting to the top surface roughness.

2.1   Flexing Rule

Space is discretized into a Cartesian *uniform* grid of cells so that each fiber in the model is represented by a single vertical planar strip one cell wide and thickness of m vertical cells. Any two nearest neighboring cells in the same layer of the fiber can make at most the maximum F vertical lattice steps allowed. We remark that this depends only on the behavior of the bottom surface layer which may be described mathematically as

$$|z_B(j) - z_B(j')| \leq F ,   \tag{1}$$

where $z_B(j)$ and $z_B(j')$ are the elevations of two nearest neighbor cells j and j' occupied by the surface bottom of a fiber and F can be any positive integer $\leq m$, which is related to fiber flexibility. Figure 1 shows a representation of a deformed fiber in 2D.

2.2   Fiber Interactions

The tendency of fibers in the suspension to concentrate around drainage sinks (those parts of the deposit that have less fibers per unit area) leads to a smoothing effect in these less dense areas in the paper sheet. This mechanism is simulated by the particle deposition rule of [8] which works over the *rejection model* introduced by [7]. The operation works as follows: A candidate fiber lands on a section of the web whose mean height is compared with a fraction of its counterpart

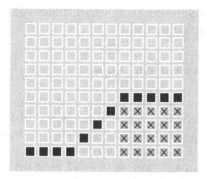

Fig. 1. Final configuration of a bended fiber with flexibility $F = 1$. The crosses represent parts of previously deposited fibers with squares denoting the bottom layer of the fiber.

of the entire paper. If the following condition is fulfilled, the attempt is always accepted:

$$h \leq \alpha H , \qquad (2a)$$

where h is the average thickness of the paper over the projected area of the trial fiber, $0 \leq \alpha \leq 1$ is a constant, and H is the average thickness of the entire paper. Otherwise, the attempt is accepted only with a probability p, called the *acceptance probability*.

In the limit $p = 1$ produces uniformly random networks for all values of α. However, for $p \to 0$ mass density uniformity is enhanced by the rule favoring depositions into the valleys within the web. Two configurations of the fiber network are shown in Figure 2.

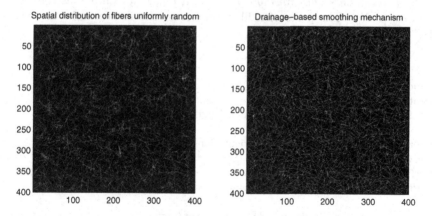

Fig. 2. Simulated X-ray image of the (x, y) plane for a paper handsheet as generated from the deposition rule, with formation control parameters set to $p = 1$, $\alpha = 1$ (left) and $p = 0.01$, $\alpha = 0.94$ (right)

We refer the interested reader to [9, Chap. 4] for a clear and simple presentation of the paper formation process.

3 Some Implementation Aspects

This section outlines the most relevant points of the implementation. For each one we give a sample code fragment and present a brief walkthrough. To focus on the principal ideas, we omit details regarding code optimization. Please note that we restrict ourselves to only one type of fiber for the sake of simplicity.

To summarize, our growth process of a 3D fiber network consists of the following steps (see Figure 3):

1. Generation of a fiber in the in-plane directions.
2. Testing the rule for particle deposition. If the fiber is not accepted, the generation trial is repeated.
3. Extraction of the out-of-plane vertical slice from the 3D network where the bending procedure occurs.
4. Fiber bending simulation for its bottom surface.
5. Filling up the remaining $m - 1$ cell layers.
6. Updating by reinsertion of the modified slice into the 3D network.

3.1 Generation of a Fiber

Each *straight* fiber is built by randomly placing the center within the boundaries of a flat surface represented by the rectangle $[0, L_x] \times [0, L_y]$ such that both position and orientation are *uniformly* distributed. This corresponds to the case of laboratory handsheets. Fiber length is characterized by a *Poisson* distribution following [8]. After this, the fiber is discretized to a chain of square cells, defined by the *Bresenham's line drawing algorithm* [1, pp.38–40], onto a discrete lattice $[1, N_x] \times [1, N_y]$. The parts of a fiber that cross the lattice limits are cut. In MATLAB this can be done with

```
XMIN = 1; YMIN = 1; XMAX = Nx; YMAX = Ny;

midpoint = unifrnd([0 0], [Lx Ly], 1, 2);
orientation = unifrnd(-1, 1, 1, 2);
half_fiber_length = poissrnd(mean_fiber_length) / 2;

orientation = orientation / norm(orientation);
mov = half_fiber_length*orientation;
startPt = midpoint - mov % Start point of segment.
endPt = midpoint + mov % End point of segment.

% Transforming from continuous to discrete coordinates.
scales = [(Nx-1)/Lx, (Ny-1)/Ly];
startPt = floor(startPt.*scales) + 1;
endPt = floor(endPt.*scales) + 1;
```

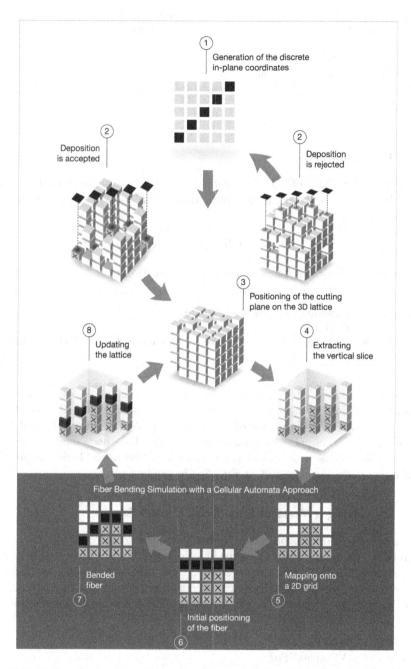

Fig. 3. Data flow diagram that illustrates the core of the sequence of computations for the fiber deposition model. Note that the step filling the layers atop the bottom one is not depicted here.

% Draw the discrete fiber segment using Bresenham algorithm.
[fiber_xcoord, fiber_ycoord] = bresline(startPt, endPt);

% Restrict the fiber segment to the rectangle [1, Nx] x [1, Ny].
clip = fiber_xcoord < XMIN | fiber_xcoord > XMAX ...
     | fiber_ycoord < YMIN | fiber_ycoord > YMAX;
fiber_xcoord(clip) = [];
fiber_ycoord(clip) = [];

3.2   Rejection Model

Notice that the origin of 2D coordinates in the vertical plane is located at the upper left corner. The trivial change of variables $h' = N_z - h$, $H' = N_z - H$ allow us to convert (2a) into

$$h' < \alpha H' + (1 - \alpha)N_z \tag{2b}$$

for the *rejection* with probability $1 - p$ of a deposition trial.

This can be done with code like

```
fiber_mask = sparse(fiber_xcoord, fiber_ycoord, true);
zPos = E(fiber_mask);
if rand > acceptanceprob && mean(zPos) < alpha*mean(E(:)) + (1−alpha)*Nz
    continue
end
```

The space is divided into $N_x \times N_y \times N_z$ cells or voxels in the form of a square parallelepiped into a regular grid of discrete locations. Each entry of the 2D array E contains the elevations of the paper web surface grid cells and those corresponding the in-plane location of the trial fiber have been selected into zPos. Because the && operator short-circuits the evaluation of the logical expression, it saves computation time to test Eq. (2b) in the last place.

3.3   Extracting a Vertical Slice from the 3D Lattice

The array web of dimension Nz-by-Nx-by-Ny is used to store information of the discretized volume elements. Once the (x, y) coordinates of an accepted fiber have been obtained in the *column* vectors fiber_xcoord and fiber_ycoord, our task is to extract the corresponding 2D vertical slice in the volume web. The sedimenting fiber bends around structures along this strip. The following is one possible way to do this:

```
firstVPos = 1; lastVPos = Nz;
z_extent = firstVPos:lastVPos;
height = length(z_extent);
width = length(fiber_xcoord);
```

X = repmat(fiber_xcoord, height, 1);
Y = repmat(fiber_ycoord, height, 1);
Z = repmat(z_extent', 1, width);
strip_idx = sub2ind([Nz Nx Ny], Z, X, Y);

strip = web(strip_idx);

Note that here we select *all* the vertical extension of web, but it is possible to find a tighter confined layer, which results in considerable savings in computing time. This will compute the (i, j, k) subscripts of web comprising a particular slice. We then use the function sub2ind to convert to one-dimensional subscripting and this can be used to index onto web.

3.4   Simulation of Bending Using a Cellular Automata Framework

The spatial discretization allow us to exploit the potential of *cellular automata* (see the book [10]). A cellular automaton (CA) is a spatial discrete time model. Each cell can exist in different states chosen from a finite set. At each time step each cell changes its state based on a set of rules or transition functions that represent the allowable physics of the phenomena.

The discrete space for the automaton maps identically onto the vertical plane in which bending takes place represented by the 2D array strip. For each cell (i, j) at time t there are three states which represent the presence or absence of fiber particles, namely:

Moving. Deforming particle covers cell.
Idle. Stopped particle covers cell.
Empty. The cell is unoccupied.

As time goes on, the new state of each cell $s_{t+1}(i, j)$ is then updated according to the following rules:

$$s_{t+1}(i,j) = \text{idle} \leftarrow s_t(i,j) = \text{moving} \wedge (s_t(i - F, j - 1) = \text{idle} \qquad (3)$$
$$\vee \, s_t(i + 1, j) \neq \text{empty}$$
$$\vee \, s_t(i - F, j + 1) = \text{idle})$$

$$\left.\begin{array}{l} s_{t+1}(i,j) = \text{empty} \\ s_{t+1}(i+1,j) = \text{moving} \end{array}\right\} \leftarrow s_t(i,j) = \text{moving} \wedge \neg\,(s_t(i - F, j - 1) = \text{idle}$$
$$\vee \, s_t(i + 1, j) \neq \text{empty}$$
$$\vee \, s_t(i - F, j + 1) = \text{idle})$$
$$(4)$$

$$s_{t+1}(i,j) = \text{idle} \leftarrow s_t(i,j) = \text{idle} \qquad (5)$$
$$s_{t+1}(i,j) = \text{empty} \leftarrow s_t(i,j) = \text{empty} \wedge (s_t(i - 1, j) = \text{empty} \qquad (6)$$
$$\vee \, s_t(i - 1, j) = \text{idle})$$

where i and j are the row and column indices and the negation of a given statement P is denoted by $\neg P$.

Via the preceding rules, particles can move only in the downward (increasing time) direction at most one cell at each time step t. We have chosen to update the cell states *asynchronously* by a line-by-line sweep of each row sequentially, so that we can eliminate a substantial amount of spurious reference to the above rules, for instance in the region "above the fiber". An example of code that would implement this behavior might look like this:

```
strip = [repmat(EMPTY, height, 1) strip repmat(EMPTY, height, 1)];
stop = false(1, width+2);
run = [false true(1, width) false ];

j = 2:(width+1);
for i = 1:(height−1)
    stop(j) = strip(i−F, j−1) == IDLE ... % Eq. (1)
            | strip(i+1, j) ~= EMPTY ...
            | strip(i−F, j+1) == IDLE;  % Eq. (1)
    strip(i, run & stop) = IDLE;        % CA rule (3)
    run = run & ~stop;                  % CA rule (5)
    if all(~run), break, end % Fiber bending stops.
    % CA rule (4)
    strip(i, run)   = EMPTY;
    strip(i+1, run) = MOVING;
end

strip( end, strip(end, :) == MOVING ) = IDLE;
strip(:, [1 end]) = [];
```

In the first part of this code segment the 2D lattice is augmented by a column vector of fictitious cells having the pre-assigned value EMPTY at the extreme left and right sides, so that the corresponding neighborhood is completed. The loop, **for** i = 1:(height−1), drives the line-by-line sweep. In each iteration the logical vector run & stop picks out those js where the particles stop to move. We can then compute vector run & ~stop whose components with value true specify the remaining particles still bending downward. The assignment of this value to the variable run implements implicitly rule (5). On leaving the loop we can return to the original dimensions of the lattice with the assignment strip (:, [1 end]) = []. Finally, notice that in this case rule (6) is not needed anymore.

Figure 4 shows the sequence of discrete steps in bending a fiber.

3.5   Filling up the Remaining Layers

Now it is time to start filling up the remaining $m-1$ cell layers by stacking one on top of the other through each point of the fiber. The fiber was modeled as a concentric assembly with lumen in the middle followed by the cellulosic wall. We distinguish three types of layers: top, bottom, and lumen. For simplicity we make both the top and bottom ones only one cell high.

After having found the i indices corresponding to the vertical coordinates z_j describing the elevation of the bottom layer, all we need is to define those for the other two. Each layer is then tagged with a label. This can be done by

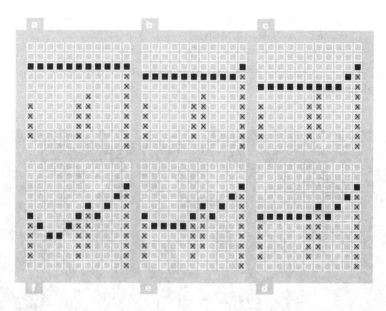

Fig. 4. (Clockwise, from top left) The time evolution of a single fiber having flexibility $F = 1$, from the initial positioning parallel to the substrate until the bending capacity is exhausted. The crosses represent parts of previously deposited fibers with squares denoting the bottom layer of the bending fiber.

```
zPos = find(strip == IDLE);
bottom_idx = sub2ind([height width], zPos, 1:width);
lumen_idx = bsxfun(@minus, bottom_idx, 1:(m−2));
top_idx    = bottom_idx − (m−1);

strip (bottom_idx) = BOTTOM;
strip (lumen_idx)  = LUMEN;
strip (top_idx)    = TOP;
```

3.6 Updating the Lattice

All we are left is to carry out the updating of the 3D array web as well as matrix E

```
E(fiber_mask) = zPos − (m−1);
web(strip_idx) = strip;
```

3.7 All Done

Now we merely have to choose the output format of the simulation

```
out = struct('web',        web, ...
             'thickness',  (Nz+1) − E, ...
             'empty',      web == EMPTY, ...
```

```
'top',     web == TOP, ...
'lumen',   web == LUMEN, ...
'bottom', web == BOTTOM);
```

Figure 5 shows an example of the 3D fiber network constructed with our proto-type implementation.

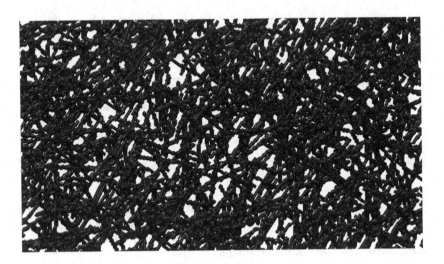

Fig. 5. Simulated 3D fiber network

4   Physical Properties of Simulated Paper

As a voxel-based approach, this has the huge advantage that it allows for easy identification of regions of interest. Furthermore, the basic method for comput-ing many paper properties lies simply on counting the number of appropriate voxels in the appropriate region. Next we present two examples of concrete im-plementations, one for sheet porosity and one for relative bonded area.

4.1   Porosity

By definition, *bulk* porosity is the volume fraction not occupied by the fibers within a paper sheet. This is simply obtained by dividing the volume of all the voids by the total volume of the sheet [12, pp. 279 and 280]. The code for the function can be written:

```
function val = porosity(x)
void_space_above_surface = sum(sum( size(x.web, 1) − x.thickness ));
pores_volume = sum(x.empty(:)) − void_space_above_surface;
total_volume = numel(x.web) − void_space_above_surface;
val = pores_volume/total_volume;
```

Note that x.empty is a 3D array with logical 1s when the corresponding position in x.web is not occupied, and their sum is the total number of empty voxels. To get the correct volume of pores, we have to subtract the contribution of the empty voxels *above* the sheet surface. The same correction has to be applied to calculate the real number of voxels in the whole paper sheet.

It is curious to note that this is the same as counting the number of black-white pixels in binarized images obtained from X-ray microtomography, as done by [4]. For a recent overview of image analysis methods for studying the internal porous structure of paper, see [3].

4.2   Relative Bonded Area

The relative bonded area (RBA) is the fraction of fiber surface in contact with other fibers. Basically, the implementation means to count the number of fiber-fiber contacts:

```
function val = rba(x)
[m, n, p] = size(x.top);

% Insure that fibers at the upper and lower sides of the paper sheet
% are not found to be adjacent.
top = cat( 1, x.top, false (1, n, p) );
bot = cat( 1, x.bottom, false (1, n, p) );

% Count each pair of adjacent top and bottom layer cells .
num_cell_contact_area = sum( bot(:) & circshift(top (:), -1) );

% Calculate RBA.
num_cell_total_area = sum(top(:));
val = num_cell_contact_area/num_cell_total_area;
```

Similarly to x.empty, x.top and x.bottom are 3D arrays with logical 1s in the elements belonging, respectively, to the top or bottom layer of a fiber. The basic idea is based on the observation that if we can reach a "bottom" voxel from a "top" one by walking up one position at the same in-plane location, these two are adjacent. To do this, vector top(:) is circularly shifted upwards by one position. Only those locations in the compound expression bot(:) & circshift (top (:), -1) that evaluate to true indicate fiber-fiber contact points. The resulting logical 1s are summed to obtain the desired number of voxels at the total contact surface. However, in addition we have to prevent that the top layer of a fiber located at the top face of the sheet is falsely found to be connected to the bottom layer of another fiber at the bottom side. This is accomplished by adding an extra level of falses on top of both x.top and x.bottom.

The procedure just described is akin to the direct determination of RBA using image analysis of sheet cross sections (see [11, pp. 884 and 885] and references therein).

5 Conclusion

We believe that this article will provides a basis for the understanding of a number of practical issues that arise in the implementation of a 3D fiber deposition model. In particular, the CA approach is an attractive paradigm by allowing the high-level bending behavior to *emerge* as a result of rules fairly straightforward to implement. Not to be overlooked is the simplicity gained in computing physical properties by using a voxel based approach.

References

1. Agoston, M.K.: Computer Graphics and Geometric Modeling: Implementation and Algorithms. Springer, London (2005)
2. Alava, M., Niskanen, K.: The physics of paper. Reports on Progress in Physics 69(3), 669–723 (2006)
3. Axelsson, M., Svensson, S.: 3D pore structure characterization of paper. Pattern Analysis & Applications (2009)
4. Goel, A., Tzanakakis, M., Huang, S., Ramaswamy, S., Choi, D., Ramarao, B.V.: Characterization of the three-dimensional structure of paper using X-ray microtomography. TAPPI Journal 84(5), 72–80 (2001)
5. Nilsen, N., Zabihian, M., Niskanen, K.: KCL-PAKKA: a tool for simulating paper properties. TAPPI Journal 81(5), 163–165 (1998)
6. Niskanen, K.J., Alava, M.J.: Planar random networks with flexible fibers. Physical Review Letters 73(25), 3475–3478 (1994)
7. Provatas, N., Haataja, M., Asikainen, J., Majaniemi, S., Alava, M., Ala-Nissila, T.: Fiber deposition models in two and three spatial dimensions. Colloids and Surfaces A: Physicochemical and Engineering Aspects 165(1-3), 209–229 (2000)
8. Provatas, N., Uesaka, T.: Modelling paper structure and paperpress interactions. Journal of Pulp and Paper Science 29(10), 332–340 (2003)
9. Roberts, J.C.: The Chemistry of Paper. Royal Society of Chemistry, Cambridge (1996)
10. Schiff, J.L.: Cellular Automata: A Discrete View of the World. Wiley, New Jersey (2008)
11. Uesaka, T., Retulainen, E., Paavilainen, L., Mark, R.E., Keller, D.S.: Determination of Fiber-Fiber Bond Properties, 2nd edn. Handbook of Physical Testing of Paper, vol. 1. Marcel Dekker, New York (2001)
12. Yamauchi, T., Murakami, K.: Porosity and Gas Permeability, 2nd edn. Handbook of Physical Testing of Paper, vol. 2. Marcel Dekker, New York (2001)

Crowd Behavior Surveillance Using Bhattacharyya Distance Metric

Md. Haidar Sharif[1], Sahin Uyaver[2], and Chabane Djeraba[1]

[1] University of Sciences and Technologies of Lille (USTL), France
[2] TC Gediz University, Cankaya Izmir, Turkey
{md-haidar.sharif,chabane.djeraba}@lifl.fr, sahin.uyaver@gediz.edu.tr

Abstract. The paper presents a simple but effective method to detect abnormal crowd behaviors from real crowd videos. The method does not depend on person detection or segmentation, instead it takes the advantages of the use of cluster analysis such as robustness against variable numbers of people in the scenes. It lies in the use of the Bhattacharyya distance to measure differences in properties of clusters over time between frames. The normalized Bhattacharyya distance measure provides the knowledge of the state of abnormality. Experiments have been conducted on different real crowd videos covering both normal and abnormal activities. The experimental results show that distances between clusters of tracked corners on movers are reasonable ways to characterize abnormal behavior as the distances vary significantly in case of abnormalities.

1 Introduction

Visual surveillance is currently one of the active research topics in computer vision. The necessity of automatic techniques which process and analysis human behaviors and activities is an increasing concern for public safety and law enforcement. However, motion detection is a fundamental processing step in the majority of visual surveillance algorithms. Motion detection algorithms mainly aim to detect moving objects while suppressing the effects caused by lighting changes, moving background, shadows, etc. In video surveillance, motion detection could take a vital role for security and safety in both public and private places e.g., town centers, parking places, airports, subways, banks, malls, etc. Abnormal motion detection would benefit from a system capable of recognizing perilous circumstances to make the system operators fully aware and attentive.

There are some works [1,2,3,5,11,12,13,17,18,19,24,26] which detect abnormalities in crowd flows. The general approach of such type of works consists of modeling normal behaviors, and then estimating the deviant behavior or attitudes between normal behavior model and observed behaviors. Those deviations are labeled as abnormal. Data of normal behaviors are generally available whereas data of abnormal behaviors are generally rare. Thus, the deviations from examples of normal behavior are used to characterize abnormality. Authors in [24] detected events which have never occurred or occur so rarely that they are not represented in the clustered activities. The method includes robust tracking,

R.P. Barneva et al. (Eds.): CompIMAGE 2010, LNCS 6026, pp. 311–323, 2010.

based on probabilistic method for background subtraction. But the robust tracking method is not adapted to crowd scene, in which it is too complex to track objects. A spatial model to represent the routes in an image has been developed in [17]. One short coming of this method is that solely spatial information is used for trajectory clustering and behavior recognition. The system cannot differentiate between a person walking and a person lingering around, or between a running and a walking person. On the other hand, a method for detecting non-conforming trajectories of objects has been proposed in [13]. A framework for automatic behavior profiling and abnormality sampling/detection without any manual labelling of the training dataset can be found in [26]. Natural grouping of behavior patterns is discovered through unsupervised model selection and feature selection on the eigen-vectors of a normalized affinity matrix. Authors in [18] considered the problem of automatically learning an activity-based semantic scene model from a stream of video data. A system for automatically learning motion patterns for anomaly detection and behavior prediction based on a proposed algorithm for robustly tracking multiple objects can be seen in [11]. Authors in [2,3] combined hidden Markov model, spectral clustering and principal component for detecting crowd emergency scenarios. But the method was experimented in simulated data. Based on an inference process in a probabilistic graphical model, the problem of detecting irregularities in visual data has been addressed by [5]. Lagrangian Particle Dynamics to detect the flow instabilities from video streams characterized by extremely high crowd density has been presented by [1]. Their framework is good to detect flow instabilities from the events where thousands of people primarily present e.g., people circling around the Kabba, marathon, etc. Still the method would not be so interest-bearing in the context of a crowd scene where the density of people is never so high e.g., airports, malls, etc. Authors in [12] presented an approach to detect abnormal situations in crowded scenes by analyzing the motion aspect instead of tracking subjects one by one, whereas the authors in [19] introduced a method by capturing the dynamics of the crowd behavior to detect and localize abnormal behaviors in concourse videos with the help of the Social Force model.

Our approach contributes to the related works of [2,3,12] with following specificities: (i) it detects all events in real videos where the motion variations are important as compared to previous events; (ii) it deals with all directional flow of crowd without imposing a coercion of the number of people in the crowd scene; (iii) it does not need any specific learning process and training data, but does expect a prior threshold. The approach estimates sudden changes and abnormal motion variations of a set of interest points detected by Harris detector and tracked by optical flow technique and classified by K-means. The overhaul of normalized Bhattacharyya distance measure over time provides the knowledge of the state of abnormal activity. Emphatically, we have noticed that distances between clusters of tracked corners on movers are a reasonable way to characterize atypical behavior as the distances change significantly in case of abnormalities.

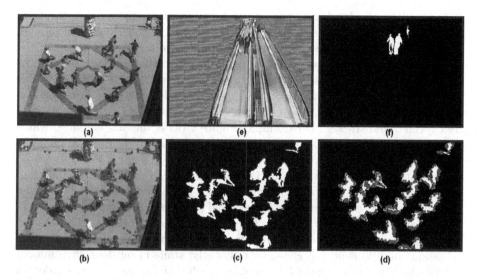

Fig. 1. The images (a) and (e) are the original frames and the results of their foreground estimation have been depicted in the images (c) and (f), successively; images (b) and (d) point to the Harris points of interest for the case of images (a) and (c), respectively

The rest of this paper: Section 2 promulgates the detailed implementation steps of the proposed framework; Section 3 reports the experimental results; and finally, Section 4 concludes the work with few inklings for further investigation.

2 Proposed Approach

In this section we will discuss detailed implementation steps of the framework.

2.1 Region of Interest Estimation

Both indoor and outdoor video surveillance would expect *region of interest* (RoI) for making video processing faster. Depending on applications and type of videos, RoI would extend from few parts of a video frame to the whole frame. In case of indoor applications (e.g., to keep under surveillance the linear passages, highway, etc.) video processing region can be fixed by using a mask instead of analyzing the whole video frame. We use a *Motion Heat Map* (MHM) as introduced in [12] for such applications. Such MHM ameliorates the quality of the results and makes the processing time faster as it is dispensable to take into account the full frame and fastidiously where there are few motion intensities or no motions.

2.2 Points of Interest Estimation

The Harris corner detector [10] is a famous point of interest detector due to its strong invariance to rotation, scale, illumination variation, and image noise [21].

It is based on the local auto-correlation function of a signal, where the local auto-correlation function measures the local changes of the signal with patches shifted by a small amount in different directions. A discrete predecessor of the Harris detector was depicted by Moravec [20], where the discreteness refers to the shifting of the patches. We deem Harris corner as a point of interest. But there is a potential problem for camera positions and lighting conditions, which allow getting an extremely large number of corner features that cannot be easily captured and tracked. For example, Figure 1 (a) is the original video frame with moving subjects, if we apply Harris detector algorithm directly then the output contains lots of unwanted corners as shown in Figure 1 (b). To avoid this situation, we prefer to use a background and foreground estimation method before applying Harris corner detector. An estimated foreground can be derived after background estimation. Ideally, residual pixels obtained on applying background subtraction should represent foreground subjects. Foreground estimation is relatively easy in an indoor environment (see Figure 1 (e) and (f)) as the illumination conditions do not change significantly; while in outdoor environment that is much more complicated, as varying weather and sunlight (e.g., shadow of each subject in the Figure 1 (a)) affect the correct detection of foreground. Some authors have adopted the adaptive Gaussian approach to model the behavior of a pixel [9,23,27]. Yet the background region of a video sequence often contains several moving objects. Thus, rather than explicitly estimating the values of all pixels as one distribution, we would prefer to estimate the value of a pixel as a mixture of Gaussians [9,23,27]. Foreground pixels obtained on applying background subtraction are shown in Figure 1 (c), in which noise, caused by shadows, which are the result of extremely strong lighting condition (e.g., sunlight); yet Figure 1 (f) is almost light invariant.

2.3   Points of Interest Tracking

Once we define the points of interest, e.g., Figure 1 (d), we track those points over the next frames using optical flow techniques. For this, we use the pyramidal implementation of Kanade-Lucas-Tomasi tracker [6,16,22]. Upon matching points of interest between frames, the result is a set of vectors over time: $\Psi = \{\Psi_1 \ldots \Psi_N | \Psi_i = (x_i, y_i, \delta_i, \alpha_i)\}$ where $x_i \mapsto x$ coordinate of a point of interest i, $y_i \mapsto y$ coordinate of the i, $\delta_i \mapsto$ displacement of the i from one frame to the next, $\alpha_i \mapsto$ direction of motion of the i. If any feature i in the frame f with its coordinate $U(x_i, y_i)$ and its matched in the frame $f+1$ with coordinate $V(x_i, y_i)$, it is easy to calculate the change of position (displacement) δ_i of the feature i using Euclidean metric as: $\delta_i = \sqrt{(U_{x_i} - V_{x_i})^2 + (U_{y_i} - V_{y_i})^2}$. Simple trigonometric function $atan$ comes into notice few potential problems, e. g., infinite slope, false quadrant. On the other hand, trigonometric function $atan2$ gracefully handles infinite slope and places the angle in the correct quadrant [e.g., $atan2(1,1) = \pi/4$, $atan2(-1,-1) = -3\pi/4$, etc.]. Thus, the accurate moving direction α_i of the feature i can be calculated as: $\alpha_i = atan2(U_{y_i} - V_{y_i}, U_{x_i} - V_{x_i})$. Furthermore, we remove static and noisy features. Points of interest having $\delta_i \cong 0$ are considered as static features. Noise features are the isolated features which

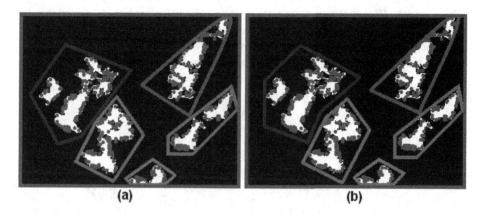

Fig. 2. Images (a) and (b) are the two consecutive frames. Polygons on the images are the resulting classification of points of interest accomplished by the K-means clustering.

have a big angle and distance difference with their near neighbors due to tracking calculation errors. The resulting points of interest are suitable for the clustering.

2.4   Classification of Points of Interest

After static error suppression points of interest, we apply k-means clustering method to accommodate with clusters. Geometric clustering method, k-means, is a simple and fast method for partitioning data points into clusters, based on the work accomplished by [15] (so-called Voronoi iteration). It is similar to the expectation-maximization algorithm for mixtures of Gaussians in that they both attempt to find the centers of natural clusters in the data. On clustering, we denote each class, which contains points of interest of an unknown distribution, as a polygon, as depicted in Figure 2. To get a quantitative measure of how separable are two classes, a distance measure is required. We calculate the Bhattacharyya distances of all the classes between video frames one after the other over time.

2.5   Calculation of Bhattacharyya Distance between Classes

The author of [14] compared the Bhattacharyya distance and the Kullback-Leibler divergence, and observed that Bhattacharyya yields better results in some respects while in other respects they are equivalent. A number of measures (e.g., Bhattacharyya, Euclidean, Kullback-Leibler, Fisher) have been studied for image discrimination and it was concluded that the Bhattacharyya distance is the most effective discriminator [4]. The Bhattacharyya distance has been used as a class separability measure for feature selection and is known provide the upper and lower bounds of the Bayes error. Upper bound of Bayes minimum error probability ε_{ij} for two classes i and j can be formulated as noted by [7]:

$$\varepsilon_{ij} = \sqrt{P(\phi_i)P(\phi_j)} \int_{-\infty}^{\infty} \sqrt{P(x|\phi_i)P(x|\phi_j)}dx \qquad (1)$$

where $P(\phi_i)$, $P(\phi_j)$, $P(x|\phi_i)$, and $P(x|\phi_j)$ are the prior probabilities and conditional probabilities of classes i and j, respectively. If the distribution of samples is unknown, the normal distribution provides a reasonable approximation. Under normal distribution assumption, the upper bound of classification error probability for two classes i and j, ε_{ij}, can be simplified as:

$$\varepsilon_{ij} = \sqrt{P(\phi_i)P(\phi_j)} \; e^{-\beta} \tag{2}$$

where the *Bhattacharyya distance*, β, is noted as [8]:

$$\beta = \frac{1}{8} [\mu_i - \mu_j]^T \left[\frac{\Sigma_i + \Sigma_j}{2} \right]^{-1} [\mu_i - \mu_j] + \frac{1}{2} log_e \frac{\left| \frac{\Sigma_i + \Sigma_j}{2} \right|}{\sqrt{|\Sigma_i||\Sigma_j|}} \tag{3}$$

where μ_i & μ_j and Σ_i & Σ_j are the mean vectors and covariance matrices of classes i & j, respectively. The first term of eq. 3 gives the class separability due to the difference between class means, while the second term gives the class separability due to the difference between class covariance matrices. In order to compute the (p,q)-th element of the Σ_i or Σ_j, we consider the following equation:

$$\Sigma_r(p,q) = \frac{1}{s-1} \left[\sum_{r=1}^{s} \Psi_r(p)\Psi_r(q) - \frac{1}{s} \sum_{r=1}^{s} \Psi_r(p) \sum_{r=1}^{s} \Psi_r(q) \right] \tag{4}$$

where m and n indicate the number of points of interest in the classes of i and j, respectively; and $r \in \{i,j\}$, $s \in \{m,n\}$, $\{p,q\} \in \{x_r, y_r, \delta_r, \alpha_r\}$. To calculate the *difference of class means*, we take into account the following conceptualization:

$$\mu_i - \mu_j = \begin{bmatrix} \frac{1}{m} \sum_{i=1}^{m} x_i - \frac{1}{n} \sum_{j=1}^{n} x_j \\ \frac{1}{m} \sum_{i=1}^{m} y_i - \frac{1}{n} \sum_{j=1}^{n} y_j \\ \frac{1}{m} \sum_{i=1}^{m} \delta_i - \frac{1}{n} \sum_{j=1}^{n} \delta_j \\ \frac{1}{m} \sum_{i=1}^{m} \alpha_i - \frac{1}{n} \sum_{j=1}^{n} \alpha_j \end{bmatrix} . \tag{5}$$

The Mahalanobis distance is a particular case of the Bhattacharyya, when the variances of the two classes are equal, this would eliminate the second term (of Eq. 3) of the distance. This term depends solely of the variances of the distribution. If the variances are equal then this term will be zero, and it will grow as the variances are different. The first term, on the other hand will be zero if the means are equal and is inversely proportional to the variances. Besides the mathematical formulation, it may be interesting to consider some of its properties. The Figure 3 shows a one-dimensional example: as a comparison of (a) and (c) we can come across that, while the Euclidean distance is the same in this two cases, β is larger in (a) than that of (c). This is because the distance between the means is scaled by the variances and expresses the degree of overlapping of the two distributions. The similar view can be viewed by considering (a) and (b): in this case β is approximately the same, while the distance between the means is different. Finally, (d) shows how the variances of the two variables may be differing in general. Upon calculating all Bhattacharyya distances among

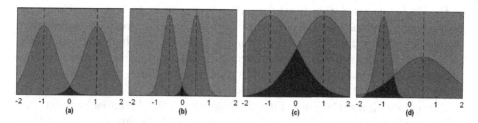

Fig. 3. Bhattacharyya distance surrounds altogether for one-dimensional example of twosomes of Gaussian distributions: (a) and (c) demonstrate twosomes with the nondescript mean Euclidean distance, nevertheless different Bhattacharyya distances between (a) and (b) have in like manner Bhattacharyya distance but miscellaneous mean Euclidean distances; (d) advances evidence for unsymmetrical distributions and distances

---

Algorithm 1. Effective Distance G_β Calculation

▷ F: total number of classes in any frame f
▷ S: total number of classes in the frame $f + 1$
▷ c_m: class counter in frame f
▷ c_n: class counter in frame $f + 1$

1 $c_m \leftarrow 1$; $c_n \leftarrow 1$
2 **while** $c_m \leq F$ **do**
3 　**while** $c_n \leq S$ **do**
4 　　using Eq. 3 calculate β between classes of c_m & c_n, and store as β_{c_n}
　　　$c_n \leftarrow c_n + 1$
5 　**end**
6 　calculate the geometric mean of β_{c_n} by means of:
$$\Omega_{c_m} = \left[\prod_{i=1}^{c_n} \beta_i\right]^{\frac{1}{c_n}} = exp\left[\frac{1}{c_n}\sum_{i=1}^{c_n} log_e \beta_i\right], \text{ and store } \Omega_{c_m}$$
7 　$F \leftarrow F - 1$
8 　$c_n = 1$; $c_m \leftarrow c_m + 1$
9 **end**
10 calculate geometric mean of Ω_{c_m} by dint of:
$$G_\beta = \left[\prod_{j=1}^{c_m} \Omega_j\right]^{\frac{1}{c_m}} = exp\left[\frac{1}{c_m}\sum_{j=1}^{c_m} log_e \Omega_j\right]$$

---

classes, we calculate the geometric means of the Bhattacharyya distances among classes and come together those means to calculate the final geometric mean (or log-average) to represent a single effective distance G_β between two consecutive frames using Algorithm 1. The advantage of using the geometric mean is that it reduces the effect of very high and low (perhaps even exponentially changing data) values in a number set. Theoretically, clustering may be very sensitive and distances between clusters may change significantly from frame to frame. The advantage of calculating single effective distance G_β between consecutive frames is that it minimizes such effect in a great amount. In the crowd scene in case of abnormal and/or emergencies situations physically there exists sufficient agitation and hence the positions, displacements, and directions of points of interest in the clustering are noticeably different between frames. In such situation, clustering configurations like 3 (a) or (b) or (d) tend to (c) between two consecutive frames. Explicitly, the value of β and hence is the G_β will be higher. Similarly, as compare to abnormal case, the clustering configurations of normal cases are almost similar between two consecutive frames. Henceforth, the value of β and hence is the G_β will be smaller, i.e., the clustering configurations like 3 (a) or (b) or (d) remain almost the same. Intuitively speaking, the distances between clusters of tracked corners on movers are a reasonable way to characterize anomalous behavior as the distances intersperse consequentially in the event of abnormalcy.

2.6 Normalization

Now, we wish to transfer each G_β into a normalized distance value between 0 and 1. For normalization purpose, we could use the simple formula like $1/(1 + log_e G_\beta)$, but the normalized values fall in a congested range (scaling problem) which will arise problem specially in threshold selection. To solve the scaling problem, we would like to use a versatile distribution which has significant effect on its shape and scale parameters. In this respect we use cumulative distribution function (cdf) of Weibull distribution which has strict lower and upper bounds between 0 and 1. Due to accurate model quality and performance characteristics of Weibull distribution and its flexibility that makes it ideal for analysis on a dataset with unknown distribution. Weibull distribution can mimic the behavior of other statistical distributions such as the normal and the exponential. If Φ_β is the normalized distance value of G_β, then Φ_β can be formulated by means of:

$$\Phi_\beta = 1 - e^{-(G_\beta/\lambda)^\nu} \tag{6}$$

where $\nu > 0$ and $\lambda > 0$ are the shape parameter and the scale parameter of the distribution, respectively. With the help of Eq. 6 and comprehending the values of ν, λ, and G_β we can explicitly estimate the value of Φ_β ranging from 0 to 1.

2.7 Threshold Estimation

A predefined threshold Γ_β value can differentiate each frame with respect to its assigned distance value whether its motion is normal or abnormal. To compute Γ_β, we consider the maximum number of distances in large videos by means of:

$$\Gamma_\beta = arg \max_{k=1...t} [\, \Phi_\beta \,]_k + arg \min_{k=1...t} [G_{error}]_k \tag{7}$$

$$G_{error} = \frac{1}{\sqrt{\pi}} \sum_{m=0}^{\infty} \left(\frac{\Phi_\beta}{2m+1} \prod_{k=1}^{m} \frac{-\Phi_\beta^2}{k} \right) \tag{8}$$

where t is the number of frames of the video database which exclusively contain normal motions and the Gauss error function G_{error} is exactly 0.5 at ∞. Any frame having value of Φ_β which is greater than the Γ_β will be considered as abnormal motion frame. The Γ_β depends on the controlled environment, namely the distance of the camera to the scene, the orientation of the camera, the type and the position of the camera, density of the crowd, varying illumination, light reflection, over head light, shadowing, day-night, indoor-outdoor, occasion, vacation, etc. The more is the distance of the camera to the scene, the less is the quantity of optical flows and blobs. Deeming these facts, we have at least one threshold by a video stream. If we have M video streams, which are the case in sites such as sporting events, political events, town centers, parking places, airports, subways, banks, malls, hospitals, hotels, etc., then we select at least M thresholds. If the environment changes, then the threshold should be regenerated.

3   Experimental Results

So as to conduct the experiments, we have predominantly relied on the *escalator dataset* and the dataset as operated by [19] also known as the *UMN dataset* [25].

3.1   The Escalator Dataset

The escalator dataset, provided by a video surveillance company[1], consists of mainly the unidirectional movement videos existing both normal and abnormal situations collected by cameras installed in an airport to monitor the situation of escalator egresses. The videos were used to provide informative data for the security team who may need to take prompt actions in the event of a critical situation such as collapsing. In this category, there are 10 different length video streams taken in spanning days and seasons. Abnormal events concern videos which contain collapsing events mostly on the escalator exits. In videos there are two escalators corresponding to two-way-traffic of opposite directions. Original video frame size is 640×480 pixels. Figure 4 (Left image) describes an example of a breakdown situation on the escalator exit point in a video stream. Two persons were standing on the moving escalator, suddenly a trolley rushed out toward them. One person escaped by running while other did not. The non-escapee was rundown by the run-away trolley, and subsequently fell down at the exit point of the moving escalator. The situation was detected by the proposed algorithm. Different video frames in normal and fortuitous circumstances have been differentiated by a threshold value ($\Gamma_\beta = 0.5$). The blue curve depicts the output of the proposed approach. The detection result has been compared with *ground truth* (the heavy blue line on the Right image in Figure 4). Ground truth is the process of manually marking what an algorithm is anticipated to output. The exhaustive evaluation of the proposed algorithm for the provided 10 video steams has been depicted in Figure 4 (Right image). The *root mean squared error* $\Upsilon = \sqrt{\frac{4^2+5^2+(-4)^2+6^2+4^2+5^2+(-5)^2+(-6)^2+4^2+(-6)^2}{10}} = \sqrt{\frac{247}{10}} \approx 5$ has been estimated using $\Upsilon = \sqrt{\frac{1}{n}\sum_{k=1}^{n}(\pm(g_t - p_a))^2}$ where, with respect to a defined threshold value, g_t and p_a denote the ground truth frame and the detected frame by the proposed approach, respectively. The quantity of $\pm(g_t - p_a)$ indicates the

---

[1] Thanks to the MIAUCE project, the EU Research Programme (IST-2005-5-033715).

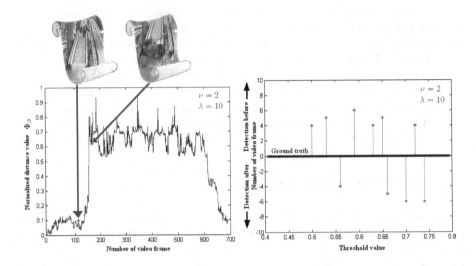

Fig. 4. *Left*: A person falling situation on the escalator exit has been detected by the proposed approach. *Right*: Performance evaluation of the ten escalator video streams.

number of frame deviations in the proposed approach from the ground truth with respective threshold level, and the signs signify the detection before (+) or after (-) the ground truth. Estimation of $\Upsilon = 0$ indicates that we have the ideal algorithm (perfect detection). Notwithstanding, estimated $\Upsilon \approx 5$ accomplishes appointively for a good deal of computer vision applications including escalators.

3.2   The UMN Dataset

This publicly available dataset of normal and abnormal crowd videos from University of Minnesota [25] comprises the videos of 11 different scenarios of an escape event in 3 different indoor and outdoor scenes. Each video consists of an initial part of normal behavior and ends with sequences of the abnormal behavior. The 320×240 frame sized videos there exist mainly omnidirectional movements of people. The shape and scale parameters of the distribution have been selected as $\nu = 1.5$ and $\lambda = 7$, respectively. The qualitative results of the abnormal behavior detection for a sample video of UMN dataset have been presented in Figure 5. In the sample video abnormal motion includes a sudden situation when a group of people start running and henceforth, the assigned distance Φ_β will be higher than any other before assigned distances. The Gaussian like curve represents the abnormal motion when the group of people is trying to leave the place with very quick motion. For explicitness, two arbitrary video frames and their corresponding positions on the output curves have been indicated by arrows. Figure 5 demonstrates that the proposed framework accomplishes something to a greater degree to distinguish aberrant sequences. The obtained results are likely a bit superior to [19] in the sense that the proposed

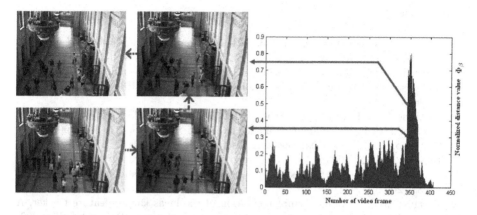

Fig. 5. Qualitative results of the proposed method for abnormality detection from a video in UMN dataset. Blue curve illustrates the output of the algorithm over frames.

approach has detected all of the anomalous sequences without reporting any false positive.

4   Conclusion

We keyed out a new and simple method for measuring normalcy and anomalies from real crowd videos. The method lies in the use of the Bhattacharyya distance to measure differences in properties of clusters over time between consecutive frames. It does not cling to person detection or segmentation, instead it takes the plus points of the use of cluster analysis such as robustness against variable numbers of people in the scenes. The normalized Bhattacharyya distance measure has been used as the judgement index for the state of abnormality. Experiments have been conducted on different real crowd videos covering both normal and abnormal activities. The experimental results show that distances between clusters of tracked corners on movers are a reasonable way to characterize abnormal behavior as the distances vary significantly in case of abnormalities.

As shortcomings, the method used the distance to measure differences between clusters or classes, assuming the same number of clusters in each frame, and compute a single value to determine the difference between activity in two frames. It would presumably have difficulties when there are multiple co-occurring activities and one changes. As a future work, one would in principle try to apply the same idea to individual clusters. It is also noticeable that the lighting condition, which causes specially shadows of moving bodies, has a severe effect on the background subtraction which has been overlooked. It would be worth interesting to count this effect in many computer vision applications. Accordingly, in future work the effect could be taken into account and minimized.

322   Md. H. Sharif, S. Uyaver, and C. Djeraba

References

1. Ali, S., Shah, M.: A Lagrangian particle dynamics approach for crowd flow segmentation and stability analysis. In: IEEE Conference on CVPR, pp. 1–6 (2007)
2. Andrade, E.L., Blunsden, S., Fisher, R.B.: Hidden Markov models for optical flow analysis in crowds. In: 18th International Conference on ICPR, vol. 1, pp. 460–463 (2006)
3. Andrade, E.L., Blunsden, S., Fisher, R.B.: Modelling crowd scenes for event detection. In: 18th International Conference on ICPR, vol. 1, pp. 175–178 (2006)
4. Bhalerao, A., Rajpoot, N.: Selecting discriminant subbands for texture classification. In: BMVC (2003)
5. Boiman, O., Irani, M.: Detecting irregularities in images and in video. IJCV 74, 17–31 (2007)
6. Bouguet, J.Y.: Pyramidal implementation of the lucas kanade feature tracker. A part of OpenCV Documentation. Int. Corporation, Micropro. Research Labs (2000)
7. Duda, R.O., Hart, P.E., Stork, D.G.: Pattern Classification, 2nd edn. John Wiley & Sons, Chichester (2001)
8. Fukunaga, K.: Introduction to Statistical Pattern Recognition, 2nd edn. Academic Press, New York (1990)
9. Hammond, R., Mohr, R.: Mixtire densities for video objects recognition. In: ICPR, vol. 2, pp. 71–75 (2000)
10. Harris, C., Stephens, M.: A combined corner and edge detector. In: Alvey Vision Conference, pp. 147–152 (1988)
11. Hu, W., Xiao, X., Fu, Z., Xie, D., Tan, T., Maybank, S.: A system for learning statistical motion patterns. TPAMI 28, 1450–1464 (2006)
12. Ihaddadene, N., Djeraba, C.: Real-time crowd motion analysis. In: ICPR, pp. 1–4 (2008)
13. Junejo, I.N., Javed, O., Shah, M.: Multi feature path modeling for video surveillance. In: ICPR, vol. 2, pp. 716–719 (2004)
14. Kailath, T.: The divergence and bhattacharyya distance measures in signal selection. IEEE Transactions on Communication Technology 15, 52–60 (1967)
15. Lloyd, S.P.: Least squares quantization in pcm. IEEE Transactions on Information Theory 28, 129–136 (1982)
16. Lucas, B.D., Kanade, T.: An iterative image registration technique with an application to stereo vision. In: International Joint Conference on Artificial Intelligence, pp. 674–679 (1981)
17. Makris, D., Ellis, T.J.: Path detection in video surveillance. Image and Vision Computing Journal 20, 895–903 (2002)
18. Makris, D., Ellis, T.J.: Learning semantic scene models from observing activity in visual surveillance. IEEE Trans. on Sys. Man and Cyb., Part B 35, 397–408 (2005)
19. Mehran, R., Oyama, A., Shah, M.: Abnormal crowd behavior detection using social force model. In: CVPR, Miami, USA (2009)
20. Moravec, H.: Obstacle avoidance and navigation in the real world by a seeing robot rover. Technical Report CMU-RI-TR-3, Carnegie-Mellon University, Robotics Institute (1980)
21. Schmid, C., Mohr, R., Bauckhage, C.: Evaluation of interest point detectors. International Journal of Computer Vision 37, 151–172 (2000)
22. Shi, J., Tomasi, C.: Good features to track. In: CVPR, pp. 593–600 (1994)
23. Stauffer, C., Grimson, W.E.L.: Adaptive background mixture models for real-time tracking. In: CVPR 1999, vol. 2, pp. 23–25 (1999)

24. Stauffer, C., Grimson, W.E.L.: Learning patterns of activity using real-time tracking. TPAMI 22, 747–757 (2000)
25. UMN: Unusual crowd activity dataset of University of Minnesota, http://mha.cs.umn.edu/movies/crowdactivity-all.avi
26. Xiang, T., Gong, S.: Video behavior profiling and abnormality detection without manual labeling. In: ICCV, pp. 1238–1245 (2005)
27. Zivkovic, Z.: Improved adaptive gaussian mixture model for background subtraction. In: ICPR, vol. 2, pp. 28–31 (2004)

Author Index

Abdoulaye, Sere   1
Alaiz-Rodríguez, Rocío   231
Albuquerque, Victor Hugo C. de   210
Alegre, Enrique   231
Andres, Eric   1, 24
Annadurai, S.   95
Arumugham, R.   119

Bajaj, Chandra   130
Balázs, Péter   242
Barneva, Reneta P.   11
Barreiro, Joaquín   231
Ben Hamza, A.   199
Brimkov, Valentin E.   11, 36

Charneau, Sylvain   60
Chen, Albert Y.C.   275
Chollet, Agathe   24
Cifone, Maria Grazia   151
Cinque, Benedetta   151
Conceição, Eduardo L.T.   299
Corso, Jason J.   275
Curto, Joana M.R.   299

Dare, V.R.   85, 95
Dhandapani, Sankari   130
Djeraba, Chabane   311
Droste, Peter   163

Falcão, Alexandre Xavier   210
Fernández, Laura   231
Fidalgo, Eduardo   231
Fiorio, Christophe   47
Franchi, Danilo   141, 151
Fuchs, Laurent   24, 60

Geetha, H.   107
Gharaibeh, Khaled   199
Giuliani, Maurizio   151
Greene, Clint   130

Itoh, Taku   263

Jebasingh, S.   72

Kalyani, T.   85, 95, 107
Kardos, Péter   287
Katyal, Sucharit   130

Lakshmi, C.   175
Largeteau-Skapin, Gaëlle   1, 24
La Torre, Cristina   151
Li, Bai   187

Macchiarelli, Guido   151
Madej, Łukasz   221
Maione, Marta   151
Maurizi, Alfredo   141, 151
Mercat, Christian   47
Miconi, Gianfranca   151
Mohamed, Waleed   199

Nagar, Atulya K.   72
Nagy, Antal   242
Németh, Gábor   287
Nguyen, Van Hieu   187
Nöh, Katharina   163

Palágyi, Kálmán   287
Papa, João Paulo   210
Pawłowski, Bogdan   221
Placidi, Giuseppe   141, 151, 254
Ponnavaikko, M.   175
Portugal, António A.T.G.   299

Rauch, Łukasz   221
Ress, David   130
Richard, Aurélie   24, 60
Rieux, Frédéric   47
Robinson, T.   72
Rodríguez, Marc   1

Samuel, Mary Jemima   85
Sharif, Md. Haidar   311
Simões, Rogério M.S.   299
Sotgiu, Antonello   151
Subramanian, K.G.   72
Sundararajan, M.   175

Tavares, João Manuel R.S.   210
Thirusangu, K.   119
Thomas, D.G.   95, 107, 119

Uyaver, Sahin   311

Varga, László   242
von Lieres, Eric   163

Wallet, Guy   24
Wiechert, Wolfgang   163